Integrated Reporting

MÜNSTERANER SCHRIFTEN ZUR INTERNATIONALEN UNTERNEHMENSRECHNUNG

Herausgegeben von Peter Kajüter

Band 15

Zu Qualitätssicherung und Peer Review der vorliegenden Publikation

Die Qualität der in dieser Reihe erscheinenden Arbeiten wird vor der Publikation durch den Herausgeber der Reihe geprüft.

Notes on the quality assurance and peer review of this publication

Prior to publication, the quality of the work published in this series is reviewed by the editor of the series.

Stefan Hannen

Integrated Reporting

Useful for investors?

PL ACADEMIC RESEARCH

Bibliographic Information published by the Deutsche Nationalbibliothek
The Deutsche Nationalbibliothek lists this publication in the Deutsche Nationalbibliografie; detailed bibliographic data is available in the internet at http://dnb.d-nb.de.

Zugl.: Münster (Westfalen), Univ., Diss., 2016

Library of Congress Cataloging-in-Publication Data
A CIP catalog record for this book has been applied for at the Library of Congress

D 6
ISSN 1868-7687
ISBN 978-3-631-73247-2 (Print)
E-ISBN 978-3-631-73323-3 (E-PDF)
E-ISBN 978-3-631-73324-0 (EPUB)
E-ISBN 978-3-631-73325-7 (MOBI)
DOI 10.3726/b11722

PL Academic Research is an Imprint of Peter Lang GmbH.

Peter Lang – Frankfurt am Main · Bern · Bruxelles · New York · Oxford · Warszawa · Wien

This publication has been peer reviewed.

www.peterlang.com

Preface

Integrated Reporting intends to address current deficiencies of corporate reporting practice – in particular information overload, redundancies and poor readability. Improvements in corporate reporting are of interest for investors, the primary addressees of corporate reports, as it may have consequences for their investment decisions. By promoting Integrated Reporting and by developing the International <IR> Framework, the International Integrated Reporting Council made a considerable effort aiming at improving corporate reporting.

However, this new holistic approach to corporate reporting raises a number of questions. This thesis deals with several of these issues, analyzing whether Integrated Reporting can achieve its objective to provide useful information for investors' decision-making. From a conceptual perspective, Stefan Hannen investigates if the IIRC's International <IR> Framework offers a suitable basis for the preparation of decision-useful reports. Moreover, the study takes a look at the practice of Integrated Reporting. Using content analysis, it examines reports in South Africa and the USA at two different points in time. Thus, this thesis documents in how far the Integrated Reporting principles had already been present in "conventional" annual reports and in how far the introduction of a quasi-obligation for firms to engage in Integrated Reporting, as in South Africa, changed this situation. In addition, Stefan Hannen investigates potential consequences of Integrated Reporting for the capital market. The study examines whether this reporting format possibly moderates an existing investor underreaction to the release of a firm's report.

These findings support the assertion that Integrated Reporting may make a difference for the corporate reporting landscape. Conceptually speaking, the International <IR> Framework introduces a useful set of requirements for firms' reports to support investors' decisions. From the empirical perspective, the descriptive study shows that reports prepared under the quasi-obligation to implement Integrated Reporting indeed yield (innovative) features that traditional reports do not exhibit. In addition, the capital-market study reveals a negative association between the degree of Integrated Reporting in firms' reports and investor underreaction following the report release.

The study contributes to the young field of literature on Integrated Reporting in several ways. In addition to providing a thorough conceptual analysis from an investor's perspective, it supplements existing research on Integrated Reporting practice, extending the range of countries examined in the literature and drawing on a solid research design. Furthermore, the capital market study contributes to the field of impact studies on Integrated Reporting while connecting this field with research on other topics such as investor underreaction. The results yield several implications, most importantly for investors. However, the study also discusses potential implications for other parties like the reporting firms or regulators.

Considering these contributions as well as the rigor of the study and the great topicality of Integrated Reporting, I am convinced that this thesis will draw a lot of attention and will be popular among academics and practitioners alike.

Münster, May 2017 Prof. Dr. Peter Kajüter

Acknowledgment

I have conducted this study during my time at the Chair of International Accounting at the University of Münster. The School of Business and Economics accepted this thesis as a dissertation in September 2016.

In this acknowledgment I want to express my gratitude for all the support I have received. First, I would like to thank my academic teacher and supervisor Prof. Dr. Peter Kajüter. Since I was a student in the bachelor's program I have been affiliated to his chair in many ways. During all these years he gave me support and encouragement, both before and during my work on the thesis. His critical thinking, high standard of demands and constructive comments and suggestions provided a fruitful basis for my work and improved my thesis considerably. Moreover, I want to thank Prof. Dr. Hans-Jürgen Kirsch and Prof. Dr. Bernd Kempa, the members of the review committee.

Likewise, I want to pay tribute to my companions at the chair. In addition to supporting me with professional advice, our great team gave me a lot of unforgettable memories. Many of these are captured in the unbelievable doctoral cap that my colleagues made for me. A special thanks goes to Dr. Martin Nienhaus who I have been sharing an office with for almost two years. The discussions with Martin about my work were of immeasurable value. Moreover, I enjoyed spending time with him outside the university, with sports, barbecues, and other activities that made us forget our work for a while. Many thanks also to Stephanie Eckerth, particularly for her feedback on my thesis, her hospitality and for all the great talks that we had, especially during the innumerable car drives between Münster and Düsseldorf. I also owe thanks to Matthias Nienaber. Besides receiving his feedback on my thesis, I enjoyed developing creative ideas with him, on the chair's PR work and beyond, which resulted in countless pieces of "art". I particularly appreciate the help of Florian Klassmann, whose thorough and constructive feedback on my study considerably improved my work. So did the remarks of Friedrich Kalden, who never failed to enrich both professional and private conversations with his cunning comments, as well as the feedback and assistance I received from Henrik Schirmacher. Henrik also appeared to be an excellent host, providing me a place to sleep in the apartment I used to live in before him.

Another dear colleague I had the pleasure to share my office with was Dr. Gregor Hagemann. Not only were we members of the same team at the chair, but we also sported the same colors in our soccer team, thus celebrating victories together on multiple levels. Furthermore, I would like to thank Alexander Schulz for the great collaboration in organizing various rounds of our annual sailing seminar. I bet we could easily run a travel agency for sailing trips together if we ever found ourselves fed up with our regular jobs. In this regard, I also want to mention Dr. Daniel Blaesing. He was (and still is) a great co-author and sports buddy, as well as a dear colleague, neighbor, and friend. The same holds true for Daniel's now-wife Christina Blaesing-Voets. Thank you very much also to my "veteran" colleagues Dr. Maximilian Saucke, Dr. Moritz Schröder and Marcel Baki, who not only helped me during my time at the chair, but were always committed to supporting our team as a whole in a multitude of ways. In addition, they are really nice and funny people. So are all my younger colleagues, namely Daniela Peters, Max Meinhövel, Kai Schaumann and Martin Vogelpohl, who continue to show the same commitment to our invaluable team.

I am also very thankful to all other fellow research assistants that made my time at the chair unforgettable, namely Dr. Kristian Bachert, Dr. Thomas Blades, Julius Hannemann, Charlotte Kaiser, Dr. Martin Merschdorf, Dr. Matthias Moeschler and Tobias Stadtbäumer. In addition, I would like to mention our student assistants who kept things ticking at the chair and supported us in so many ways. In particular, I want to highlight the work of Robert Beukmann, Johannes Effenberger, Manuel Herkenhoff and Nils Nürnberg, who were of major assistance during different phases of my study. Finally, I would like to show my gratitude for our colleagues in the secretary's office, Ashly Bills, Tobias Langehaneberg and Leila Prousch, who were always there to guide me through the university's administrative jungle.

Beyond the chair, I am also very thankful for the dear friends I have got to know in Münster. We had a great time with many unforgettable experiences, but I am more than glad that our friendship did not end with our time in the Westphalian metropolis. Instead, we still manage to spend time together as often as possible (e.g., at our annual Christmas party or on vacation), even though we live in different places all over the world. The same holds for those friends that have been by my side since I went to school or even before. Some of you also spent your studies in Münster, and some have also faced, or are still facing, the challenge of writing doctoral theses on a variety of different topics. It is always a pleasure to exchange our views on these and other topics over a couple of beers, to indulge in memories of the good old times, or to simply fool around. I could not imagine a better group of friends.

Most importantly, however, I want to express my gratitude to my family, in particular to my parents Ursula and Peter Hannen. You have been there for me during my entire life and have enabled me to become the person I am today, backing me in whatever I wanted to do. Thank you so much for this unconditional support, and most of all for your love. But my parents would not have been able to do so without the help of my grandparents, Maria and Josef Hannen and especially Käthe and Walter Schmidt. In particular, I want to address the influence of my grandfather Walter. You taught me the value of being curious by exploring my surroundings with me when I was a child and setting the example of how important it is to never stop learning. You gave me the mindset that enabled me to conduct this study. So I dedicate this thesis to you. I also want to mention my brother Andreas, my sister Katharina and her boyfriend Nils, as well as my parents-in-law Angelika Banik-Bürger and Michael Bürger, my brothers-in-law Max and Christoph, my sister-in-law Alexandra and her boyfriend Philipp as well as my godfather Hans Stenert and his wife Sylvia. Thank you for your patience, as almost all of our conversations over the last years reflected my study.

Eventually, I want to say thank you to my beloved wife Kathi. I am so grateful that you never lost faith in me no matter how tough my work was, nor how strenuous it could be for myself and for us as a couple. Not only did you tolerate my strange ideas and work habits, but you became involved with my research itself, from discussing my thoughts to proofreading the thesis along the way. After these years, I cannot wait for my future with you, when I can finally redirect the dedication I have spent on my thesis to all the things that really count in our life. Nobody deserves this more than you.

Münster, May 2017 Stefan Hannen

Contents overview

Contents

List of figures

List of tables

List of abbreviations

A4S	Accounting for Sustainability (project initiated by HRH The Prince of Wales)
ACCA	Association of Chartered Certified Accountants
ACFA	Annual Conference on Finance and Accounting
AECI	AECI Limited (formerly "African Explosives and Chemical Industries")
AFGRI	AFGRI Limited
AIA	American Institute of Accountants
AICPA	American Institute of Certified Public Accountants
AIR	Annual (integrated) report
AKEU	Arbeitskreis Externe Unternehmensrechnung der Schmalenbach Gesellschaft für Betriebswirtschaft e.V.
AKIW	Arbeitskreis "Immaterielle Werte im Rechnungswesen" der Schmalenbach-Gesellschaft für Betriebswirtschaft e.V.
ANC	African National Congress
APB	Accounting Practices Board
AS	Auditing Standard(s) (PCAOB)
ASC	Accounting Standards Codification
ASCG	Accounting Standards Committee of Germany
ASISA	Association for Saving & Investment South Africa
ASR	Accounting Series Release(s)
ASX	Australian Securities Exchange
AT	Attestation Standard(s) (AICPA)
AU	Auditing Standard(s) (AICPA)
BaFin	Bundesanstalt für Finanzdienstleistungsaufsicht (Federal Financial Supervisory Authority)
BASF	BASF SE (formerly "Badische Anilin und Soda Fabrik" – Baden Aniline and Soda Factory)
BC	Basis for Conclusion
BEE	Black Economic Empowerment
BIS	Department for Business Innovation & Skills
BP	BP plc (formerly "British Petroleum")
BUSA	Business Unity South Africa
CA	California
CA ANZ	Chartered Accountants Australia and New Zealand
CAP	Committee on Accounting Procedure

CD IR	Consultation Draft Integrated Reporting ("Consultation Draft of the International <IR> Framework")
CEO	Chief Executive Officer
Cf.	Confer
CF	Conceptual Framework for Financial Reporting
CFR	Code of Federal Regulations
Chemserve	Chemical Services Limited
CIMA	Chartered Institute of Management Accountants
CIS	Chartered Institute of Secretaries and Administrators
CLP	CLP Group (formerly "China Light & Power Company")
CLT	Cognitive Load Theory
CO_2	Carbon dioxide
CON	Contrary to expectations
CPA	Certified Public Accountant
CSR	Corporate Social Responsibility
CSSA	Chartered Secretaries Southern Africa
CT	Connecticut
DAX	Deutscher Aktienindex (German Stock Index)
D.C.	District of Columbia
Dec	December
DP IR	Discussion Paper Integrated Reporting ("Towards Integrated Reporting – Communicating Value in the 21st Century")
Dr.	Doctor
DRS	Deutscher Rechnungslegungs Standard (German Accounting Standard)
Ed.	Editor
EDGAR	Electronic Data Gathering, Analysis, and Retrieval
E-DRS	Entwurf Deutscher Rechnungslegungs Standard (Draft German Accounting Standard)
E.g.	Exempli gratia (for example)
Eds.	Editors
EITF	Emerging Issues Task Force
EMH	Efficient Market Hypothesis
ESG	Environmental, social and governance
Et al.	Et alii
Etc.	Et cetera
e.V.	Eingetragener Verein (registered association)
EVA®	Economic Value Added

EY	Ernst & Young (accounting network)
FAQ	Frequently Asked Questions
FASB	Financial Accounting Standards Board
FRSC	Financial Reporting Standards Council
FSB	Financial Services Board
FTSE	Financial Times Stock Exchange
FY	Financial year
GA	Georgia
GAAP	Generally Accepted Accounting Principles
GAS	German Accounting Standard
GASB	Governmental Accounting Standards Board
GDP	Gross Domestic Product
GHG	Greenhouse gas
GICS	Global Industry Classification Code
GRI	Global Reporting Initiative
GWh	Gigawatt hour(s)
HGB	Handelsgesetzbuch (German Commercial Code)
HR	Human resources
HRH	His Royal Highness
http	Hypertext Transfer Protocol
IAS	International Accounting Standard(s)
IASB	International Accounting Standards Board
IASC	International Accounting Standards Committee
IBEX	Índice Bursátil Español (Iberia Index; Spanish Exchange Index)
ICA	Intellectual Capital Accounting
ICAEW	Institute of Chartered Accountants in England and Wales
ICB	Industry Classification Benchmark
IDW	Institut der Wirtschaftsprüfer in Deutschland e.V.
I.e.	Id est (that is)
IFAC	International Federation of Accountants
IFRS	International Financial Reporting Standard(s)
IIRC	International Integrated Reporting Committee; International Integrated Reporting Council
IL	Illinois
IMF	International Monetary Fund
Imug	Institut für Markt-Umwelt-Gesellschaft

Inc.	Incorporated
Incl.	Including
IND	Indifferent
IODSA	Institute of Directors in Southern Africa
IR	Integrated Reporting
IR F	Integrated Reporting Framework ("The International <IR> Framework")
IRCSA	Integrated Reporting Committee of South Africa
IRCSA DP	Integrated Reporting Committee of South Africa Discussion Paper ("Framework for Integrated Reporting and the Integrated Report – Discussion Paper")
IRH	Incomplete Revelation Hypothesis
IRRCI	Investor Responsibility Research Center Institute
JSE	Johannesburg Stock Exchange
JSE AltX	Johannesburg Stock Exchange Alternative Exchange
JSE LR	Johannesburg Stock Exchange Listings Requirements
Jun	June
Kg	Kilogram
KPI	Key Performance Indicator
KPMG	KPMG International (accounting network) (formerly "Klynveld, Peat, Marwick and Goerdeler")
LLC	Limited Liability Company
LLP	Limited Liability Partnership
Ln	Logarithmus naturalis (natural logarithm)
Ltd.	Limited
MA	Massachusetts
Max	Maximum
mbH	mit beschränkter Haftung (of limited liability)
MD&A	Management's Discussion and Analysis of Financial Condition and Results of Operations
MI	Michigan
MN	Minnesota
MSc	Master of Science
MSCI	Morgan Stanley Capital International Inc.
MVO	maatschappelijk verantwoord ondernemen (corporate social responsibility)
MWh	Megawatt hour(s)

NA	Not available
NACD	National Association of Corporate Directors
NASDAQ	Nasdaq, Inc. (formerly "National Association of Securities Dealers Automated Quotations")
NBA	Koninklijke Nederlandse Beroepsorganisatie van Accountants (The Royal Netherlands Institute of Chartered Accountants)
n.d.	No date
NGO	Non-Governmental Organization
NJ	New Jersey
No.	Number
NY	New York
NYSE	New York Stock Exchange
NYSE Arca	New York Stock Exchange Archipelago Exchange
NYSE MKT	New York Stock Exchange MKT LLC
OB	Objective
OCBOA	Other comprehensive basis of accounting
OFR	Operating and Financial Review and Prospects
OH	Ohio
OLS	Ordinary Least Squares
p.	Page
PA	Pennsylvania
par(s).	paragraph(s)
PAT	Positive Accounting Theory
PCAOB	Public Company Accounting Standards Board
PCC	Private Company Council
PDF	Portable Document Format
PEAD	Post-Earnings Announcement Drift
PF IR	Prototype Framework Integrated Reporting ("Prototype of The International <IR> Framework")
P.L.	Public Law
plc	Public limited company
pop.	Population (as used in a World Economic Forum indicator)
pp.	Pages
PPC	Pretoria Portland Cement Company Limited
PPG	PPG Industries, Inc. (formerly "Pittsburgh Plate Glass Company")
Prof.	Professor

PwC	PricewaterhouseCoopers International Limited (accounting network)
QC	Qualitative Characteristics
Q-Principle	Quantity Principle
R&D	Research and development
RESET	Regression Equation Specification Error Test
ROA	Return on assets
R-Principle	Relation Principle
RSA	Republic of South Africa
SAB	Staff Accounting Bulletin
SACOB	South African Chamber of Business
SA-GAAP	South African Statements of Generally Accepted Accounting Practice
SAICA	South African Institute of Chartered Accountants
SAP	SAP SE (formerly "Systemanalyse und Programmentwicklung" – Systems, Applications & Products in Data Processing)
SASB	Sustainability Accounting Standards Board
Sasol	Sasol Limited (formerly "Suid-Afrikaanse Steenkool-, Olie- en Gasmaatskappy")
SE	Societas Europaea (European Company)
SEC	Securities and Exchange Commission
SEC	Swaziland Electricity Company (as used in *Illovo* (2013))
Si2	Sustainable Investments Institute
SICS	Sustainable Industry Classification System
SME	Small and Medium-Sized Entities
S&P	Standard & Poor's Financial Services LLC
SOX	Sarbanes Oxley Act
SRI	Socially Responsible Investment
Std. Dev.	Standard Deviation
STI	FTSE Straits Times Index (Singapore Exchange Index)
SUPP	Supportive of expectations
tCO_2e	Tons of carbon dioxide equivalent
TN	Tennessee
TSE	Tokyo Stock Exchange
TX	Texas
Txt	Text File (filename extension)

UK	United Kingdom
UPS	United Parcel Service, Inc.
URL	Uniform Resource Locator
US	United States
USA	United States of America
U.S.C.	United States Code
USD	United States Dollar(s)
US-GAAP	United States Generally Accepted Accounting Principles
VA	Virginia
VIF	Variance Inflation Factors
Vol.	Volume
Vs.	Versus
WEF	World Economic Forum
WICI	World Intellectual Capital Initiative
WU	Wirtschaftsuniversität Wien (Vienna University of Economics and Business)
www	World Wide Web
XBRL	Extensible Business Reporting Language
ZAR	Zuid-Afrikaanse Rand (South African Rand)

List of symbols

α	Constant Regression Term
β	Regression Coefficient
ε	Error Term
*	Significance Level
&	And
$	Dollar
#	Number
H	Hypothesis
i	Item in the Company Index
<IR>	Integrated Reporting (official IIRC denotation)
k	Item in the Control Variables Index
m	Item in the Market Index
N (n)	Number of Observations
τ	Item in the Day Index
t	Item in the Period Index
Σ	Sum
§	Section
®	Registered Trademark
™	Trademark
✓	Guiding Principle or Content Element covered by national regulations; results in line with expectations
☒	Guiding Principle or Content Element not covered by national regulations; results contrary to expectations
[illegible]	Mixed results

1 Introduction

1.1 Motivation and objective of the study

Annual (financial) reports have been considered the **centerpiece of corporate communication** for a long time (*Hütten* (2000), p. 84, with further references). While the capital providers and other stakeholders of private firms often have access to insider information and thus do not rely on the firms' reporting (e.g., *Hope et al.* (2013), p. 1716), corporate reports represent a way to gain and enhance investors' confidence for public firms (*Subramanian et al.* (1993), p. 59).[1] The reports enable investors to assess how effectively managers discharge their fiduciary duties and carry out their stewardship function (*Kohut/Segars* (1992), p. 7; *Epstein/Pava* (1993), p. 18), in addition to providing meaningful information on both the firms' past performance and future opportunities (*Kohut/Segars* (1992), p. 7). Capital-market-oriented companies may therefore put considerable effort into preparing their reports to present themselves in a transparent and open way (*Simpson* (1997), p. 16).

Shortcomings of corporate reporting

In contrast to these purposes and to the intended importance of financial reports, current reporting practice is only of limited assistance for investors' decision making, as lengthy reports and disclosures of low substance require their readers to undertake a long process of filtering the necessary information when analyzing a firm (*Peñarrubia Fraguas* (2015), pp. 597-598). At the same time, alternative ways to communicate (e.g., analyst presentations) gain importance so that **financial reports are struggling to remain relevant** (*CA ANZ/EY* (2015), pp. 6-7).

Dissatisfaction and complaints about these communications have a history almost as long as that of the reports. *Girdler* (1963) provokingly characterized the annual reports that firms send to their shareholders as "*18,000,000 books nobody reads*".[2] Referring to the mentioned effort firms put into the preparation, *Jones* (1988) asked the question "*Annual corporate reports: A waste of time and money?*". Most explicitly, *Bruce* ranted about the reports in an article in Canadian Business from 1987:

> "*Usually they're dreary, repetitive, pretentious, self-congratulatory and even ungrammatical. They seem to be the work of whole committees of stuffed shirts and illiterates. Printing this stuff on expensive paper is like delivering loose horse manure from the back seat of a Jaguar. Billion-dollar corporations that reward competence in other disciplines somehow can't produce annual reports that demonstrate competence in writing.*"
>
> (*Bruce* (1987), p. 84)

---

1 This study deals with the reporting of public (listed) firms if not explicitly indicated differently.

2 In a similar vein, financial analysts from Germany state that they use management reports (Lageberichte) as a comprehensive reference work that they use selectively rather than reading it completely (*Kajüter et al.* (2010), p. 459).

Analyzing the **reasons for this mismatch** between the intended purpose of corporate reports and their perception by users reveals that one central shortcoming of corporate reporting is that reports often are not **understandable** for their readers (e.g., *Warren E. Buffett* in *SEC* (1998), p. 1). This problem occurs in various ways. First, reports are frequently just not written well. There is a lot of evidence that corporate reports were **insufficiently readable** and became even less legible over the years (e.g., *Smith/Smith* (1971); *Barnett/Leoffler* (1979); *Jones/Shoemaker* (1994); *Cox* (2007); *KPMG* (2011)). Due to this flaw, the reports require considerable expertise to read and may thus fail to address a wide audience among (potential) shareholders without specific knowledge, in particular in countries with deficiencies in education (*Rensburg/Botha* (2014), p. 150).

A second aspect of this problem is **information overload**, meaning that the reports provide information in excess of the readers' processing capacity (*Snowball* (1979), p. 22). In turn, this overload affects the quality of the decisions that users make on the basis of the respective report (*Iselin* (1988), p. 147), contradicting the purpose of financial reporting to convey decision-useful information, as stated in the Conceptual Framework (CF) for Financial Reporting (CF. OB2).[3] The excess of information results from an increasing number of disclosures in the reports, both in response to growing information demand (*Fertakis* (1969), p. 680) and in compliance with manifold regulations (*Simpson* (1997), p. 17).

Users consider the resulting increase in report length as an impairment to the usefulness of the information (*Stainbank/Peebles* (2006), p. 78). This increasing volume is also driven by a third aspect of the problem: the rising number of **redundancies** in the reports (*KPMG* (2011), p. 12). While at some points, repetition may assist readers' understanding, it may also be distractive and thus hamper the readers' information processing (*KPMG* (2011), p. 12).

In addition to a lack of understandability, annual reports suffer from a **too narrow focus.** One issue in this regard is their concentration on financial aspects. As a central part of the annual report, the financial statements – in line with their name – amply cover this perspective. However, there have been early complaints that the reports only insufficiently deal with **non-financial** data (*Fertakis* (1969), p. 683). Today, this problem persists in a similar way. Rather than non-financial aspects in general, in particular non-physical aspects lack coverage in the reports (*Stubbs et al.* (2014), p. 6). Along with a growing importance of intangible assets, the percentage of firms' market value represented by financial and physical assets has decreased to 19% in 2009, coming from 83% in 1975, measured for the American S&P 500 index[4] (*Ocean Tomo* (2010)). Figure 1-1 illustrates this development over time. Non-financial and intangible factors often do not appear in the statement of financial position or elsewhere in the annual report, in particular due to their treatment in accounting

---

[3] This study refers to the purpose of financial reports under IFRS and US GAAP. The parts of the CF that outline the purpose and the Qualitative Characteristics of financial reporting have been elaborated in a joint project by the International Accounting Standards Board (IASB) and the Financial Accounting Standards Board (FASB). After the development of these parts, the two bodies suspended their collaboration and continued the work on their respective frameworks separately (*IASB* (2016); *FASB* (2016)). The jointly developed parts are still effective under both regimes. Other national GAAP or regulations in different countries may prescribe additional or deviating purposes for financial reports.

[4] Section 4.3.1 provides a short introduction of the S&P 500 index.

regulations.[5] Hence, this communication fails to inform about a substantial portion of a firm's value.

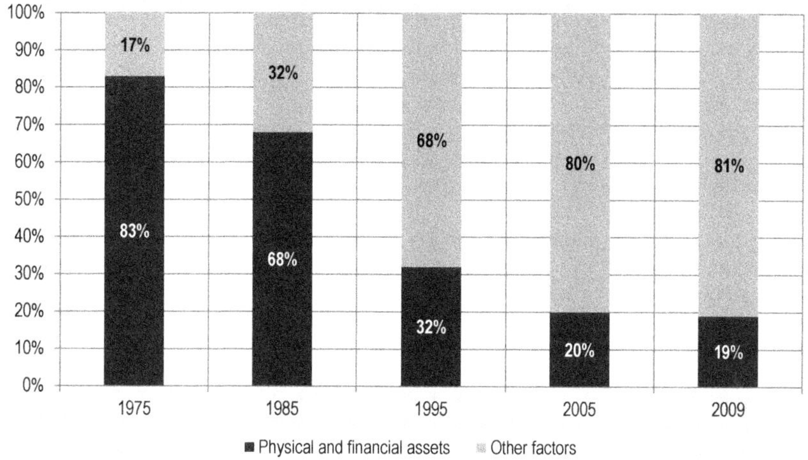

Figure 1-1: Components of S&P 500 market value (based on *Ocean Tomo* (2010) and DP IR, p. 4)

Moreover, annual reports often do not satisfy their users' needs for **forward-looking information.** While single countries, such as Germany, prescribe the disclosure of forecast information in annual reports (GAS 20.118), corporate communication in many countries lacks future-orientation. As firms in the latter group of countries fear litigation in case that they do not meet communicated targets or forecasts (*Johnen/Ganske* (2002), columns 1529-1530), many reports use boilerplate language (i.e., highly generic information) to present future-oriented contents (*Iannaconi/Rouse* (1996), pp. 72-73). This language also hampers the informative value of the reports, as forward-looking disclosures have been identified as one of the key aspects for reports to consider in satisfying users' changing information needs (*AICPA* (1994), p. 5).

Attempts to improve corporate reporting

Some initiatives, on the national and international level, have addressed these issues. In **different countries,** projects attempted to stimulate the understandability of reporting and/or more disclosures about non-financial aspects. For instance, the introduction of the Strategic Report in the UK drew on the notion that report users wanted a **clear focus** on

---

5 For instance, IAS 38.52-67 define special criteria for the recognition of internally developed intangible assets. The requirements include the firm's intention, technical feasibility and (financial) resources to complete the development of the asset, the firm's ability to reliably measure the expenditure of the development, the ability to use or sell the asset and an assessment of the future economic benefits. These criteria are susceptible to creative accounting and reporting (*Finch* (2006), p. 19).

material and relevant information (*BIS* (2010a; 2010b; 2011; 2012a; 2012b)). Moreover, the new requirements, among other things, included the disclosure of environmental and social matters for listed firms (The Companies Act 2006 (Strategic Report and Directors' Report) Regulations 2013, Part 2, Chapter 4A, Section 414C (7) (b)) in the "front-end" of the annual report (*ICAEW* (2014), p. 2). In other European countries, different approaches particularly dealt with the disclosure of **intangibles**, including the Austrian "Wissensbilanz" or several models from Scandinavia, such as the "Skandia Navigator".[6] Basing upon these models and on Danish guidance for Intellectual Capital Statements (Guideline for Intellectual Capital Statements (2000) and Intellectual Capital Statements – The New Guideline (2003)), the German "Arbeitskreis 'Immaterielle Werte im Rechnungswesen' der Schmalenbach-Gesellschaft für Betriebswirtschaft e.V." (AKIW) developed a recommendation for Intellectual Capital Statements in the German management report (Lagebericht) (*AKIW* (2003; 2004)). The Accounting Standards Committee of Germany (ASCG) even included a recommendation for the disclosure of intangible items in the former accounting standard on group management reporting (GAS 15.169-173), drawing on a taxonomy of different capitals that the *AKIW* (2001) developed to represent intangible value. On an international level, the upcoming idea of Value Reporting confirmed the importance of non-financial issues as drivers of shareholder value (*Eccles et al.* (2001)).

Moreover, different projects in the **USA** intended to **enhance the understandability** of corporate reports. For instance, the idea of Summary Annual Reports, which only include a condensed version of the financial statements, in particular of the notes (*Nair/Rittenberg* (1990), p. 25), was supposed to reduce information load and improve readability, but showed only slow adoption (*Schneider* (1988), p. 21) and little of the expected improvement (*Schroeder/Gibson* (1992), p. 37). To further address the problem of readability, the Securities and Exchange Commission (SEC) started the plain English initiative (*SEC* (1998)), which aimed at promoting the use of plain English in firms' shareholder communication for a better understandability. However, this project did not have much impact, either (*KPMG* (2011), p. 18). Other approaches **addressed the too narrow focus** of the reports and their lack of future orientation. A study by the American Institute of Certified Public Accountants (AICPA) in 1994, the so-called "Jenkins Report", yielded recommendations for better business reporting, in particular more forward-looking information, a stronger focus on factors that create long-term value and a better alignment of internally and externally reported information (*AICPA* (1994), p. 5). After further promotion of forward-looking information by the SEC through an Interpretative Release (SEC Release 33-8350 (2003)), slight changes toward more future-oriented disclosures were visible in annual reports (*Muslu et al.* (2015), p. 935). Furthermore, the FASB carried out the Business Reporting Research Project (*Velte* (2008), pp. 375-376), developing a framework for voluntary disclosures[7] for firms in different industries (*FASB* (2001)). These disclosures

[6] Cf. *Velte* ((2008), pp. 367-413) for a presentation and discussion of several approaches of reporting on intangible values.

[7] The disclosures were to be provided primarily outside the financial statements, but e.g. in Management's Discussion and Analysis of Financial Condition and Results of Operations (MD&A), thus inside the firms' annual report (Form 10-K) (*FASB* (2001), p. 5).

include information about unrecognized intangible assets (*FASB* (2001), pp. 10-11). Nonetheless, US firms are still reticent on voluntary disclosures due to remaining concern about additional liability risk (*AICPA* (2014), p. 3).

In **South Africa**, the King Committee developed three consecutive reports on corporate governance and corporate governance reporting, including codes for good governance practice (see section 3.1). Besides governance (reporting) issues, the second version of the report (King II) included various requirements and principles for reporting, such as the principle of clarity (King II Code, par. 5.1.3), accompanied by recommendations for better **understandability**, such as the avoidance of jargon (King II Report, section 4, chapter 2, recital 12 (pp. 99-100)). Moreover, this version extensively addressed reporting on **non-financial issues**, in particular stakeholder or sustainability issues (e.g., King II Code, par. 5.1.1). The third version even included a requirement for integrating financial and sustainability reporting in the same report (King III Report, Introduction and background, recital 9 (p. 14)), thus for preparing integrated reports (King III Code, pars. 9.1-9.3).

Despite these efforts, the aforementioned shortcomings of corporate reporting could not be remedied. Although the initiatives helped to address particular issues in different countries, the **lack of a holistic approach to tackle all deficiencies** and to provide a standardized basis for reporting internationally persisted. Furthermore, the outlined regulations and recommendations add to a confusing hotchpotch of guidance that reporting firms face, complicating the preparation of the reports and resulting in difficult and partly repetitive communications (*Kajüter et al.* (2013a), p. 199).

The Integrated Reporting approach

The international approach of **Integrated Reporting** (IR) aims at providing a holistic method of resolution, tackling the presented problems and providing guidance for reports that are supposed to better enable investors to assess the firm's value creation and make according investment decisions. In 2010, the International Integrated Reporting Committee (IIRC)[8] started its mission to develop a framework for IR (*IIRC* (2010a), p. 1).[9] What began with an intention to develop a framework for sustainability reporting (*IIRC* (2010b), p. 1) would soon become the idea to install a whole "*new approach to corporate reporting*" (*IIRC* (2011b), p. 1). Basing upon the developments in South Africa, a discussion paper called "Towards Integrated Reporting – Communicating Value in the 21st Century" (DP IR) gave a first impression of the IIRC's plans in September 2011. It outlined the shortcomings of traditional reporting and the changes in the conduct of business over time that reporting has to depict. As a response to these challenges, the paper presented the key aspects of IR, which were supposed to address these issues.

According to the DP IR, an integrated report should become a company's primary channel of communication with investors and other users, explaining the firm's ability to create and sustain value. It should combine the information that was traditionally reported in different

[8] In November 2011 the IIRC changed its name to International Integrated Reporting Council. It kept the official abbreviation IIRC, though (*IIRC* (2011f)).

[9] Chapter 2 presents the IIRC and its mission, as well as the Framework it has developed, in detail.

strands (e.g., financial reports, management commentaries, governance and remuneration reports and sustainability reports). The paper defined different Content Elements to determine what the report should contain, including an outlook to **address the firm's future.** Different Guiding Principles should govern the disclosures, combining principles known from both financial and sustainability reporting. Among these principles were Conciseness, to **overcome long and difficult reports**, as well as Connectivity of Information, intending to reveal the linkages and interdependencies between different aspects of reporting. A major purpose of the new approach was to **tackle the silo thinking** behind traditional reporting (*Adams/Simnett* (2011), p. 293), which was a result of the various reporting strands and the multitude of reporting regulations. Moreover, the DP IR used the concept of six different capitals for a comprehensive depiction of the company's business model and value creation. In addition to financial capital, it suggested to use manufactured, human, intellectual, natural and social capital. This concept **broadened the financial focus of traditional corporate reporting.**

The IIRC also showed possible impacts of the new reporting format for the different parties involved in corporate reporting, both in terms of **potential benefits and challenges of IR.** According to the Council, investors could benefit from integrated reports, which could enhance their capital allocation decisions, but would need to adapt their analysis techniques to process the new type of information (DP IR, p. 22). Better access to and lower cost of capital could be examples of benefits for the reporting firms, while the firms would face the challenge to establish the necessary systems and structures for the new approach (DP IR, p. 21). Furthermore, the approach could allow the harmonization of reporting regulations, given the will and effort of the different regulators (DP IR, p. 23).

With this perspective in mind, the IIRC developed the intended Framework in a transparent process under surveillance of an interested public and with the participation of numerous commentators responding to different draft versions, including the DP IR. Nevertheless, the development process advanced quickly, ending with the release of the **International <IR> Framework** (IR F) in December 2013. This Framework conveys a substantial part of the ideas that the DP IR had introduced, including the six capitals and the Connectivity and Conciseness principles. In line with the IIRC's intention stated in the DP IR (DP IR, p. 2), the Framework guides the preparation of integrated reports to provide meaningful information for investors (and, subordinately, other stakeholders) about the firm's value creation (IR F. 1.3; 1.7-1.8). Altogether, the final guidance document presents three Fundamental Concepts (value creation for the organization and for others, the capitals, the value creation process), seven Guiding Principles (Strategic Focus and Future Orientation, Connectivity of Information, Stakeholder Relationships, Materiality, Conciseness, Reliability and Completeness, Consistency and Comparability) and eight Content Elements (Organizational Overview and External Environment, Governance, Business Model, Risks and Opportunities, Strategy and Resource Allocation, Performance, Outlook, Basis of Preparation and Presentation) to determine the information in an integrated report and how it is presented.

Focus and research questions of the study at hand

The study at hand analyzes this new reporting approach. Taking into regard the outlined shortcomings of annual reports, which mitigate the usefulness of these reports for their readers (in particular investors), as well as the focus of the IR Framework on investors, this study takes an investor perspective. It deals with the overall **research question** whether IR is useful for the providers of financial capital. Following the IIRC's reasoning, integrated reports provide an enhanced basis for their analysis of the firm and for their investment decisions (DP IR, p. 22). Two sub-questions constitute this examination:

- Research question 1: Do the IIRC regulations improve the usefulness of corporate reports?
- Research question 2: Do integrated reports improve their users' decision making?

Figure 1-2 illustrates the conception of this study, presenting the different parts with their respective goals and methods, as well as the way these parts interact. A **conceptual analysis** deals with research question 1. It builds the foundation of the study. The regulations of the IIRC Framework are investigated and assessed against their declared purpose to inform investors about the firm's value creation and against the principles that shall contribute to this purpose by governing the regulations. This examination allows an assessment of the general potential of the Framework to promote reports that are useful for investors.

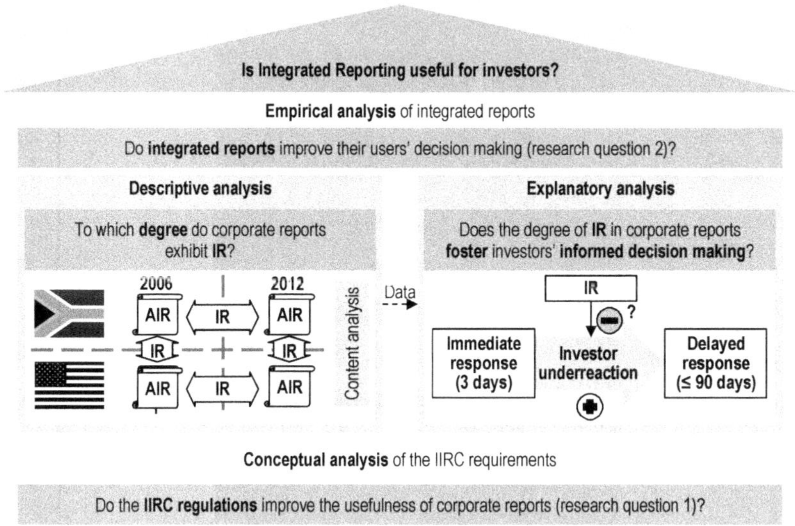

Figure 1-2: Conception of the study

Subsequently, an **empirical analysis** takes a look at the actual reporting practice. This empirical part is further divided into two sub-studies. First, a **descriptive study** gives an impression of the degree to which corporate reports exhibit IR. It employs content analysis to derive an IR score that captures the adherence of the reports to the IR Guiding Principles.

The reports stem from a balanced sample of South African and US firms, covering financial years 2012 and 2006. Contrasting these two countries could yield promising insights, given the differences in their approach to corporate reporting. While South Africa plays a pioneering role for IR and shows a tradition of stakeholder and sustainability orientation, the USA have an established and developed system of corporate reporting with a rather standardized reporting approach. The US system has shown its usefulness for investors, firms and other parties in the economy, though. South African firms had to use IR on an apply-or-explain basis beginning in 2010, whereas US firms did not face a requirement to apply IR in either of these years.[10] Hence, the country comparisons in 2012 and 2006 draw on changed circumstances in the two countries. In addition to this **country dimension**, the setting allows comparisons over time in both countries (**time dimension**). For South Africa, the research design makes it possible to examine the presence of the IR principles in firms' reports before and after the introduction of the IR requirement. For the USA, the study compares reports for two points in time without a structural change. Resulting from the two-dimension setting, the design also allows a comparison of the differences over time in each country.

In conjunction with archival data on firms' characteristics and stock returns, the IR scores from the descriptive study represent the inputs for the **explanatory analysis,** which constitutes the second empirical sub-study. This part investigates the capital market reaction to the aforementioned corporate reports. Employing an event study design, the analysis examines **investor underreaction**, i.e. delayed market reaction to the report release, depicted by the alignment of long-term market reactions with market movements immediately following the report release. **IR may exert a moderating influence** on the potential underreaction. As the approach intends to make corporate reports a better basis for investors' analysis of the firm and for their investment decisions, the degree of IR in a report can be expected to decrease a potential underreaction to the information from the report. The question whether this is the case, and whether IR thus fosters investors' informed decisions making, guides this explanatory study. In conjunction with the descriptive study, the explanatory part shall therefore answer research question 2, assessing the potential of integrated reports to improve users' decision making.

As the study takes an investor perspective, it particularly yields **implications** for this group. The conceptual analysis allows shareholders and lenders to assess the IR Framework and to build expectations toward reports that are prepared in abidance by this IIRC guidance. Most importantly, these expectations regard the ability of the reports to present the firm's value and thus support investors with their capital allocation decision. Furthermore, the empirical study gives an impression of the degree to which existing reports already exhibit IR in terms of the Guiding Principles. Moreover, the results from the capital market study may provide evidence that IR has an impact on investment decisions, in so far as it may impact investor underreaction. This would contribute to an assessment of the IIRC's expectation that IR may facilitate investors' decision making and send a respective signal to

[10] Industry-specific SASB standards provide non-mandatory guidance on including sustainability issues in financial reports, which may represent a first step toward IR in the USA (see section 3.2). However, the standards were issued gradually after the release of the examined reports, starting on 31 July 2013.

the market participants. In addition to the investors themselves, the outlined features of this study may be helpful for other parties. The findings could inform report preparers in their assessment of whether the implementation of IR (or of selected features of the IR idea) is an option for their firms, or in their estimation of the impacts that their reports have on the firms' investors. As mentioned before, the study also helps to evaluate in how far the IIRC's expectations are met. So it would contribute to the IIRC's and other regulators' assessment of the reporting format and of resulting decisions for rules and standards.

Furthermore, this study **contributes to the literature** in different ways. Owing to the young age, IR is not yet explored in detail. Nevertheless, there are already several reviews of the practice of this new reporting approach. The descriptive study goes beyond this existing research due to its measurement of IR and its design. In particular, the IR variable captures the adherence to the Guidance Principles. It draws on both manually collected items and on data that was collected by software, embedding constructs that have been used in prior literature on a standalone basis (e.g., the similarity of reports to depict the use of boilerplate disclosures). The design allows statistically sound comparisons across two countries and between two points in time, but also a comparison of the changes over time in the two countries (difference-in-differences). Research on the economic consequences of IR is sparse, even though some early studies examine the relationships of IR with the cost of capital or information asymmetry. However, extant literature does not provide insights on investor underreaction to integrated reports. This study thus sets in at the cross-section of the literature on the economic consequences of IR, on the impact of reporting formats and on investor underreaction to reduce this research gap. It uses a measure of capital market response that closely relates to the report release and that is independent of unobserved interdependencies between different economic influences, as opposed to other measures of economic consequences.

The following section describes the scientific positioning of the study and section 1.3 outlines its organization.

1.2 Scientific research strategy

Science is a process of detecting, formulating and solving problems in a systematic way (*Lingnau* (1995), p. 124).[11] It aims at advancing and accumulating knowledge (*Fülbier* (2004), p. 266; *Kornmeier* (2007), p. 4). In requiring verification of certain assertions, science differs from belief or intuition (*Kornmeier* (2007), p. 4). The **philosophy of science** is a meta-science that deals with the concept and objective of science and with how knowledge is gained (*Fülbier* (2004), p. 266; *Kornmeier* (2007), pp. 6-8). A direct predecessor of the philosophy of science is epistemology, the theory of knowledge, which can be traced back to antique Greek philosophers (*Kornmeier* (2007), p. 6).

According to *Schweitzer* ((1978), pp. 3-9) science has four different **objectives**. The descriptive objective aims at a definition of occurring phenomena and at their systematic documentation. Explanative science exceeds this approach by depicting (causal) relationships.

[11] *Raffée* ((1974), pp. 13-17) uses a more differentiated definition of science, distinguishing between science as an institution, as a process and as the outcome of this process.

Furthermore, the pragmatic objective of science is to use these relationships for predictions and decision making, whereas the normative objective intends to render value judgments and derive recommendations.

In business economics research, there are two prevailing epistemological approaches: constructivism and critical rationalism (*Fülbier* (2004), p. 268)[12]. **Constructivism** is particularly associated with the Erlangen School around Paul Lorenzen and bases the gain of knowledge upon deductive argument, from which experts derive their conclusions (*Lorenzen* (1974), pp. 113-118, *Fülbier* (2004), p. 269). However, since human arguments are fallible, the derived knowledge cannot be considered to be an ultimate truth (*Fülbier* (2004), p. 269).

This fallibility of human knowledge is also the basic idea behind **critical rationalism**, which goes back to *Popper* (1934).[13] Knowledge can be erroneous at any time and is thus only of a temporary nature, while an eventual and ultimate verification is impossible (*Lingnau* (1995), p. 124; *Popper* (2005), pp. 16-17). *Popper* does not consider this a reason for pessimism, though, but concludes that scientists can approximate the truth by falsifying different positions and notions (*Popper* (2005), pp. XXXIII-XXXIV, 16-19). The process of gaining knowledge under the critical rationalism works as follows (*Fülbier* (2004), p. 268; *Kornmeier* (2007), p. 42): First, an observable phenomenon that needs an explanation (problem) is addressed by developing hypotheses (solution). The next step constitutes an empirical test of these hypotheses, which potentially falsifies and eliminates some of them. A steady iteration of this process eventually leads to nomological hypotheses, i.e. universal, well-tested statements occurring under defined conditions (*Lingnau* (1995), p. 125). However, hypotheses or theories[14] in general are only of temporal validity until they are falsified (*Bartel* (1990), p. 58).

Although critical rationalism is the dominant approach in recent business economics studies, constructivism is still of non-negligible importance for the research and the gain of knowledge in this subject (*Fülbier* (2004), p. 269). As empirical research bears several limitations (*Frank* (2003), p. 283), it is doubtful to merely rely on critical rationalism. Instead, scientists may use both approaches as **complements.** Financial reporting research is an example in this regard (*Nienhaus* (2015), p. 9): Empirical research may analyze the effects of accounting and reporting standards on the capital markets. At the same time, deducting useful rules based on a specific set of standards (e.g., the IASB's Conceptual Framework) can benefit the development of accounting and reporting standards.

This study follows the critical rationalism as the scientific approach. Rather than deductively deriving recommendations on the use of IR as under constructivism, the study develops hypotheses about IR practice and about the capital market consequences of IR. In the next step, these hypotheses are tested empirically.

---

12 The two approaches have historically developed from the earlier approaches classical rationalism, empiricism, positivism and neo-positivism (*Fülbier* (2004), p. 268).

13 Cf. *Albert* (2000) for an extensive depiction of critical rationalism.

14 Various nomological hypotheses that connect without contradiction constitute a theory (*Lingnau* (1995), p. 125).

In addition to the scientific approach, researchers need to select a strategy. There are three different **research strategies** that dominate in business economics: the conceptual, the analytical and the empirical research strategy (*Grochla* (1978), p. 71).

Based upon plausibility, **conceptual** research (*Grochla* (1978), pp. 72-78) uses logical reasoning to analyze a problem and derives implications, as well as a basis for actions. This strategy mostly yields definitional or descriptive statements. They may construct relationships and explain circumstances so that they have a hypothetical character. Nonetheless, conceptual research does not consider empirical tests of the hypotheses.

The most distinctive feature of the **analytical** research strategy compared with other strategies is its focus on a specific problem (*Grochla* (1978), pp. 85-93). Analytical research analyzes such specific problems by abstract modeling. To this end, the researcher depicts a generalized real situation in a mathematical model and combines it with the occurring problem, trying to derive solutions on this basis. While the emphasis of analytical research is on finding such solutions, this research strategy does not necessarily provide an accurate depiction of reality.

In contrast, the **empirical** research strategy (*Grochla* (1978), pp. 78-85) aims at a confrontation of hypotheses and theories with reality, which either results in the support or the rejection of these hypotheses. Statements on reality can be of a descriptive or explanatory nature. The latter group of statements presents (causal) relationships between variables. Various methods are applicable to collect the necessary data for making these statements. These methods include case studies, field studies, experiments (in the field or in a laboratory setting) and action research, but also historical research with archival data (*Grochla* (1978), pp. 80-81; *Smith* (2015), p. 53).

After a conceptual analysis of the International <IR> Framework as the regulatory basis of IR, **this study** follows an empirical research strategy. It provides both a description of reality (IR practice in different countries and at different points in time) and an empirical-cognitive explanation of relationships between two variables (the impact of IR on investor underreaction). The results from the description and explanation serve as a basis to derive implications for investors as well as for the reporting firms and regulators. However, it is not the intention of the study to give normative recommendations for these parties.[15]

1.3 Outline of the study

This study is organized along six chapters. Figure 1-3 shows the outline. The **first chapter** provides the introduction of the study, motivating the topic and showing its relevance for research and practice. A central aspect is the presentation of the research questions for this study. In addition, the chapter sets out both the scientific research strategy that the study applies and the organization that the thesis follows.

The **second chapter** develops the conceptual basis for this research project. It introduces the approach of IR. After elaborating the historical and institutional background, it presents

[15] Cf. e.g. *Nienhaus* (2015) for a similar approach.

the International <IR> Framework, which contains the objective and other general characteristics of IR, the Fundamental Concepts underlying this reporting format, Guiding Principles that govern reporting and the particular requirements on the Content Elements. A conceptual analysis of the Framework requirements against the background of the objective of integrated reports and the Guiding Principles concludes this chapter.

Supplementing the institutional and regulatory background of the second chapter, the **third chapter** introduces the reporting landscape in South Africa and the USA. At the same time this part sets out basic information for the empirical analyses, as the two subsequent chapters of this study analyze the reporting practice in these two countries and the impact of this practice on capital markets. The chapter begins with a presentation of the historical and institutional background of South African reporting, before it outlines the relevant regulations and compares them with the IR requirements. The same analysis follows for the US reporting landscape.

Representing the first sub-study of the empirical analysis, the **fourth chapter** describes the IR practice in South Africa and the USA for the years 2006 and 2012 respectively, i.e. before and after the introduction of an apply-or-explain requirement for South African listed firms to use IR. It reviews the literature on IR disclosures and identifies a research gap and potential for improvement, which this study addresses with its research design. Based on theoretical reasoning, it subsequently posits hypotheses on the disclosure practices in the two countries for the different years and on their relationships. This reasoning includes Principle Agent Theory, Positive Accounting Theory (PAT) and different systems-oriented theories (Legitimacy Theory, Stakeholder Theory and Institutional Theory). Following a description of the sample and the method of data collection, i.e. content analysis, the descriptive results are presented. The chapter concludes with a discussion of these results against the extant literature and the theoretical reasoning and hypotheses.

Following a similar organization, the **fifth chapter** provides the second empirical part, the explanatory study. As in the previous chapter, a review of the extant literature and the deduction of the research gap provide the starting point for the analysis, after which the chapter derives the hypothesis for the explanatory study. Both the literature and the theories section distinguish between impacts of IR features, effects of reporting formats on investor reaction and the underreaction effect. Theoretical reasoning stems from rational structural uncertainty and behavioral approaches, both of which contradict the Efficient Market Hypothesis (EMH), as well as from Cognitive Load Theory (CLT) and Pragmatics, two theoretical approaches from psychology and linguistics, respectively. After that, the methodology for this part of the study is introduced, followed by a presentation of the results of the main analysis and of various tests that specify and/or supplement the findings of the main treatment. These results are eventually discussed, in particular in light of the stated hypothesis and the underlying theoretical reasoning.

The **last chapter** merges the conceptual analysis and the two empirical studies, by summarizing and combining their conclusions to an overall line of reasoning. Moreover, it derives implications for investors, as the main users of integrated reports, as well as for reporting firms and regulators from the conceptual and empirical results. From remaining limitations of the analysis, the chapter develops suggestions for future research. The study ends with an outlook on the further advancement of IR.

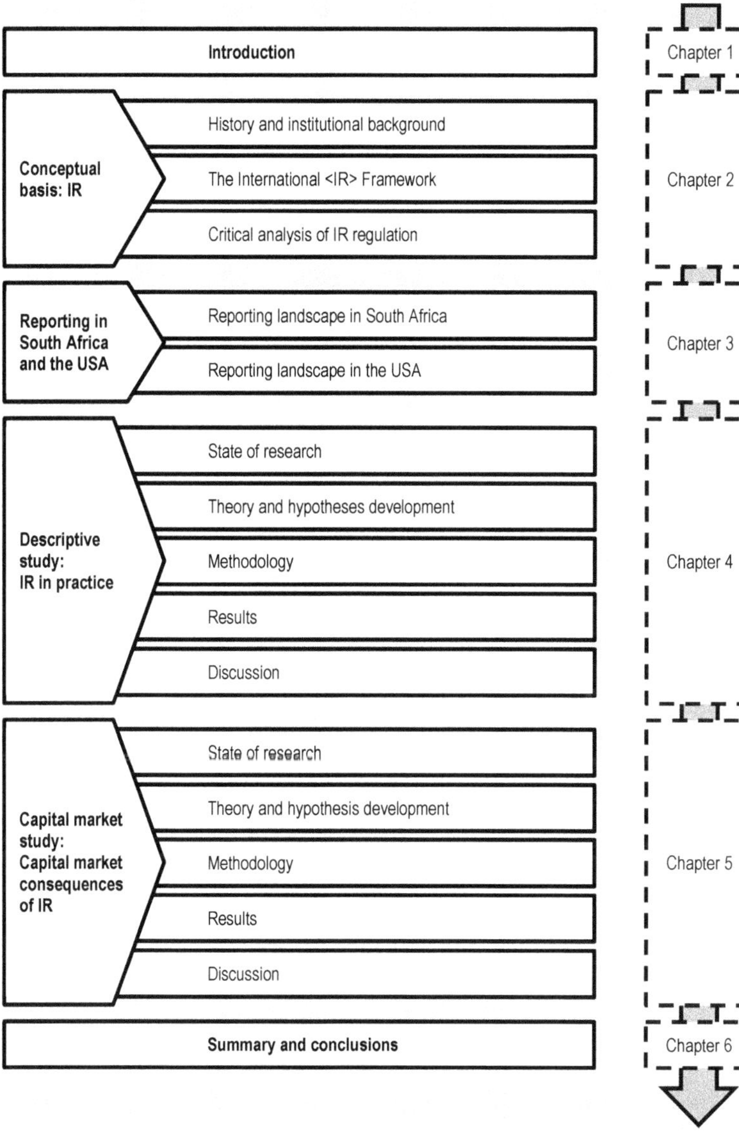

Figure 1-3: Outline of the study

2 The Integrated Reporting approach

This chapter deals with the approach of IR. The first section sheds light on where IR comes from and how it developed. Both the young history of the IR movement[16] and the institutions that played or still play a role in its advancement are introduced, with particular focus on the IIRC and the development of the International <IR> Framework as the main output of the Council's work. The second section describes this Framework. A critical discussion of the regulations follows in the third section.

2.1 History and institutional background

Various movements in corporate reporting already dealt with different inadequacies of corporate reporting and with reporting topics outside the focus of traditional (financial) reports. These movements laid the foundation for IR. However, it was the formation of the IIRC that brought together different approaches and topics for a joint proceeding toward IR and a common Framework.

The background of Integrated Reporting

The idea of IR has its **roots** in the insight that traditional financial reporting suffers from the different shortcomings depicted in section 1.1. As outlined in that section, several approaches, both on national and international level, tried to overcome these insufficiencies. For instance, they included the promotion of Intellectual Capital Statements in different European countries. Besides, after the recommendations of the Jenkins Report in 1994, the SEC tried to promote the use of forward-looking information in US firms' reports with an Interpretative Release 2003 (SEC Release 33-8350 (2003), Part III.B.3). In South Africa, the King Committee released three consecutive versions of the King Report on corporate governance, dealing with governance aspects, but also with sustainability and stakeholder issues and how reporting can include them (King II). The third version (King III) even introduced the requirement for firms to apply IR (or to explain why they do not). On an international level, the upcoming idea of Value Reporting conveyed that non-financial issues are important drivers of shareholder value (*Eccles et al.* (2001)). It contributed to the discussion toward the development of IR (*PwC* (2015b), p. 3).

Particular non-financial issues that play a role in this regard are sustainability aspects. The Global Reporting Initiative (GRI), headquartered in Amsterdam, has been working on the standardization of **sustainability reporting** since its foundation in 1997 and has provided several versions of guidance on this form of corporate reporting so far (*Blaesing* (2013), pp. 41-44; *Maniora* (2013b), p. 479; *Kajüter* (2014b)). In addition, the Prince's Accounting for Sustainability (A4S) initiative, set up by HRH The Prince of Wales in 2004 (*A4S* (n.d.)), deals with this topic. The initiative's work has – among other things – yielded a guidance document on Connected Reporting in 2009. This document follows three objectives: to connect the business strategy with sustainability, to connect KPIs for measurement with actions to address the measured issues and to report performance against the

[16] Cf. also *Eccles/Krzus* (2015), who give an overview of the movement, dividing it into four phases.

target KPIs, together with a commentary on progress. This guidance thus represents a predecessor of the IR Framework.

Some firms from various countries already began to publish **reports** that included both their financial and sustainability report. Among the earliest examples were the reports of the Danish biotechnology firm Novozymes in 2002 and the Brazilian cosmetics and fragrances company Natura in 2003 (*Eccles/Serafeim* (2011), p. 70). This is in line with the "*One Report*" approach that *Eccles/Krzus* (2010) promoted in their book of the same name. It represents the first book published on IR (*Eccles/Krzus* (2015), p. 10). Further **publications** had already dealt with the combination of traditional financial and sustainability reporting (e.g., *Solstice* (2005); *Mammatt* (2009)) and helped to advance the development of IR.[17] On 17 December 2009, both the A4S and the GRI announced their intention to establish an international body that develops an accepted integrated reporting framework (*HRH The Prince of Wales* (2009); *King* (2009)) at the A4S Forum seminar. To this end, they established the IIRC, officially announcing the formation on 2 August 2010 (*IIRC* (2010b), p. 1; *Druckman* (2010), p. I). This new body then started to work on its mission to develop the mentioned framework (*IIRC* (2010a), p. 1). Figure 2-1 summarizes the milestones of this development.

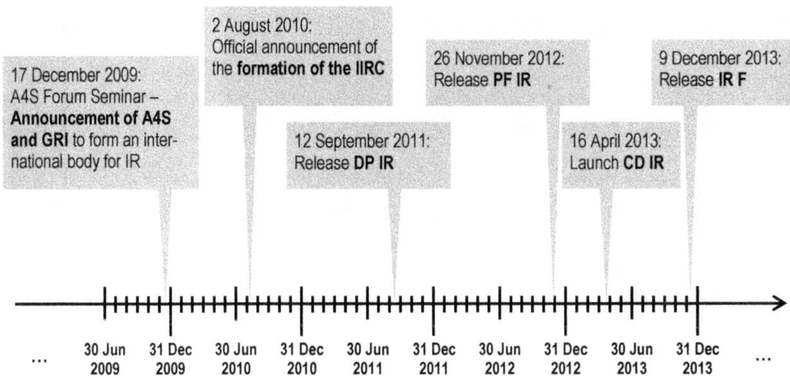

Figure 2-1: The development of the IR F – major milestones

Organization and structure of the IIRC

Initially, the London-based **IIRC** consisted of a Steering Committee and a Working Group (*IIRC* (2010b)). Sir Michael Peat, Principal Private Secretary to HRH The Prince of Wales and the Duchess of Cornwall, was chairman of the Steering Committee, with Mervyn E. King being deputy chairman. The latter already was chairman of both the GRI and the King Committee in South Africa, but he also chaired the Integrated Reporting Committee

[17] *Müller/Stawinoga* (2015) provide an overview of the development of financial and sustainability reporting and how these two streams led to IR.

of South Africa (IRCSA)[18], which had been founded in May 2010 (IRCSA DP 1.4 (p. 5)). Two co-chairmen presided over the Working Group: Paul Druckman, A4S Executive Board Chairman, and Ian Ball, CEO of the International Federation of Accountants. In 2011, King became chairman of the IIRC (*IIRC* (2011c)), while Druckman turned CEO (*IIRC* (2011d)). The Committee also changed its name to International Integrated Reporting Council, while keeping the official abbreviation IIRC (*IIRC* (2011f)).

From the beginning, the IIRC had **members from various parties**, including companies, investors, regulators, NGOs, the accounting profession, civil society and academia (*IIRC* (2010a), p. 1) to consider the interests of all material stakeholders in the development of the IR Framework (*Beyhs/Barth* (2011b), pp. 2857-2858). Among the members were the heads of major accounting bodies like the IASB, the FASB or the CEOs of the Big Four accounting firms – a composition that gave the IIRC a high power (*Flower* (2015), p. 2) and ensured support for IR by these institutions. Moreover, various **memoranda of understanding** with influential institutions arranged mutual support and cooperation as well as an alignment of the competencies between the IIRC and the respective partners. Among these partners are the IFRS Foundation (*IIRC/IFRS Foundation* (2013)), the GRI (*IIRC/GRI* (2013); *IIRC* (2013a)) or the Sustainability Accounting Standards Board (SASB) (*IIRC/SASB* (2013)). This variety of allies reflects the common dissatisfaction with the status of the reporting practice, which is characterized by the aforementioned shortcomings (*Fink et al.* (2013), p. 35; *Kajüter* (2013), pp. 125-126).

Figure 2-2 shows the **structure of the IIRC** as of today, as documented by the Constitution[19] of the IIRC (*IIRC* (2015c)). Representatives of the various parties mentioned before (coalition parties) sit on the Council[20] (*IIRC* (2015c), p. 1). The Council is the primary institutional forum for the coalition parties to express their views, interact with each other and provide advice and input for the IIRC (*IIRC* (2015c), p. 7). A private company limited by guarantee (Operating Company) registered in England and Wales has been established in addition to the Council (*IIRC* (2015c), p. 6). It provides the IIRC with a legal personality for conducting all initiatives and activities (*IIRC* (2015c), p. 2). The Council appoints the members of the Governance and Nominations Committee. Subject to the Council's direction, this committee monitors the organization's governance practices and has the power to appoint and remove the directors of the Operating Company (*IIRC* (2015c), pp. 10-12). Neither the members of the Council nor those of the Governance and Nominations Committee receive financial benefits for their work (*IIRC* (2015c), pp. 9; 12).

It is the responsibility of the Board of Directors to run the activities of the **Operating Company** (*IIRC* (2015c), p. 12). To this end, the Board may also form committees (Board Committees) for support in the discharge of duties (IIRC (2015c), p. 15). The directors

[18] Section 3.1 describes the King Committee and the IRCSA in more detail.

[19] The constitution contains the Charter (Part I), which governs the basis for the institutional embodiment of the organization, the Articles of Association of the Operating Company (Part II), which govern the relationship between the members of the Operating Company, and various Annexes (Part III).

[20] For the description of the structure of the IIRC, the term "Council" refers to the respective body of the organization. Throughout the remainder of this thesis, the term "Council" is considered as a synonym for the IIRC, unless a different meaning is explicitly indicated.

also designate the members of the <IR> Framework Panel, which operates autonomously and elaborates revisions, modifications and updates to the IR Framework as well as other IR guidance materials for Board sign-off (*IIRC* (2015c), pp. 15-16). Moreover, the Board appoints a CEO who is responsible for the organization's strategy and operational issues, leading the IIRC team (*IIRC* (2015c), pp. 16-17). For appropriate purposes, this IIRC team can establish and monitor advisory groups and task forces that elaborate guidance and can provide expertise and experience for particular topics (*IIRC* (2015c), p. 17).

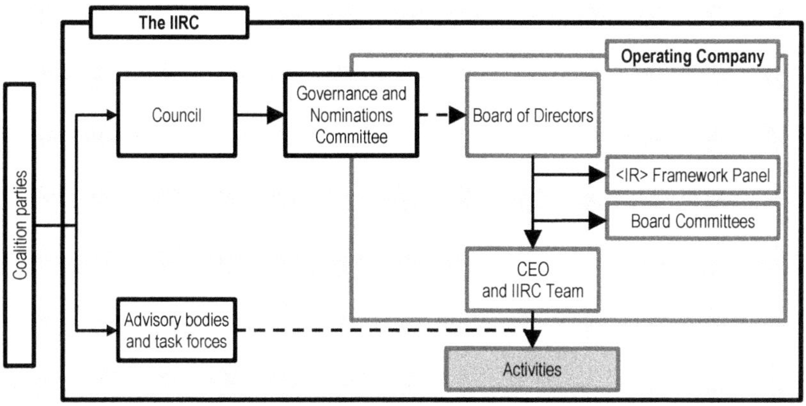

Figure 2-2: Structure of the IIRC (based on *IIRC* (2015c), p. 2)

The Board is also responsible for the **funding of the organization** (*IIRC* (2015c), pp. 17-18). Funds are raised from different sources, including kind contributions from supporting entities, such as those represented on the Council. However, in determining the funding, the Board needs to avoid dependencies from single parties while ensuring the transparency of the monetary flow.

The work of the IIRC

One of the first steps on the way to establish a framework for IR was the release of the DP IR on 12 September 2011, roughly eight months after the release of a **discussion paper on IR** in South Africa (see section 3.1). On 32 pages, the DP IR provides the motivation for IR and a definition of the concept, introduces the model of six different capitals, specifies five Guiding Principles and six Content Elements that an integrated report is supposed to address, gives best practice examples from existing reports and lists benefits and challenges related to IR for the different participants in the reporting process (i.e., the reporting firms, the investors, regulators and others). The paper raised a lot of attention, as was visible in the high number of comment letters that the IIRC received in response, which were analyzed by the Committee, published on its website and considered for the further development of the framework (*IIRC* (2012a), p. 1).[21] Both the five Guiding Principles (Strategic Focus, Connectivity of Information, Future Orientation, Responsiveness and Stakeholder Inclusiveness, Conciseness, Reliability and Materiality) and the six Content Elements (Organizational Overview and Business Model, Operating Context including Risks and Opportunities, Strategic Objectives, Governance and Remuneration, Performance, Future Outlook) were already close to the principles and contents that the eventual framework included (see section 2.2.4). Among the benefits that the DP IR expects IR to deliver are lower cost of capital through improved disclosures for the reporting firms (DP IR, p. 21), more effective investment decisions and capital allocation and therefore better long-term returns for investors (DP IR, p. 22) and better identification of occurring risks for regulators, as well as a harmonized and consistent basis to deal with these risks (DP IR, p. 23).

Alongside the framework development, the IIRC set up its so-called "**Pilot Programme**" in October 2011 (*IIRC* (2011a; 2011e)). This program formed a network of participating companies that worked as a peer group for IR by exchanging knowledge and experience as well as by testing the application of IR (*IIRC* (2011e)). The program started with about 75 companies from various sectors and countries (*IIRC* (2012c), p. 3), but over the years the number grew to more than 100 in September 2014, the time that the program ended (*IIRC* (2013c), pp. 10-11; *Eccles/Krzus* (2015), p. 16). A list of the participants (*IIRC* (2014a), pp. 6-8) includes various renowned companies from around the globe. For instance, German firms BASF and SAP, Sainsbury's, Unilever and Marks & Spencer from the UK, Danone from France, Telefónica from Spain or the Swedish Volvo Group are some examples of European participants. Furthermore, the Chinese energy firm CLP, Hyundai from South Korea, Tata Steel from India, the oil and gas firms Rosneft from Russia and Petrobras from Brazil as well as New Zealand Post took part in the Pilot Programme. Moreover, several firms from the countries that this study examines appear in the list. Among the businesses that joined the program were the South African firms AngloGold Ashanti Limited, Gold Fields Limited (Gold Fields) or Sasol Limited (Sasol) as well as The Clorox Company (Clorox), Microsoft Corporation or PepsiCo and The Coca-Cola Company from the USA. In addition to this Business Network, the IIRC's Investor Network assisted the framework development by providing helpful feedback on innovations as well as input for the process from the investor perspective (*IIRC* (2012c), p. 3; *IIRC* (2013b)).

In terms of time planning, the IIRC had the ambitious goal to publish the final Framework in 2013 (*IIRC* (2012b)). During the course of 2012, the IIRC provided several working documents of the framework on its website, which enabled interested stakeholders to closely follow the development process. These documents included the **Prototype Framework** (PF IR) that was made available on 26 November 2012. It represented the pre-stage to the **Consultation Draft** of the International <IR> Framework (CD IR), which was released on 16 April 2013. The latter constituted the next phase of interaction with the public, as the CD IR once more provided the opportunity for any interested party to give feedback in the

[21] The IIRC received 214 comment letters in response to the DP IR, all of which were published online (*IIRC* (2012a), p. 1). *Maniora* (2013a) analyzes the distribution and the remarks of the comment letters. *Reuter/Messner* (2015) examine the comment letters from a lobbying perspective.

form of a comment letter (CD IR, p. 1). Following up on the responses to the DP IR, the IIRC had specified the requirements on the Guiding Principles and in particular on the Content Elements and had rearranged both categories. Furthermore, the CD IR included a revised and more concise definition of IR (CD IR 1.2-1.4; compared with DP IR, p. 6) and a separate chapter "Fundamental Concepts" that merged the guidance on the different capitals, on the business model and on value creation (CD IR, chapter 2). The 359 responses to the CD IR even outnumbered the comment letters responding to the DP IR by far and the IIRC again provided all comment letters online, analyzed them and worked the results into the eventual version of the framework (*IIRC* (2013d), pp. 5-7). On 9 December 2013, this final **International <IR> Framework** was released, together with a Basis for Conclusions (IR F. BC). This date constitutes a cornerstone in the short history of IR, since it represents the accomplishment of the IIRC's mission to develop such a framework.

In addition to the aforementioned stages on the way to the final framework, the IIRC, in cooperation with various partners, provided in-depth information, discussions and **guidance material** on issues that had raised attention in the comment letters on the DP IR and CD IR, the so-called "Background Papers". These papers covered the topics Business Model (*IIRC et al.* (2013a)), Capitals (*IIRC et al.* (2013b)), Materiality (*IIRC/AICPA* (2013)), Value creation (*IIRC/EY* (2013)) and Connectivity (*IIRC/WICI* (2013)). The IIRC continued to publish background materials after the release of the Framework. Among them is the "Creating Value" series, which elaborates the ways in which IR can provide additional value for different parties like firms' boards (*IIRC* (2014b)) or investors (*IIRC* (2015a; 2015d)). Moreover, the Council provided further guidance on materiality and its determination (*IIRC/IFAC* (2015)). Such publications are part of the activities that the IIRC undertakes in its "**Breakthrough Phase**" from 2014 to 2017 (*IIRC* (2014c), p. 4), for which it changed its now accomplished mission of creating a framework to establishing IR as a norm in mainstream business practice (*IIRC* (2014c), p. 3). To support the distribution of IR, the IIRC now runs various further **networks** with many organizations from around the globe. Besides the aforementioned Business and Investor networks, these include networks for the public sector, pension funds, technology, banking and insurance.[22] However, the International <IR> Framework remains the critical element for the global acceptance of IR (*IIRC* (2012c), p. 3). Section 2.2 presents this Framework.

2.2 The International <IR> Framework

The International <IR> Framework constitutes the centerpiece of IR regulation worldwide. This section presents the provisions of the Framework in detail. The organization of the section follows that of the IIRC document. At the beginning, an overview of different basic characteristics of IR, the IR Framework and its use gives an impression of the new reporting approach in general. The section goes on by describing the Fundamental Concepts, which deal with the way the Framework defines value and how it is created. After that, the seven Guiding Principles that determine the preparation and presentation of an integrated report are explained, followed by a presentation of the eight Content Elements.

[22] The IIRC gives an overview of the different networks on its website: http://integratedreporting.org/ir-networks/ (last accessed on 29 August 2016).

2.2.1 Overview of basic characteristics of IR, the IR Framework and its use

It is the **objective** of the International <IR> Framework to define Guiding Principles and Content Elements for an integrated report and to provide an explanation of Fundamental Concepts as a basis for reporting (IR F. 1.3). Instead of prescribing specific indicators for reporting, the Framework follows a principles-based approach, which intends to balance the comparability of the reports and the flexibility to consider firm-specific circumstances (IR F. 1.9-1.10). As a private initiative, the IIRC has no legal authority so that the **use of the Framework is not binding** (*Kajüter/Hannen* (2014), p. 75).[23] If a firm choses to apply the guidance, however, it needs to apply all requirements that the Framework prints in bold italic type[24] to claim its communication to be an integrated report in accordance with the Framework; the only exceptions are the unavailability of the necessary information, legal prohibitions or competitive harm[25] through the disclosure of information (IR F. 1.17). As it is voluntary, the **application** is possible since the very release of the document in December 2013. Similarly, there is no restriction in terms of the users. Both for-profit companies and not-for-profit or public-sector organizations of any size can use the guidance, although the Framework primarily has a private-sector focus (IR F. 1.4). The IIRC has the long-term vision that IR becomes "*the corporate reporting norm*" (IR F., p. 2).

The Framework bases upon the following **definition of an integrated report:**

> *"An integrated report is a concise communication about how an organization's strategy, governance, performance and prospects, in the context of its external environment, lead to the creation of value over the short, medium and long term."*
>
> (IR F. 1.1)

Consistent with this definition, IR F. 1.7 states that the **purpose of an integrated report** is to explain how the organization creates value over time. It explicitly refers to "*providers of financial capital*" as the **addressees** of the integrated report, while IR F. 1.8 adds that the report also benefits all other stakeholders.

An integrated report needs to be a designated and identifiable communication (IR F. 1.12), that exceeds a mere summary of information from other reports (e.g., financial statements or sustainability reports) and elaborates the connectivity of the information from these sources (IR F. 1.13).[26] Hence, **integrated thinking**, which the IIRC defines as the consideration of the relationships between an organization's units and the capitals that the organization affects, and which leads to integrated decision making (IR F., pp. 2, 33), represents a major foundation for IR. As the Background Paper on Connectivity explains, IR can in turn enhance managers' understanding of the business and its strategy (*IIRC/WICI* (2013),

---

23 The IRCSA endorsed the International <IR> Framework as guidance for integrated reports in South Africa (*IRCSA* (2014)). This is only for guidance, however, and does not constitute an obligation to use the Framework. Section 3.1 presents the institutions and regulations in South Africa in detail.

24 In its Appendix, the IR Framework summarizes all these minimum requirements in a compact list.

25 Matters sensitive of competitive harm only need to be described in a way that avoids the loss of competitive advantage (IR F. 3.51).

26 This constitutes an essential distinction between an integrated and a combined report (*IIRC/IFAC* (2015), p. 8).

recital 9 (p. 3)) and may therefore benefit their decision making. Thus, the IIRC speaks of the "*cycle of integrated thinking and reporting*" (IR F., p. 2).

There are several ways how an integrated report can **relate to the firm's other communications**. It can be either a standalone document or a distinguishable part of another communication, e.g., a report that includes the financial statements (IR F. 1.15). Furthermore, it may overlap with reports that the firm prepares to comply with existing regulations, such as management reports, if it is also in line with the requirements of the International <IR> Framework, and if additionally provided information does not dilute the conciseness of the report (IR F. 1.14). Irrespective of its form, the integrated report can link to more detailed information in other communications (IR F. 1.16).

Moreover, the report needs to include a **statement on the responsibility** for its preparation (IR F. 1.20). In this declaration, the people responsible for the report acknowledge this responsibility and confirm that they have ensured the integrity of the report, having applied their collective minds to its preparation. In addition, they give their opinion in how far the report is in accordance with the Framework. If an integrated report comes without this statement, it needs to include an explanation of the role that "*those charged with governance*" have in the report's preparation and of the steps and timeframe to include the statement in reports on future periods. The third report that claims to be abiding by the Framework needs to include this declaration at the latest. This "apply-or-explain" rule gives the reporting firms a transition period for abiding by the Framework requirements (*Kajüter/Hannen* (2014), p. 77).

2.2.2 Fundamental Concepts

As a basis underlying the integrated report and as a help to understand the contents of the report, the Framework provides **three Fundamental Concepts**: value creation for the organization and for others, the capitals and the value creation process. These three concepts are connected and interdependent.

The value created by an organization is determined by the changes in the different capitals that the organization's activities and outputs cause (IR F. 2.4). It comprises the **value for the organization itself**, which leads to financial returns for the organization's investors (i.e., the providers of financial capital) **and value for others** (i.e., other stakeholders). Both aspects of value interrelate, as creating value for others (e.g., customer satisfaction) eventually affects the value for the firm through financial returns (IR F. 2.5-2.6). In particular, these interdependencies may occur over different time horizons, where the maximization of one capital at the cost of another (e.g., increasing financial capital by decreasing human capital) is unlikely to lead to a long-term maximization of the value for the organization (IR F. 2.9).

Underlying this value concept is the idea of six different **capitals** that all organizations depend on. The capitals are stocks of value that may vary in response to the firm's activities and outputs, with their changes representing the creation of value (IR F. 2.10-2.13). This value creation does not necessarily mean an overall net increase in the stock of capitals, though, as different stakeholders may value the flow between the capitals differently (IR F. 2.14). The six capitals are

- financial capital, being the funds that are obtained through financing and that are available for the firm's activities,
- manufactured capital, representing manufactured (as opposed to natural) physical objects available for the firm's activities,
- intellectual capital, meaning knowledge-based intangibles like intellectual property, but also systems and procedures ("organizational capital"),
- human capital, i.e. the employees' capabilities, experience and motivation,
- social and relationship capital, determined by the institutions and relationships within and between communities or stakeholder groups and by the ability to share information for the sake of individual and collective welfare, and
- natural capital, comprising (renewable or non-renewable) natural resources that support the firm's prosperity (IR F. 2.15).

The Framework admits that not all capitals are relevant to the same degree for all organizations (IR F. 2.16). Moreover, firms do not necessarily have to comply with this categorization, as they might define capitals differently (IR F. 2.17-2.19).[27]

Figure 2-3 shows a firm's **value creation process** according to the Framework, founding on the six capitals. They represent both the inputs and the outcomes of the firm's business model, which is the centerpiece of the process (IR F. 2.23-2.25). The firm transforms the different inputs from the capitals through its business activities (including planning and manufacturing of products or deploying skills to provide services) into outputs (i.e., products and services, but also by-products or waste), which in turn affect the different stocks of capitals as outcomes[28] of the model. The remaining Content Elements[29] besides Business Model also influence the value creation process. Economic, societal and environmental conditions set the context for the firms operations, representing the external environment, while the mission and vision provides a purpose for the whole organization (IR F. 2.21). Governance constitutes the oversight structure that the firm follows, which supports the ability to create value (IR F. 2.22). Among other things, this structure includes bodies and procedures to deal with risks and opportunities, stemming e.g. from the external environment (IR F. 2.26). The firm's strategy defines objectives and identifies how to mitigate the aforementioned risks and maximize the opportunities, allocating the necessary resources accordingly (IR F. 2.27). Monitoring the performance provides information that can be useful for further decision making (IR F. 2.28). The same holds for prospective information from an outlook, which may help to refine and improve the components of the process

[27] The Capitals Background Paper discusses the categorization of the capitals in detail, including their interdependencies (*IIRC et al.* (2013b), section 4 (pp. 5-15)).

[28] The Background Paper on the Business Model further explains the distinction between outputs and outcomes, giving the example of a car manufacturer: While the car represents the output, outcomes include mobility, safety or status for customers or emissions for the environment (*IIRC et al.* (2013a), recital 19 (p. 5)).

[29] Section 2.2.4 describes the disclosures regarding the Content Elements in detail.

(IR F. 2.29). According to the Value Creation Background Paper, various Content Elements hold so-called "*value drivers*". Among them are financial drivers (e.g., pricing strategy, operational efficiency, brand equity or cost of capital), non-financial drivers (e.g., customer relations, societal expectations, environmental concerns, innovation or corporate governance) and values (in the sense of behavioral standards or principles: e.g., integrity, trust or teamwork) (*IIRC/EY* (2013), recital 47 (p. 13)).

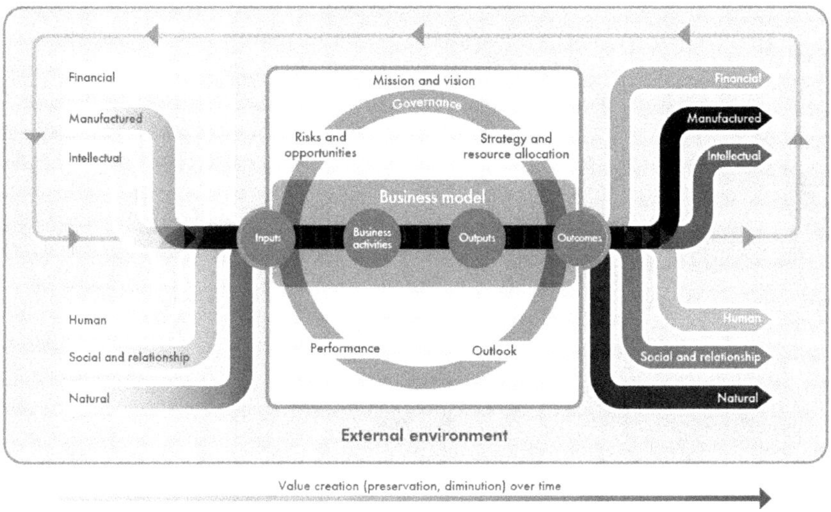

Figure 2-3: The value creation process
(IR F., p. 13)

The interaction of all Content Elements eventually allows the readers to assess the value created by the organization (IR F. 2.4). The **integrated report** encompasses all of the firm's interactions, activities and relationships that finally affect the value for the firm, which includes considering the effects on capitals the firm does not own (externalities) (IR F. 2.7-2.8). However, it is not possible to measure the movement of all capitals, as the Background Paper on Value Creation points out (*IIRC/EY* (2013), recitals 53-55 (p. 14)). Thus, the integrated report does not necessarily intend to quantify the value (IR F. 1.11).[30] Instead, a combination of quantitative and qualitative information may be the best way to report on the movement of the capitals (IR F. 1.11, 4.55).

[30] The Background Paper on Capitals, however, mentions various examples of quantitative indicators representing different capitals, including CO2 emissions (natural capital), the firm's investment in training (human capital), a customer satisfaction index (social and relationship capital) or the number of filed patent applications (intellectual capital) (*IIRC et al.* (2013b), recital 6.4 (p. 21)).

2.2.3 Guiding Principles

In line with the principles-based approach of the Framework, seven principles provide guidance on how to prepare an integrated report and how to present its contents, namely

- Strategic Focus and Future Orientation,
- Connectivity of Information,
- Stakeholder Relationships,
- Materiality,
- Conciseness,
- Reliability and Completeness and
- Consistency and Comparability (IR F. 3.1).

These **Guiding Principles** apply both individually and collectively, but the Framework admits that there may be tensions between them, calling for judgment in these cases (IR F. 3.2). Figure 2-4 gives an overview of all Guiding Principles in combination with the Content Elements.

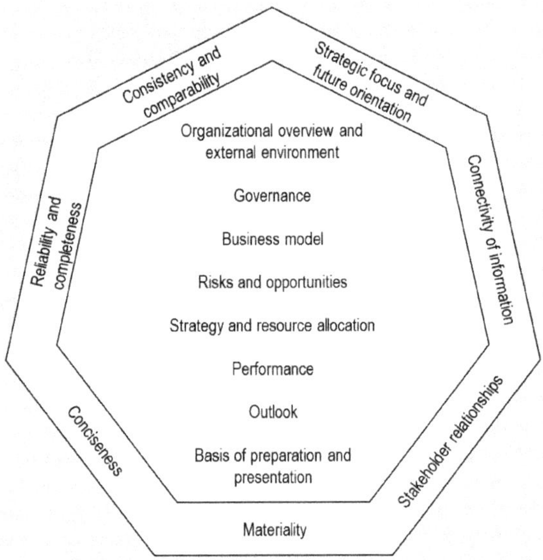

Figure 2-4: Guiding Principles and Content Elements of IR (based on DP IR, p. 12)

The **Strategic Focus and Future Orientation** principle requires the integrated report to give insight into the firm's strategy and into how the firm makes use of the different capitals to create value (IR F. 3.3). In particular, the report needs to present significant risks and opportunities resulting from the firm's market position and business model as well as the board's (i.e., "*those charged with governance*") views on the relationship of the firm's past and future performance, on its balance of short-, medium- and long-term interests and on lessons learned from past experiences for the firm's future strategy (IR F. 3.4). Furthermore, IR F. 3.5 requires information on how the different capitals contribute to the firm's ability to reach its strategic objectives and therefore to create value.

According to the **Connectivity of Information** principle, an integrated report shows a holistic picture of how the different factors affecting the firm's ability to create value combine, interrelate and depend on each other (IR F. 3.6). The aforementioned integrated thinking provides a foundation for the connectivity in reporting (IR F. 3.7). According to IR F. 3.8, different aspects may by connected. First, these aspects include the Content Elements, such as the effects of resource allocation on targeted performance or the adaption of the strategy in response to risks and opportunities. Second, reports connect time dimensions, revealing the connections between the firm's activities and performance in the past, present and future. The third aspect that integrated reports need to connect are the different capitals, to show their interdependencies and trade-offs as outlined in the previous section. Fourth, the reports show connections between financial and other information, e.g. the revenue and cost effects of R&D, HR or environmental policies or of customer satisfaction. As a fifth aspect, the reports include connections between quantitative and qualitative information, presenting a combination of KPIs and narrative explanations. Sixth, the connectivity refers to the alignment of the information in the external report with internal (management and board) information, consistent with the management approach known from financial reporting (*Merschdorf* (2012)). Seventh, the integrated reports link to other communications. Effective navigation devices like cross-references help to realize the latter, but other characteristics like a logical structure or a clear, understandable and jargon-free language also enhance the connectivity and usefulness of the report,[31] for which information technology can play a helpful role (IR F. 3.9). The Background Paper on Connectivity mentions the Extensible Business Reporting Language (XBRL)[32] standard for the exchange of business information as such an enhancing technology (*IIRC/WICI* (2013), recital 50 (pp. 11-12)).

The integrated report also informs about the firm's **Stakeholder Relationships**, in particular about how the firm considers and responds to its key stakeholders' legitimate needs and interests (IR F. 3.10). This Guiding Principle bases upon the notion that value is created not only by the organization itself, but also through its relationships with its key stakeholders (IR F. 3.11). As the Framework refers to the "*key stakeholders*" (IR F. 3.10-3.11) only, the report does not need to satisfy the information needs of all stakeholders. Through its day-to-day interaction with these stakeholders, the company can get insights about their needs, e.g. how they perceive value or what risks may be linked to the relationship, and can derive according decisions from that (IR F. 3.12-3.13). By presenting these interests as well as the firm's responses in the form of communication or decisions, actions and performance, the integrated report enhances transparency and accountability (IR F. 3.14). Thus, it helps

31 *Kajüter et al.* (2013a) also mention verbal explanations, a logical structure and references as ways to connect information, furthermore supplementing the use of tables or graphics as additional means of connectivity (pp. 201-202).

32 The official website of the XBRL project provides introductory information and guidance for filers, developers, regulators and governments on the language: https://www.xbrl.org/ (last accessed on 29 August 2016).

management and the board to fulfill its stewardship responsibility of the capitals, be it a legal or a purely moral responsibility (IR F. 3.15-3.16).

Materiality is a Guiding Principle that mainly refers to the determination of the information included in the report, although providing some related disclosure requirements itself. The principle states that the integrated report needs to disclose matters substantively affecting the firm's ability to create value (IR F. 3.17). To find these matters, the Framework presents a process to determine materiality (IR F. 3.18-3.29). Furthermore, it provides guidance on how to detect the reporting boundary, which is important to determine materiality. An additional guidance document on Materiality (*IIRC/IFAC* (2015)) combines these issues in the following process, referring to the respective paragraphs of the Framework (Figure 2-5).

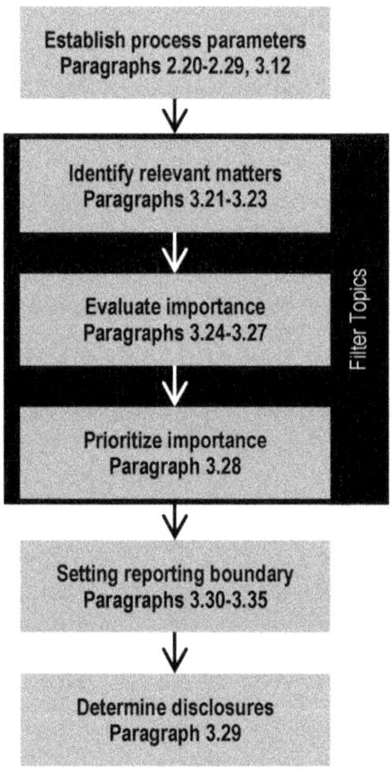

Figure 2-5: Determining materiality
(based on *IIRC/IFAC* (2015), p. 13)

The first step is the **establishment of process parameters.** This step is not mentioned explicitly in the Framework, but is considered implicitly. It defines the scope of the materiality determination process[33] by identifying the activities, performance and impacts of the firms

[33] The scope of the materiality determination process needs to be distinguished from the scope of the report (the reporting boundary), which represents the boundary of the disclosures in the report (*IIRC/IFAC* (2015), p. 14).

in the financial reporting entity – a step that helps to reveal both the inputs, business activities and outputs for value creation and the relationships with key stakeholders (*IIRC/IFAC* (2015), p. 14). After that, the topics of the report need to be filtered. Thus, the next step is to **identify relevant matters**. Matters are relevant if they (may) have an effect on the entity's ability to create value, determined by their effect on strategy, governance, performance or prospects (IR F. 3.21). In the following step, the firm needs to **evaluate the importance of these relevant matters** by assessing their magnitude and likelihood (IR F. 3.24). This evaluation may take place on the basis of an individual matter or an aggregate of matters (IR F.3.25). Both quantitative and qualitative aspects play a role for assessing the magnitude (IR F. 3.26). For instance, a qualitative evaluation of a matter may be an explanation of the influence on strategic objectives or how it has triggered a re-assessment of the firm's business model (*IIRC/IFAC* (2015), p. 17). Moreover, the nature (financial, operational, strategic, reputational or regulatory), area (internal or external) and time frame (short-, medium- or long-term) of an effect need to be considered to evaluate its magnitude (IR F. 3.27; *IIRC/IFAC* (2015), pp. 17-20). The next step of the process then requires the firm to **prioritize the matters** according to this magnitude to generate a focus on the most important aspects for reporting (IR F. 3.28).

In addition to the topics of the report, materiality determination also requires the definition of the **reporting boundary**. The Framework distinguishes between two aspects: the financial reporting entity on the one hand and risks and opportunities as well as outcomes of entities beyond the financial reporting entity on the other (IR F. 3.30). As it can be derived from the applicable financial reporting standards, the financial reporting entity forms the basis of the reporting boundary: It is the reference for financial capital investments and for the performance data from the financial statements (IR F. 3.31-3.33). However, risks, opportunities and outcomes of other entities may also impact the firm's ability to create value so that it is useful to include their effects in the integrated report (IR F. 3.34-3.35).

After applying the aforementioned stages, the final step is to **determine the disclosures** in the integrated report (IR F. 3.29). They can be distinguished into three categories (*IIRC/IFAC* (2015), p. 23): a summary of the materiality determination process (IR F. 4.40-4.42), a discussion of the results of this process, i.e. the material matters (IR F. 3.17, 4.50), and a comment on the role of those charged with governance in preparing and presenting the content (IR F. 1.20; 4.42).

A Guiding Principle closely related to Materiality is **Conciseness**. It deals with the balance that an integrated report needs to have between sufficient information to understand the firm's strategy, governance, performance and prospects on the one hand and avoiding less relevant information on the other hand (IR F. 3.37). To ensure the conciseness of the report, the guidance document on materiality (*IIRC/IFAC* (2015), p. 8) suggests a "*layered approach*". This approach sees the integrated report as an overarching or umbrella document that provides the necessary information on value creation, but references other communications like regulatory filings or voluntary reports for detailed information. Irrespective of this format approach, IR F. 3.38 lists various characteristics of the report to achieve conciseness. The list includes the application of the materiality determination process, a logical structure and the use of "*as few words as possible*", cross-references and links to more detailed information, but also the avoidance of repetition, boilerplate disclosures and jargon.

Reliability and Completeness are two related principles that the Framework embraces in one Guiding Principle, stating that an integrated report needs to include all (positive and negative) material matters in a balanced way and without material error (IR F. 3.39). Internal control and audit, external assurance or stakeholder engagement can enhance the balance of information and its freedom from material error – thus its **reliability**[34] (IR F. 3.40). **Balance** implies that no bias, weighting, offsetting or other manipulation underlies the data (IR F. 3.44). By selecting an appropriate format, by equally considering both increases and decreases in the capitals, both strengths and weaknesses and both positive and negative performance, and by reporting current performance against previous targets and future expectations, the firm can adhere to this concept of balance (IR F. 3.45). **Freedom from error** means that appropriate processes and controls minimize the risk of material misstatement in the information and that the report transparently informs the reader about the use of estimates (IR F. 3.46). However, the Framework acknowledges that is impossible to present the information in a perfectly accurate way in all respects. Those charged with governance are responsible for ensuring the reliability of the information, while the integrated report is considered an appropriate means to document their approach (IR F. 3.41-3.42). The report also needs to explain a potential omission of certain information, together with the reasons for the omission and the firm's steps to overcome it in the future (IR F. 3.43 in conjunction with 1.18).

To assess the **completeness** of the report, which implies that the report includes all (i.e., both positive and negative) material information, a firm may find reports released by other firms in the same industry to be helpful indicators (IR F. 3.47). This assessment also entails considerations about the extent of the information and the level of preciseness, for which the firm may take into regard concerns about the cost/benefit trade-off, about impacts on the competitive position and about future-oriented information (IR F. 3.48). Regarding the cost/benefit aspect, IR F. 3.49 states that costs may not be a factor in failing to collect critical data, as long as the respective matter is important for managing the business. Besides, while cost/benefit considerations may influence the specificity of the information, they must not lead to a complete omission of material information (IR F. 3.50). Similarly, the reporting firm needs to balance the specificity of the information between the need to fulfil the primary purpose of the integrated report and the risk of losing competitive advantage by providing too specified information (IR F. 3.51). Uncertainty is inherent in future-oriented information, but does not constitute a reason to omit such information (IR F. 3.53). The Framework points out that various regulatory requirements determine forward-looking information, in particular the types of disclosures, the need for updates of the data and requirements for cautionary statements (IR F. 3.52).

[34] IR F. 3.40 clarifies that Reliability is the equivalent of Faithful Representation, as it is used in other reporting regulations, such as the IASB's Conceptual Framework (CF. QC12-QC16). The IASB used the term "Reliability" in its previous Framework of 1989. However, *Kirsch et al.* (2012) reveal that as opposed to the IASB's intention, the two versions of the principle do not only differ in the name, as changes in the structure of the Qualitative Characteristics in fact lead to a degradation vis-à-vis the Relevance principle. For the sake of simplicity, this study assumes the IIRC's perspective and considers Reliability and Faithful Representation as synonymous principles.

Finally, the **Consistency and Comparability** principle states that the presentation of information in the integrated report needs to have a consistent basis over time and needs to enable readers to compare the firm with other organizations (IR F. 3.54). Consistency refers to the reporting policies and to KPIs (IR F. 3.55). The firm should use the same set of KPIs over time or explain the reasons for and effects of changes in the selection, should such changes be necessary (IR F. 3.55). While the particular information in the reports of different firms will always vary to some degree, the requirements on the Content Elements are supposed to apply to any organization and may thus allow certain comparisons between firms (IR F. 3.56). To enhance this comparability, an integrated report uses regional or industry benchmark data, presents the information in the form of ratios and reports KPIs that are common in the firm's industry or even defined by an independent (industry) body (IR F. 3.57).

2.2.4 Content Elements

In addition to the Guiding Principles, the International <IR> Framework lists eight Content Elements (Figure 2-4) that govern the particular disclosures an integrated report needs to provide:

- Organizational Overview and External Environment,
- Governance,
- Business Model,
- Risks and Opportunities,
- Strategy and Resource Allocation,
- Performance,
- Outlook and
- Basis of Preparation and Presentation (IR F. 4.1).

However, this sequence is not prescriptive as a standard structure for the report, since the elements link to each other and accordingly need to be presented in a way that reveals their connections – consistent with the Connectivity of Information principle (IR F. 4.2). Considering the individual circumstances of different organizations, the Framework states the **Content Elements** in the form of questions so that judgment and the application of the Guiding Principles are required to determine the disclosures and the way to present them (IR F. 4.3).

The first Content Element, **Organizational Overview and External Environment**, asks the question "*What does the organization do and what are the circumstances under which it operates?*" (IR F. 4.4). Its requirements are twofold (IR F. 4.5). First, the report needs to contain the firm's mission and vision, as well as aspects like ethics and values, the ownership structure, activities and markets, the competitive landscape and the position within the value chain, but also quantitative information (e.g., the number of employees). Second, it is supposed to convey factors that influence the external environment. The latter may impact the firm directly or indirectly and include aspects from the legal (e.g., the regulatory environment), commercial (e.g., economic stability or customer demand), social (e.g., demographic change or human rights), environmental (e.g., climate change) and political context, as well as the stakeholders' legitimate needs and interests (IR F. 4.6-4.7).

Governance, the second Content Element, asks the question how the firm's governance structure supports the ability to create value (IR F. 4.8). In particular, the report needs to include the organization's leadership structure, processes to make strategic decisions, the board's approach to risk management and its actions to impact the strategic direction, while also covering how the firm's culture and ethics influence its use of the capitals, governance practices beyond legal requirements, the board's responsibility for enabling innovation and how the firm's remuneration and incentives consider value creation (IR F. 4.9).

Moreover, the integrated report needs to answer the question what the firm's **business model** is (IR F. 4.10). The Framework provides the following definition:

> *"An organization's business model is its system of transforming inputs, through its business activities, into outputs and outcomes that aims to fulfil the organization's strategic purposes and create value over the short, medium and long term."*
>
> (IR F. 4.11)

In **presenting the Content Element Business Model**, the report identifies the key elements of the model and highlights them with a simple diagram, identifies stakeholder and other dependencies, provides logical narrative flow and connects the presentation to the other Content Elements (IR F. 4.13). The descriptions of both the inputs and the outcomes need to relate to the affected capitals, including those that the organization does not own or control (IR F. 4.14, 4.20). The list of inputs includes only those that are material, rather than providing an exhaustive enumeration (IR F. 4.15). In terms of the business activities, the report shows how the firm differentiates itself in the market, its reliance on revenues after the point of sale, its approach to innovation and its design in terms of adaptability to change (IR F. 4.16). Furthermore, the report presents the impact of process improvement, employee training or relationships management (IR F. 4.17). The Framework requires a discussion of the outputs, being products and services, by-products and waste (IR F. 4.18), but also a description of the outcomes, comprising both internal and external outcomes as well as both positive and negative ones (IR F. 4.19). In case that a firm employs more than one business model, the report needs to present the different models separately, but include the connections between them (IR F. 4.21). Internal top level reporting may indicate the right balance of disclosure and complexity in this case (IR F. 4.22).

For the Content Element **Risks and Opportunities**, an integrated report needs to answer the question what the specific risks and opportunities are that affect the firm's ability to create value and how the firm deals with them (IR F. 4.23). The risks and opportunities that the report identifies include those that relate to the firm's effects on and the availability, quality and affordability of the capitals (IR F. 4.24). In addition to the risks and opportunities as such, the disclosures comprise their respective (internal and/or external) sources, their likelihood of occurrence and magnitude of effect as well as the steps that the firm takes to mitigate the risks or create value from the opportunities (IR F. 4.25). The Framework gives particular consideration to those risks that fundamentally affect the organization's ongoing ability to create value and that could have extreme consequences, by requiring the report to include them even in case of a very small likelihood of occurrence (IR F. 4.26).

The question "*Where does the organization want to go and how does it intend to get there?*" (IR F. 4.27) underlies the Content Element **Strategy and Resource Allocation.** This element requires the identification of the firm's strategic objectives, the related strategies, the resource allocation plans and of how the firm measures its achievements and targets (IR F. 4.28). The requirement includes a depiction of the linkages of these issues with information from other Content Elements (e.g., the relationship with the business model), the explanation of differentiating factors that give the firm a competitive advantage (e.g., the role of innovation) and the description of stakeholder engagement features used in the development of the strategy (IR F. 4.29).

An integrated report also needs to answer the question to what extent the firm has achieved its strategic objectives for the period and how this shows in terms of the capitals (IR F. 4.30). Both the use of qualitative and quantitative information serve the purpose to report on the Content Element **Performance**, including quantitative indicators with regard to targets, risks and opportunities, in combination with an explanation of their significance and compilation, but also the effects on the capitals along the value chain, the state of stakeholder relationships and the linkages between past, present and future performance (IR F. 4.31). Reporting on the capitals can particularly be achieved through KPIs that combine financial and non-financial measures (e.g., the ratio of greenhouse gas emissions to sales), through the monetization of certain effects (e.g., water use) or through narrative explanations on the financial implications of effects on the capitals (e.g., expected revenue growth resulting from human capital policies) (IR F. 4.32). Another important feature in the performance discussion may be the report on the effects of regulations or non-compliance with regulations on the firm's performance (IR F. 4.33).

In addition to the performance in the current period, an integrated report also addresses expectations for the future according to the Content Element **Outlook.** The report needs to answer the question what challenges and uncertainties the firm expects to face in the pursuit of its strategy and how they could affect the business model and future performance (IR F. 4.34). Expectations about the external environment, together with their potential effects on the organization and the firm's current equipment to face these effects need to be disclosed (IR F. 4.35). All expectations that the report presents need to carefully ground in current reality (IR F. 4.36). A discussion of the implications for future financial performance implies the effects of the external environment and of risks and opportunities on the achievement of strategic objectives, as well as the availability, quality and affordability of capitals, including stakeholder relationships (IR F. 4.37). The Outlook disclosures comprise lead indicators, KPIs or objectives, information from external sources and sensitivity analyses, but also forecasts, together with an explanation of the underlying assumptions (IR F. 4.38). These forecasts or targets need to be presented against the actual performance in the respective period, while the current performance compares with previously identified targets (IR F. 4.38). All disclosures on Outlook need to consider the firm's regulatory requirements (IR F. 4.39).

The last Content Element is **Basis of Preparation and Presentation.** To address this element, the report must answer the question how the organization determines the matters to include in the report and how it quantifies or evaluates these matters (IR F. 4.40). The answer to this question yields three issues: the materiality determination process, the (determination of the) reporting boundary and the significant frameworks or methods used to evaluate the material matters (IR F. 4.41). Disclosures on the materiality determination comprise the description of the process as outlined in IR F. 3.18-3.20 (see section 2.2.3), which also identifies the role of those charged with governance and may include a link to an external detailed description of the process (IR F. 4.42). In terms of the reporting boundary (as defined in IR F. 3.30-3.35 and outlined in section 2.2.3 of this study) the report shows the boundary itself and its determination (IR F. 4.43). Besides, the risks, opportunities and outcomes both of the firms included in the financial reporting entity and – in so far as they affect the firm's ability to create value – of other entities or stakeholders are shown (IR F. 4.44-4.45). However, these and other disclosures may face limits that the integrated report needs to address, like unavailable data or the inherent inability to identify the material risks, opportunities and outcomes (IR F. 4.46). Lastly, the report covers a summary of the significant frameworks and methods to quantify and evaluate the material matters (e.g., the respective financial reporting standards), while the firm may provide and reference details in other communications (IR F. 4.47). The IR Framework remarks that the information in the report needs to ground on the same basis and needs to be reconcilable with similar other information that the organization has published (IR F. 4.48).

General reporting guidance

Supplementing these eight Content Elements, the Framework provides general reporting guidance that refers to all Content Elements and supports the presentation of various aspects regarding both form and content (*Kajüter/Hannen* (2014), p. 79). IR F. 4.50-4.52 present the requirements for the disclosure of **material matters.** Integrated reports need to explain the matter itself, potential uncertainty about the matter and the related assumptions. Moreover, firms need to indicate the unavailability of information. In case of a potential loss of competitive advantage, general nature information rather than specific details on the respective matter suffices. The report may present these matters on their own or in conjunction with others, depending on their nature, and needs to consider the specific circumstances of the matter to avoid generic disclosures.

For the reporting of **quantitative indicators**, IR F. 4.53 provides various characteristics to consider. They need to be relevant, consistent with internally used and previously reported indicators and regional or industry benchmarks, but also connected, focused on material matters and presented with their current and previous targets as well as with previous actual values and narrative explanations (e.g., measurement methods, assumptions or explanations of variation).

Disclosures on the **capitals** are determined by their effects on the firm's value creation, irrespective of whether the firm owns them, and include factors that have an impact on the availability, quality and affordability of the capitals as well as the firm's expected flows from them (IR F. 4.54). If not meaningful or practicable, a quantification of the movements is dispensable and qualitative information suffices, instead (IR F. 4.55). In particular, the report needs to show the interdependencies and trade-offs between the capitals and over time, in so far as they influence value creation (IR F. 4.56).

The Framework also gives guidance on the **time frames** for reporting, distinguishing between the short, medium and long term. However, it does not provide a standard length for each time frame, but leaves this to the discretion of each organization, only stating that this length depends on the firm's industry and on the nature of the firm's outcomes (IR F. 4.57-4.58). While the length of a time frame and the reason for it influence the nature of information in the integrated report, the report does not have to present disclosures for each time frame (IR F. 4.59).

Similar to the time frame, the Framework also leaves open the appropriate level of disclosure **aggregation** (IR F. 4.60). The IIRC acknowledges that while aggregation may lead to the loss of information in some cases, disaggregation can result in unnecessary clutter if the information is not material (IR F. 4.61). Applying the management approach, IR F. 4.62 thus refers to the internal organization for aggregation purposes. If the integrated report uses this internal structure as a benchmark for the aggregation of the reported data, this will commonly result in a presentation that bases upon business or geographical segments.

2.3 Critical discussion of the Framework

This critical discussion analyzes the International <IR> Framework conceptually. In line with the investor focus of this study, the overarching question is whether the **Framework constitutes a basis for integrated reports to be useful for investors** (research question 1). To this end, the analysis assesses the rules that the Framework lays down against the purpose of integrated reports. The discussion follows a **three-step structure**.

Step 1 scrutinizes the **purpose of integrated** reports and breaks it down into different components, as well as comparing it with the purpose of financial reporting. Step 2 deals with the IR **Guiding Principles** and checks for their coherence with the purpose of integrated reports and with interdependencies and trade-offs across the principles. These principles determine the preparation and presentation of information in an integrated report (IR F. 3.1-3.2). By analogy with the Qualitative Characteristics of the Conceptual Framework for Financial Reporting[35] the Guiding Principles can be argued to identify the information that is most useful for serving the purpose of integrated reports, if they are in line with this purpose (CF. QC1). Similar to these Qualitative Characteristics[36] the Guiding Principles thus constitute the criteria for the analysis of the provisions for the particular contents of the reports.[37] Therefore, step 3 assesses the requirements of the Framework on the **Content Elements** against the Guiding Principles. If both the Guiding Principles turn out to align with the purpose of integrated reports and the Content Elements turn out to align with the principles, the Content Elements can be argued to be in line with the purpose of integrated reports, resulting in a coherent system overall. Hence, the analysis can be depicted by a cascade system (Figure 2-6). All in all, the discussion evaluates this **coherence of the system**.

35 See section 3.2 for a detailed comparison of the Guiding Principles and the Qualitative Characteristics.

36 Conceptual work that deals with particular provisions for financial reporting often uses the Qualitative Characteristics of the Conceptual Framework as the criteria for the analysis. Cf. e.g. *Kessler* (2005).

37 *Eccles et al.* ((2015), p. 126) also point out the parallels between the CF and the IR F in establishing the architecture for the respective reports.

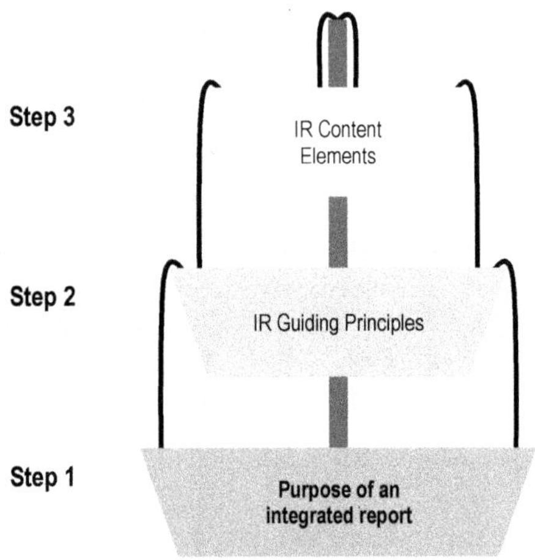

Figure 2-6: Three-step cascade system of the critical discussion

2.3.1 The purpose of an integrated report

The purpose of an integrated report as stated in the Framework represents the first step of the analysis and the **reference point for the following steps**. It reads:

> *"The primary purpose of an integrated report is to explain to providers of financial capital how an organization creates value over time."*
>
> (*IR F. 1.7*).

A **breakdown of this purpose** specifies the underlying idea and allows a better understanding as well as a comparison with the purpose of traditional financial reports. This breakdown reveals three different components that the purpose of an integrated report refers to: (1) the role and appearance of the report, (2) information about value creation and (3) the addressees of an integrated report. Figure 2-7 presents these components.

(1) The role and appearance of the integrated report

As a first component, it is necessary to understand the role of the integrated report. The Framework offers different ways how the report can **relate to the firm's other communications.** This issue raised some controversy. In the DP IR, the IIRC stated that the integrated report was supposed to be "*an organization's primary reporting vehicle*" (DP IR, p. 2). During the further development of the Framework, the suggested role has changed in response to various remarks on this topic in the comment letters (IR F. BC 2.3).

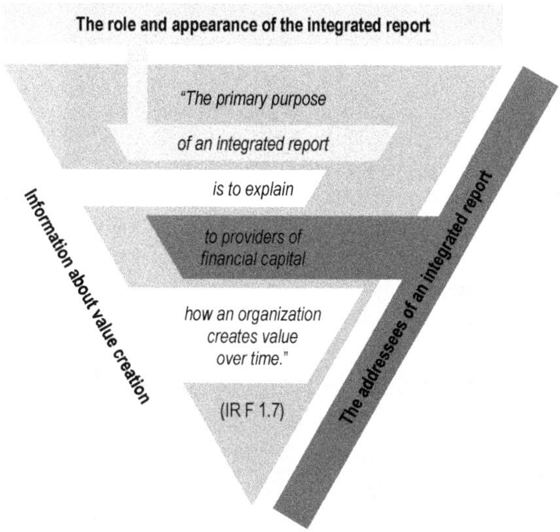

Figure 2-7: The purpose of an integrated report

By not mandating a particular form for the report in the final Framework, the IIRC avoids conflict with requirements of other regulations and gives firms the flexibility to **embed the integrated report into existing communications** (*Kajüter/Hannen* (2014), p. 80; *Roberts* (2014), p. 28), which in turn may prevent unnecessary redundancies (*Stawinoga* (2015), p. 206). While potentially promoting the acceptance of IR among the reporting firms, this flexibility may impede the standardization and comparability of the reports (*Kajüter/Hannen* (2014), p. 80). Furthermore, embedding the integrated report in a particular communication, such as the management report, contrasts the original idea of using it as the primary reporting vehicle. Instead of integrating different topics and strands of reporting, the report would itself be integrated.

However, merging various communications in a single document is in line with the simplest form of the **One Report** approach (*Eccles/Krzus* (2010)). Rather than seeing the integrated report as a part of the document, this approach considers the document in its entirety as the integrated report (*Eccles/Krzus* (2010), pp. 10-11). The South African King Committee called such a combined communication the "*truly integrated report*" (King III Report, chapter 9, recital 1 (p. 108)). However, it almost inevitably opposes the definition of an integrated report as a "*concise communication*" (IR F. 1.1), if this communication is supposed to replace other reports without losing information (*Flower* (2015), p. 5).

To maintain conciseness, the IIRC's guidance document on Materiality suggests that the integrated report can be an overarching "*umbrella*" document (*IIRC/IFAC* (2015), p. 8). Thereby the integrated report may provide the necessary information on value creation, but reference other communications like regulatory filings or voluntary reports for detailed information. These detailed communications could serve the purpose of a comprehensive reference work, as this is a purpose that corporate reports also serve for their addressees (*Kajüter et al.* (2010), p. 459). This approach became known as the "Octopus Model" (Figure 2-8). Like the head of a metaphorical octopus, which is connected with its arms, the integrated report connects the various detailed reports (*Armbrester et al.* (2011), p. 29; *IRCSA* (2014), p. 6; *IRCSA* (2015); *King/Roberts* (2013), p. 72). This picture also illustrates the Connectivity of Information principle that underlies the report. So rather than a single all-embracing report, the **Octopus Model** may present a solution to the trade-off between the broader perspective of the integrated report and the Conciseness principle. Yet, this model adds another report to the multitude of existing communications.[38]

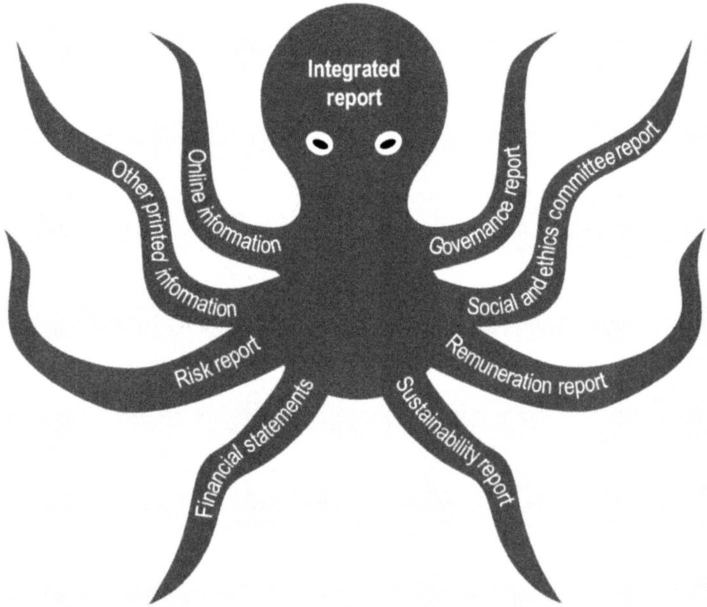

Figure 2-8: The Octopus Model

(2) Information about value creation

Explaining the firm's value creation is the second component of the purpose of an integrated report. According to this core component, an integrated report serves an **information purpose.**

[38] Note that this practice does not conflict with the One Report approach, as the latter is not necessarily limited to cases of only one single report (*Eccles/Krzus* (2010), p. 10). However, the name "One Report" would be misleading in this case.

The three **Fundamental Concepts** (value creation for the organization and for others, the capitals and the value creation process) deal with the understanding of **value creation** under IR. These concepts are inseparably linked. Value creation manifests itself in changes of the capitals, which in turn are induced by the firm's activities and outputs (IR F. 2.4), or as Roberts puts it briefly:

> *"Value creation is essentially the company's outcomes"*
>
> (*Roberts* (2015), p. 36).

This **idea of value and different capitals** has also raised considerable discussion, in particular on the definition of the concept, on the question for whom the value in question is created and on a potential quantification of this value (IR F. BC 5.1). The idea challenges managers and investors that merely think in financial terms and requires them to take a more holistic view to make use of the approach (*Stubbs et al.* (2014), p. 10). Ensuring awareness of the different kinds of resources, the concept of six capitals may help in taking such a holistic perspective so that it allows a complete picture of value creation (*Roberts* (2015), p. 36). However, the concept holds some subjectivity, as it is particularly difficult to distinguish certain capitals whose concepts overlap, like human and intellectual capital (*Cheng et al.* (2014), p. 98; *Flower* (2015), p. 3).

Neither the **conception of the non-financial capitals** as such, nor their consideration for corporate reporting purposes is entirely new, though. In addition to financial capital, manufactured capital classically appears in a firm's statement of financial position in the form of tangible assets. *Victor* ((1993), with further references) gives an overview of different conceptions of capital in economics, with particular focus on how this manufactured capital is different from natural capital[39]. The latter in turn has so far only been present in sustainability reporting. Instead, several concepts on a national or international level intended to establish reporting on intellectual capital as a supplement to merely financial reporting, beginning in the late 1980s (*Larsen et al.* (1999), p. 16). This Intellectual Capital Accounting (ICA) developed from goodwill accounting and intangibles accounting, both of which may also affect the financial statements (*Petty/Guthrie* (2000), pp. 158-160). Examples of initiatives to establish ICA include approaches from Scandinavia (e.g., the Danish Guideline for Intellectual Capital Statements (2000) and Intellectual Capital Statements – The New Guideline (2003)) or Germany (e.g., *AKIW* (2003; 2004) or Intellectual capital statement – Made in Germany by the Federal Ministry of Economics and Labour (2004)). As the definitions of intellectual capital underlying these approaches mostly draw on several dimensions of capital, in particular human capital and structural capital (*Petty/Guthrie* (2000), pp. 158-160), but also customer capital (*Stewart* (1997), pp. ix-x), the IIRC opted for a different definition. To avoid a two-tiered model and promote a better understanding (*IIRC et al.* (2013b), recital 4.22 (p. 8)), the IIRC's definition of intellectual capital concentrates on the structural (or organizational) capital and on intellectual property (IR F. 2.15), whereas human capital[40] as well as social and relationship capital[41] cover the

---

[39] Cf. e.g. *Pearce et al.* ((1989), p. 3) or *Holland* ((1994), p. 169) for definitions of natural capital from prior literature.

[40] Cf. e.g. *Schultz* (1961) or *Becker* (1964) for a discussion of human capital.

[41] Cf. *Coleman* (1988) for a discussion of social capital.

other mentioned dimensions. The IIRC distinguishes these three capitals by means of different "carriers":

- The carrier for human capital is the individual person,
- the carrier for social and relationship capital is intra- or extra-organizational networks and
- the carrier for intellectual capital is the organization (*IIRC et al.* (2013b), recital 4.23 (p. 8)).

All in all, the taxonomy that the IIRC uses is close to those used by sustainability initiatives (e.g., *The SIGMA Project* (2003); *Global Development and Environment Institute* (2003)).

The broader perspective that the non-financial capitals bring into reporting **benefits the readers**, who get **more information** about different impacts on the firm's competitive position than from traditional reporting, which required them to make excessive supplementary analyses to come up with non-financial information (*Peñarrubia Fraguas* (2015), p. 598). This information is particularly useful when assessing a firm's value, seeing that physical and financial assets only determine less than 20% of a firm's market value, while this rate used to exceed 80% in the 1970s (*Ocean Tomo* (2010)). Current findings underline that investors increasingly consider non-financial aspects to inform their decision making (e.g., *Stubbs et al.* (2014); *EY* (2014; 2015)). At the same time, there are concerns that the idea of the six capitals might lead to the misconception that IR equals environmental, social and governance (ESG) reporting, which is not the case (*Stubbs et al.* (2014), p. 12).

These concerns relate to the questions **for whom the organization creates value**. The Framework states that the firm creates value for itself and for others. Value for the firm itself can be interpreted as value to investors, as IR F. 2.4 explicitly refers to the financial returns that this value entails (*Flower* (2015), p. 6). However, the value for investors is linked to the value for others, seeing that factors like the external environment or stakeholder relationships contribute to the value creation for the firm (IR F. 2.6). Investors generally are interested in value for others if it affects the value creation for the firm or if it is one of the firm's objectives, e.g. for charities (IR F. 2.5). Value for others is thus only relevant for the integrated report in so far as it impacts the value for the firm (IR F. 2.7). Hence, this value for others can neither be interpreted as "*value to society*" nor as "*value to stakeholders*", nor can it be considered as "*value to present and future generations*" (*Flower* (2015), p. 5).

Consistently, the Framework follows a similar approach in terms of the question in how far the integrated report covers **the capitals that the firm does not own**. Neither capital is within the scope of the integrated report for its intrinsic value, as the report only covers the capitals to the extent that they affect the firm's value creation. In particular, this holds for externalities (IR F. 2.7-2.8). The degree to which the non-owned capitals affect the firm's value creation leaves room for interpretation, though. *Flower* ((2015), pp. 6-7) provides various examples of manufactured (e.g., schools in the firm's surroundings being destroyed by pollution emanating from the firm), human (e.g., people dying from poisonous gases that the firm releases) or natural (e.g., rising sea levels due to the firm's emission of greenhouse gases) capital that would not be reported according to his interpretation of the respective paragraphs of the Framework. However, the aforementioned holistic perspective that the concept of capitals entails also allow a different point of view. Severe externalities, as given in Flower's examples, bear the risk of losing reputation, i.e. declining social and relationship capital, which in turn can substantially affect the value for the firm. The report would thus need to include the underlying effects on the capitals. For instance, the shareholders of the British oil giant BP faced a massive drop of the firm's stock market value after the Deepwater Horizon oil disaster in 2010 (*Armitstead/Butterworth* (2010)), in addition to penalties, costs for cleaning up, payouts to individuals etc. that the firm had to bear (*Breen* (2010)). Moreover, various BP gas stations in the USA had to deal with enormous sales declines, in response to which a discussion arose whether changing the name of the brand would mitigate the loss of reputation (*Weber* (2010)). Although not affecting the capitals that the firm owned directly, the indirect implications of this pollution on the firm's value would require reporting on this issue.

Rather than reporting on the creation of value only, a balanced integrated report also deals with a potential diminution (*Roberts* (2014), p. 29). While positive value creation means an increase in capitals, a decrease in capitals represents a negative development of value. In this regard, IR F. 4.56 remarks that there may also be **interdependencies and trade-offs** between the capitals. Thus, this paragraph requires the integrated report to disclose these trade-offs if they affect value creation. In the literature, there is doubt about whether a decline in natural capital can be offset by an increase in financial capital at all, as well as suspicion that the depiction of trade-offs may be an easy justification for firms' negative environmental impacts (*Flower* (2015), p. 8). However, this criticism seems to be misplaced in so far as it is beyond the scope of corporate reporting to judge the trade-offs. Instead, a report rather needs to inform on the fact that the firm trades off different capitals and thus enable the readers to form an opinion.

An issue that this topic affects, however, is a potential **quantification** of the capitals and thus of value. Instead of providing particular guidance on measurement, the Framework states that in case of impracticability to quantify the capitals, qualitative information suffices to explain their movements (IR F. 4.55). The IIRC did not substantially change the provisions that the CD IR had already included in this regard, although various comment letters had remarked the lack of quantification (e.g., *University of Münster* (2013), p. 2) and the resulting lower comparability across firms (IR F. BC 8.1). Universal provisions on measurement seem to be impracticable, though, as the underlying matters are widespread and complex, and as too specific guidance would contradict the idea of a principles-based Framework (*Kajüter et al.* (2013b), p. 1685). Nevertheless, the IIRC considers developing guidance on this issue outside the Framework, with a database that includes specific measures from external sources (IR F. BC 8.2). Such sources could be financial reporting regulations like the IFRS, but also standards on non-financial reporting issues like the GRI or others (*IDW* (2013), p. 4). If firms look for a way to provide quantitative disclosures on the capitals, a starting point to get a feeling for a potential quantification may be internal tools to manage the respective issues, in particular budgets (*Phillips* (2013), p. 18). This practice would also be consistent with the management approach. Nonetheless, the focus of the integrated report is on the description of value creation as such, rather than on measuring the impacts (*Adams* (2015), p. 26). Standardization and quantification of non-financial aspects would be essential for the decision-usefulness of the information, however

(*Velte* (2008), p. 367). If firms monetize the different capitals, the awareness for the multi-dimensional impacts of their business may increase and external pressure to create value may rise (*imug* (2015), p. 42). On the one hand, this monetization always requires discretion and may thus be subject to manipulation, whereas on the other hand, the readers may develop an own opinion and valuation if the firm itself does not monetize the capitals (*imug* (2015), p. 42).

With their information purpose, **integrated reports align with the purpose of financial reports** to provide decision-useful information (CF. OB2). Similar to financial reports, integrated reports are intended to lead to better-informed decisions (*Stubbs et al.* (2014), p. 8).[42] To this end, integrated reports explain the firm's value creation. Financial reports instead do not present the value itself, but the information they convey shall enable readers to estimate the firm's value (CF. OB8). Despite this likeness, the two concepts of value differ essentially, albeit with some overlap. Financial reports deal with financial and manufactured capital, but also include intellectual capital to some degree. Moreover, approaches in various countries have attempted to include disclosures on intangible values (e.g., human capital) in corporate reports as supplements to the financial statements. Integrated reports do not generally refer to all capitals to the full extent, but only in so far as they affect the value for the firm. Nevertheless, the concept of value under IR goes beyond the value definition of financial reports and thus constitutes an innovation over financial reporting. This broader approach may provide additional useful information for the readers.

(3) The addressees of an integrated report

The third component of the purpose of an integrated report is the **target audience** of the report. As IR F. 1.7 states, the main addressees are (potential) providers of financial capital. The question whether IR should primarily address investors or all stakeholders was another controversial issue, particularly in the comment letters to the CD IR (IR F. BC 3.2). Despite criticism, the IIRC did not change its opinion and continued considering investors as the primary addressees and all other stakeholders as secondary addressees, although the Council slightly changed the wording of the respective paragraphs to lessen emphasis on the difference (IR F. BC 3.1-3.5). As the owners of financial capital, investors have the right to be informed by management, which has a stewardship responsibility (IR F. 3.15) for the capitals (*Moxter* (1976), p. 95). Moreover, the allocation of financial capital eventually also determines the allocation of the other capitals, so that investors play an essential role for the firm overall (IR F. BC 3.4). Aiming at all stakeholders could contrast the intention of the integrated report to deal with the value creation for the firm and could also reduce focus, thus hampering conciseness (IR F. BC 3.4). In addition, while investors will always be present in a firm's life cycle, the groups of other stakeholders may change over time and differ between firms so that aligning reporting with their needs would possibly also impede consistency and comparability (*Stawinoga* (2015), p. 199). At the same time, however, the distinction between two groups of addressees bears the risk that other stakeholders make less use of the integrated report as a source of information (*Stawinoga* (2015), p. 189).

---

[42] On aggregate, these better-informed decisions may also lead to a more efficient market.

Investors instead welcome the integrated report, as it substantially overlaps with their information needs (*Peñarrubia Fraguas* (2015), pp. 600-601; *Stubbs et al.* (2014), p. 3). It is necessary to distinguish both between short and long-term **providers of financial capital** and between share- and debtholders, though. IR mainly benefits long-term shareholders, who may use the holistic information of an integrated report as a leading indicator for future cash flows or may even have an original interest in non-financial aspects (e.g., sustainable funds) (*Stubbs et al.* (2014), p. 5; *Lachnit/Müller* (2015), pp. 547-548). Furthermore, some players in the investment supply chain (i.e., certain analysts) do not necessarily welcome IR, since the presumably more transparent reports might reveal firm-specific information that they had for themselves before, and since the transparency may thus destroy their competitive advantage (*Stubbs et al.* (2014), p. 6). Interested investors need some time to adapt to the new reporting format, as it requires them to question and potentially adapt their decision making (*Haller/Zellner* (2014), p. 257), but according to Nick Topazio, head of corporate reporting policy at CIMA, there is already a growing number of investors who understand the concept (*Orton-Jones* (2015), p. 37).

With regard to its addressees, the purpose of an integrated report is therefore **similar to the purpose of financial reports**, which is to provide information that is useful to shareholders, lenders and other creditors in making decisions (CF. OB2). Conversely, ESG or sustainability reporting usually take a stakeholder perspective (e.g., GRI G4, p. 3). As stated before, there is also a strong overlap in terms of the information object. In summary, the purpose of integrated reports is thus closely related to the purpose of financial reporting, albeit with a stronger focus on the value of the firm and with a broader definition of this value.

2.3.2 Guiding Principles

As the Guiding Principles determine how the information in integrated reports is prepared and presented, they may help to identify such information that is useful for investors and that is thus in line with the purpose of integrated reports. To be such an aid to orientation, the principles themselves need to **align with the purpose of integrated reports**. In addition to assessing whether the principles actually do align with this purpose, the second step of the Framework analysis in this section reveals the relationships between different Guiding Principles, including interdependencies or tensions.

Before analyzing the seven Guiding Principles, the principles-based nature of the Framework in general is worthy of discussion. As IR F. 1.9 points out, there is a trade-off between firms' flexibility to describe their individual situation on the one hand and prescribed disclosures to meet standardized information needs on the other hand, thus between the Relevance[43] principle and the Consistency and Comparability principle (*Müller/Stawinoga* (2013), p. 309). Under the **principles-based approach,** it is left to the firms to derive the relevant information according to their readers' needs, which may prove useful

[43] While not explicitly considering it as a separate Guiding Principle, the Framework implicitly bases upon the Relevance principle, as the selection of relevant information lays the foundation of the materiality determination process (IR F. 3.21-3.23). References to the Relevance principle in this analysis thus imply a reference to the IR Guiding Principle of Materiality.

for the addressees, but also represents a major challenge for managers (*Müller/Stawinoga* (2013), pp. 307-308). At the same time, this freedom yields room for discretion that managers could misuse for purposeful misinformation, such as a generally restrictive disclosure practice (*Kajüter/Hannen* (2014), p. 80; *Flower* (2015), p. 9). Sector-specific guidance could be a compromising attempt to deal with this issue, as it considers both the relevance and the comparability of the information (*Aebersold/Suter* (2012), p. 384). While taking into account the individual circumstances of a firm's business at least on industry level, such guidance would enable users to compare different reports across firms from the same field. This practice would in particular align with IR F. 3.57, which requires companies to use industry benchmark data and to reflect measures that other firms in the industry use or that an industry body stipulates.

The alternative of requiring specific disclosures from all firms would in turn not necessarily yield more comparability, as the informative value of a piece of information varies with the firm's business model. For instance, information about manufactured capital, e.g. property, plant and equipment, is important if the firm has a classical industrial business model like car manufacturers, for which these assets constitute an essential foundation of value creation. For a service provider like a consulting firm instead, the same piece of information would be of minor importance, as the underlying business model rather bases upon inputs from other capitals (in particular human or intellectual capital). Hence, **specific disclosure requirements** could constrain a firm's ability to tell its individual story and might rather trigger reporting to be a compliance exercise, with firms adhering to the letter of the law more than to its spirit (*Eccles/Krzus* (2015), p. 13). The minimum requirements that the Framework sets out in bold italic type are an attempt of a compromise in this regard. However, their generic nature leaves considerable room for interpretation on whether or not a specific report is in line with the Framework. Therefore doubt persists about the reliability and completeness of the information, especially since the involved discretion also represents a challenge for external assurance providers (*Kajüter/Hannen* (2014), p. 80). *Eccles/Krzus* ((2015), p. 16) suggest that the IIRC could also address this problem itself, by installing a process for a voluntary official certification of the reports.

Turning to the Guiding Principles, the principle named first is **Strategic Focus and Future Orientation.** It represents a reflection of investors' information needs, as they consider information on a company's strategy and future important for assessing the firm's value (*Peñarrubia Fraguas* (2015), pp. 615-616) and allocating their resources accordingly (*Daily* (1971), p. 686; *Steinmeyer* (2008), p. 1). Strategic information is thus relevant for investors, but is at the same time sensitive by its nature. By allowing the omittance of disclosures that would cause competitive harm (IR F. 1.17), the Framework sets a limit to this Guiding Principle, taking the firms' competitive interests into account. Another issue with this principle is its close relation to the two Content Elements Strategy and Resource Allocation and Outlook (formerly called "Future Outlook" in the CD IR). Responding to confusion about this relation in the comment letters to the CD IR, the IIRC states that while the Guiding Principle addresses the selection and presentation of information (which may also stem from other Content Elements than these two), the two Content Elements deal with the specific disclosures in the form of questions to be answered by the report (*IIRC* (2013d), pp. 32-33). Nonetheless, it seems questionable whether it is useful to have future orientation as a Guiding Principle at all: The report also contains information on the past and present so that the idea of the principle is not generalizable for the entire report (*Kajüter et al.* (2013b), p. 1685). As information on the past may also prove useful with regard to the purpose of integrated reports (e.g., by serving as comparative values or by indicating trends), this Guiding Principle only partly constitutes a guideline for useful information for investors.

The **Connectivity of Information** principle represents a centerpiece of IR. Aiming at overcoming the silos in traditional reports (*Adams/Simnett* (2011), p. 293), it constitutes the main innovation that this reporting format entails (*Kajüter et al.* (2013a), p. 199) and is essential for achieving the objective of IR (*Aebersold/Suter* (2012), p. 383). IR F. 3.8 lists various **elements** to be connected: the Content Elements, past, present and future, the capitals, financial and other information, quantitative and qualitative information, information that is used internally and information reported externally as well as the integrated report and other communications. These elements represent only one dimension of connectivity, though. *Kajüter et al.* ((2013a), pp. 200-202) present two further dimensions to categorize connections. Figure 2-9 depicts these three dimensions. In addition to the elements, they analyze the nature and the means of connectivity. Regarding the **nature**, they generally distinguish formal and substantial connections. Formal connections exist when two or more aspects are mentioned in the same context, while their interrelatedness is not explained. This includes instances where a report just names a different source of information for a described issue or where it provides a comparative value next to a reported indicator without further analysis of their relationship. Instead, substantial connections outline the essence of the interrelatedness, like interdependencies or cause-and-effect relationships. Following *Küpper et al.'s* ((2013), pp. 473-475) categorization of KPIs, substantial connections can be further divided into logical, empirical and hierarchical connections.[44] The **means** of connections cover the technical view on connectivity. *Kajüter et al.* (2013a) name verbal explanations, graphics and tables, the structure of a report and references or links as different means to create connectivity. Formulae might be another means in this regard. *Abeysekera* ((2013), pp. 234-235) illustrates that a combination of these different means may even result in an enhanced informative value overall.

This categorization helps to better understand the connectivity of information and its novelty for corporate reporting. Some of the mentioned features have already been common in corporate reporting before the occurrence of IR. In the dimension of means, e.g. cross-referencing (*Cole* (1990), p. 127) or graphs (*Penrose* (2008), pp. 165-166) have been used for a long time, especially in US reporting. Regarding the nature of connections, formal connections are also present in firms' reports, e.g. the parallel use of financial and non-financial data in the same report (*AKEU* (2013), pp. 875-876). The Connectivity of Information principle now **combines the different dimensions** and their categories. An integrated report contains both formal and substantial connections (*Kajüter et al.* (2013a),

[44] Logical connections connect elements by reason, in particular by mathematical transformations, while empirical connections show observably related elements without necessarily a logical connection, and hierarchical connections represent a (subjectively) ranked order between elements (*Kajüter et al.* (2013a), p. 201).

p. 201) between the different elements listed in IR F. 3.8 and employs various means to present them (e.g., IR F. 3.9 makes clear that the use of references contributes to the connectivity of information). This creates a holistic reporting format (*Abeysekera* (2013), p. 243), which facilitates the analysis of the provided information for the users (*Peñarrubia Fraguas* (2015), p. 603). The Connectivity principle therefore yields support for the purpose of integrated reports.

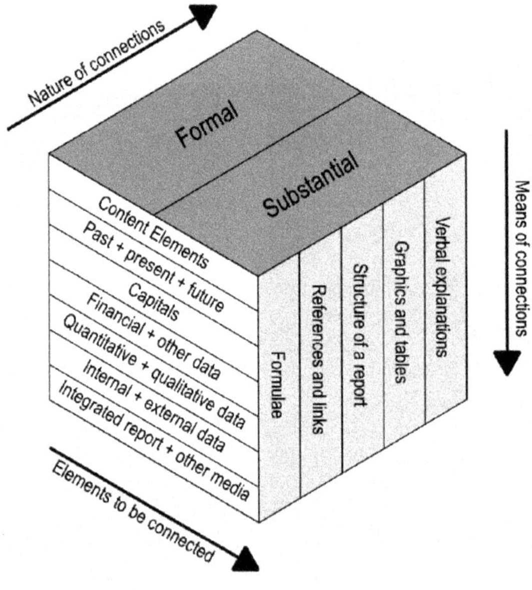

Figure 2-9: Three dimensions of connectivity

Conversely, connecting different pieces of information may also drive the difficulty to understand the report and hamper the conciseness of the document. There may thus be a tension between the Connectivity and the Conciseness principle. Arguably, a potential decrease in understandability stems from the nature of the underlying transactions itself rather than from presenting information on these issues in a connected way, though. A connected presentation instead enables users to derive implications from the interrelation of the issues, while non-connected information would possibly neglect this interplay. Providing a more complete and cohesive picture therefore promotes the **understanding** of the report rather than complicating it.

Integrated thinking plays an important role in realizing the benefits of the Connectivity Guiding Principle, since a useful depiction of connections in the report requires the awareness and consideration of these connections in managing the firm. As integrated thinking is a management rather than a reporting issue, the Framework hardly provides guidance on this topic, however (*Kajüter/Hannen* (2014), p. 81). Moreover, integrated thinking seems to be rare in actual management practice (*Kajüter* (2013), p. 148). For instance, many firms that use the Balanced Scorecard[45] do not identify the cause-and-effect relationships between the four dimensions, while many applicants see it as a performance measurement system in which the different perspectives merely represent groups of financial and non-financial strategic measures (*Speckbacher et al.* (2003), pp. 372-373). Without considering substantial connections when managing the firm, it is difficult to present them in the report and thus fulfill the Connectivity of Information principle. An essential requirement to reach the "*cycle of integrated thinking and reporting*" (IR F., p. 2) that the Framework speaks of is a consistent communication between management accounting and corporate reporting, including uniform concepts and definitions, which will be a central task for firms when implementing and applying IR (*Weißenberger* (2014), pp. 444-445).

As mentioned in the Framework, the **Stakeholder Relationships** principle helps managers and directors to fulfill their stewardship responsibility of the different capitals to the respective stakeholders that own them (IR F. 3.15-3.16). Nonetheless, an integrated report does not need to satisfy the information needs of all stakeholders (IR F. 3.11). Instead, the principle requires the report to present the stakeholders' needs and the company's responses to them only in so far as they affect the firm's value creation (IR F. 3.12). The name of the principle, which changed over time, also reflects this focus. It used to comprise the term "inclusiveness" in the DP IR, which was consistent with the GRI (e.g., GRI G4, p. 16), where this principle was present before. This term signaled a stronger involvement and meaning of stakeholders for the firm's value creation than the neutral expression "relationships" in the final Framework (*Flower* (2015), p. 14). The latter in turn more clearly aligns with the overall purpose of an integrated report and its definition of users. Due to potential changes in the stakeholder structure over time, this concentrated approach fosters the consistency and comparability of the report. Moreover, as opposed to extensive disclosures on all stakeholders, this focus is in line with the Conciseness principle. Compared with the merely financial view of traditional reporting, this principle still gives IR a broader perspective, though, which is consistent with the IIRC's conception of value and the different capitals, as well as with the principle of Completeness. Thus, this Guiding Principle is supportive of the purpose of integrated reports.

Although the principle of materiality plays an important role for corporate reporting in general, there is no universal legal definition of the term (*Eccles et al.* (2015), p. 119). However, basing upon U.S. Supreme Court decisions, *Eccles et al.* ((2015), pp. 119-120, with further references) elaborate different substantial characteristics of **materiality**: The materiality of a matter is a binary question (there are no "degrees" of materiality). Furthermore, it is management's and ultimately the board's decision whether or not a matter is material for the firm. Finally, these decisions have to be made on a case-by-case basis and have to

45 The Balanced Scorecard is a strategic planning and management system that provides managers with information from four different perspectives through a limited number of indicators for each of them: the Customer Perspective, the Internal Business Perspective, the Innovation and Learning Perspective and the Financial Perspective (*Kaplan/Norton* (1992)).

consider both quantitative and qualitative factors. The materiality determination process under IR (see section 2.2.3) considers these **characteristics**. Nevertheless, the definition of materiality in the IR Framework is not fully in line with materiality conceptions in other existing reporting frameworks (IR F. BC 4.1).[46] During the development of the Framework, the Materiality principle was therefore also subject to controversy. Almost 30% of the respondents to the CD IR were concerned about the aforementioned misalignment. Although the IIRC acknowledged these concerns (IR F. BC 4.3), it only slightly changed the wording, but not the substance of the respective paragraph for the final Framework (*Müller/Stawinoga* (2014), p. 42). As a consequence, however, the Council set up a project on materiality (IR F. BC 4.4), resulting in the release of a guidance document (*IIRC/IFAC* (2015)). The document explains the misalignment by stating that e.g. for financial reporting, materiality decisions anchor to financial matters, whereas IR has a wider perspective (*IIRC/IFAC* (2015), p. 10). According to the guidance, using other reporting frameworks may nevertheless be helpful for determining the material issues from the respective area for the integrated report.

Despite the misalignment, Materiality is an essential principle for IR. The **materiality determination process** documents the interplay between the reporting firms and the addressees of their reports. As different stakeholders and their respective capitals determine the firm's value creation (see section 2.3.1), the board has to consider the relationships with the different parties in determining the material matters for managing the firm and for the integrated report. In turn, the integrated reports informs the readers about the respective matters (IR F. 4.50-4.53) and about the process how the matters were determined (IR F. 4.42). The latter information is important for the addressees, as it provides guidance on how the board judges importance and allows an evaluation of the board's ability to exercise this judgment (*Eccles et al.* (2015), p. 133). Hence, these disclosures assist the readers in assessing how managers have fulfilled their stewardship responsibility. In particular, the information is of importance for investors. Being the owners of the firm's financial capital, they are the recipients of the value created for the firm (IR F. 2.4). As the IIRC ties the determination of materiality to the firm's value creation, the materiality concept is thus implicitly geared to the investors' interests. In this regard, it aligns with the materiality definition under IFRS (*Eccles et al.* (2015), pp. 124-125). Moreover, the IIRC's materiality determination process includes an assessment of the relevance of the matter (IR F. 3.21-3.23). Considering the Relevance principle constitutes another parallel with IFRS, as Relevance represents a Fundamental Qualitative Characteristic in the Conceptual Framework (CF. QC6-QC11).

Materiality is closely related to the **Conciseness** principle. In the CD IR and prior versions of the Framework, Materiality and Conciseness formed a single Guiding Principle (CD IR 3D). However, the IIRC decided to split it into two, as Conciseness refers to the entire report instead of just relating to the materiality determination process (*IIRC* (2013d), p. 27). Hence, while Materiality deals with the determination of what is included in the

[46] Cf. *Eccles et al.* (2015), pp. 123-127 for a comparison of materiality definitions across different reporting approaches, e.g. including IFRS or the GRI.

report, Conciseness refers to the presentation of the matters. The importance of the Conciseness principle for IR is evident from the fact that it is included in the definition of an integrated report ("*a concise communication*") in IR F. 1.1. It is a principle that has hardly been present in existing reporting frameworks[47] and it represents a direct response to the shortcoming that traditional reports are too long and difficult for users (*Stubbs et al.* (2014), p. 3). Thus supporting the understandability of the reports, Conciseness aligns with the purpose of integrated reports to provide useful information. As integrated reports seek a balance between comparability, conciseness and completeness (*Stubbs et al.* (2014), p. 11), this principle trades off against the requirement that reports need to contain all material information (*IIRC* (2013d), p. 26), which is part of the following principle.

The **Reliability and Completeness** Guiding Principle is known from financial reporting. As the IR Framework remarks, the IASB Conceptual Framework uses the term "Faithful Representation" instead, but the underlying concepts of balance (or "neutrality" in the CF), freedom from error and completeness are alike (IR F. 3.40; CF. QC12).[48] The principle used to be named "Reliability" in the financial reporting framework as well, where it represents the counterpart to the Relevance principle, against which it trades off (*Whittington* (2008), p. 146). As there is no separate Guiding Principle for relevance in IR, the tension between these principles is reflected in the aforementioned trade-off between the Materiality and Conciseness Guiding Principles on the one hand and Reliability on the other. While the former two ensure that management – and in turn the integrated report – considers the matters that are important for the firm's value creation and enable users to assess this value, the Reliability and Completeness principle (in combination with the concept of consistency) is essential for the firm to gain and retain the investors' trust and long-term credibility for itself (*Aebersold/Suter* (2012), p. 383). This Guiding Principle therefore supports the purpose of integrated reports.

Among other **mechanisms for the firms to strengthen their credibility,** the Framework mentions internal control systems and external assurance[49] (IR F. 3.40). In addition, the statement on the board's responsibility for the integrity of the report (IR F. 1.20) constitutes a mechanism to support the readers' trust. To include the requirement for this statement and thus a potential signal of credibility to the readers (*Müller/Stawinoga* (2014), p. 42), the IIRC accepts a potential hampering effect of the statement for the adoption of IR (IR F. BC 6.2-6.5). The Council intends to mitigate this effect with the "*scaredy cat*" exception (*Roberts* (2014), p. 28) in IR F. 1.20, which allows a delayed application of the

[47] E.g. chapter 3 of this study includes a direct comparison of the Guiding Principles with the principles in South Africa and the USA respectively, which cover this principle only partially. So do the principles underlying the German Lagebericht (management report) (*Wulf et al.* (2014), p. 152).

[48] Cf. *Kirsch et al.* (2012) for a discussion of different interpretations of reliability and completeness as well as the hierarchy of the underlying concepts.

[49] IR, in particular due to its principles-based approach, presents assurance providers with special problems and challenges (*Kajüter/Hannen* (2014), p. 80). The IIRC has started a debate on this topic, receiving feedback from various affected parties, which is intended to provide a starting point for developments undertaken by the IIRC itself and other parties toward a concept for assurance on IR (*IIRC* (2015b)). As this study analyzes IR from the investors' perspective, it does not focus on the development of assurance. E.g. *Nolden/Richter* (2012) or *Oprisor* (2015) discuss assurance on IR in detail.

statement in the firm's second or third integrated report. One issue that the mentioned mechanisms need to prevent is the lack of transparency regarding negative aspects. *Stubbs et al.* ((2014), pp. 10-11) reveal a potential tendency toward a non-disclosure of negative issues (e.g., the challenges that the firm faces). This practice collides with both the balance and completeness dimension of this Guiding Principle.

Also common in financial reporting, the **Consistency and Comparability** Guiding Principle governs IR as well. As mentioned before, this principle affects various other principles and further aspects of IR. It provides two different contributions to the informative value of the report. On the one hand, investors require data that is comparable within the respective sector and consistent over several periods (*Peñarrubia Fraguas* (2015), p. 596; *Lachnit/Müller* (2015), p. 546). In this regard, both consistency and comparability add to the relevance of the information. On the other hand, the principle assists more reliable disclosures and helps to gain the users' trust, in particular through the consistency aspect (*Aebersold/Suter* (2012), p. 383). The principles of Materiality (including the relevance aspect), Conciseness, Reliability and Completeness as well as Consistency and Comparability are thus mutually supportive. A useful integrated report manages to balance them (*Stubbs et al.* (2014), p. 11). The comparability aspect, however, remains in the aforementioned tension with the principles-based approach and the related freedom for firms to select the appropriate disclosures for their individual value creation story. These individual disclosures on a firm's value are also a reflection of relevant information. Hence, the relationship between comparability and relevance is ambivalent. *Higgins et al.* ((2014), p. 1112) confirm this notion with their insights from interviews with managers of early-adopting firms, who experienced this trade-off in practice.

Overall, the Guiding Principles of the IR Framework draw on various principles that have already been established by traditional reporting. With these principles, IR also takes over the trade-offs between them. In particular, the tension between reliability and relevance, persists, with relevance being present in IR's Materiality principle. Due to its principles-based rather than rules-based nature, the IIRC's approach also implies a tension between the Comparability principle and firms' flexibility to report their individual situation. Supplementing the set of principles from traditional financial reporting, IR puts the ideas of future orientation and conciseness into particular focus, takes a broader perspective toward reporting on stakeholders (as known from sustainability reporting) and promotes the connectivity of information. These innovative features add to the importance of the Guiding Principles for IR and represent useful aspects for reporting in general. Taken together, the seven IR Guiding Principles align with the purpose of integrated reports despite the mentioned trade-offs. The principles serve as an aid to orientation in identifying useful contents for the integrated reports. It is therefore not surprising that Matt Chapman, head of KPMG UK's better business reporting group, expects many Guiding Principles to be adopted, irrespective of the name of IR (*Orton-Jones* (2015), p. 38).[50]

[50] Chapter 4 of this study examines in how far existing reports from two countries already adhere to the Guiding Principles and how this adherence changes with the requirement for firms to adopt IR.

2.3.3 Content Elements

This third step of the analysis **assesses the requirements on the Content Elements against the Guiding Principles.** By analogy with conceptual analyses of the provisions of financial reporting against the Qualitative Characteristics of the Conceptual Framework, the principles represent the criteria to evaluate the Content Elements and their alignment with the purpose of integrated reports.

Consistent with the outlined principles-based approach that the Framework follows, the requirements regarding the Content Elements are not very specific and do not even constitute an authoritative structure for the report (IR F. 4.2). The flexibility that this lack of authority entails is supposed to better demonstrate the connections between the different contents, which is in line with the Connectivity of Information principle. Potential overlaps and redundancies between the elements (Figure 2-10)[51], as criticized in response to the DP IR (*IIRC* (2012a), p. 9), are not necessarily problematic for the structure, clarity and conciseness of the report, while at the same time the IIRC avoids conflicts with other regulations that govern the respective contents (*Kajüter et al.* (2013b), p. 1686). Indeed there are various rules, standards and guidance documents that already cover the contents that the Framework suggests (see chapter 3). Hence, as opposed to some of the aforementioned Guiding Principles, the **eight Content Elements** do not yield particular innovation. Nevertheless, they show considerable conformity with the information needs that investors have when analyzing securities (*Peñarrubia Fraguas* (2015), pp. 602-603).

From the requirements on the **Organizational Overview and External Environment**, in particular the description of the firm's **mission and vision** is of interest for investors. Understanding a firm's core values, its reason to exist and its vision represents a first step in business analysis, as it helps investors to assess the firm's ability to manage continuity and change (*Peñarrubia Fraguas* (2015), pp. 604). For companies it is important to understand how to distinguish between a core ideology (i.e., the firm's core purpose and core values) that does not change over time and an envisioned future that includes the aspired achievements and creations and for which progress and change is necessary – together they form the company's vision (*Collins/Porras* (1996), pp. 65-66). Furthermore, a clear ideology can assist a company in connecting with stakeholders, since it increases the likelihood to link with people (e.g., employees) that share the firm's values (*Collins/Porras* (1996), p. 71). Investors and other stakeholders therefore get a general impression of what they can expect from the firm (*Peñarrubia Fraguas* (2015), pp. 604). Information on the mission and vision is thus relevant for them on its own, while also providing a reference for assessing the reliability of other information that the firm presents. Moreover, it is decisive for the comparability with other firms, because organizations with entirely different missions and visions may be incomparable.

Information about the company's **external environment** provides a background for analyzing the firm, helping users to evaluate its opportunities and risks (*AICPA* (1994), p. 31).

---

[51] Basing upon *Eccles et al.* ((2015), p. 205, with single modifications), the figure gives an impression of the multitude of relationships among the Content Elements. It does not show a collectively exhaustive picture of these relationships, though. For instance, Basis of Preparation and Presentation is not included at all.

For their analysis investors use frameworks like *Porter's* (1979) Five Forces, which include the force from current competitors jockeying for position, the bargaining power of customers, the bargaining power of suppliers, the threat of new market entrants and the threat of substitute products or services (*Peñarrubia Fraguas* (2015), p. 611). The IR Framework requires an integrated report to make according disclosures (e.g., information on competitors in IR F. 4.7) that can help the investors with this analysis and may therefore turn out to be relevant for them. As a lot of publicly available information exists on political, industry or environmental issues in the firms' environment (e.g., World Bank data) this type of information is likely to be verifiable[52] and thus reliable, in particular if the report references such data. The latter practice is also in line with the Connectivity principle and may at the same time enhance Conciseness (IR F. 3.38).

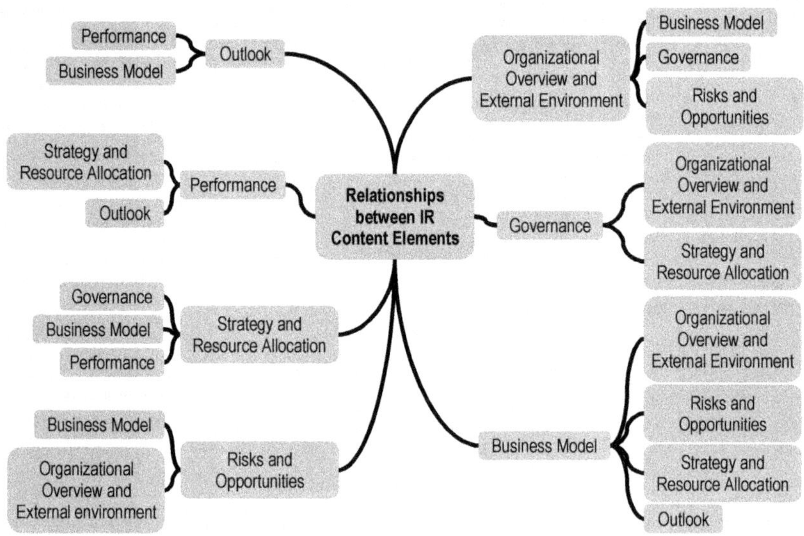

Figure 2-10: Relationships between the IR Content Elements (based on *Eccles et al.* (2015), p. 205)

Various traits of good corporate **governance** connect with the risk-adjusted return of an investment, including the expertise, experience and independence of the board, the appropriateness of how the board controls management, remuneration policies, the firm's ownership structure etc. (*Peñarrubia Fraguas* (2015), p. 611). Empirical evidence confirms that governance is both directly related to firms' results and value (e.g., *Gompers et al.* (2003);

52 As opposed to the Conceptual Framework, Verifiability does not constitute a separate Guiding Principle or an explicit feature of a principle in IR. Nevertheless, the verifiability of information adds to its reliability.

Ammann et al. (2011)) and has a positive effect on accounting quality (e.g., *Ashbaugh-Skaife* (2008)). Hence, information on these aspects is relevant for investors, helping them to select firms that create and sustainably increase value and to assess the quality and reliability of other disclosures in the report. Management's remuneration is of particular importance in this regard. If – in line with integrated thinking – the salary connects with the firm's performance (e.g., through bonus payments based on certain performance KPIs), managers are incentivized to act in the investors' interest and increase firm value (*Deegan/Unerman* (2011), pp. 276-280, with further references). In turn, reporting on (the results and) management's remuneration enables investors to assess how managers have fulfilled their stewardship responsibility (IR F. 3.15) and if they are appropriately motivated for future performance (*Peñarrubia Fraguas* (2015), p. 613). Depending on the remuneration system, the disclosures in the integrated report may thus be particularly useful for investors, given that this information is in line with the principles of Connectivity and Strategic Focus.

The DP IR already acknowledged the central role that disclosures on the organization's **business model** play for IR, as they support investors' resource allocation by providing relevant information on the firm's long-term success (DP IR, p. 10). In particular, this information assists investors in understanding the nature and scope of the firm's activities, which represents the foundation for their analysis of the business. By describing the inputs the company uses, the report enables investors to assess the impacts of global and industry trends for the firm's stakeholders and for the financial power, while a description of the business activities allows them to identify sources of revenues and cost structures so that they can evaluate the firm's profitability (*Peñarrubia Fraguas* (2015), pp. 605-606). The outputs, as the value generated for customers (*Magretta* (2002)), are central to the business. By distinguishing them from the outcomes, the IIRC makes investors consider not only the financial results from the sale of these outputs, but also the changes in the other capitals, to assess the generated value and its sustainability for the growth of the company (*Peñarrubia Fraguas* (2015), pp. 607-609). Thus, investors get a more complete picture of the firm's value creation. Although critics note that business models are typically static so that their disclosure may cause repetition over time and contradict the idea of conciseness, the important context that this information provides for strategy, risks and opportunities, capitals and particularly value creation made the IIRC retain this disclosure requirement (*IIRC* (2013d), p. 20).

With their forward-looking nature, disclosures on **risks and opportunities** are in line with the Future Orientation principle and represent relevant information for investors. Providers of financial capital bear the risk of investing and thus need to take the risk profile of the firms in their portfolio into account (*Linsley et al.* (2008), p. 187). Disclosures on risks and opportunities directly affect the valuation of the firm, e.g. the determination of multiples or discount rates (*AICPA* (1994), p. 30). Hence, investors require information on risks and opportunities (*Solomon et al.* (2000), p. 464). At the same time, there is also room for improvements regarding a better quantification of the risks through the potential consequences and likelihood of the risks (*Peñarrubia Fraguas* (2015), p. 614). IR F. 4.25 requires an integrated report to provide such information.

A critical issue of risks and opportunities information is their balance and completeness. Investors' views (*Stubbs et al.* (2014), pp. 12-13) and empirical results from management reports (*Kajüter et al.* (2010), p. 463) show that disclosure practice often focuses on risks rather than opportunities. However, to get a complete picture of the firm's situation, readers need to know both potential negative (risks) and positive (opportunities) deviations from the firm's forecasts or objectives (Figure 2-11). As the described one-sided reporting practice contrasts the Reliability principle, the Framework explicitly requires a balanced disclosure of both risks and opportunities (IR F. 4.24) so that integrated reports provide a different picture. It remains to be seen whether IR may actually change the disclosure practice in this regard, as the requirement of balance is not new and the Framework thus provides no innovative solution to this problem (*Kajüter* (2013), pp. 148-149). Moreover, even if one considers the Framework to be good guidance, practice guidelines alone are unlikely to change risk reporting behavior (*Linsley et al.* (2008), p. 206). **Useful reporting requires the willingness of the firms** to actually disclose the information in question. If the reporting firm considers reporting as an exercise of abiding by regulations or guidelines without arousing (proprietary) costs, the firm could also employ cheap talk[53], i.e. costless, non-verifiable, non-binding information (*Farrell* (1987), p. 34). Disclosures of this kind would impede the informative value of the respective content and would not be qualified to influence users' decisions.

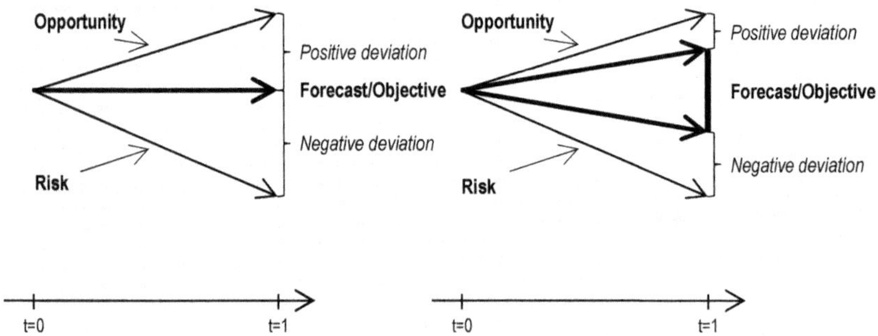

Figure 2-11: Risks and opportunities (based on *Fink et al.* (2013), p. 182)

Cheap talk may also be a problem for disclosures on the Content Element **Strategy and Resource Allocation**. Since disclosures on this topic are sensitive of revealing information that could result in a loss of competitive advantage (*Greinert* (2004), p. 54), managers are not necessarily willing to provide them. In response to this problem, the Framework clarifies that firms only need to describe the essence of a matter, without being so specific that competitors could gain an advantage (IR F. 3.51; 4.50). Hence, the forward-looking and inherently uncertain character of strategic information and its subjectivity – as a reflection of

[53] Cf. e.g. *Crawford/Sobel* (1982); *Farrell* (1987); *Farrell/Gibbons* (1989); *Farrell/Rabin* (1996).

managers' intentions – put the reliability of this information into doubt (*Ferreira/Rezende* (2007), p. 165). However, like the description of the external environment and the business model[54], strategic content provides background information for investors' analysis of the firm, helping them to understand the company's broad objectives and strategies (*AICPA* (1994), p. 31). At the same time, these disclosures are highly relevant and therefore beneficial for investors. Knowledge about how the firm allocates its resources helps investors to assess the company's ability to invest its scarce capital in profitable activities (*Peñarrubia Fraguas* (2015), p. 614).

Disclosures on a firm's **performance** are a classical element of corporate reporting. However, the respective IR Content Element yields some new features compared to traditional performance reporting in financial statements. In line with the different aspects of the Connectivity principle, the IR Framework requires reporting against the strategic objectives (IR F. 4.30) and against past and future information (IR F. 4.31). Furthermore, the IIRC prescribes disclosures on the different capitals (IR F. 4.31) as a combination of quantitative and qualitative disclosures (IR F. 4.32). In general, these connected disclosures yield a holistic perspective on the firm's performance. They enhance the relevance of the report for investors, as they help to overcome the narrow focus of financial statements and show a more complete picture of the firm's market value (see section 1.1).

The new aspect of disclosures on the firm's non-financial performance led to a discussion about the **need of explicit guidance on indicators** and on other ways to measure and report non-financial information, which would provide more comparability between firms (IR F. BC 8.1). Such guidance could establish a minimum standard for performance disclosures (*Kajüter et al.* (2013b), p. 1686). However, the IIRC positioned itself at the other end of the noted trade-off and opted for a non-prescriptive approach that leaves room for individual disclosures. The Council keeps the issue of guidance out of the Framework itself, while considering to undertake the aforementioned project for a database with external sources of KPIs (IR F. BC 8.2). Moreover, there are suggestions in the literature how investors can use non-financial data. *Lachnit/Müller* ((2015), pp. 551-555) list four different options:

- Using non-financial measures as (subjective) knockout criteria or thresholds beyond which the investor stops following the firm,
- using a scoring model by assigning (subjective) scores to the values of different indicators and combining them in an aggregate overall score,
- using KPIs that put non-financial values into meaningful relations with other indicators (e.g., emissions relative to sales) to better interpret them and make them more comparable with other firms' values and

[54] In response to comments on potential confusion between strategy and the business model, the IIRC tried to clarify the distinction between the two elements by outlining the role of all Content Elements for value creation in IR F. 2D (*IIRC* (2013d), p. 20). While the business model represents the aforementioned process of transforming inputs from the different capitals into outputs through the firm's business activities, which leads to outcomes that in turn affect the capitals (IR F. 2.23), the strategy identifies the approach to manage risks and opportunities and sets out strategic objectives and the related strategies to achieve them by allocating resources accordingly (IR F. 2.27).

- combining the different indicators in a market value added calculation[55], which requires a relative comparison with average values from other firms as well as monetization.

This and other models (e.g., *Mook* (2006)) have in common that the firm needs to overcome the difficulty of finding **appropriate measures of the six capitals** in the first place. Combining them in a useful way is then often affected by subjectivity so that the final conclusion may base upon a lack of both reliability and comparability.

Forward-looking information, as provided under the Content Element **Outlook**, meets investors' information needs, since it assists them in their future-oriented task to assess the firm's value (*Peñarrubia Fraguas* (2015), pp. 615-616). Even though the Framework does not require the disclosure of particular forecasts, the information in the integrated report is supposed to allow an evaluation of the firm's prospects, (*IIRC* (2013d), pp. 39-40), for which investors usually make their own forecasts (*AICPA* (1994), p. 30). This information is thus highly relevant, but at the same time uncertain and therefore not necessarily reliable. Although regulations in some countries mandate forward-looking disclosures,[56] regulation constraints in other countries may keep future-oriented information from appearing in the reports (*Stubbs et al.* (2014), p. 7). Similarly, managers' fear of personal liability (*Stubbs et al.* (2014), p. 10; *IIRC* (2013d), p. 39)) and the indirect costs of reporting, like competitive disadvantage or negative stock price reactions (*Kajüter et al.* (2013b), p. 1687), may impede such disclosures. The guidance that recommends general rather than specific disclosures in response to potential competitive harm (IR F. 3.51; 4.50), as mentioned in the context of strategy information, also holds for these cases (*IIRC* (2013d), p. 40).

The Content Element **Basis of Preparation and Presentation** was not present in the CD IR, but was introduced for the final Framework, as it presents rather general information that is supposed to assist readers in understanding the integrated report (*IIRC* (2013d), p. 36). This information had been summarized under a separate part in the CD IR, which was probably more systematical, as the informational value of this element in practice remains to be shown (*Kajüter/Hannen* (2014), p. 80).

To sum up, the Content Elements leave room for flexibility in the disclosures due to their unauthoritative structure, as the IIRC avoids conflicts with other regulations that already govern particular contents. Due to these existing regulations, the elements as such are hardly an innovation. However, in line with a more holistic depiction of value, the concept of six capitals yields a new dimension for some of the contents, even though different capitals have already been considered to a varying degree in some forms of corporate reporting or in several countries (e.g., in sustainability reporting or in ICA). In particular, this broader

[55] This model aggregates weighted single indicators (e.g., an index of employee satisfaction, the labor turnover rate etc.) to index values that represent certain success factors (e.g., a human capital index or indices for the other capitals). These factors add up to the market value added, which in turn can be derived from the discounted future residual profits (*Lachnit/Müller* (2015), pp. 553-555). Market value added is also known from the EVA® concept (*Stewart* (1991)).

[56] For instance, GAS 20.118 requires German parent entities to assess and discuss management's forecasts about the course of business and the position of the group in their group management report (Konzernlagebericht).

approach may impact the description of the business model and the performance disclosures. In line with the Framework's investor orientation, this additional dimension makes the provided information more relevant for investors and their capital allocation decisions. At the same time, it requires them to develop new methods and tools to use the additional data for their analysis. As in financial reporting, the relevance of the Content Elements is in tension with the reliability of the information. It remains doubtful whether the Framework requirements and their inherent flexibility can ensure the latter. Additional guidance for some areas outside the Framework, as intended by the IIRC, might help in this regard, and might furthermore enhance the comparability with other firms' reports.

The freedom involved in the Content Elements is consistent with the principles-based approach of the Framework. Given this freedom, the **Guiding Principles** may serve as an aid to orientation in the preparation of the report. The seven principles that the Framework presents combine established ideas from financial reporting with a consideration of stakeholders' views as known from sustainability reporting. This combination broadens the perspective of the reports compared with traditional communications and is in line with the concept of the six capitals. However, the consideration of both the other stakeholders' interests and the capitals is limited by the shareholder primacy of IR. Consistent with the overall purpose of an integrated report, only contributions to the value for the firm and its owners are relevant for disclosures. Nevertheless, the broader perspective of IR due to these aspects constitutes an innovation compared with financial reporting. So does the particular emphasis on future orientation to overcome the retrospection of traditional reports and on the Conciseness principle, which aims at tackling the length of corporate reports and the difficulty to process them. Moreover, the new Connectivity principle, which intends to reveal the trade-offs and interactions among the different elements of a firm's business for a better understanding of the latter, represents a novelty of IR.

Overall, the Framework provides a coherent reporting approach. The Guiding Principles represent the purpose of integrated reports and serve as an aid to orientation for the contents of integrated reports. In turn, the Content Elements largely align with these principles and thus with the purpose of integrated reports. Nonetheless, tensions between the principles and critical issues regarding certain contents (e.g., the sensitivity of future-oriented disclosures), which were already present in traditional financial reporting, persist. The non-binding character of the Framework and the high degree of discretion that it offers to the reporting firms question the reliability and comparability of the information and thus the conceptual benefits for investors. Moreover, these characteristics leave doubt about a widespread implementation of the IR approach. The question whether IR – in line with the IIRC's vision – may become "*the corporate reporting norm*" (IR F., p. 2) depends on how both preparers and users of the reports accept the idea (*Kajüter* (2014a), p. 222). However, irrespective of the overall approach, the innovative ideas of IR, e.g. the Connectivity Guiding Principle, may be adopted on their own and enhance the usefulness of corporate reports (*Orton-Jones* (2015), p. 38). Rather than initiating a "*revolution*" (*Beyhs/Barth* (2011a)), IR would thus contribute to the evolutionary advancement of corporate reporting (*Kajüter* (2014a), p. 226). The study at hand intends to shed light on the implementation of IR in practice in terms of the adherence to the Guiding Principles (see chapter 4).

3 Corporate reporting in South Africa and the USA

This chapter presents the institutional and regulatory setting in South Africa and the USA. These two countries constitute a **promising setting to examine the corporate reporting practice** with a view to the use of IR, as they yield certain differences in various regards. With strong personal and institutional involvement in the IIRC and in the development of the International <IR> Framework, as well as with the introduction of the requirement to apply IR in the King III regulations, South Africa is a pioneer for the development of IR (*Güleş* (2014)). Stakeholder orientation and sustainability issues had already been established in the South African reporting environment by prior versions of the King rules (*Rensburg/Botha* (2014), p. 146). The perspective of corporate reporting was thus broader than that of traditional financial reporting, which makes the country an adequate setting for IR and thus for an empirical study on this reporting approach. As opposed to South Africa, the USA do not play a pioneering role in the development of IR. However, the USA have a developed and established system of (financial) reporting, which is considered to be useful for firms, investors and other participants in the economy.[57] Contrary to IR, which puts a lot of weight on the firms' individual situation, this system bases upon standardized reporting to a high degree, particularly driven by the different Forms that firms have to file with the SEC. Thus, it appears useful to reflect the South African reporting practice against firms' reporting in the USA.

The subsequent empirical analysis of this study therefore examines reports from these two countries. To provide an understanding of the basis upon which these reports are prepared this chapter **introduces the countries' corporate reporting environment**. After a presentation of the South African reporting landscape in the first section, the second section outlines the corporate reporting system in the USA.

3.1 Corporate reporting in South Africa

Presenting **the South African reporting landscape** requires special consideration of the economic situation and some historical developments in this country. After their presentation, the section introduces the institutions involved in reporting regulation and the regulations that influence the reporting practice. The respective provisions are compared with the requirements on principles and contents of the International <IR> Framework. As the introduction of the King III Code and its apply-or-explain approach brought the requirement for listed firms to engage in IR, this code marks an essential turning point for IR and for this study. Hence, this section focuses on this regulation and the related guidance on IR. Moreover, to enable an assessment of the reporting practice before IR, also other regulations that have been in place before King III, including the predecessor King II, are introduced. The section ends with a summary.

---

[57] Many studies provide evidence on positive economic consequences of US (financial) reporting. E.g., *Griffin* (2003) documents investor reaction to Form 10-Ks, thus showing their informative value. *Barron et al.* (1999) evidence a positive relationship of MD&A quality and analysts' earnings forecast quality. *Botosan* (1997) finds an association of disclosure level with reduced cost of capital.

3.1.1 Economic and historical background

Both the country's **economic situation** and several developments in its relatively young history substantially shaped the reporting landscape of South Africa. The economy is one of extreme ends. Great poverty, widespread health issues, limited access to education and massive unemployment on the one hand oppose financial wealth in line with phases of booming capital markets and enormous natural resources (farmlands and mineral resources) on the other hand (*Rensburg/Botha* (2014), p. 145). Recent numbers from the *World Economic Forum* ((2014), p. 341) back these notions. South Africa ranks among the top 25 (out of 144) countries for indicators referring to investors' interests (e.g., "Protection of minority shareholders' interests" or "Financing through local equity markets"). At the same time, it occurs among the bottom 25 countries in terms of various health indicators (e.g., "Tuberculosis cases/100,000 pop." or "Life expectancy, years"), education scores (e.g., "Quality of primary education" or "Quality of math and science education") or labor relation indicators (e.g., "Cooperation in labor employer relations" or "Hiring and firing practices"). Hence, South Africa shows some typical traits and problems of a developing country (*Oberholster* (1999), pp. 223-224, with further references).

In terms of the country's **history**, the colonial past and the apartheid era had a remarkable influence on the economic situation as well as on today's accounting and reporting landscape. Dutch merchants brought accounting techniques to the region, which British **colonial influence** later refined (*Oberholster* (1999), p. 224; *Verhoeff/Van Vuuren* (2012), pp. 136-143).[58] The British Companies Acts of 1844, 1856 and 1867 also formed the basis for various Companies Acts in the South African colonies. These South African acts manifested the formation of companies, the compilation and auditing of financial statements and the formation of an annual general meeting of shareholders including the firm's requirement to submit income statements to this meeting and compile balance sheets according to a prescribed schedule (*Verhoeff/Van Vuuren* (2012), pp. 141-143). So the colonial era laid the foundation for today's accounting and reporting system in South Africa.

The second phase with a major influence on the business and reporting situation was the **apartheid** era from 1948 to 1991[59], which established a racial hierarchy in favor of white South Africans. This policy was considered a "crime against humanity" by the United Nations (UN) General Assembly in 1966 (Resolution 2202, p. 20) and caused anti-apartheid movements internationally. One of the most important activities in this regard was the US divestment movement (*Arnold/Hammond* (1994)). US (institutional) investors massively divested from firms doing business in South Africa (*Stevenson* (1990)). Even though the white minority rule prevented substantial political changes in response to these actions, it became clear that the apartheid system constituted a hindrance for firms to do business and invest money in the country (*Van Staden* (2003), p. 233).

---

[58] Early accounting records provide evidence of farmers' bookkeeping, with not only slaves, but also hired apprentices being included in the balance sheet (*Verhoeff/Van Vuuren* (2012), pp. 139-140). It could thus be argued that there was an awareness for the importance of human capital for the business from the initial stages of accounting in South Africa.

[59] Cf. e.g. *Clark/Worger* (2016) or *Dubow* (2014) for an overview and detailed background information on the apartheid era.

When the African National Congress (ANC) was elected as the governing party in the first democratic elections after the end of the apartheid era in April 1994, the new government passed many **laws strengthening labor rights** (*Cahan/Van Staden* (2009), pp. 44-45; *Catchpowle/Cooper* (1999), pp. 719-723). Most prominent among them was probably the Black Economic Empowerment (BEE) legislation (*Krüger* (2011)), which aimed at a transformation in terms of more economic participation of black people. These laws also resulted in an increasing power of trade unions (*Jamerson* (2004), p. 41). Moreover, this political turn of events put more focus on firms' ethical conduct as well as on the necessity to be transparent and provide the necessary disclosures in this regard (*Druckman* (2013)). The foundation of the King Committee with the development of the first King Report on corporate governance (King I) was one reflection of these developments.

3.1.2 Institutions regulating corporate reporting

Founded in 1887, the **JSE** is the only licensed full service securities exchange in South Africa (*JSE* (2015), p. 4), while being the largest stock exchange in Africa and the 19th largest in the world by market capitalization.[60] With an international investor base and tradable instruments from the entire African continent and elsewhere, it has a global reach (*JSE* (2015), p. 5). The World Economic Forum Global Competitiveness Report 2014-2015 ranks South Africa first worldwide as regards securities exchanges regulation (*World Economic Forum* (2014), p. 341). Important factors for the quality of the securities exchange regulation may be the JSE's deliberate reaction to the financial crisis and its sound working relationship with the Financial Services Board (*Minney* (2010)), an independent institution to oversee the Non-Banking Financial Services Industry in South Africa (*FSB* (n.d.)). Firms that want to list their securities on the JSE need to comply with the JSE Listings Requirements (par. 1.2 of the JSE Listings Requirements). These Listing Requirements set out legal, reporting and other criteria, also including several minimum disclosure standards.

The **Financial Reporting Standards Council (FRSC)** is the legally constituted standard setter in South Africa (*FRSC* (n.d.), p. 2). Section 203 of the Companies Act No. 71 of 2008 (the Companies Act) obliged the Minister of Trade & Industry to establish this institution and prescribed the background of the members. Among them are auditors, preparers of financial statements for public and private firms, investors, company law professionals and several persons nominated by banks, stock exchanges and the Financial Services Board. However, regulation 27 (4) to the Companies Act prescribes the use of IFRS or IFRS for SMEs for almost all companies, leaving the FRSC with the function to issue financial reporting pronouncements, consider the need for interpretations of the standards (*FRSC* (n.d.), p. 3) or to respond to Exposure Drafts on standards issued by the IASB (*FRSC* (n.d.), Section A, recital 4 (p. 6)).

After its formation in October 2011, the FRSC cooperated closely with its predecessor, the **Accounting Practices Board (APB)**, which was supposed to wind up after transferring its knowledge to the FRSC (*APB/FRSC* (2012), pp. 1-2). Founded in 1973, the APB had developed generally accepted accounting principles, the SA GAAP, and had harmonized them

[60] Cf. https://www.jse.co.za/about/history-company-overview (last accessed on 29 August 2016) for general information on the JSE.

from 2003 on with IFRS (*APB/FRSC* (2012), p. 1).[61] As the Johannesburg Stock Exchange (JSE) required listed firms in 2004 to comply with IFRS from 1 January 2005 on, the APB even issued IFRS texts without amendments as SA GAAP, beginning in February 2004 (*Verhoeff/Van Vuuren* (2012), p. 174). As a result, for the reporting firms no substantial changes occurred with the replacement of SA GAAP by IFRS, effective for years beginning on or after 1 December 2012 (*APB/FRSC* (2012), p. 1).

Another relevant institution in the reporting landscape is the **Companies and Intellectual Property Commission** (sections 185-192 of the Companies Act).[62] The Commission is responsible for the investigation of alleged non-compliance with the financial reporting standards, thus for the enforcement of the standards. Furthermore it may recommend amendments of the standards to the FRSC. According to the Companies Act, the Commission is a regulatory agency, a statutorily established juristic person that is independent, with only the Minister of Trade & Industry having power to direct the Commission to initiate investigations. Apart from these directed investigations, the Commission can investigate companies on its own initiative or on complaint. These investigations and procedures are governed by sections 168-179 of the Companies Act. Any company can be subject to these enforcement procedures. Typically, the Commission appoints an inspector to carry out the inquiries and deliver an investigation report on the non-compliance. By issuing a compliance notice (and sending a copy to the JSE in case of a listed company), the Commission puts the company under pressure to rectify the issue(s) of non-compliance. When the reporting firm has corrected their financial statements, the Commission issues a compliance certificate. If the firm fails to do so, the case may be taken to a court or to the National Prosecution Authority. For recidivist companies, the Commission may even apply to a court for an order to wind up the company (section 81 (1) (f) of the Companies Act).

At the political turning point that the end of the apartheid era marked, it was Nelson Mandela himself who convinced former Supreme Court judge Mervyn E. King in 1992 (*Stewart* (2010)) to found and chair the **King Committee**, aiming at providing corporate governance guidelines for South Africa (*West* (2009), p. 11). Formed in July 1993 at the instance of the Institute of Directors in Southern Africa (IODSA), the Committee received support from different institutions. In particular the South African Chamber of Business (SACOB), the Chartered Institute of Secretaries and Administrators (CIS), the South African Institute of Chartered Accountants (SAICA), the JSE and the South African Institute of Business Ethics assisted the development of the governance framework with their advice in a transparent process (King I Report, The Background to Corporate Governance, recitals 2-5 (pp. 3-4)). The team consisted of 15 members from various areas and professions, including for instance politicians, managers, accounting professionals, academics and judges, who formed five task groups on the issues of Directors, Audit, Stakeholder Links, Ethic and Conformance/Compliance (King I Report, Appendix I, pp. 40-43). The result-

61 The harmonization turned out to be relatively easy, however, as the IASC (i.e., the predecessor of the IASB) had collaboratively contributed to the development of the SA GAAP (*Verhoeff/Van Vuuren* (2012), p. 167).

62 Cf. *Schmidt et al.* (2011) for a detailed presentation of the Commission and the South African enforcement system.

ing King Report on corporate governance (King I), including the Code of Corporate Practices & Conduct[63], was published in November 1994. It paved the way for further developments in the South African business and reporting landscape. The aforementioned laws passed by the new ANC-led government, amendments in the Companies Act (No. 61 of 1973) and changes in the JSE listings requirements led to the implementation of various ideas from the King I Report into binding laws (King II Report, Introduction and background, recitals 10 and 11 (p. 9)), which was one of the reasons for the King Committee to develop a new version of the regulations (King II), released in 2002. Even after the release of the third edition (King III) in 2009, which requires the application of IR or an explanation of non-application, the Committee continues to exist[64] and has even developed a fourth version of the governance rules (King IV), effective for financial years starting on or after 1 April 2017.[65]

Although King III required the application of IR and the JSE Listings Requirements mandated all listed firms to apply the principles set out in the King Code or to disclose the non-application and the underlying reasons, there was a lack of guidance for reporting firms on how to apply IR. The King III provisions hold some explanations on IR itself,[66] but on a rather general level and only comprising three and a half pages in the report.[67] In May 2010 several South African institutions[68] founded the **IRCSA** under the chairmanship of Mervyn E. King (IRCSA DP 1.4 (p. 5)). The Committee formed a working group to develop guidance on good IR practice and cooperated closely with the IIRC after the latter's formation on 2 August 2010 (IRCSA DP 1.4, p. 5). The working group's effort resulted in the release of a discussion paper on a "Framework for Integrated Reporting and the Integrated Report" (IRCSA DP) on 25 January 2011 and constituted a first step for the planned IR guidance. The IIRC considered both this discussion paper and the 40 comment letters received in response (*IRCSA* (2011b)) for their work on the international discussion paper and the later work on the Framework (*IRCSA* (2011c)). After the IIRC had finished and released its International <IR> Framework in December 2013, the IRCSA endorsed the IIRC Framework (*IRCSA* (2014), p. 1), making it the relevant guidance on IR for South Africa and thus replacing the IRCSA DP.

---

63 The code holds the governance provisions, while the other parts of the report include background information and best practice recommendations beyond the provisions of the code.

64 However, the members of the Committee changed over time and different numbers and kinds of task groups were created for the development of the different King versions, cf. King II Report, Appendices I and II (pp. 156-164); King III Report, The King Committee (pp. 136-139).

65 For this study, only the requirements of King I, II and III have been considered.

66 Cf. King III Report, chapter 9 (pp. 107-111). *Makiwane/Padia* (2013) use the King III requirements (in combination with GRI requirements) as indicators representing IR.

67 In addition, King III gives the impression of considering an integrated report as a combination of the financial and the sustainability report (e.g., principle 9.2 and the related explanations; cf. King III Report, chapter 9 (pp. 109-110)), whereas the IIRC and this study take a broader view, seeing an integrated report as a communication about the firm's value creation, with regard to its strategy, governance, performance and prospects in the context of its external environment (IR F. 1.1). *Flower* (2015) criticizes that an integrated report does not include sustainability reporting.

68 The institutions to form the IRCSA were the Association for Saving & Investment South Africa (ASISA), Business Unity South Africa (BUSA), the IODSA, the JSE and SAICA (*IRCSA* (2011a)).

3.1.3 Regulations on corporate reporting

Given these institutions, South African firms face a variety of regulations they have to consider for their reporting. Table 3-1 provides an overview.

	Companies Act No. 71 of 2008	JSE Listings Requirements (JSE LR)	International Financial Reporting Standards (IFRS)	King Report on Governance for South Africa 2009 (King III)	The International <IR> Framework (IR F)
Focus	Stipulation of general legal framework (particularly, IFRS focus)	Requirements for listing at the JSE, including disclosures	Standards for financial reporting	Corporate impact on communities; sustainability and risk-related issues	Guidance on IR (as required e.g. by King III)
Effective date of current version	1 May 2011	30 September 2014	Different effective dates for the different standards; amended on an ongoing basis	1 March 2010	9 December 2013
Binding character	Binding by law	Binding for firms listed at the JSE	Mandatory use for almost all South African firms (Alternative: IFRS for SMEs)	Not legally binding; apply-or-explain approach if JSE-listed	Not legally binding

Table 3-1: Overview of reporting regulations in South Africa

Companies Act

The **Companies Act** regulates – among other things – the incorporation, registration, organization and management of firms, their relationship with shareholders or merger and acquisition matters. But in conjunction with the Companies Regulations 2011[69], it also provides a framework for financial record-keeping and reporting. Financial reporting needs to be in line with IFRS or IFRS for SMEs for all firms except companies of minor public interest (regulation 27 (4) to the Companies Act). In addition to setting the stage for the financial reporting standards, the Companies Act also prescribes particular contents of the financial statements and disclosures itself. For instance, this includes the auditor's report, the directors' report, i.e. a narrative statement by the directors on the firm's state of affairs and profit or loss, and certain disclosures on the directors' and officers' remuneration (section 30 (3) (a) and (b) as well as (4) of the Companies Act). Moreover, this comprises the requirement for regulated companies[70] to provide a list of shareholders with a stake of 5% or higher (including their respective share) in their financial statements (section 56 (7) of the Companies Act) or a report on the work of the audit committee (section 94 (7) (f) of the Companies Act).

[69] Section 223 of the Companies Act empowers the Minister of Trade & Industry to make Regulations on various issues to supplement the Companies Act. Like the Companies Act itself, these Companies Regulations 2011 came into effect on 1 May 2011.

[70] The term "regulated companies" refers to all public companies as well as certain state-owned and private companies (section 117 (1) (i) in conjunction with section 118 (1) of the Companies Act).

Furthermore, section 30 (2) of the Companies Act prescribes that all public companies need to have their **financial statements audited.** Other profit or non-profit companies need to undergo an audit or an independent review based on their economic and social significance (measured by their turnover, workforce as well as the nature and extent of their activities). Regulations 28 and 29 to the Companies Act in conjunction with section 30 (7) of the Companies Act provide more detailed provisions on the kinds of companies that need to have their financial statements audited.

After the State President had signed the Companies Act No. 71 of 2008 on 9 April 2009, several amendments were necessary to correct errors so that the act finally became effective on 1 May 2011 (*Stein* (2011), p. 7) and replaced the **previous Companies Act** No. 61 of 1973. The latter in turn had also been subject to various amendments. These amendments had made it difficult to use the Act, but had not changed the outdated basic philosophy of this piece of legislation (*Stein* (2011), p. 6). However, as the previous Companies Act required financial statements to be in line with generally accepted accounting practice (section 286 (3) of the Companies Act of 1973) and as SA GAAP being was similar to (and later even harmonized with) IFRS, the change did not impact financial accounting materially. Besides, except the report on the work of the audit committee, all the particular content- and disclosure-related requirements listed above were already part of the previous act (as of 2004)[71] so that the replacement hardly affected financial reporting overall.

JSE Listings Requirements

Firms listed on the JSE have to comply with the **JSE Listings Requirements** as a necessary condition for their listing (par. 1.2 of the JSE Listings Requirements). In addition to legal and governance criteria, these rules require public firms to provide a lot of information (section 8), including historical financial information, pro forma financial information or profit forecasts, and they refer to various reporting instruments, such as pre-listing statements or cautionary announcements (section 11). Par. 8.63 also sets out minimum contents for annual financial statements and the annual report. Financial statement disclosures include the aforementioned requirements set out in section 30 of the Companies Act, disclosures to be made under IFRS and various items listed in par. 8.63, inter alia directors' interests (par. 8.63 I), share incentive schemes (par. 8.63 (f)) or explanations of deviations from profit forecasts of 10% or greater (par. 8.63 (f)). Minimum disclosures to be made in the remaining annual report comprise a report on the compliance with various corporate governance issues listed in par. 3.84 of the Listings Requirements, special disclosures on mineral resources and reserves for mining companies (par. 8.63 (l)) and in particular a narrative statement on the application of the principles from the King Code and on instances of non-application with their respective reasons (par. 8.63 (a)).[72]

---

[71] The requirements for the auditor's report and the directors' report to be part of the financial statements are set out in Section 286 (2) (c) and (d) of the Companies Act No. 61 of 1973, the provisions for remuneration disclosures are (although with differences in the detailed requirements) set out in sections 295-297 and section 140A (8) (a) requires the list of shareholders.

[72] Differences to prior versions regarding these disclosures are negligible for the purposes of this study.

International Financial Reporting Standards

Both the Companies Act and the JSE Listings Requirements prescribe the preparation of financial statements in accordance with **IFRS.** In addition to outlining the rules on how to account for different types of transactions, the regulations issued by the London-based independent standard-setting body IASB include requirements for the format of the statements as well as manifold requirements for disclosures to provide the users of financial statements with comprehensive information on the firm's situation.[73] These rules on report format and disclosures include certain requirements that are somewhat similar to some IR requirements.[74] For instance, they comprise: comparative information from the preceding period for the financial statements and potentially for narrative disclosures (IAS 1.38-1.38(D)), consistent presentation of financial statement information (IAS 1.45-1.46), separate (i.e., non-offset) disclosure of financial statement items (IAS 1.32), in particular of cash receipts and payments in the cash flow statement (IAS 7.21), a statement on the compliance with IFRS (IAS 1.16), a description of the basis of presentation (IAS 1.112 (a)) and of the used accounting policies with the related judgments (IAS 1.117-1.124) as well as information about estimation uncertainties and assumptions made for financial statements items (IAS 1.125-133), but also disclosure of information enabling the users to understand the group composition (IFRS 12.10 (a) (i)).

King governance framework

Until 2016, the **King Committee** developed three reports on corporate governance (King I, II and III). Each of them comes with a **code of governance practices** that includes principles and provisions on good corporate governance, while the **reports** also provide background information and best practice recommendations beyond the principles of the code. The King I and II Reports include this code, whereas the latest version holds two separate documents: the code, containing the provisions (i.e., the principles with detailed sub-principles), and the report, which delivers further information (King III Report, Introduction and background, recital 13 (p. 17)). The three editions also differ in terms of their intended users. King III, being effective from 1 March 2010 on, addresses all entities on an "apply-or-explain" basis (King III Report, Introduction and background, recitals 13-14 (pp. 17-18)), while the prior versions only aimed at selected companies.[75]

---

[73] For a comprehensive overview of financial accounting under IFRS, cf. e.g. *Lubbe et al.* (2014), *Grünberger* (2015) or *Petersen et al.* (2016). *Petersen et al.* (2016) also provide a comprehensive checklist of the disclosure requirements in particular. Similar checklists are provided online by different accounting firms.

[74] In addition to the rules in the standards, the Conceptual Framework sets out the purpose and principles for financial reporting. Section 3.2.3 presents this framework, which the IASB partly developed in cooperation with the American FASB and which is thus also partly valid for firms reporting under US GAAP.

[75] In particular, King I was to be applied by all firms listed on the JSE main board as well as by large entities (i.e., entities with an equity greater than ZAR 50 million) and firms from the financial sector, while all other companies were also encouraged to apply the code (King I Code, pars. 1.1-1.3). King II applied to all JSE-listed firms, firms from the financial sector and certain public sector enterprises and agencies, but also encouraged all other companies to use the framework (King II Code, pars. 1.1-1.2).

In addition to provisions dealing with ethical leadership, the boards and directors, audit committees and information technology, as well as with compliance issues and internal audit, the **King III** Code holds principles on **"Integrated reporting and disclosure"** (King III Code, pars. 9.1-9.3). The King III Report provides additional guidance on these provisions, which are of a rather general nature, and gives recommendations that exceed the principles of the code.

King III **defines an integrated report** as a "*holistic and integrated representation of the company's performance in terms of both its finance and its sustainability*" (King III Code, Glossary, p. 54). Supplementing this definition, chapter 9, recital 1 of the King III Report (p. 108) states that an integrated report can take the form of one or more documents, even though "*a truly integrated report should be presented in one document*".

Principle 9.1 of the King III Code requires the board to ensure the **integrity of the integrated report**, with five sub-principles (King III Code, pars. 9.1.1-9.1.5) stating that internal controls and the audit committee should help to safeguard this integrity and that the report itself should be prepared each year with a "substance over form" focus, conveying adequate information on the firm's financial and sustainability performance. Moreover, the report should be independently assured (principle 9.3), with the audit committee assisting and overseeing this (external) assurance process (pars. 9.3.1-9.3.3).

It is notable that the King III framework uses **different capitals** at various instances in the report, albeit without providing an explicit and structured taxonomy for the capitals as in the IIRC Framework. Namely, King III differentiates between "human and monetary capital" (King III Report, Introduction and background, recital 6 (p. 10)), but also speaks of "social capital" (chapter 1, recital 29 (p. 24)).

The King III framework holds different rules on reporting principles and on the contents of an integrated report, although the provisions in the code and the report are not explicitly organized along principles and contents. Various paragraphs scattered across both the code and the report provide the respective guidance, instead. In terms of **reporting principles**, financial and sustainability disclosures should be "integrated" according to principle 9.2 of the King III Code and should include both positive and negative aspects of the company's operations (King III Code, par. 9.2.4). Moreover, the information in an integrated report should be complete, timely, relevant, accurate, honest, accessible and comparable with past performance, with some information being forward-looking (King III Report, chapter 9, recital 7 (p. 109)). These criteria of transparency do not only apply to the financial disclosures in an integrated report. Sustainability disclosures should also follow the principle of transparency, to allow an assessment of both the issues affecting the company and the firm's (positive and negative) impacts on its surroundings (King III Report, chapter 9, recital 13 (p. 109)).

In addition to these explicit principles, King III generally takes a **"stakeholder inclusive" perspective** on governance and reporting. According to this perspective, a firm considers the legitimate interests and expectations of its stakeholders, taking into account that this is also in the best interest of the firm itself (King III Report, Introduction and background, recital 9 (p. 13)). In terms of reporting, the code's principles on "Governing stakeholder relationships" include the requirement to disclose the nature and outcome of the firm's dealings with stakeholders in the integrated report (King III Code, par. 8.2.6) and suggest publishing the firm's stakeholder policies, if appropriate (par. 8.2.2). For the communication with stakeholders (which includes the integrated report), the code prescribes a clear and understandable language, in addition to the criteria outlined above for information in the integrated report (pars. 8.5.1-8.5.2). Besides these provisions, the King III Report also suggests a publication of the different stakeholder groups if this is appropriate (chapter 8, recital 12 (p. 101)).

As regards the **contents of an integrated report**, firms are recommended to report on their objectives and strategies, as well as on their economic, social and environmental performance, to further align with the interests of their stakeholders (King III Report, chapter 9, recital 6 (p. 108)). Financial disclosures should comprise the financial statements and the board's comment on the financial performance so that the users can assess the firm's value and future value creation, as well as the risks that might interfere with the prospects (recitals 9-10 (p. 109)). Paragraphs 9.2.1 through 9.2.4 of the King III Code state that the board is required to comment on the financial results and the firm's going concern status. In addition, the board needs to ensure that the report describes the firm's operations and conveys both positive and negative impacts, as well as the firm's plans to manage them in the future. Sustainability reporting is not fully standardized, although it becomes more formalized through the influence of initiatives like the GRI. Thus, the respective indicators in the firm's report need additional explanation and benchmarks to put them into context (King III Report, chapter 9, recitals 14-15 (pp. 109-110)). Moreover, the report highlights the notion that sustainability issues need to be considered in conjunction with the firm's other business activities and managed on a daily basis, rather than just being a reporting topic at the end of the year (recital 16 (p. 110)).

In addition to the provisions that explicitly relate to IR in the King III sense, the King III Code requires also several **risk disclosures**. Principle 4.10 states the need for complete, timely, relevant, accurate and accessible risk disclosure to stakeholders. In particular, this should include undue, unexpected or unusual risks as well as the boards view on the risk management process (pars. 4.10.1-4.10.2). Moreover, the King Report recommends to disclose the losses connected with unexpected risks and their causes, together with their impact on the company and the firm's responses, albeit with due regard to commercially privileged information (King III Report, chapter 4, recital 54 (p. 80)). A further recommendation for the integrated report is to disclose risks that threaten the firm's long-term sustainability (recital 55 (p. 80)).

The outlined regulations from King III are consistent with King III's definition of an integrated report as a communication that connects financial and sustainability reporting (King III Report, chapter 9, recital 1). Sustainability reporting in turn was already an issue in the **previous version (King II)**. King II was effective for eight years, beginning on 1 March 2002 and ending when King III came into effect in 2010. The second edition of the King Code was applicable on a comply-or-explain basis[76] by firms listed on the JSE and

[76] This comply-or-explain approach slightly differs from the apply-or-explain approach of King III. The former expects the application of all requirements to be in full compliance with a regulation, whereas the latter assesses the application of single requirements on an individual basis (*Walker/Meiring* (2010), p. 1).

certain public and financial sector entities, while it encouraged all firms to apply the regulations (King II Code, pars. 1.1-1.2). King II took a triple bottom line approach[77] (King II Report, Introduction and background, recital 17 (pp. 10-11)) and required the disclosure of the firm's social, safety and environmental policies (King II Code, par. 5.1.1). It outlined the principles of Reliability, Relevance, Clarity, Comparability, Timeliness and Verifiability for non-financial reporting and referenced the GRI (G3) guidelines for further regulation in this regard (par. 5.1.3). In line with the Reliability principle, the code held the provision that the annual report should contain a statement on the directors' responsibility to prepare the financial statements (par. 8.4.1). Besides, the King II Report recommended explanations and benchmarks for quantitative information and the avoidance of jargon (King II Report, section 4, chapter 2, recital 12 (pp. 99-100)). Regarding stakeholders, this governance framework also followed the "stakeholder inclusive" approach (Introduction and background, recital 5.3 (p. 8)), which constitutes a major difference between South African corporate governance and the Anglo-American model (*West* (2009), p. 12). Communication with stakeholders was required to be open, balanced and material (King II Code, par. 8.1). Concerning risks, King II required disclosures on the process of risk management only, rather than on the risks themselves (par. 3.2.6). Moreover, human capital was an issue in the second edition of the King regulations, as the code required the consideration of several disclosures on human capital development (par. 5.1.4). Hence, many of the requirements set out in the King III governance framework were already present in a similar form in its predecessor, King II.

Discussion paper of the Integrated Reporting Committee of South Africa

More detailed guidance[78] on IR than in the King III regulations stems from **the discussion paper on IR** that the **IRCSA** published in January 2011. The paper presents various reporting principles and elements that an integrated report should address. In addition, it provides some **general features** to introduce the concept. The definition of an integrated report differs from the one in King III, as it considers the report to be a document on the firm's strategy, performance and activities that enables stakeholders to assess the firm's ability to create and sustain value (IRCSA DP 1.7 (pp. 6-7)). Like the IIRC Framework, this discussion paper focuses on the documentation of the overall value creation rather than on a mere connection of financial and sustainability reporting. Unlike King III, which recommends to present an integrated report in a single document (King III Report chapter 9, recital 1), the IRCSA DP follows the Octopus Model. It considers an integrated report as a strategic overview document, while other documents possibly hold more detailed information (IRCSA DP 1.1 (p. 9)). The IRCSA framework employs the concept of different

[77] A triple bottom line perspective takes into account economic, environmental and social aspects of a firm's activities, as opposed to the classical single bottom line view, which only considers the financial perspective (*Slaper/Hall* (2011), p. 4).

[78] The discussion paper is not legally binding. It was supposed to be guidance material only and it did not even represent the final intended guidance document. Nevertheless, it turned out to be helpful for the reporting firms as one of the first detailed guidance materials on the new concept of IR. Several firms examined in this study state to have used the IRCSA DP as guidance for their report (e.g., *Datatec* (2013), p. 3; *Illovo* (2013), front matter).

capitals,[79] although not explicitly using the term in particular reporting requirements. Instead, it requires the report to provide information on the firm's "resources" and on how the company uses them (IRCSA DP 1.6 (p. 6), 3.2 (p. 12)).

The reporting principles that the IRCSA uses show some **overlap with the Guiding Principles of the International <IR> Framework.**[80] Figure 3-1 summarizes the principles of both regulations and shows how they relate.

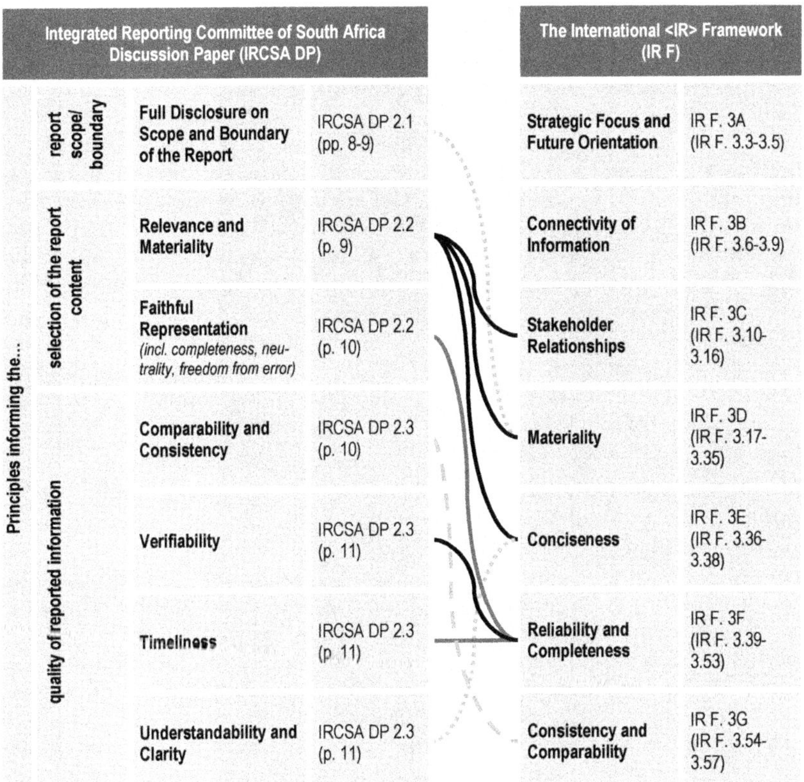

The connecting lines are shaded and dotted differently for the purpose of better distinctiveness. This involves no distinction in the type of connection.

Figure 3-1: Reporting principles under the IRCSA DP and Guiding Principles under the IR F

[79] The introduction of the IRCSA DP speaks of five "*capital assets – financial, human, manufactured, social or natural*", which determine a firm's value (IRCSA DP 1.1 (p. 3)).

[80] Cf. *Roberts* (2011) for a comparison of the IRCSA DP and the IIRC's DP IR from the same year.

Although the order and sequence of the **requirements on the reporting principles** is different in the two frameworks, the underlying idea is similar. As the name suggests, the first IRCSA principle, called "Full Disclosure on Scope and Boundary Setting", requires the identification of the reporting boundary. The discussion paper points out that this boundary may be different from the one used for the financial statements or other reporting instruments (IRCSA DP 2.1 (p. 8)). As opposed to the IIRC Framework, the provision on the boundary is not part of the Materiality principle, here. Moreover, the concept of materiality from the IRCSA DP bases upon the capability of an item to influence stakeholder decisions so that it relates to both the concept of relevance and to the Stakeholder Relationships principle (IRCSA DP 2.2 (p. 9)).[81] The IIRC uses the capability of a matter to influence the firm's value creation as the basis for the determination of materiality, instead (IR F. 3.17). There is no separate Conciseness principle in the IRCSA DP, but the principle of Understandability and Clarity provides some of the requirements from the respective section in the IIRC Framework, in particular the avoidance of jargon (IRCSA DP 2.3 (p. 11)). The Faithful Representation principle, which requires complete, neutral and error-free information (IRCSA DP 2.2 (p. 10)), is in line with the requirements of the IIRC's Reliability Guiding Principle. However, the latter also includes the concepts of Timeliness and Verifiability, which constitute two separate principles in the IRCSA DP (IRCSA DP 2.3 (p. 11)). In particular, the Verifiability principle also holds the requirement to supplement the outlined information with a presentation of the underlying assumptions and with a description of the method of compiling the information. Lastly, the principle of Comparability and Consistency is similar to the IIRC Framework, requiring comparability of the report both over time and with other firms' reports. This principle even demands the consideration of industry benchmarks in the integrated report to put the provided information into context (IRCSA DP 2.3 (p. 10)).

The IIRC Guiding Principles Strategic Focus and Future Orientation, Stakeholder Relationships, Conciseness and in particular Connectivity of Information are **not addressed as separate reporting** principles in the IRCSA DP. As outlined above, Stakeholder Relationships and Conciseness are covered by requirements from other reporting principles, though. Besides, the ideas underlying these principles are present in various requirements throughout different other parts of the regulation. For instance, the introduction states that the report should take a forward-looking perspective (IRCSA DP 1.6 (p. 6), which is in line with Future Orientation. Moreover, consistent with the IIRC's Stakeholder Relationships and Conciseness principles, it requires that the stakeholders' legitimate interests and expectations should be considered and that the report should be "as concise as possible" (IRCSA DP 1.5 (p. 6)). Connectivity of Information (as well as a reference to the Strategic Orientation) is also addressed, but only in rather general terms in the foreword:

---

81 The reference to stakeholders' decision-making also constitutes a difference to the IASB's CF, which considers shareholders as the primary addressees of financial reporting. Apart from this and other minor differences, the principles informing the selection of the report content from the IRCSA DP overlap with the Fundamental Qualitative Characteristics in the CF, while the principles informing the quality of reported information match the Enhancing Qualitative Characteristics in the CF. The Qualitative Characteristics in the CF also underlie the IASB's Practice Statement Management Commentary.

"An integrated report should provide stakeholders with a concise overview of an organization, integrating and connecting important information about strategy, risks and opportunities and relating them to social, environmental, economic and financial issues."

(IRCSA DP, Foreword (p. 1))

The distinction between various kinds of connections from the International <IR> Framework is not present here, though.

Compared with the reporting principles, the requirements on the **contents of an integrated report** are even more similar in the IRCSA DP and the IIRC Framework (Figure 3-2). The description of the report's scope and boundary is required under the heading "Report Profile" in the South African guidance (IRSCA DP 3.1 (p. 12)), while being part of the Content Element Basis of Preparation in the IIRC Framework (IR F. 4H). Organizational Overview, Business Model and Governance Structure constitute a single element in South Africa (IRCSA DP 3.2 (pp. 12-13)), but three different Content Elements internationally (IR F. 4A, 4B and 4C). The provisions from the element Understanding the Operating Context in the IRCSA regulations (IRCSA DP 3.3 (pp. 13-14)) can be found in the Content Elements Organizational Overview and External Environment (IR F. 4A) and Risks and Opportunities (IR F. 4D). Furthermore, the elements on strategy (IRCSA DP 3.4 (p. 14) and IR F. 4E) and performance (IRCSA DP 3.5 (p. 14) and IR F. 4F) are more or less identical in both frameworks as well as the Future Outlook element (IRCSA DP 3.6 (p. 15) and IR F. 4G, respectively). While Remuneration Policies represent a separate element in the South African discussion paper (IRCSA DP 3.7 (p. 16)), the IIRC Framework subsumes them under Governance (IR F. 4B). The Analytical Commentary element in IRCSA DP 3.8 (p. 16) has no direct international equivalent. Such comments by management are required here as well, but under the provisions of the Guiding Principle Strategic Focus and Future Orientation (IR F. 3.4).

Conclusion

With the manifold requirements on the general content, the format and on particular disclosures, the South African reporting regulations show a high degree of overlap with the IIRC Framework. As the IRCSA and the IIRC cooperated, it is not unexpected that the two IR frameworks are similar. Likewise, with Mervyn E. King chairing both the King Committee and the IIRC, it is not surprising that many of the ideas from King III match those in the IIRC Framework. Both the reporting principles and the prescribed contents of an integrated report are highly comparable in the two regulations. But even before the King III rules and the subsequent IR guidance from the IRCSA DP, the existing reporting requirements (i.e., King II and the explicit format and disclosure requirements in the IFRS, the JSE Listings Requirements and the Companies Act) were already consistent with the later idea of IR to some extent. For instance, the requirement of open and balanced communication with stakeholders, the provision to provide a directors' responsibility statement, guidance for reporting on sustainability issues or the awareness of different capitals from King II are requirements that also form part of the International <IR> Framework. Furthermore, the provision of comparative disclosures from preceding periods and of explanations on estimations and assumptions from IFRS, reporting against previous forecasts from the JSE Listings Requirements as well as the necessity of remuneration disclosures as set out in the (amended) Companies Act of 1973 are examples of issues that are also present in the IIRC Framework.

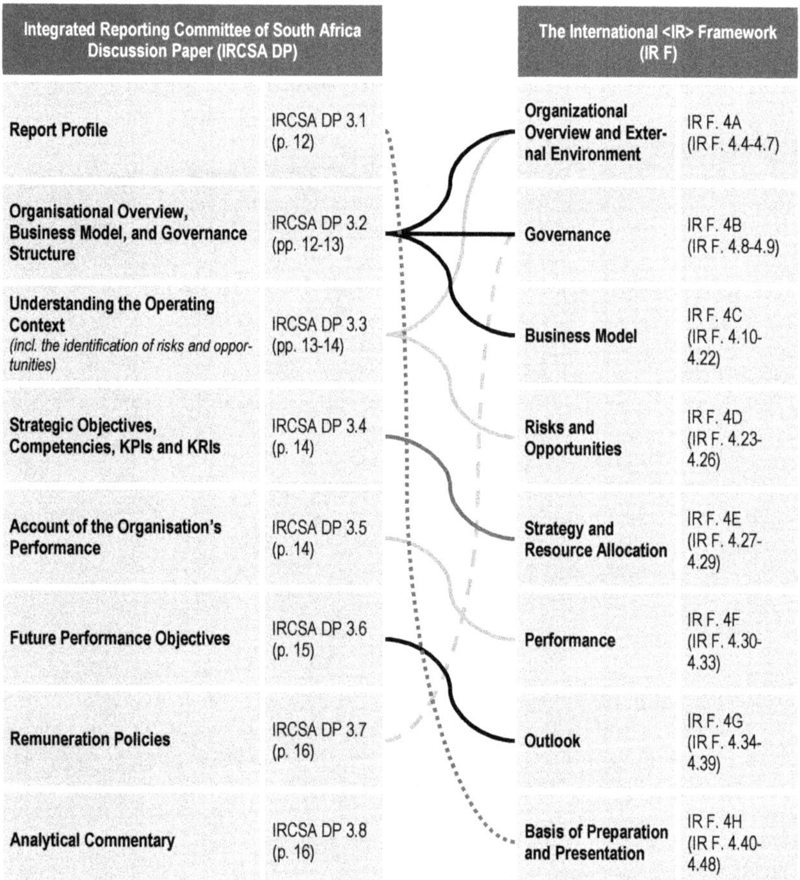

The connecting lines are shaded and dotted differently for the purpose of better distinctiveness. This involves no distinction in the type of connection.

Figure 3-2: Report contents under the IRCSA DP and Content Elements under the IR F

3.1.4 Summary of the South African reporting landscape

South Africa's economic situation is typical for a developing country. It faces unequal distribution of capital, severe health issues and a lack of education for many, but at the same time richness of natural resources. Labor unions have considerable power, which is also a consequence of historical developments. After the apartheid era, laws strengthened the power of workers and minorities. The divestment of foreign capital from South African firms during this era also raised **awareness for the social issues and for the importance of transparent reporting** by firms to document a change in their conduct. This paved the way for major advances in governance regulations like the King Codes and subsequently also for IR.

Financial reporting also has a long history in South Africa, rooting in the developed British accounting system, which found its way to the South African colonies and had a long-lasting impact. A multitude of institutions determine the country's accounting and reporting landscape, which does not only include government regulations, but also rules from private institutions like the JSE, the King Committee or the IRCSA. In particular large companies listed on the JSE face **many regulations**, which determine the incorporation (the Companies Act), stock exchange dealing (the JSE Listings Requirements) or management and governance issues (the King Code), but also accounting and reporting questions (IFRS, the IRCSA DP or IIRC guidance, respectively, but also the aforementioned other regulations to some degree).

In terms of both the principles and the content requirements for reporting, the outlined regulations on firms' reporting show remarkable **overlap with the International <IR> Framework** that was developed later. This similarity was expectable to some degree, given the institutional and personal interdependence during the development of several regulations, in particular the influence of Mervyn E. King. Even before the King III framework, various requirements from the IIRC Framework were already established in the South African reporting requirements (in particular in King II). Thus, it is not surprising that South Africa is considered to play a pioneering role in the development of IR. Turning to a country without this trailblazer role in terms of IR, but with a highly developed and established economic and financial reporting system, the following section describes the reporting landscape in the USA.

3.2 Corporate reporting in the USA

The US reporting landscape is distinct from the South African one in various regards, both in the economic and historical basis and in the principles and orientation of corporate reporting. This section presents the **US reporting landscape** and elaborates these differences. In parallel with the depiction of the South African system, this description starts with the economic and historical background, followed by the rulemaking and standard-setting institutions. The section continues with a presentation of the regulations that govern the principles and contents of corporate reporting against their counterparts in the IR Framework. A summary completes the section.

3.2.1 Economic and historical background

Constituting 16% of the world's GDP (*IMF* (2015), p. 147), the USA are one of the strongest **economies** on earth. The *World Economic Forum* (2014) Global Competitiveness Report 2014-2015 places the USA third (of 144 countries) in the overall ranking. They were constantly among the top ten in previous years. Two particular areas of strength are Business sophistication and Innovation, where the USA rank among the top ten countries in almost all indicators (*World Economic Forum* (2014), p. 379). While not being among the top countries in each area, the USA hardly have any indicator in which they rank in the bottom 25, whereas South Africa shows particular weakness in terms of health, education or labor market efficiency. No urgent need to regulate these issues or firms' reporting on them appears evident from these statistics for the USA. However, regarding environmental issues, the USA have hardly taken political actions, e.g. in fighting climate change, and start to face the costs ("The cost of doing nothing" (2014)).

Economic growth has been strong throughout major parts of the country's **history**, especially after the ratification of the Constitution in 1789, with the formation of the New York Stock Exchange (NYSE) in 1792 boosting the development of larger companies even more (*Moehrle/Reynolds-Moehrle* (2011), p. 106). It enabled these firms to **raise capital at the stock market** – a way of financing that the Supreme Court made more attractive for investors by strengthening property rights (*Previts/Merino* (1998), pp. 33-34). The enlargement and increased complexity of firms also raised the importance of sophisticated accounting and led to an **advancement of accounting** systems from ledger balances to financial reports (*Moehrle/Reynolds-Moehrle* (2011), p. 107). For a long time, the focus of capital funding was rather on short-term bank loans, though, so that the reports mainly addressed bankers' information needs (*Chatfield* (1977), p. 72). But at the end of the 19th century, increasing information needs of the shareholders of non-owner led firms ultimately made the NYSE require periodic financial statements from listed firms (NYSE Corporate Governance Guide, p. vi; *Schultz* (1936), pp. 17-18).

However, the stock market crash in 1929 and the following Great Depression, with a subsequent high-profile fraud, decreased investor confidence and revealed the necessity of stronger **investor protection** (*Moehrle/Reynolds-Moehrle* (2011), p. 117). These developments resulted in the enactment of the Securities Act of 1933 and the Securities Exchange Act of 1934, as well as in the establishment of the **SEC** to regulate financial reporting for publicly traded firms (*Moehrle/Reynolds-Moehrle* (2011), p. 118). A main characteristic of US financial reporting was – and still is – conservatism, which inter alia reduces management's opportunities to report opportunistically, besides decreasing litigation risk and political attention (*Watts* (2003a; 2003b)).

In 1938, the SEC deferred[82] its authority for **accounting guidance** to the American Institute of Accountants (AIA – now known as the American Institute of Certified Public Accountants (AICPA)), which in turn created the Committee on Accounting Procedure (CAP) to fulfill this task (*Moehrle/Reynolds-Moehrle* (2011), p. 121; *Bragg* (2010),

---

[82] Notwithstanding differing depictions in the literature, the SEC did not "delegate" its authority to other entities, as it has not been empowered by Congress to do so (*Zeff* (2010)).

pp. 19-20). After the CAP and its successor, the Accounting Principles Board[83], failed to gain wide acceptance, the FASB was established in 1973 (*Previts/Merino* (1998), pp. 365-366) and still exists today. However, available accounting guidance that had been issued by the predecessors continued to be effective until the FASB restructured and recodified the numerous guidance materials from CAP, the Accounting Principles Board, FASB, AICPA and the Emerging Issues Task Force (EITF) in 2009 and united them in one volume (without revision) (*Moehrle/Reynolds-Moehrle* (2011), p. 137). Through this FASB Accounting Standards Codification®, the FASB is the single source of authoritative US GAAP as of 2009. Basing upon a four-layer hierarchy of topics, subtopics, sections and subsections, this codification assigns an unambiguous number to every guidance item, (*FASB* (2014), pp. 12-15).[84] Moreover, from 2002, the FASB has been cooperating with the IASB, attempting to align US GAAP and IFRS over time (*FASB/IASB* (2002)).

The AICPA also contributed to the improvement of financial accounting and reporting. From 1973 on, the institute started several initiatives. Most notably, the AICPA formed the Trueblood Committee in 1971, which studied the **objectives of financial statements** and published a report (*AICPA* (1973)) on the results. By maintaining that the primary purpose of financial reports was to provide decision-useful information, this committee helped to target nonprofessional financial statement users and to expand the disclosure horizon from financial statements to financial reports (*Previts/Merino* (1998), pp. 366-367).

Furthermore, the work of the Jenkins Committee was of major importance for the development of reporting. This committee conducted research on the **information needs of financial reporting users**. In its "Jenkins Report" (*AICPA* (1994)), the committee established the term "business reporting", meaning the "*information a company provides to help users with capital-allocation decisions about a company*" (*AICPA* (1994), p. 2). In addition, the report provides recommendations for better reporting, in particular more forward-looking information, a stronger focus on factors that create long-term value and a better alignment of internally and externally reported information (*AICPA* (1994), p. 5).

Following several high-profile financial frauds at the beginning of the new millennium, the government enacted the Sarbanes-Oxley Act of 2002 (SOX) in response to calls for reform and to restore **investor confidence** (*Moehrle/Reynolds-Moehrle* (2011), p. 136). Most importantly, the act introduced the Public Company Accounting Oversight Board (PCAOB) to oversee the audits of public companies (*Bragg* (2010), p. 22), but it also required additional governance-related disclosures.

In April 2016, the SEC issued a Concept Release (SEC Release 33-10064 (2016)), seeking public comment to assess whether the business and financial disclosure requirements in Regulation S-K continue to lead to reporting that meets **investors' information needs**. Due to the facts that ecological and social constraints determine today's economy and that over the last decades, the percentage of a firm's value represented by its financial report

---

[83] This study avoids the use of the official abbreviation of the Accounting Principles Board, APB, as this abbreviation overlaps with that of the South African Accounting Practices Board as introduced in section 3.1.

[84] For instance, disclosures on goodwill are in section 350-20-50, with a sequential number added in the end indicating the respective items of regulation.

decreased substantially (see chapter 1), investors are only incompletely informed by financial reporting. Intending to restore a true and fair view of the firms for investors, the Sustainability Accounting Standards Board (SASB) was founded in 2011, as a response to results of Harvard University research (*SASB* (n.d.)). The SASB develops standards for sustainability accounting for each industry, to complement the companies' financial reporting. By reporting according to these standards, the firms shall enable their investors to get a complete view of corporate performance. Thus, the standards are supposed to provide a basis for effective capital markets.

Given the traditional and current importance of these capital markets for firms' financing (*Nobes/Parker* (2012), pp. 32-36) as well as the outlined emphasis on investor protection and investors' information needs, accounting and (financial) reporting primarily play a role for listed firms. Against this background, **private companies** mostly only have to satisfy minor reporting requirements (see section 3.2.3).

3.2.2 Institutions regulating corporate reporting

As the capital market is essential for firms' financing in the USA (*Nobes/Parker* (2012), pp. 32-36), stock exchanges are important institutions in the country's economy. The aforementioned **NYSE** is the world's leading exchange, with a high market quality in terms of liquidity, traded shares and bid-ask spreads.[85] In addition to the bond market, the exchange runs three different equity markets. Besides the NYSE, which is the primary market for large and medium-sized firms, there is the NYSE MKT for younger, small-cap firms and the NYSE Arca, an all-electronic exchange. In the comprehensive Listed Company Manual, the NYSE sets forth rules and policies for the listed companies, on issues including corporate governance or shareholder communications.

Given this importance of the capital market, the **SEC** plays a central role for the regulation of market rules and corporate disclosures, but also for enforcement issues and various other topics (*Bragg* (2010), pp. 28-31). In pursuance of Section 4 of the Securities Exchange Act of 1934, the SEC came into existence on 2 July 1934, as a successor to the Federal Trade Commission, which was administering the Securities Act of 1933 (*Atkins/Bondi* (2008), pp. 368-369). At a time when the country's economy was struggling in the Great Depression, the Commission was provided with the mission of investor protection. The SEC is responsible for interpreting and enforcing federal securities laws, issuing new and amending existing rules, overseeing the inspection of securities firms and other parties in the financial markets, overseeing private regulatory organization in the securities, accounting and auditing fields and coordinating securities regulation with federal, state and foreign authorities (*SEC* (2013)). Headquartered in Washington D.C., the SEC is organized around five divisions (Corporation Finance, Enforcement, Economic and Risk Analysis, Investment Management and Trading and Markets) and 23 offices (including e.g. Administrative Law Judges, Compliance Inspections and Examinations, Minority and Women Inclusion or Information Technology) (*SEC* (2013)).

---

[85] Cf. https://www.nyse.com/markets/nyse (last accessed on 29 August 2016) for general information on the NYSE.

In particular, the **Division of Corporation Finance** reviews the documents that public firms have to file with the SEC, including annual reports to shareholders, annual (Form 10-K) and quarterly (Form 10-Q) filings, proxy materials etc. (*SEC* (2013)).[86] Moreover, the SEC provides guidance to (prospective) registrants for compliance with the laws, usually by issuing different types of commission releases, which are legally binding (*Hüfner* (2007a), pp. 291-293). Furthermore, the SEC enacts rules, regulations and forms.[87] Of particular importance are Regulations S-X and S-K as well as Form 10-K.[88] However, as a consequence of the aforementioned deferral of authority, the private sector organization FASB is responsible for regulating financial accounting. The SEC officially recognizes the FASB's standards as authoritative according to Section 19(b)(1)(B) of the Securities Act of 1933, as added by Section 108 of the Sarbanes-Oxley Act of 2002 (SEC Financial Reporting Release No. 1, Section 101, as cited in *Bragg* (2010), pp. 20-21; SEC Release 33-8221 (2003); *FASB* (n.d.b)). In case of gaps in the accounting regulation and literature or for matters that may require the use of more conservative accounting or extended disclosures, the Division of Corporation Finance and the Office of the Chief Accountant jointly issue Staff Accounting Bulletins (SABs) (*Bragg* (2010), pp. 44-47). Since 1975, the SEC has released over one hundred of these Bulletins, giving their views and interpretations on different topics. For instance, the quantification of financial statement misstatements (SAB 108) or the GAAP definition of materiality (SAB 99) have been subject of this guidance.

Another SEC division, the **Division of Enforcement**, is responsible for the supervision of security issuers and transactions on the financial market. This includes the monitoring of compliance with transparency requirements (*Litsoukov* (2015)). Drawing on the SEC's mission to protect investors, the purpose of enforcing the securities laws is to provide remedies for aggrieved investors and to deter from future violations, although the nature of the Commission's actions changed from remedial to punitive over time (*Atkins/Bondi* (2008), pp. 368-369, 383). The Division of Enforcement was created in 1972, taking over its responsibilities from other SEC divisions (*Atkins/Bondi* (2008), p. 374). In case of suspicion relating to a violation of regulations, this division investigates the respective instances, basing upon the work of its own staff (e.g., interviews, even using subpoenas) or upon external information (*Bragg* (2010), p. 28). The division prosecutes violations either in the form of civil suits in federal courts or through administrative proceedings (*SEC* (2007)). In civil suits, the Commission seeks injunctions, civil money penalties or the disgorgement of illegal profits, while the courts may also suspend individuals from working as corporate officers. Administrative proceedings, which are heard by independent administrative law judges or by the Commission itself, may result in cease and desist orders, bars from employment or

[86] Firms file their documents with the SEC via the commission's Electronic Data Gathering, Analysis, and Retrieval system (EDGAR), which automates the collection, validation and indexing and provides investors, analysts and other interested users an almost immediate and convenient online access to the filings (*Bragg* (2010), pp. 31-32).

[87] Generally, there are four levels of capital-market-oriented regulations in the US corporate reporting landscape (in order of decreasing binding force): statutes, regulations and forms, commission releases and also staff advice, the latter not being legally binding (*Miller/Robertson* (1989), pp. 240-248).

[88] The following section presents the respective provisions.

suspensions of registration, as well as in civil penalties or disgorgement. Money penalties follow a three-tier sanction system provided by the Securities Act, with the size of the penalty depending on the severity of the violation, the size of the loss and on whether the subject of the penalty is a company or a natural person (*Litsoukov* (2015)). The SEC describes recent litigation in releases that are available on its website (*SEC* (2007)).

Officially designated by the SEC, the FASB is the national standard setter for accounting and financial reporting standards. It develops and improves US GAAP for non-governmental entities[89] in an open, orderly process (*FASB* (2013), p. 5), but has no enforcement power and therefore needs the SEC to ensure their implementation (*Bragg* (2010), pp. 20-21). In addition to the standards, the **FASB** releases Statements of Financial Accounting Concepts, which are not authoritative, but lay out fundamentals as a basis for the standards (*FASB* (2013), pp. 20-21). Moreover, the FASB has the right to address "other topics" (SEC Release 33-8221 (2003), II.B) by issuing Discussion Papers, Special Reports or other communications (*FASB* (2013), pp. 21-22). Since 2002, the FASB cooperates with the IASB to converge US and international financial reporting. As outlined in a joint memorandum of understanding – the "Norwalk Agreement" (*FASB/IASB* (2002)) – this cooperation includes several projects, such as a short-term convergence project or the joint development of standards, but also collaboration through a liaison board member.[90]

The SASB, a standard setter for sustainability accounting standards across all industries[91], is based in San Francisco (*Eccles et al.* (2015), p. 73). It was formed as a (501I) non-profit organization in July 2011, following positive response to Harvard University research (*Lydenberg et al.* (2010)) on industry-specific materiality determination and associated performance indicators (*SASB* (n.d.)). The board's mission is to define materiality of sustainability information for corporate reporting and to provide guidance on how this information should be reported in Form 10-Ks (*IRRCI/Si2* (2013), p. 25). Thus, the **SASB** intends to integrate sustainability issues with financial reporting. In a memorandum of understanding with the IIRC (*IIRC/SASB* (2013)), the board therefore declared its collaboration with the IR standard setter, since the SASB's work possibly represents a stepping stone toward the implementation of IR in the USA. Michael Bloomberg – former mayor of New York City – and Mary Schapiro – former SEC chairwoman – chair the SASB, while different large foundations (e.g., Ford or Rockefeller) provide financial support for the board's mission (*White* (2016)).

3.2.3 Regulations on corporate reporting

Depicting the regulations on corporate reporting in the USA requires a clear distinction between public (listed firms inside the perimeter of the SEC) and private (non-listed) firms. For private firms, there is no central financial reporting framework (*IFRS Founda-*

---

89 Reporting standards for governmental entities are provided by the GASB, instead. Cf. *Bragg* (2010), pp. 19-25, for an overview of the different current and former standard-setting organizations.

90 Cf. *FASB* (n.d.a) for a comprehensive depiction of the cooperation between FASB and IASB.

91 As of April 2016, the SASB had developed provisional accounting standards across all 11 sectors and 79 SICS industries.

tion/SEC (2016), pp. 4, 6). Their reporting often only comprises reports to particular stakeholders, such as lenders, regulators or tax authorities, as well as reports for internal purposes (*Blue-Ribbon Panel* (2011), p. 6). These reports do not necessarily have to comply with GAAP. Instead, private companies may select an accounting framework that is suitable for the purpose of their financial statements (*IFRS Foundation/SEC* (2016), p. 6). Several accounting institutions have released guidance materials that private firms can use. For instance, these materials include the FASB Private Company Council's (PCC) Private Company Decision-Making Framework, AICPA's Financial Reporting Framework for Small- and Medium-Sized Entities or the Other Comprehensive Basis of Accounting (OCBOA) under AU Section 623 (*Ratcliffe* (2003)). However, in line with this study's investor perspective, this section focuses on the US reporting regulations for public firms.

Similar to the presentation of the South African regulations in section 3.1.3, Table 3-2 gives an overview of the relevant regulations on (financial) reporting that public US firms need to comply with. The subsequent paragraphs in this section present the regulations depicted in the table.[92]

Conceptual Framework

Public firms in the USA have to deal with a variety of regulations regarding their corporate reporting. Although not being a binding reporting regulation itself, the **FASB's Conceptual Framework** (CF) provides a basis for financial reporting, giving a direction and structure (FASB Statement of Financial Accounting Concepts No. 8, front matter). This framework is a product of the FASB's and IASB's aforementioned joint activities. The two standard setters intended to develop a principles-based[93] Conceptual Framework. After publishing the parts of the Framework that elaborate the purpose and the Qualitative Characteristics of financial reporting in 2010 (FASB Concepts Statement No. 8), the two bodies suspended this collaboration and continued to work on their respective frameworks separately (*IASB* (2016); *FASB* (2016)). However, the jointly developed parts are still effective under both regimes. The Framework is not only applicable to financial statements, but also provides a basis for financial reporting (CF. BC1.4). As an overall purpose, it requires financial information to be useful for investors' decision making (CF. OB2). Even though not mentioning the term explicitly, this objective also acknowledges the importance of the reports for stewardship, i.e. for enabling investors to assess management's use of the firm's resources (CF. BC1.28). The Conceptual Framework clarifies that investors are seen as the only primary addressees, while the reports may nonetheless be useful for other parties (CF. OB10). Thus, the Conceptual Framework aligns with the International <IR> Framework in terms of the addressees. Moreover, the document sets out Qualitative Characteristics for reporting that are similar to the Guiding Principles in the IIRC Framework. Figure 3-3 compares the reporting principles in the two frameworks.

---

[92] *Miller/Robertson* (1989) give a more comprehensive overview of the different regulations and their interactions.

[93] Usually, the FASB follows a rules-based approach with its standards. This faced some criticism (e.g., *Benston et al.* (2006)), inter alia due to the complexity of this convolute of different rules, and led to the restructuring and recodification of the standards in 2009.

	FASB Conceptual Framework (CF)	NYSE listing standards	Form 10-K	Regulation S-K	Regulation S-X	United States Generally Accepted Accounting Principles (US GAAP)	Report of the NACD Blue Ribbon Commission on Director Professionalism	SASB standards
Focus	Principles and objective underlying the standards for financial reporting	Requirements for listing at the NYSE, including disclosures	Minimum disclosure requirements for annual report	Information requirements in addition to the financial statements (for registration statements, annual reports, proxy solicitations)	Accounting and auditing requirements	Standards for accounting and financial reporting	Guidance for governance and governance-related reporting	Guidance for potentially material industry-specific sustainability information and accounting metrics
Effective date of current version	28 September 2010 (as of release)	Different effective dates of the different rules, which are amended on an ongoing basis	1 April 2015 (Code of Federal Regulations)	1 April 2015 (Code of Federal Regulations)	1 April 2015 (Code of Federal Regulations)	Different effective dates for the different standards, which are amended on an ongoing basis	November 1996 (as of release)	Different effective dates of the different industry standards
Binding character	Not legally binding	Binding for firms listed at the NYSE	Mandatory for listed firms with total assets exceeding USD 10 million and more than 2,000 equity security holders (or more than 500 that are not accredited investors)	Mandatory for listed firms	Mandatory for listed firms	Mandatory for listed firms	Not legally binding	Not legally binding

Table 3-2: Overview of reporting regulations in the USA

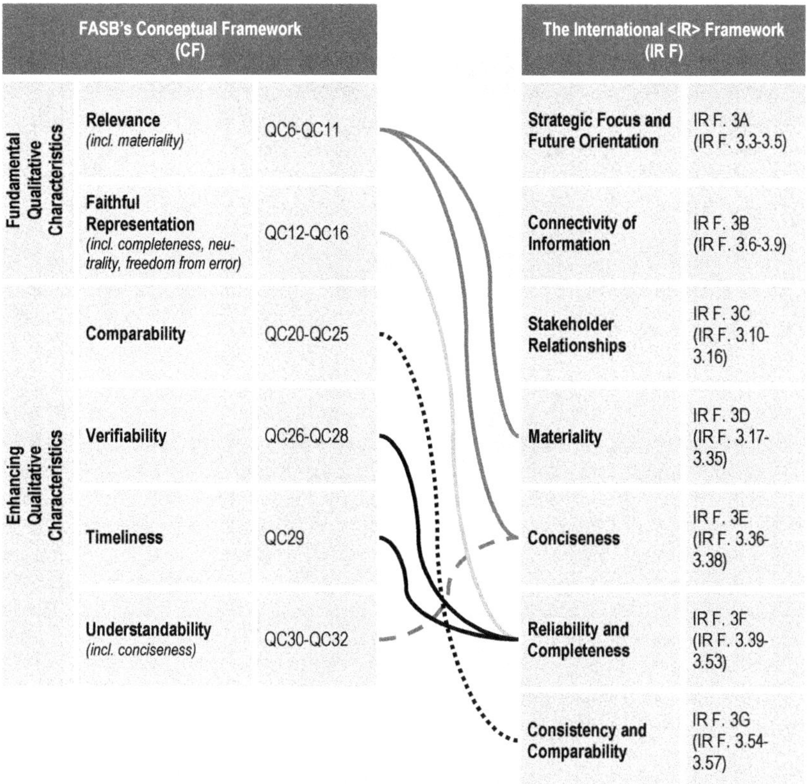

The connecting lines are shaded and dotted differently for the purpose of better distinctiveness. This involves no distinction in the type of connection.

Figure 3-3: Qualitative Characteristics under the CF and Guiding Principles under the IR F

The Conceptual Framework distinguishes between the **Fundamental** and the Enhancing **Qualitative Characteristics.** Relevance and Faithful Representation constitute the former category. As in the IRCSA DP, information is considered material if its omission could influence users' decision making (CF. QC11) and thus influence the relevance of the information (CF. QC6). The Relevance characteristic is therefore comparable to the IIRC's Materiality Guiding Principle (and implicitly to the related Conciseness principle, too). Also similar to the IRCSA DP, Faithful Representation comprises completeness, neutrality and freedom from error (CF. QC12). Hence, it corresponds with the IIRC's Reliability and Completeness Guiding Principle. The Conceptual Framework does not mention the substance over form approach explicitly, but nevertheless regards it as considered in the Faithful

Representation principle (CF. BC3.26). Conservatism or prudence are no aspects of Faithful Representation, as they contrast the idea of neutrality (CF. BC3.27-BC3.29).

In terms of the **Enhancing Qualitative Characteristics**, there are strong similarities between the aforementioned South African IR framework and the FASB's Conceptual Framework. Firstly, the Conceptual Framework sets out Comparability (CF. QC20). However, as opposed to the IIRC Framework, Consistency is not part of the principle here, as the FASB and IASB consider it as a help to achieve comparability rather than a characteristic on its own (CF. QC22). Nevertheless, the relation to the IIRC's Consistency and Comparability principle is obvious. Both the second characteristic, Verifiability (CF. QC26), and the third one, Timeliness (CF. QC29), are covered by the Reliability and Completeness Guiding Principle in the IIRC's Framework. The former also includes the requirement to provide underlying assumptions and methods of compiling of the disclosed information (CF. QC28). Finally, the Understandability characteristic requires a clear and concise presentation (CF. QC30) so that it relates to the IR Conciseness principle.

Similar to the IRCSA DP, the **Conceptual Framework does not explicitly cover** the four IIRC **Guiding Principles** Strategic Focus and Future Orientation, Connectivity of Information, Stakeholder Relationships and Conciseness. Also similar to the South African IR guidance, the provisions of the Conciseness principle are covered by the requirements of the Relevance (Materiality) and Understandability Qualitative Characteristics. Furthermore, in terms of future orientation, the Relevance characteristic states that to be relevant, information needs either confirmative or predictive value, the latter meaning that it may serve as a basis for users' forecasts (CF. QC7-QC10). The Conceptual Framework does not mention a consideration of the firm's strategic orientation. Certain contents of US firms' reports do provide a future-oriented focus, though. Moreover, there is no mention of connectivity in the Conceptual Framework. However, specific contents of the report may show some aspects of connectivity, in particular between past, present and future. In addition to these connections, the use of references, both inside a report and between different documents, is a common concept in US reports (Item 10(d) of Regulation S-K). Under the aforementioned primacy of investors, reports are not required to consider and disclose the interests of the different key stakeholders and on the firm's relationships with them. Hence, they do not address the IR Stakeholder Relationships Guiding Principle. Besides, the Conceptual Framework uses the terms "capital" and "resources" in their economic or financial dimension, only. The concept of different capitals is thus not present, either.

Form 10-K and underlying regulations

Pursuant to Section 13 or 15(d) in conjunction with Section 12(g) of the Securities Exchange Act of 1934, reports on Form 10-K have to be **filed annually** by firms with total assets exceeding USD 10 million and with more than 2,000 security holders (or 500 that are not accredited investors). These reports are among the principal documents for firm disclosures and are often included in firms' annual reports or even sent to shareholder in lieu of the annual reports (*SEC* (2011)). Stock exchanges like the NYSE also draw on these forms in their **listing standards**, as they require the listed firms to file these reports, referring to the respective SEC documents (e.g., NYSE Listed Company Manual, Section 203).

The SEC's Form 10-K guidance document (document SEC 1643) combines the different mandatory reporting requirements from the underlying Regulations S-K and S-X and puts them into the pattern required for the filing. It references the pertinent items of the Regulations for each 10-K item. Figure 3-4 gives an overview of the different **contents of Form 10-K** and contrasts them with the Content Elements of the International <IR> Framework.

Form 10-K **item 1** Business refers to Item 101 of Regulation S-K. It requires a description of elements that would fall under the IIRC Content Element Business Model, like the firm's principal products and services, the sources and availability of raw materials or the importance of patents and licenses (as inputs to the business model), but also the firm's form of organization, the markets it works or potential seasonality of its operations, which would rather be summarized under the Content Element Organizational Overview and External Environment. Moreover, issues like potential dependencies on a small number of customers need to be disclosed under item 1. While this last example refers to a situation that could eventually be a risk for the company, the next item in part I of the Form 10-K explicitly aims at a disclosure of risk factors (**item 1A**). The referenced Item 503(c) of Regulation S-K substantiates that this does not refer to risks which could apply to any issuer. Instead, the item specifies examples for risk factors like a lack of operating history, a lack of profitability or a lack of a market for common equity securities. Unlike IIRC Content Element Risks and Opportunities, these disclosures focus on the negative side of risk. Nevertheless, item 1A corresponds with this Content Element.

Item 2[94] of Form 10-K requires the description of the firm's material physical properties, e.g. plants or mines (Item 102 of Regulation S-K). As these properties represent inputs to the business model (under the IIRC's definition), this item corresponds with the respective IR Content Element. Instead, the disclosure of Legal Proceedings (**item 3** of Form 10-K) under Item 103 of Regulation S-K rather overlaps with the description of the legislative and regulatory environment under the IIRC's Content Element Organizational Overview and External Environment, if anything. **Item 4** Mine Safety Disclosures applies only to firms from the mining sector and requires them to disclose[95] violations of health or safety standards in these mines and related issues like fatalities (Item 104 of Regulation S-K and Section 1503(a) of the Dodd-Frank Wall Street Reform and Consumer Protection Act). While also relating to the regulatory environment, these disclosures can at the same time be seen as describing the firm's safety performance so that they relate to the IR Content Element Performance.[96]

---

94 Item 1B Unresolved Staff Comments is not relevant for the course of this study so that it is neglected, here. So are item 5 Market for Registrant's Common Equity, Related Stockholder Matters and Issuer Purchases of Equity Securities, item 9 Changes in Disagreements With Accountants on Accounting and Financial Disclosures, item 9B Other Information and item 14 Principal Accounting Fees and Services.

95 Precisely, the item requires the firm to disclose the necessary information on mining safety issues in Exhibit 95 and only requires a statement referencing this exhibit under item 4.

96 Safety performance could be seen as performance affecting social and/or human capital (IR F. 4.30-4.31). Introduced by SEC Release 33-9286 (2012), this requirement represents an issue of social reporting in Form 10-K.

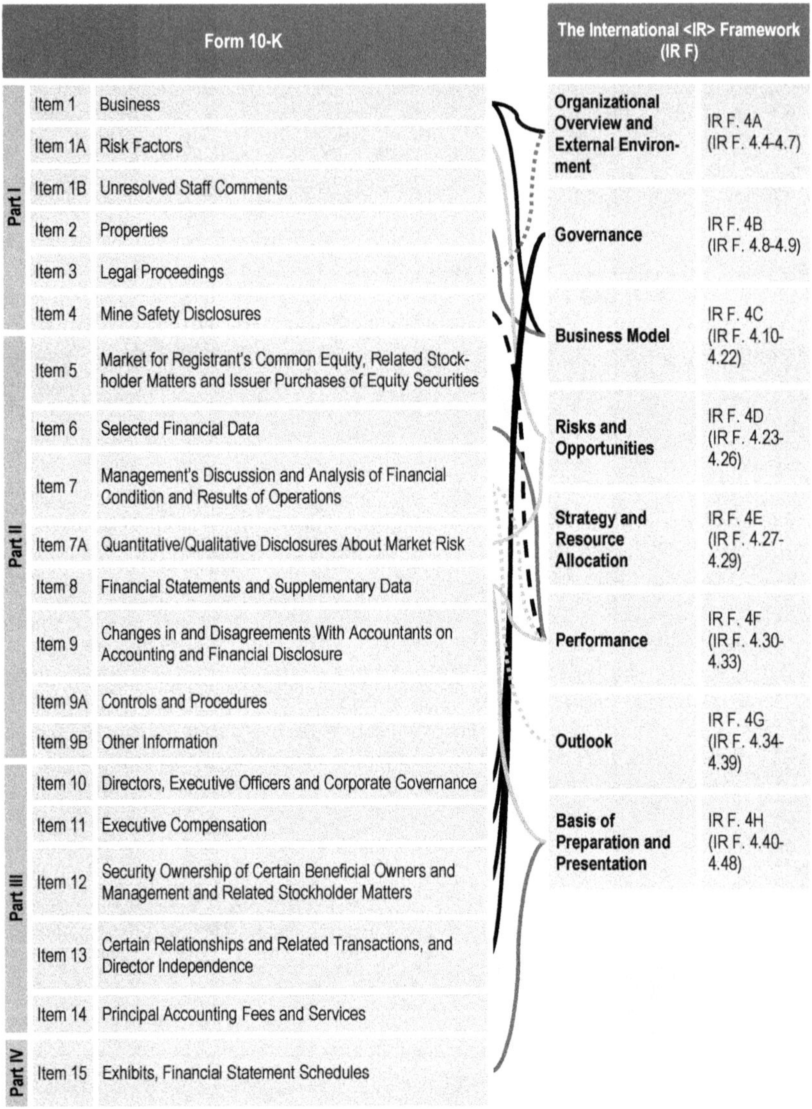

The connecting lines are shaded and dotted differently for the purpose of better distinctiveness. This involves no distinction in the type of connection.

Figure 3-4: Items of Form 10-K and Content Elements under the IR F

In **part II** of Form 10-K, **item 6** (Selected Financial Data) also corresponds with the Performance Content Element. The underlying Item 301 of Regulation S-K requires the disclosure of various financial indicators (e.g., revenues, income or total assets) for five years, including a discussion. This is one example of a disclosure requirement that conveys the Connectivity of Information principle, both regarding the time dimension (five years) and the connectivity of quantitative and qualitative information, as the item also prescribes a discussion of factors that influence their comparability.

Item 7 refers to the **MD&A**. Written from management's perspective, this narrative reporting instrument is widely read and considered important, while also being reputable internationally (*Hüfner* (2007b), pp. 58-59). The purpose of the MD&A is to enable investors and other users to assess the firm's financial condition and results of operation by providing relevant information (Instruction 2 to Item 303(a) of Regulation S-K). This discussion covers the topics that its name includes. In particular, regarding the financial condition, the MD&A deals with the firm's liquidity and capital resources (Item 303(a)(1) and (2) of Regulation S-K). In terms of the results of operations, it includes unusual events or economic changes that affect income from continuing operations, and possibly also particular revenues and expenses (Item 303(a)(3)). For both the financial conditions indicators and the results of operations indicators, known trends and uncertainties with a potential future material impact on the indicators need to be disclosed. This requirement intends to give the information predictive value, thereby introducing future-orientation to the MD&A. However, despite SEC guidance and safe harbor rules to stimulate firms to provide such information,[97] direct forward-looking information (such as forecasts) can hardly be expected in the MD&A in practice (*Hüfner* (2007b), pp. 72-74). Empirical findings support this expectation.[98] In addition, the MD&A has to include disclosures on off-balance sheet arrangements and contractual arrangements (Item 303(a)(4) and (5) of Regulation S-K). In their entirety, the disclosure requirements of the MD&A correspond with the Content Elements Performance and – slightly limited – Outlook. Besides, the MD&A is one part of the Form 10-K that may include environmental information. SEC Release 33-9106 (2010) sets out that climate change and its physical effects or subsequent technical development may represent factors which influence the firm's financial position or results. Hence, the MD&A needs to report on these issues. Moreover, information relating to climate change may also be provided in items 1 (Business), 1A (Risk Factors) or 3 (Legal Proceedings).

---

97 SEC Releases 33-6835 (1989) and 33-8350 (2003) provide guidance on forward-looking disclosures in the MD&A. They also reference the safe harbor rules under the Securities Act of 1933 (Rule 175) and under the Securities Exchange Act of 1934 (Rule 3b-6), which are also referenced in Instruction 7 to Item 303(a) of the Regulation S-K. These rules preserve management from litigation resulting from forward-looking information that turns out to be untrue.

98 *Clarkson et al.* (1994) document that only about 36% of their sample firms include a forecast of operating results somewhere in the report. A third of the forecasts is exclusively allocated in the MD&A (pp. 430-431). *Muslu et al.* (2015) find 39 MD&A sentences being forward-looking on average, while the MD&A in total has 301 sentences on average. The mean forward-looking intensity (forward-looking sentences divided by total sentences) is 13%.

As opposed to the financial statements (see item 8), the **MD&A** is not required to be audited. Instead, an auditor may be engaged to perform an examination or review of the MD&A, irrespective of the auditor's responsibility in an audit of the firm's financial statements (AT Section 701). Similarly, par. 04 of AU Section 550[99] states that other information in the document that contains the audited financial statements may only be relevant to the **audit** in so far that the auditor can check this information for consistency with the financial statements. However, the auditor's responsibility does not extend beyond the financial information that he identifies in the auditor's report.

Only referring to the negative side of risk, but nonetheless relating to the Content Element Risks and Opportunities, **item 7A** of the Form 10-K requires quantitative and qualitative **disclosures about market risk.** Item 305 of Regulation S-K offers three different options for the disclosures: a tabular presentation, a sensitivity analysis or a value at risk calculation. As the name suggests, this item yields connectivity between quantitative and qualitative information, since it prescribes an adjacent explanatory discussion to the quantitative risk information, e.g. comprising the underlying assumptions (in each of the three format options).

Item 8 Financial Statements and Supplementary Data refers to Regulation S-X, which governs the form and content of financial statements. Rule 3 of Regulation S-X (in conjunction with item 8(a) of Form 10-K) requires the filing of **consolidated, audited financial statements.** Subsequently, Rule 3A of Regulation S-X provides general principles of consolidation and requires the disclosure of these principles in the notes to the financial statements (Rule 3A-02 and 03(a) of Regulation S-X). The financial statements are to be in accordance with US GAAP or are presumed to be inaccurate or misleading (Rule 4-01).[100] In addition, Rule 5 prescribes the elements of the balance sheet (Rule 5-02) and income statement (Rule 5-03) for all "Commercial and Industrial Companies", meaning all firms except those listed in Rule 5-01. The exceptions comprise different kinds of firms from the financial services sector, for which Rules 6 through 9 provide special guidance. Balance sheet and income statement are the classical reporting instruments for the firm's results, so that item 8 of Form 10-K clearly relates to the IR Content Element Performance.

Moreover, Rule 4-08 of Regulation S-X sets out the different disclosures in the notes, beginning with the aforementioned principles of consolidation and furthermore including information on shares and dividends, but also taxes and other issues. The US GAAP, which regulate the balance sheet and income statement items, also prescribe **formal issues and various disclosure requirements**, similar to the IFRS (section 3.1.3). For instance, the formal requirements state that offsetting is improper (ASC 210-20-05-2), while the disclosure provisions require an explanation of changes in the compilation and measurement methods (ASC 205-10-50-1). These provisions partly overlap with those required by the Content

[99] Note that the PCAOB reorganized its auditing standards on 31 March 2015. According to the new organization, former AU Section 550 will be known as AS 2710. The SEC approved these amendments on 17 September 2015. They will be effective as of 31 December 2016.

[100] Despite the FASB's close cooperation with the IASB, domestic firms are not allowed to use IFRS in preparing their financial statements; foreign private issuers are allowed to do so, instead (IFRS Foundation/SEC (2016), p. 3).

Element Basis of Preparation and Presentation in the IIRC Framework. As supplementary data to be provided in the Form 10-K, Item 302(a) of Regulation S-K prescribes quarterly financial data on various performance figures like sales or profits.

Besides, Item 302(b) of Regulation S-K requires **oil and gas firms** to describe their producing activities, referencing ASC Topic 932. This in turn names the items to be disclosed, including information on the capitalization of the costs for these activities, in particular exploratory well costs, and (for public companies) also on the oil and gas reserves and their changes, the results of operations for these activities and a standardized measure of discounted future cash flows from these areas (ASC 932-235-50). The oil and gas industry faces special disclosure provisions as it plays an exceptional role for the national energy supply.[101] This is also visible in the even more detailed additional disclosure requirements introduced by SEC Release 33-8995 (2008), including among other things, (optional) disclosures on the sensitivity of the oil and gas reserves to price (Item 1202(b) of Regulation S-K), and also affect items 1 (business) and 2 (properties) of Form 10-K. Thus, these disclosures provide information about the natural resources the firm uses in its activities and can be seen as a parallel to IR requiring environmental information, in particular information about natural capital. Further information on environmental matters or other issues not included in the aforementioned explicit reporting requirements may be included in the Form 10-K of firms from any sector via Exchange Act Rule 12b-20 (17 CFR § 240.12b-20). This rule stipulates that material **additional information** be provided as far as necessary to make the required statements not misleading.

Item 9A of Form 10-K prescribes disclosures on controls and procedures. The underlying Items 307 and 308 of Regulation S-K require management's conclusions on the disclosure controls and procedures and a report on the internal controls over financial reporting and on their changes, including a statement of responsibility, but also the auditor's attestation report. This corresponds with the requirement of a similar statement in the International <IR> Framework (IR F. 1.20).

The items of **part III of Form 10-K** mostly deal with governance issues and are thus related to the IIRC Content Element of the same name. **Item 10** Directors, Executive Officers and Corporate Governance prescribes the disclosure of identification data on the directors, executive officers and other important employees, including their name, age, all positions and much more personal data (Item 401 of Regulation S-K). Moreover, the item requires data on directors' trading with the firm's securities if they hold a share of more than 10% (Item 405 of Regulation S-K) and on other governance-related issues, like the adoption of a code of ethics or disclosures on the audit committee (Items 406 and 407(d)(4) of Regulation S-K, respectively). Detailed information on the remuneration of certain directors and officers (Item 402 of Regulation S-K) and information on the compensation committee (Item 407I of Regulation S-K) is disclosed under 10-K **item 11** Executive Compensation, whereas **item 12** prescribes reporting on security holdings and equity compensation plans

[101] First oil and gas disclosure requirements were introduced by the SEC pursuing a directive in the Energy Policy and Conservation Act of 1975 (SEC Release 33-8995, p. 7), which in turn intended to install a comprehensive energy policy and attempted to secure the national energy supply ("The Energy Policy and Conservation Act" (1976), p. 2).

according to Items 403 and 201(d) of Regulation S-K, respectively. **Item 13** supplements this with detailed information on directors' independence (Item 407(a) of Regulation S-K) and on the firm's transactions with related persons (Item 404 of Regulation S-K).

In part IV at the end of the 10-K filing (**item 15**), there are various exhibits (or at least references to them if they are incorporated by reference according to Exchange Act Rule 12b-32 ((17 CFR § 240.12b-32)). An index for the exhibits precedes the documents (Item 601(a)(2) of Regulation S-K). Among other things, exhibits include a list of subsidiaries (Item 601(b)(21) of Regulation S-K), from which users get an indication of the financial statement entity[102] and thus in many cases the reporting boundary. This list thus relates this 10-K item to the IR Content Element Basis of Preparation and Presentation. Moreover, exhibits include a certification from the directors on their responsibility for and review of the report as well as their oversight over internal reporting controls (Item 601(b)(31) of Regulation S-K).

Corporate governance and governance reporting guidance

Regarding corporate governance in the USA, there is no central guidance document with particular prominence like the King framework in South Africa. Instead, several sources of governance regulation and guidance exist. Paralleling SEC regulation, the **NYSE listing standards** (or comparable standards at other stock exchanges, e.g. the NASDAQ) set out requirements on the firms' governance. Moreover, several **private guidance** reports, such as the Report of the NACD Blue Ribbon Commission on Director Professionalism, summarize governance principles or best practice.[103] However, (at least in terms of disclosures) both the listing standards and the private guidance documents essentially refer to the SEC regulations or set out the same requirements rather than going beyond them. As regards SEC regulation, SOX yielded new and stricter requirements on governance issues and related disclosures for public firms when enacted on 30 July 2002 as a reaction to major corporate and accounting scandals (*Jackson* (2010)). For instance, the aforementioned requirements to disclose off-balance sheet arrangements and contractual obligations in the MD&A or the provision to disclose the signing officers' responsibility for internal controls have been introduced by the SEC in response to SOX[104]. Not only the respective Form 10-K items, but also the SEC disclosure requirements (NYSE Listed Company Manual Section 303)

---

[102] ASC 810 regulates the consolidation of entities. *Alves* ((2011), pp. 183-214) summarizes the regulations of group accounting and financial reporting under US GAAP, including the reporting entity. The notes to the financial statements need to include a description of these principles of consolidation (Rule 3A-03(a) of Regulations S-K, see above).

[103] Examples of other private governance guidance in the USA are the American Law Institute's Principles of Corporate Governance (from 1994), Business Roundtable's Principles of Corporate Governance 2012 or the Findings and Recommendations of The Conference Board Commission on Public Trust and Private Enterprise (from 2003). *Weil* (2013b; 2013a) provide a comparison of these and other guidance documents and an international comparison of corporate governance regulation, respectively.

[104] The SEC fulfilled the requirement of Section 302(a) of SOX, which required the commission to introduce a regulation on such a statement, with SEC Release 33-8124 (2002) on 29 August 2002. On 28 January 2003, the SEC then introduced the off-balance sheet and contractual obligations requirements (Item 303(a)(4) and (5) of Regulation S-K) with SEC Release 33-8182 (2003), carrying into execution the provision of Section 401(a) of SOX.

and the NACD Report mostly refer to Items 407 or 601 of Regulation S-K. Substantially, the disclosures in the firms' annual reporting documents (Form 10-K or proxy statement) stemming from corporate governance regulation or guidance deal with director independence, the nominating/governance committee and its members, the used governance guidelines, the firm's code of ethics, the compensation committee and its members, the compensation of directors and executives as well as the audit committee and its members.

Sustainability reporting

As a basis for sustainability accounting standards, the **SASB** has issued a **Conceptual Framework** (SASB CF) in 2013.[105] It outlines the concepts and definitions for sustainability accounting and shall serve as additional guidance beyond the industry-specific standards (SASB CF, p. 3). According to the framework, the purpose of sustainability accounting and disclosure is to inform investors about the environmental, social and governance performance of a company, thereby complementing financial reporting to provide a complete picture of the firm's performance (SASB CF, p. 3). Thus, the primary beneficiary and target audience of the SASB standards is the "reasonable investor", irrespective of his or her investment horizon or investment strategy (SASB CF, p. 5). Eventually, the SASB standards shall increase the decision-usefulness of the firm's reports for this investor (SASB CF, p. 10). Corresponding with the target audience, the intended users of the standards are firms that engage in public securities offerings and are thus required to file periodic reports (e.g., Form 10-K or Form 20-F) with the SEC, although the SASB guidance may also be applicable to the disclosures of other entities (SASB CF, p. 4). To determine the sustainability disclosures that firms have to include in their filings, the SASB employs an industry-specific approach based on materiality, following the materiality definition adopted by US securities laws and case laws (SASB CF, pp. 8-9). The standards are intended to provide guidance for firms in determining their own material issues for disclosure (SASB CF, pp. 19-20). This guidance follows a two-step approach. First, an SASB standard sets out (potentially) material sustainability topics for the respective industry. In determining these topics, the SASB considers the following factors: applicability to investors, relevance across an industry, potential to affect value creation, benefits exceeding the perceived costs, practicability by the companies and reflectiveness of stakeholders' views (SASB CF, p. 12). Second, the SASB recommends particular "activity metrics" to report on the different topics. To ensure that these metrics produce decision-useful information, the framework requires them to satisfy the following criteria: relevance, usefulness, applicability, cost-effectiveness, comparability, completeness, directionality, auditability and neutrality.

The **SASB standards** for each industry generally comprise (1) disclosure guidance, identifying sustainability topics that may be material for the firms in the respective industry and (2) accounting standards on sustainability topics, providing standardized accounting metrics to account for and depict the firm's performance on industry-level sustainability topics. At the beginning, the standards also include a description of the particular industry they

[105] A draft version of a revised SASB Conceptual Framework has been published in April 2016 and was open for comment until July 2016. As regards the contents of the framework outlined here, the 2016 draft version differs only marginally from the 2013 version.

have been developed for. The SASB draws on certain provisions in Regulation S-K or certain items of Form 10-K, respectively. In particular, sustainability disclosures may occur in the description of the business (Item 1 of Form 10-K), of legal proceedings (Item 3 of Form 10-K), of risk factors (Item 1A of Form 10-K). Moreover, Item 303(a)(3)(ii) of Regulation S-K is of particular importance. According to this item, a firm has to disclose known trends or uncertainties with a (potential) material impact on sales or income in the MD&A (Item 7 of Form 10-K). The SASB recommends to make the respective MD&A disclosures under the separate heading "Sustainability Accounting Standards Disclosures". In addition, Securities Act Rule 408 (17 CFR § 230.408) and Exchange Act Rule 12b-20 (17 CFR § 240.12b-20) require firms to add to the information that is explicitly required by law or regulation the material information that is necessary to avoid a misleading character of the required statements. Hence, the determination of materiality is key for sustainability disclosures.

To assist firms in determining material issues for disclosure, the SASB standards thus provide a list of **sustainability topics** that are potentially material for the respective industry. For instance, the standard for the Construction Materials industry names the following topics: Greenhouse Gas Emissions, Air Quality, Energy Management, Water Management, Waste Management, Biodiversity Impacts, Workforce Health, Safety and Well-Being, Product Innovation and Pricing Integrity & Payments Transparency. For each of these topics, the standard names various **accounting metrics**, which may be quantitative or qualitative in nature and may include a discussion and analysis. Examples include the following metrics: For the Biodiversity Impacts topic, the standard recommends the disclosure of the terrestrial acreage disturbed and the percentage of impacted area restored as well as a description of environmental management policies and practices for active sites. For Waste Management, the suggested metrics are the amount of waste from operations, the percentage of hazardous waste and the percentage of recycled waste. For each of the listed metrics, the standard provides an identification number, the unit of measure (if applicable) and detailed guidance on how to report on the metrics.

As the sustainability information that the SASB standards recommend may include **forward-looking information**, such as environmental, social, regulatory or political trends, the standards also refer to the aforementioned safe harbor rule that can preserve management from litigation relating to such statements. Moreover, the standards encourage the reporting firms to use **independent assurance** for the sustainability disclosures.

Conclusion

The Qualitative Characteristics in the FASB's Conceptual Framework show a remarkable overlap with the Guiding Principles of the International <IR> Framework. The two Fundamental Qualitative Characteristics Relevance and Faithful Representation and the four Enhancing Qualitative Characteristics Comparability, Verifiability, Timeliness and Understandability all find their equivalents in the IR guidance document. Similar to the IRCSA DP, there is no direct corresponding principle with the IR Guiding Principles Strategic Focus and Future Orientation and Connectivity of Information, though. Moreover, the clear focus on investors in US reporting also results in a lack of alignment with the

Guiding Principle Stakeholder Relationships, which also distinguishes the Conceptual Framework from the South African guidance.

The contents of a Form 10-K filing and thus of an annual report are prescribed in detail by various regulations. These include Regulations S-K and S-X, the rules on the Securities Act and Securities Exchange Act, SEC Releases as guidance materials and US GAAP governing accounting and financial reporting. The SEC's Form 10-K guidance document puts the different contents into a defined structure and refers to the underlying regulations for the different 10-K items. Moreover, voluntary disclosures may supplement the information in Form 10-K, e.g. specific information on sustainability issues as outlined in the SASB standards. Taken together, the contents cover the IR Content Elements and even go beyond these in some regards. Moreover, several contents even address aspects of certain IR Guiding Principles that are not explicitly covered by the Qualitative Characteristics of the Conceptual Framework. Examples include disclosures on trends in the MD&A, the reporting of financial data from previous periods or explanations on some financial data, which cover Future Orientation and aspects of the Connectivity of Information principle. However, the actual disclosure of forward-looking information is limited and the connectivity aspects only refer to some features of the IR Guiding Principle. The Strategic Focus and Stakeholder Relationships principles remain unaddressed.

3.2.4 Summary of the US reporting landscape

The USA are a wealthy economy with a history of business that has strongly been influenced by financing through capital markets from early stages, triggering an **investor protection** perspective of regulations. In this regard, the USA differ from South Africa, where regulations show a broader perspective on all stakeholders, consistent with the country's economic and historical development. The **SEC**, which was formed as a response to the Great Depression, follows the mission of investor protection in the USA. The commission provides rules and interpretations on firms' listing issues, security trading and financial reporting, besides dealing with the enforcement of financial reporting. It has deferred the task of providing detailed guidance for accounting issues, however. After less successful efforts of the CAP and the Accounting Principles Board, the **FASB** took over the job of issuing accounting standards. The FASB is now the single source of US GAAP and has unified and structured the standards in the FASB Accounting Standards Codification®. However, as the occurrence of corporate fraud had destroyed investors' trust in the firms and their reporting to a noticeable degree, laws and guidance on corporate governance and on governance reporting have been issued or strengthened to re-foster investor confidence and provide a basis for the capital markets to work. Moreover, as doing business today is determined by social and ecological constraints and as a firm's value is only insufficiently depicted by traditional financial report, reporting on sustainability issues shall enable investors to get a complete picture of the firm's value. Therefore, the **SASB** has issued standards that provide guidance on sustainability reporting, following an industry-specific approach.

The FASB's **Conceptual Framework** is also in line with the investor focus, as it names investors as the primary addressees of financial reports and decision usefulness for investors as the overall purpose of the provided information. Although not being a mandatory reporting regulation itself, this framework provides a principles-based foundation for firms' reporting. The Qualitative Characteristics that the framework holds address various IR Guiding Principles. Both the Fundamental (Relevance and Faithful Representation) and Enhancing Qualitative Characteristics (Comparability, Verifiability, Timeliness and Understandability) have their equivalents in the International <IR> Framework, whereas the IR Guiding Principles Strategic Focus and Future Orientation, Connectivity of Information, Stakeholder Relationships and Conciseness are not explicitly covered by the Qualitative Characteristics of the Conceptual Framework. Some of these Guiding Principles are only partly covered by the requirements of other Qualitative Characteristics (as it is the case for Conciseness) or by particular content provisions in the disclosure regulations (as with some aspects of Connectivity as well as with Future Orientation), while some aspects remain unaddressed after all (Strategic Focus and Stakeholder Relationships). As opposed to the Conceptual Framework, the South African IR guidance takes these remaining principles into account. While listing the almost same set of **principles** as the Conceptual Framework in terms of their names, the detailed guidance on the principles and in the remaining IRCSA DP cover the stakeholder approach and the strategic and future orientation, but also the connectivity of information, at least in general terms.

The **contents** of the **Form 10-K** that the SEC prescribes, referencing a magnitude of different reporting requirements in the 10-K guidance document, are very extensive and detailed. With the exception of Strategy and Resource Allocation, they cover all IR Content Elements in more or less detail (similar to the South African IR guidance) and also go beyond the IIRC requirements in the detailed provisions on the 20 different 10-K items.

Table 3-3 summarizes in how far the **Guiding Principles and Content Elements of the International <IR> Framework are covered** in the discussed regulations from both countries. The sets of principles are generally almost the same in South Africa and the USA, at least in terms of the names. However, due to differences in the particular requirements of principles that carry the same name and due to some differences in the stated objectives of the report, the Guiding Principles from the IR Framework are not covered equally in both countries. While both frameworks deal with Materiality, Conciseness, Reliability and Completeness, as well as with Consistency and Comparability, US regulations do not address Connectivity of Information and Stakeholder Relationships, and slightly consider Future-Orientation, but not Strategic Focus. Instead, the South African Framework covers these latter three aspects, although not as extensively as the International <IR> Framework. The regulations in both countries cover almost all Content Elements, though, the only unaddressed element in the USA being Strategy and Resource Allocation. However, traditionally Form 10-K does not take the perspective of different capitals so that not all dimensions of e.g. Performance are addressed to the same degree as under the IR Framework. The IRCSA DP does consider (five) different capitals instead. Voluntary reporting on social and ecological issues, as recommended e.g. by the SASB standards, may broaden the narrow focus of Form 10-K in terms of the capitals, though. Although such an inclusion of sustainability issues in Form 10-K does not satisfy the IIRC's definition of an integrated report, this may even constitute a first step toward IR in the USA (*Eccles et al.* (2015), p. 74).

All in all, the South African IR discussion paper is nevertheless more in line with the International <IR> Framework than the US Conceptual Framework for financial reporting. Consistent with the principles-based approach of IR, the principles rather than the contents account for the major differences between the regulations of the two countries.

The International <IR> Framework (IR F) – Coverage by South African and US regulations			
Panel A: Guiding Principles			
IR F		**South Africa: IRCSA DP**	**USA: CF**
Strategic Focus and Future Orientation	IR F. 3A (IR F. 3.3-3.5)	indirectly covered (not directly by the requirements from the principles): forward-looking perspective; strategic objectives to be reported (✓)	indirectly covered (not directly by the requirements from the principles): predictive value of relevant information; Strategic Focus not considered ~
Connectivity of Information	IR F. 3B (IR F. 3.6-3.9)	covered ✓	not covered ☒
Stakeholder relationships	IR F. 3C (IR F. 3.10-3.16)	covered ✓	not covered ☒
Materiality	IR F. 3D (IR F. 3.17-3.35)	covered ✓	covered ✓
Conciseness	IR F. 3E (IR F. 3.36-3.38)	covered ✓	covered ✓
Reliability and Completeness	IR F. 3F (IR F. 3.39-3.53)	covered ✓	covered ✓
Consistency and Comparability	IR F. 3G (IR F. 3.54-3.57)	covered ✓	covered ✓
Panel B: Content Elements			
IR F		**South Africa: IRCSA DP**	**USA: CF**
Organizational Overview and External Environment	IR F. 4A (IR F. 4.4-4.7)	covered ✓	covered ✓
Governance	IR F. 4B (IR F. 4.8-4.9)	covered ✓	covered ✓
Business Model	IR F. 4C (IR F. 4.10-4.22)	covered ✓	covered ✓
Risks and Opportunities	IR F. 4D (IR F. 4.23-4.26)	covered ✓	covered ✓
Strategy and Resource Allocation	IR F. 4E (IR F. 4.27-4.29)	covered ✓	not covered ☒
Performance	IR F. 4F (IR F. 4.30-4.33)	covered ✓	covered ✓
Outlook	IR F. 4G (IR F. 4.34-4.39)	covered ✓	covered ✓
Basis of Preparation and Presentation	IR F. 4H (IR F. 4.40-4.48)	covered ✓	covered ✓

Table 3-3: IR F coverage by South African and US regulations

4 Integrated Reporting in practice

Following the presentation of the IR Framework and the reporting landscape in South Africa and the USA, the two empirical parts of this study shall assess the potential of integrated reports to improve users' decision making (research question 2). This chapter investigates the reporting practice in these two countries descriptively, aiming at an answer to the question in how far IR is present in firms' reports. In line with the IIRC's principles-based approach, this study interprets IR as the alignment of the reports with the Guiding Principles of the International <IR> Framework. This allows an assessment of IR presence in the reports, irrespective of whether they are named integrated reports and whether they are prepared in compliance with a requirement to apply IR (South Africa) or not (USA). Examining reports from two different years, 2006 and 2012, permits comparisons of the IR practice between the countries at two points in time and in each country over time, in particular before and after the release of King III in South Africa, which introduced the requirement for listed firms to apply IR or explain why they would not.

The chapter begins with an analysis of prior research on IR practice. Next, theoretical reasoning on the drivers of corporate reporting sets out the basis to derive hypotheses on the reporting practice in the two countries and years. After an explanation of the methodology for this study, which describes the sample and the data collection on IR, the chapter presents the results and contrasts them for the different years and countries. The last section of this chapter discusses the findings against the hypotheses and theoretical reasoning.

4.1 State of research

Since IR emerged, various studies have examined the practice of this new reporting format empirically.[106] This section gives an overview of the extant literature on this topic, concentrating on **descriptive evidence**[107] **about IR practice**, in particular analyses of best practice or the degree or quality[108] of IR in different countries. The findings reveal where the literature leaves room for improvement and further research, including diverging approaches of examination. So this first part of the chapter elaborates in how far this study is distinct from extant literature and may thus add value to the research on IR practice.

---

[106] As chapter 2 has shown, this study – in line with the IR Framework – understands IR as a holistic reporting format rather than as an advancement of ESG reporting or a combination of financial and ESG reporting. This section thus focuses on studies that address IR in terms of this definition, instead of also portraying extant ESG reporting literature. Cf. e.g. *Panzer/Ergün* (2015) or *Martinez* ((2016), with further references) for a diverging practice that also encompasses literature on ESG reporting.

[107] Setting the context for the explanatory analysis, section 5.1 presents literature on the impacts of IR, instead. Hence, in line with the overall focus of this study, both empirical parts of the study take a report readers' perspective. For a review that includes studies which deal with the preparation of the reports from the firms' perspective, cf. *De Villiers et al.* (2014) or *Velte/Stawinoga* (2016).

[108] Other literature, in particular research on the determinants of IR, uses dummy variables indicating whether or not a company practices IR. These studies include *Jensen/Berg* (2012), *Frías-Aceituno et al.* (2013a; 2013b; 2014), *García-Sánchez et al.* (2013) and *Lai et al.* (2016). The KPMG Survey of Corporate Responsibility Reporting (e.g., *KPMG* (2013; 2014; 2015b)) or *Bernardi/Stark* (2015) provide data on the same aggregation level. Due to this high-level perspective on IR, the descriptive statistics of these studies are not comparable to the results of the study at hand. Thus, they are not presented here.

Europe

Several studies and other publications, in particular reviews and surveys by accounting firms, document the practice of IR in European **settings**. Countries under examination are Austria (*PwC/WU* (2014)), Belgium (*PwC* (2014a)), the Czech Republic (*Havlová* (2015a)), Germany (*PwC* (2012b; 2013d; 2014f)), the Netherlands (*PwC* (2013e); *Deloitte* (2014); *Deloitte/MVO Nederland* (2015)), Spain (*PwC* (2012a; 2013b; 2014b; 2015a)), Sweden (*PwC* (2013a; 2013f)) and the UK (*Robertson/Samy* (2015); *Deloitte* (2015)). The reviews cover different financial years between 2010 and 2014/2015. In Germany (2011-2013), the Czech Republic (2012-2014), the Netherlands (2012-2014), Spain (2010-2013), Sweden (2011 and 2012) and the UK (2013 and 2014/2015), studies on different financial years exist, while the reviews from other countries only cover one year (2012/2013 for Austria and 2012 for Belgium).

The **findings** reveal that the most widespread weaknesses in terms of reporting **principles** occur in terms of connectivity in the reports (in all countries) and of conciseness (e.g., in the Netherlands). However, many reviews only examine linkages between the **contents** or between financial and non-financial aspects, while generally focusing on the IR Content Elements. In this regard, the most common weaknesses are the reporting on Governance (in all countries except the Netherlands in financial year 2014), Business Model (e.g., in Belgium or the Netherlands in 2014) and External Environment (e.g., in Belgium, Spain or Sweden). Common areas of strength are reporting on Risks and Opportunities (e.g., in Germany, the Netherlands, Spain and Sweden, whereas this field represents a weakness in the Czech Republic) as well as strategy reporting (e.g., in Spain and Sweden). Although all countries that are reviewed for several years show improvement in firms' reporting, in particular the lack of linkages is a persistent issue. Comparing the different countries, reporting in the UK and Germany is often considered as a benchmark for IR by other European countries (e.g., *PwC* (2013e), p. 8; *PwC* (2014b), p. 5). However, the reviews do not employ statistically sound comparisons between the countries. Small sample sizes (e.g., the Swedish sample for 2012 contains 28 firms, the Dutch sample for 2012 contains 25 firms, the UK sample for 2013 contains 22 firms and the Belgian sample for 2012 contains 20 firms) would hamper such comparisons. Another problem in this regard is data collection. Even though the criteria of data collection may be comparable to some extent due to a common approach within the same international accounting firm, differences in scoring the reports may occur between the countries and/or the different reviewers. In addition to being exposed to such a bias, research by accounting firms[109] might also implicitly be driven by the firms' or their clients' business interests.

Asia and Oceania

Further reviews of this kind examine the IR practice in Asia and Oceania, in particular in Japan (*KPMG* (2015a)), Malaysia (*PwC* (2014c; 2015c)) and Singapore (*PwC* (2014e)), as well as in Australia (*ACCA/Net Balance Foundation* (2011)) and New Zealand (*Stent/Dowler* (2015)). The covered **settings** include years between 2010 (Australia) and 2014 (Japan

[109] The only European studies not conducted by accounting firms are those on reporting in the Czech Republic by *Havlová* (2015a) and in the UK by *Robertson/Samy* (2015).

and Malaysia). Malaysia is the only country with reviews on two consecutive financial years (2013 and 2014).

The **results** for both the 30 firms in the Singapore Straits Times Index (STI) (for financial year 2013/2014) and Bursa Malaysia's Top 30 (for 2013) or Top 50 (for 2014) firms reveal that the reports are mostly backward-looking and compliance driven, including boilerplate disclosures and lacking linkages as well as non-financial aspects. From 2013 to 2014, slight improvements are visible in Malaysia in some areas. However, this may be driven by the changes in the sample. Australian reports in 2010 show similar shortcomings in terms of integration and coverage of non-financial issues. In addition to these **principles**-related findings, the surveys yield insights about the coverage of different **contents**. Malaysian firms address aspects that are related to many IR Content Elements, but mostly on a generic basis (e.g., many firms describe the process to identify risks, but few describe the risks themselves). In Singapore, companies hardly provide effective disclosures on the Content Elements, the weakest areas being Governance, Performance and Future Outlook. An overarching issue is the lack of non-financial aspects. Weaknesses in reporting on governance and non-financial aspects are also common among Japanese (mostly TSE-listed) firms in financial year 2014. In addition, their reports show little adoption of the label "integrated" and little reference to the IR Framework. Despite some room for improvement in the Outlook section, the examined firms from New Zealand present very high scores. These results are likely to be driven by the sample selection, however, as the sample contains only four firms, all of which participate in the IIRC Pilot Programme. Hence, they constitute a small and at the same time biased selection. The other mentioned studies use larger samples (30 firms in Singapore and Malaysia 2013, 50 in Malaysia 2014 and Australia 2010, 142 in Japan 2014), but face the same problems in terms of data collection as described for the European reviews.

America

Although Brazil is among the countries where IR is developing (*De Villiers et al.* (2014), p. 1054), no empirical data on the IR practice in this country is available so far. Similarly, no data exists for other **South American** countries. Turning to **North America**, no data is available for Canada, either. For the near future, the adoption of IR is unlikely in this country, mainly due to litigation concerns among the firms (*Hao* (2014), p. 34). Comparable concerns exist in the USA (*AICPA* (2014), p. 3). However, a single study examines the use of IR in US reports.[110]

Serafeim (2015) provides data on the use of IR for a sample of 1,114 **US firms** (5,762 firm-year observations from the period between 2002 and 2010). He employs this data to analyze associations of IR use and the characteristics of the firm's investor base. The IR score stems from the Thomson Reuters Asset 4 database. It can be interpreted as a measure of the

[110] A second study, *IRRCI/Si2* (2013), analyzes the disclosure practice of the S&P 500 firms in their 2012 reports, taking aspects of IR into regard. However, despite describing the work of the IIRC and the development of the IR Framework, the study examines IR only as a combination of financial and sustainability reporting rather than as a holistic reporting approach in the sense of the IIRC Framework. Even in the former sense, the study finds that the adherence to IR is low among the examined firms.

firm's management commitment and effectiveness toward creating an overarching vision and strategy while integrating financial and non-financial aspects. In addition, it reflects the firm's ability to convincingly communicate the integration of economic, social and environmental aspects into daily business decisions. The mean IR score (in a range of 0 to 100) for this sample is 39, with a standard deviation of 29. However, it is questionable if this score can actually depict the use of IR. Compared to a database measure, a self-constructed metric is more likely to capture what it intends to do (*Healy/Palepu* (2001), p. 427). To this end, *Serafeim* – in a robustness test – uses scores for the Content Elements, Guiding Principles and capitals, which he collects manually by content analysis from 97 reports of global companies with fiscal year end 2012. The average score, which also ranges between 0 and 100, is 70 (57; 68) for the Content Elements (Guiding Principles; capitals). Although representing a more direct measure to depict IR than the data from the database that the study uses, these hand-collected scores are presented on an aggregate level and do not yield detailed insight into the reporting practice for the respective IR dimension.

Africa

The pioneering role of **South Africa** in the development of IR determines the research on the IR practice in Africa. Various studies and other publications examine the reporting practice of South African companies, whereas there is only one study on the IR practice in another African country, namely Malawi. Due to the pioneering role of the country, the coverage of South Africa is also broad in comparison with the research on countries from other continents. Figure 4-1 illustrates the distribution of the research considered by the study a hand over all continents.

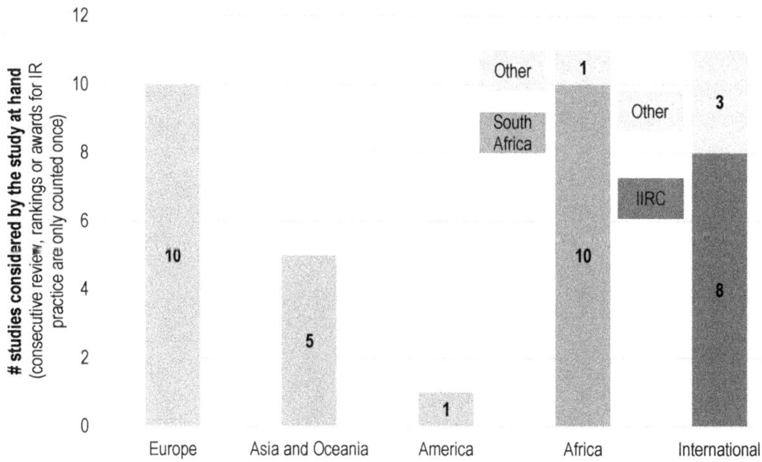

Figure 4-1: Studies on IR practice – Global coverage

As in Europe and Asia, the literature on South Africa includes **reviews by accounting firms**. *PwC* (2013c; 2014d; 2015d) has surveyed the top 40 JSE-listed firms for three consecutive years (financial years 2012-2014), assessing their reporting in terms of the IR Content Elements[111]. The study identifies room for improvement in the disclosure on all Content Elements. In most cases, the percentage of firms with effective disclosure on the Content Elements increases over the years, though. For instance, 16% of the firms make effective disclosures on Strategy and Resource Allocation in financial year 2012. This number increases to 28% in 2013 and 36% in 2014. While Governance (3%) and Performance (6%) are the Content Elements with the lowest percentage of effective disclosures in 2012, Outlook shows the lowest percentage in 2014 (8%), although the disclosures on this element are better in 2012 (13%) and 2013 (18%). However, in comparison with other countries, the South African reports yield the highest scores overall (e.g., *PwC* (2013f), p. 18). As mentioned for the European studies, these comparisons are not statistically sound. Besides, the surveys face the other aforementioned shortcomings of the reviews by accounting firms. A further issue with these and other reviews that focus on the Content Elements is that a focus on the Guiding Principles would seem more suitable to depict the use of IR. As elaborated in chapters 2 and 3, IR follows a principles-based approach and the principles constitute the main distinctive features compared to traditional and existing reporting requirements.

EY's Excellence rating is another Big Four survey on the IR practice in South Africa. Since 1997, *EY* has been reviewing annual reports of South African companies, **ranking** them according to a self-developed scoring plan that bases upon the expertise of academics (e.g., *Ernst & Young* (2011), p. 11) and on the IR guidance from King III and the various IIRC guidance documents – thus changing over the years (e.g., *EY* (2013), p. 15; *EY* (2015), p. 28). Initially named "Excellence in Corporate Reporting", the survey is called "Excellence in Integrated Reporting" from the 2012 version on. Based on the scoring process, the surveys categorize the examined reports[112] into four different groups in terms of report quality[113] and rank the top ten reports. Sasol often took the first place in the 2000s, including the 2006 and 2007 rankings, still placing among the top ten reports regularly in more current issues of the ranking. In 2012 and 2013, ABSA Group Ltd. and Gold Fields were the winners, respectively. *Barth et al.* (2015) and *Martinez* (2016) use the ranks as proxies for IR quality to analyze different economic consequences of IR. Although the scoring plan is more distinctive and – in the latest version – assigns scores from 0 to 10 for each Content Element and each Guiding Principle (*EY* (2015), p. 26), the published results (and the data employed by *Barth et al.* (2015) and *Martinez* (2016)) only provide the ranks or quality groups. Therefore the data remains on a rather aggregate level.

[111] While the 2013 survey uses the Content Elements of the Consultation Draft, the 2014 and 2015 versions use the Content Elements of the final International <IR> Framework.

[112] The sample regularly includes the top 100 JSE-listed companies. In a separate category, state-owned companies are also ranked.

[113] From a conceptual point of view, the quality of disclosure is sometimes considered to be immeasurable, however (*Botosan* (2004), p. 290). Section 4.3.2 briefly discusses the impacts of this issue for the data collection of this study.

Similarly, the *Chartered Secretaries Southern Africa (CSSA)* Annual Report Award also decorates firms that provide the **best annual (integrated) reports.** Established in 1956, it awards firms in different categories, based on size and listing status (e.g., top 40, mid cap, small cap, public sector firms etc.). Accounting professionals judge the reports in nine different categories of criteria (*CSSA* (2013)). In 2006 and 2007, Edgars Consolidated Stores Ltd. and Sasol were the overall winners, respectively. Group Five Limited (Group Five) and Nedbank Group Ltd. won in 2012 and 2013.[114] Here, too, only very aggregate data is provided to the public, as the *CSSA* only names the award winner, albeit in different categories. This provides a benchmark for best practice in reporting, but hardly allows distinguished comparisons between firms.

A third ranking of South African firms' reporting is *Nkonki Inc.'s* (2011; 2012; 2013; 2014; 2015) "Top 100 JSE Listed Companies IR Awards". For five consecutive years (financial years 2010-2014), the South African accounting firm has reviewed the Top 100 firms listed on the JSE (by market capitalization) in terms of their reporting, evaluating the annual reports against the requirements of the King III Code, the JSE Listings Requirements and the IRCSA DP, but also against IIRC guidance. While the latest version of the **award** concentrates on IR and on the IR Framework requirements, earlier versions assessed IR usage as a section in a catalogue of various other criteria. The criteria to rate IR base upon the Guiding Principles, the Content Elements and the Fundamental Concepts, in addition to considering special matters. Although the changes in the scoring mechanism over the years hamper the consistency of the assessment, a positive trend in the average IR score is visible over time. The IR score increases from 46% in financial year 2011[115] to 53% in 2012 and 59% in 2013, the (overall) score for financial year 2014 being 62%. More than 80% of the firms score between 50% and 79% in 2013, coming from 45% in 2011. In line with these developments, an increasing percentage of firms (from 66% in 2011 to 88% and 87% in 2013 and 2014, respectively) uses the term "integrated" in the title of their reports. The latest version shows an established application of almost all Guiding Principles in financial year 2014. All principles have average scores of at least 69%, the only exception being Conciseness, which had a mean of 54%. The Content Elements overall show an average score of 72% in financial year 2014. Throughout the years, Sasol and PPC Limited (PPC) are firms that regularly occur in the top 10 ranks. PPC is also the winner in the ranking for year 2012, with Exxaro Resources Limited placing first in year 2013. Besides the flaws in terms of consistency, Nkonki Inc.'s award and the two aforementioned rankings also suffer from the shortcomings outlined for the reviews made by accounting firms. In particular, this includes potential biases in data collection due to inconsistencies or due to conflicting interests.

Makiwane/Padia (2013) **compare the level of reporting** in South African reports "*as far as integrated reporting is concerned*" (*Makiwane/Padia* (2013), p. 427) **pre and post the release of King III.** They use a sample of 92 listed firms, assigning reporting scores to the respective reports based on content analysis. Their indicators stem from the King Report and the

[114] Cf. http://www.chartsec.co.za/index.php?option=com_content&view=article&id=257&Itemid=344 (last accessed on 29 August 2016) for an overview of all award winners over the years.

[115] The average IR score in 2010 was 56.4%, but referred to the Top 40 firms, only.

GRI 3.1 requirements. The results show improvements in many indicators between the pre-King III base year 2009 and the first post-King III year (2010/2011), in particular in the indicators from the King III "Integrated Reporting" category. Especially firms that label their report "integrated" show large differences compared with those that do not. Moreover, a detailed analysis in terms of the IR components reveals that larger percentages of companies provide a high degree of detail on these components in the post-King III period compared with the pre-King III year. While the comparison of pre- and post-King III implementation yields fruitful insights, the measurement of IR via the indicators from the King Report and the GRI are not necessarily representative of the understanding of IR, as these guidance documents take a stakeholder-oriented and ESG reporting perspective.

For a sample comprising the top 40 JSE-listed firms, *Marx/Mohammadali-Haji* (2014) **analyze the IR practice**, using a content analysis of the firms' annual (integrated) reports[116] and their website reporting. The disclosure checklist bases upon literature and a discussion with experts. While the findings reveal that almost 80% of the sample firms do not explain their materiality determination and almost 90% do not describe their capitals, the study also shows that two thirds of the firms explicitly name the basis on which they prepare the report. However, 60% do not identify a body with oversight responsibilities for IR and no firm has any form of assurance provided for their report. 90% of the firms use a clear language. Regarding the different contents, almost all companies explain their business model and value creation as well as the circumstances of their operations. While more than 80% provide key risks, less than 40% explain key opportunities. Similarly, only 30% name strategic objectives, but 70% explain their strategies. Almost all firms describe their governance structures, but only 40% relate them to their objectives, risk management and remuneration approach. In contrast, 80% report their performance against their strategies. In terms of an outlook, almost 90% of the firms explain likely opportunities, risks and challenges, but merely 30% derive the implications from these for the strategy and future performance. As in the studies discussed above, the mainly **content-oriented** disclosure catalogue seems debatable in so far as a focus of data collection on the Guiding Principles might be more fruitful to capture the nature of IR. The results only allow indirect conclusions on the Guiding Principles, by relating the findings on the contents to the different principles, such as Connectivity, Strategic Focus or Reliability/Balance. As these principles constitute a centerpiece of IR (see chapter 2), a more direct reflection of the Guiding Principles in the analysis of the reports might characterize IR better.

Similar to *Makiwane/Padia* (2013), *Setia et al.* (2015) compare the reporting practice of the South African firms before the release of King III (using reports from 2009/2010) and after this introduction (using reports from 2011/2012). Unlike the former paper, they base their content analysis on a coding scheme derived from IIRC guidance. It comprises 37 items that deal with the **disclosures on four different capitals**: human (eight items), natural (three items) social and relationship (17 items) and intellectual capital (nine items). The sample consists of the 25 top JSE-listed companies. The study finds a significant increase in social and relationship capital disclosures from the pre to the post-King III period, but

[116] The authors analyze the firms' most recent report at the time of inspection, i.e. March 2013 (*Marx/Mohammadali-Haji* (2014), p. 239).

not in the disclosures on the other capitals.[117] Moreover, the results show the largest increase in disclosures for firms with a below-average disclosure level before the King III introduction. From this finding, the authors derive a decrease in the dispersion of disclosures induced by IR regulation. Overall, however, 10 out of 25 firms reduce (or do not change) the level of disclosures from 2009/2010 to 2011/2012. IR takes a broader perspective on capitals compared to traditional reporting, which is a substantial distinctive feature of this reporting format. Nonetheless, the concept of capitals might not be a fruitful basis for content analysis. At least, it requires a careful interpretation, as the use of the different capitals and thus also the disclosures per definition depend on the firm's business model. So these disclosures are not necessarily comparable across different firms.[118]

A study conducted by *Clayton et al.* (2015) also analyzes the reporting practice of South African firms over time, with a focus on the change from King II to King III. The authors examine the reports of eight JSE-listed firms from 2008 to 2013. The results show that both the number of reports with an integrated structure and the number of reports labelled "integrated" grow over time. Besides, the reports become more stakeholder oriented and show an increase in both the quantification and assurance of non-financial issues. With non-financial information being integrated to a higher degree, the reports also yield more repetitions. Overall, the authors consider IR rather as a **compliance exercise** than an improvement of communication. The low number of sample firms prevents statistically valid inferences, though.

Zhou et al. (2016) present **IR scores** that depict the alignment of the firm's report with the PF IR. The authors derive the scores from a self-developed disclosure catalogue based on this preliminary version of the Framework, with 31 items across eight dimensions, each scored with 0 or 1 point. For a sample of 443 firm-year observations from 132 unique JSE-listed companies with fiscal years ending between 2009 and 2012, they find a median score (mean; standard deviation) of 5 (6; 4), with 0.25 being the minimum and 18 the maximum score reached, respectively. In relation to the maximum possible score of 31 points, this equals percentages of 17% (20%) for the median (mean) as well as 1% and 58% for the minimum and maximum. The study further builds a **connectivity sub-score** from the components that reflect the Connectivity principle. The mean connectivity score (for a reduced sample with 430 observations) is 2 out of 31 (equaling 5%), whereas the minimum is 0 and the maximum 6 (19%). Due to various validations, most notably an investor survey that confirms the importance of the components used, the score shows a high degree of reliability. However, the study does not report all single components of the score with their results so that the descriptive information remains on a somewhat aggregated level.

Another study with a South African sample is *Lee/Yeo* (2016). This sample comprises 822 firm-year observations of JSE-listed firms for the period 2010-2013. The IR score bases upon the eight **Content Elements** of the final IIRC Framework. Five questions per Content Element assess the quality of IR disclosures, each of which yields a score from 0 to 5. Hence, the score ranges between 0 and 200. Overall, the mean (median) score is 93 (84),

[117] While disclosures on natural capital also increase by 19%, the difference is not significant due to the low number of items on this category, however.

[118] A comparison of the same firm over time seems less problematic, though.

with a standard deviation of 35. The study does not provide detailed data on the single Content Elements. Moreover, as mentioned before, a data collection that bases upon the Guiding Principles would be more representative of the idea of IR. For instance, conclusions about the connectivity, conciseness or future orientation of the reports under examination are not possible with these findings.

In addition to this large number of studies from South Africa, *Lipunga* (2015) examines the role of IR in the developing African country **Malawi**. The study draws on the annual reports for financial year 2013 of twelve listed firms at the Malawi Stock Exchange. Basing upon a mainly content-oriented disclosure checklist, *Lipunga* finds an IR index score of 0.43 (ranging from 0 to 1). Again, both the small sample size and the reflection of the contents rather than the principles of IR hampers the soundness of the inferences.

International

While the aforementioned literature mainly analyzes the disclosure practice in single countries (referencing comparative values from other countries at some points), *Wild/Van Staden* (2013) use an international sample of 58 firms participating in the IIRC Pilot Programme, with their reports published as at January 2013. The study provides the number and percentage of companies that address the different Guiding Principles, Content Elements and capitals described in the IIRC's DP IR and PF IR. Regarding the **Guiding Principles**, they find that Strategic Focus is the principle that most firms address (76%), while Stakeholder Responsiveness is the one with least addressing firms (33%). Roughly between 40% and 60% of the companies in the sample respond to the Future Orientation, Conciseness/Reliability/Materiality and Connectivity of Information principle, respectively. In terms of the **Content Elements**, only 5% report on each Governance/Remuneration and Future Outlook. 21% provide disclosures on Performance, 33% on Operating Context, 43% on Organizational Overview and 45% on Strategic Objectives. More than half of the companies (57%) address only one Content Element. The firms in *Wild/Van Staden's* (2013) sample use many of the different **capitals** to a high degree. Not surprisingly, nearly 90% of the sample firms use financial capital, but almost as many firms report on human, natural or social capital. Around 40% provide disclosures on intellectual or manufactured capital. With 80% using four or more of the six different capitals, the broad idea of capitals that IR entails seems to be familiar among the early adopters, already. While the study covers the capitals, Guiding Principles and Content Elements, it only delivers limited insight into each of these dimensions, as it considers each element as a binary variable. Moreover, the international sample yields a broader perspective than studies focusing on a single country, but the small number of companies from each country does not allow statistically valid conclusions on the respective countries and their differences. In a similar vein, the fact that all companies are participants of the Pilot Programme may prohibit conclusions for firms that are not voluntary early adopters of IR.

Using a larger sample of 2,000 firms from around the world (listed on the S&P Global Broad Market Index), *Churet/Eccles* (2014) examine the presence of IR in the firms' 2011 and 2012 annual reports. The study draws on evidence for IR from the RobecoSAM database. This database particularly refers to examples of sustainability indicators impacting financial performance, which represents a specific feature of the **connectivity of information**. The findings reveal that only 12% of the firms provide at least one connecting indicator in their 2012 report. This means a 50% increase compared to the 8% with at least one such indicator in 2011, however. For the most part, the respective examples refer to cost savings or additional revenue caused by environmental initiatives, in particular energy consumption issues. As mentioned above, the use of database data may lead to a less accurate picture of IR than hand-collected data. Moreover, the focus on the connecting indicators only gives insight on a singular aspect of IR rather than a complete picture, even though connectivity constitutes a central feature of the reporting format.

Mio/Fasan (2014) focus on **disclosures about materiality**. For financial year 2012, the study analyzes the annual reports of 65 companies from the IIRC Pilot Programme, thus using a similar sample as *Wild/Van Staden* (2013). The results show that the firms refer to words like "material" or "materiality" 0.41 times per 100 words at the maximum. The mean relevance score, which documents the intensity of materiality disclosures throughout the report, is 1.5 (out of a possible 5). In addition to facing the mentioned bias resulting from the voluntary participation in the Pilot Programme, these findings only provide a narrow detail of IR by concentrating on the materiality disclosures.

Another study that analyzes IR practice on an international level is *Eccles et al.* (2015).The authors examine the reports of 100 firms from different countries, sourced from the GRI Sustainability Disclosure Database, in addition to the largest 24 South African firms. To assess the quality of IR, the study uses a score that bases upon 20 factors, yielding 0 to 3 points each. The factors stem from the CD IR and represent the seven Content Elements of the CD IR, the six capitals and seven special factors, which largely cover the Guiding Principles. Across all **capitals**, the average score is 2.0, with little variation between the capitals. Only manufactured (1.83) and intellectual (1.93) capital show scores below 2.0. South African companies have a higher mean (2.29) than the international firms (1.98). Similarly, South African firms score higher on average (2.35) than the international firms (2.06) across the **Content Elements**, while the overall mean in this regard is 2.1. Except Outlook, all elements yield average scores that exceed 2.0. For the special factors, the scores are substantially lower in total, signaling that the **Guiding Principles** are more challenging to adhere to than the other aspects. The spread between South African and other firms is larger, here. While the overall mean is 1.68, South African firms score 2.09 on average, non-South African firms 1.58. This large spread is also visible in various single factors, such as the connectivity of information (2.33 compared with 1.62). In the depiction of stakeholder engagement, there was hardly a difference (1.79 and 1.74, respectively). Although these comparisons give an impression of the differences in the reporting practice between South Africa and other countries, they do not allow statistically meaningful inferences, especially not between two particular countries. Moreover, the results are once more biased by the selection of companies only from the Pilot Programme.

Also drawing on a sample from the IIRC Pilot Programme, *Havlová* (2015b) analyzes the reports of 48 firms from different countries for financial years 2010 to 2014, covering a period beginning before and ending after the firms' entry to the program. The study finds a reduction in the number and length of reports over time. Besides, the examined firms show an increase in their use of information technology, publishing more interactive reports over the years. In terms of **adopting the IIRC's requirements**, *Havlová* also finds a strong increase of her rating. While 16 companies show full adoption of the requirements in 2010, 37 of the 48 sample firms fully adopt the IIRC's requirements in 2014, at the end of the examined period. These results remain on a general level, however, and face the aforementioned bias induced by using only Pilot Programme companies.

Employing a sample of the best 25 reports of participants in the IIRC Pilot Programme, *imug* (2015) provides an international best practice analysis of integrated reports. The study examines in how far the reports, which were released before 16 January 2015, adhere to the different **Guiding Principles** of the IIRC Framework. While Strategic Focus and Future Orientation is the principle that the highest number of companies follow, the firms show only little adherence to the Consistency and Comparability principle as well as to Connectivity. South African firms in the sample obey the principles to a particularly high degree. Due to the small sample size, assertions about country comparisons from this study do not yield statistically sound conclusions, though. In addition, the findings only give an impression of the best practice of IR.

For all reports available on the IIRC's website as of 31 May 2014 (n=52 after exclusions), *Melloni* (2015) examines both the content and linguistic attributes (e.g., the tone) of **intellectual capital disclosures** in IR, using a manual content analysis. In terms of the content, *Melloni* finds a focus on relational capital for the most part, and only a small degree of quantification and future-orientation. As regards the tone, the intellectual capital disclosures are more optimistic than other disclosures in the reports. However, these results only give insights to a singular feature of IR and are biased by the sample selection. All firms' are voluntary early adopters, resulting in the aforementioned problems.

As opposed to *Melloni* (2015), *Arguelles et al.* (2016) use a sample that includes a control group in addition to voluntary adopters of IR. Besides 960 firm-year observations from 357 unique firms that are voluntary early adopters of IR (either in the IIRC's Pilot Programme or self-declared), the study employs the same number of propensity-matched control observations. Like *Serafeim's* (2015) work on a US sample, *Arguelles et al.* draw on data from the Asset 4 database. From this data, the authors derive scores for four different capitals, as well as a score to depict the integrativeness of reporting, which reflects the IR Content Elements and the firm's level of integration. For all of these scores, as well as for an additional score that aggregates all of them, the early adopters show significantly higher values than the control firms. While the mean scores for all of the variables are around 60% for the early-moving firms (the financial capital score is even higher than 70%), all scores for the non-early-moving firms are between 40% and 50% on average. The study uses this data to derive implications for the value relevance of disclosures in conjunction with signaling an early movement. It is debatable whether the data depicts IR adequately, in particular for two reasons that have been outlined for other studies as well. First, the use of database data is less likely than hand-collected data to depict the intended phenomena. Second, even though the authors derive customized scores for the capitals to overcome this issue, the measures do not necessarily depict IR adequately, as they do not reflect the IR Guiding Principles. Instead, they draw on the Content Elements as well as on the capitals. Moreover, the capitals are not applicable to all firms to the same degree.

Melloni et al. (2016a) examine the **disclosures on the business model** for all reports that were available in the examples database on the IIRC website. This sample comprises 54 reports (after exclusions) on financial years 2011, 2012 and 2013, released by 51 firms from all continents, from different industries and with a different listing status. Of the business model disclosures in these reports, 43% have a positive tone, 57% are negative or neutral. 12% of the disclosures are forward-looking and 26% convey quantitative information. In terms of the topics, 41% relate to the outcomes, while the remaining 59% deal with inputs, business activities and outputs. The study uses this data to find that managers manipulate the tone of business model disclosures for impression management. As in *Melloni* (2015), the focus on a single aspect of IR and the sample selection leave doubt about the generalizability of these inferences.

Focusing on the **relation between the Conciseness and the Completeness principle**, *Melloni et al.* (2016b) investigate another specific feature of integrated reports. The study analyzes 148 annual reports on financial years 2013 and 2014 of the Pilot Programme members (74 firms). To capture the conciseness of the reports, the authors use the length of the text and the Fog Index[119], whereas an optimism index and the coverage of specific topics, for which the authors use Bloomberg ESG disclosure scores, represent the Completeness principle. On average, the reports contain more than 71,500 words, while yielding a mean Fog Index of 16, meaning that they are very difficult to read. At the same time, the optimism score is relatively high compared with other studies. The ESG scores (48 out of 100) reveal that the reports convey less than half of the disclosures expected by the Bloomberg score. From the scores and their correlations, the authors derive empirical evidence for the trade-off between the Conciseness and the Completeness principle. Like *Melloni et al.* (2016a), this study furthermore shows that firms use the examined features for impression management. However, the study suffers from the same shortcomings as the aforementioned research, preventing generalizable conclusions about IR practice: a narrow focus on particular aspects of IR and a biased sample.

Turning to a study that **compares the IR practice in two different countries**, *Müller et al.* (2016) analyze the alignment of corporate reports with IR, both in Switzerland and South Africa. The sample includes the 16 largest firms (based on market capitalization as of February 2015) listed on the Swiss Market Index and the 16 largest listed on the JSE Top 40 Index, respectively. Using content analysis that bases upon a set of 62 binary criteria reflecting the Content Elements (47 criteria) and Guiding Principles (15 criteria) from the International <IR> Framework, the authors examine the firms' annual reports on financial year 2014. For the Swiss firms, scores range from 23 points (37%) to 48 points (77%), with a mean score of 40 points (65%). Scores for South Africa are higher, reaching from 31 points (50%) to 58 points (94%) and showing an average of 51 points (82%). Despite the small sample size, the study finds these differences between the two countries to be significant. As a potential explanation, *Müller et al.* name the differences in regulatory pressure. The study rules out the influence of accounting standards and other regulations by narrowing down the score to elements only covered by IR, namely various groupings of capital and the principles of Connectivity and Future Orientation. The difference in these

119 The Fog Index is a measure of text readability. See section 4.3.2.3 for an explanation of this measure.

alternative scores between the countries is also significant. Nevertheless, unobserved pre-existing country differences may be a driver of these findings.

To analyze the quality of IR, *Pozzoli/Gesuele* (2016) examine the reports that 11 Pilot Programme firms from different countries published in 2013. The study employs content analysis, drawing on criteria that reflect the Fundamental Concepts and the Guiding Principles from the CD IR. In particular, the authors focus on the **relationship between content and length of the report.** The results reveal a lack of conciseness in the documents. Judging from the frequency of certain keywords (normalized by report length) the study finds little consideration of sustainability, environment or stakeholders, whereas keywords that relate to relationships with parties or aspects outside the firm (e.g., "link" or "network") show high frequencies. However, both the reliance on keywords to draw conclusions on the quality of IR and the small and biased sample leave room for doubt about the inferences about IR from these results.

Conclusions from extant descriptive research

An **overall analysis** of the outlined research on IR practice reveals a mixed **coverage of different countries in the literature.** Various studies, in particular reviews by accounting firms, analyze the practice in several European, Asian and Oceanian countries, while studies that deal with the IR practice in America are rare. Due to South Africa's pioneering role in terms of IR, the majority of the IR literature examines the IR practice of South African firms. The findings from the different countries show potential for improvement in several areas of the firms' reports, for instance in terms of connectivity and conciseness, or for specific contents, such as governance disclosures. Comparisons mentioned in some single-country reviews as well as the results of some international studies indicate a higher degree of IR in South African firms' reports compared to reports from other countries.

Many of these country comparisons do not allow statistically sound conclusions, however, mostly due to too small sample sizes in each country (as in *imug* (2015)). *Müller et al.* (2016) is the only study to reveal statistically significant differences (between Switzerland and South Africa). These results may be driven by pre-existing country differences, though. Moreover, various studies use samples that draw on the IIRC's Pilot Programme and are thus implicitly biased, as they only include voluntary early adopters of IR (e.g., *Havlová* (2015b)). Different issues concerning data collection represent further **flaws in the existing evidence.** First, the latter include the reliance on database data (as with *Serafeim's* (2015) main IR measure), which is less likely than a self-constructed metric to actually capture what it intends to do. Second, while the used database data does not reflect IIRC guidance, most studies base their data collection upon the Council's provisions, but not necessarily upon the final IR Framework (e.g., *Zhou et al.* (2016)). Although many of these documents are not substantially different from the Framework, this practice may yield slight dissimilarities from the IIRC's eventual idea of IR. Third, the data collection in many studies reflects the Content Elements (e.g., *Marx/Mohammadali-Haji* (2014)) so that they only give limited insight into the degree of IR. While the contents of integrated reports are not new, the Guiding Principles (e.g., Connectivity of Information or Conciseness) rather represent innovations compared to traditional reports and thus characterize IR better (see chapters 2 and 3). The data collection in other studies reflects the capitals (e.g., *Setia et al.* (2015)), which impedes a comparable application to all reports. Fourth, the numerous reviews by accounting firms (e.g., *Nkonki Inc.* (2014)) may suffer from a bias induced by different researchers as well as from the risk that the firms' or their clients' business interests implicitly drive the results. Finally, a rather general level of results presentation in some studies prevents detailed insights into IR practice (as in *Wild/Van Staden* (2013)). Hence, the extant literature leaves room for studies that allow further inferences. Figure 4-2 summarizes the analysis of the literature, including the elaborated flaws, and shows the focus of the study at hand.

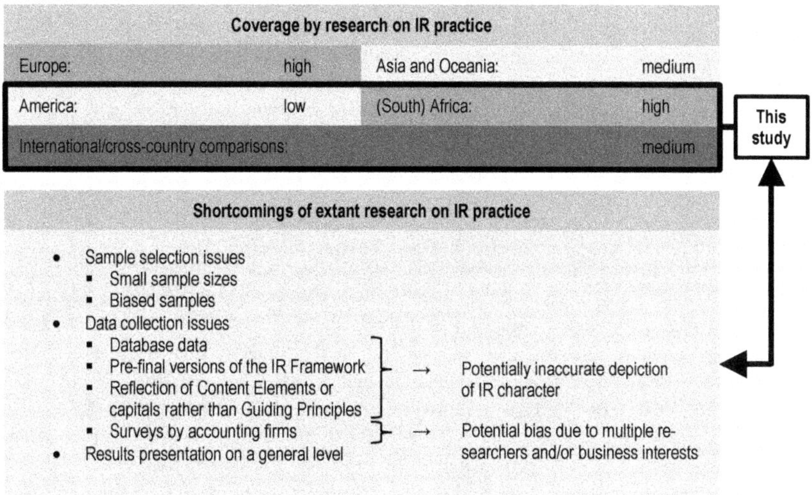

Figure 4-2: The relationship of the study at hand to extant empirical literature on IR practice

This study addresses the outlined shortcomings and aims at reducing the resulting research gap. Given the low coverage of America in the literature on IR practice, the study examines the presence of IR in US firms' reports. To put these findings into context, an analysis of the IR practice in South African reports contrasts the US results. According to the reasoning based on the regulatory situation in these countries (see chapter 3) and to the indications from the extant literature presented here, the IR practice in South Africa and the USA may differ not only in the coverage by extant literature, but also in the presence of IR in firms' reporting practice. While the examination of the South African reports supplements existing studies, the cross-country comparison addresses the lack of sound conclusions on country differences. In addition, an analysis at two different points in time allows a comparison of the pre- and post-King III status in South Africa and a comparison between the two countries at both these points in time. The balanced panel design makes it possible to use a difference-in-differences approach. Compared with one-dimensional comparisons this approach is more likely to produce results that can be ascribed to the change of regulation in

South Africa (King III). Moreover, the research design takes the flaws of the existing studies into account. In addition to employing a sample size that allows statistically valid inferences, the study uses a self-constructed measure that reflects the Guiding Principles of the final IR Framework. Thereby it intends to capture the idea of IR and to ensure a comparable applicability to all reports. The results are presented on a detailed level. Section 4.3 provides an in depth presentation of the research design for this descriptive study.

4.2 Theory and hypotheses development

This section presents theoretical approaches that intend to explain why a firm's management may choose to provide certain disclosures, in particular why it may use IR. After introducing Principal Agent Theory, the section describes Positive Accounting Theory (PAT) and different systems-oriented theories, specifically Legitimacy Theory, Stakeholder Theory and Institutional Theory. In conjunction with the differences between the South African and the US reporting environment and the development of the two reporting regimes over time as described in chapter 3, these theories build the foundation to derive hypotheses on differences in the use of IR.

4.2.1 Principal Agent Theory

Principal Agent Theory[120] (*Jensen/Meckling* (1976)), being part of the new institutional economics[121], describes the relationship between two parties, one of which – the principal – engages the other – the agent – to carry out work in his or her name (*Eisenhardt* (1989), p. 58). The contract on this engagement, which includes the delegation of decision-making authority from the principal to the agent, is called "**agency relationship**" (*Jensen/Meckling* (1976), p. 308). However, presumably information asymmetries and partially conflicting objectives exist between the two parties (*Spremann* (1990), pp. 562-563; *Pfaff/Zweifel* (1998), p. 184). In the relationship between a firm's owners (principals) and managers (agents)[122], the managers might pursue the objective of maximizing their personal compensation or power (empire building), while shareholders are interested in maximizing shareholder return (i.e., stock value and dividends). Management is better informed due to their participation in the daily business activities, which leaves room for discretion and opportunistic behavior (*Ross* (1973)).

This constellation thus gives rise to **agency problems**. Before the conclusion of the contract, the principal may have difficulties to assess the quality of the agent's services (**hidden characteristics**) (*Spremann* (1987), p. 11; *Picot* (1991), p. 152). In turn, the principal will only be willing to pay an average compensation (*Horsch* (2005), p. 86), which may cause agents with quality above average to cease to offer. This "adverse selection" problem continuously reduces the average compensation as well as the service quality, and eventually leads to a market breakdown (*Akerlof* (1970)). In addition, principals could be subject to moral hazard of two different types (*Arrow* (1985), p. 38). After contract conclusion, agents might

[120] This reasoning bases upon the positive rather than the normative branch of Principal Agent Theory.

[121] Cf. *Furubotn/Richter* (2005) for an overview of new institutional economics theories.

[122] Other agency relationships can be found between employer and employee, citizen and state, voters and politicians, patient and doctor (*Nienhaus* (2015), p. 58).

engage in **hidden actions** (*Hartmann-Wendels* (1989), p. 714). They could use the firm's resources for their own purposes (consumption on the job) or reduce their efforts (shirking), which is unobservable for the principals (*Decker* (1994), p. 20). Moreover, due to **hidden information**, the principals cannot assess if all of the agents' actions are beneficial to the principals or if they happen for the purpose of self-maximization (fringe benefits), although they may be able to observe the actions as such (*Stiglitz/Weiss* (1981), pp. 393-398; *Arrow* (1985), pp. 38-39).

These problems lead to **agency costs** (*Jensen/Meckling* (1976), p. 308). The principals may align the agents' action with their own interest by harmonizing the objectives (e.g., through incentive payments) or by reducing information asymmetries (e.g., by signaling or reporting), which gives rise to **bonding costs.** Principals could also supervise the agents' actions, which causes **monitoring costs.** Since a complete alignment of interests is not possible, however, the principals will in most cases face a reduction in their welfare, the so-called "**residual loss**". The sum of these three components amounts to the agency costs.

Both parties are able to mitigate agency problems. Principals, on the one hand, can reduce information asymmetries before the conclusion of the contract by carefully observing the agents' behavior (**screening**) (*Stiglitz* (1975)) and by supervising the agents after contract conclusion (**monitoring**) (*Göbel* (2002), p. 112). On the other hand, the agents can avoid a hidden characteristics problem by **signaling** their characteristics before the conclusion of the contract (*Spence* (1973), p. 357). After signing the contract, they may report their actions on a regular basis, which yields transparency (**reporting**) (*Spence* (1973), p. 355). Table 4-1 presents the different agency problems and their potential solutions.

Agency problems and possible mitigations				
Appearance	**Problem**	**Issue**	**Possible solutions**	
			Principal	**Agent**
Before contract	Hidden characteristics	Adverse selection	Screening	Signaling
After contract	Hidden action	Shirking, consumption on the job	Monitoring	Reporting
	Hidden information	Fringe benefits		

Table 4-1: Overview of agency problems and their possible mitigations (based on *Göbel* (2002), pp. 100, 110)

Corporate reporting in general and **IR** in particular represent means for managers (agents) **to tackle agency problems by reducing information asymmetries.** In terms of signaling, managers can indicate to future investors (principals), which have not yet concluded a contract with the firm, that the firm is a quality investment. Moreover, managers can confirm current investors in the quality of the investment through IR. The latter practice represents the agent's reporting after the conclusion of the contract.

4.2.2 Positive Accounting Theory

PAT, which is closely related to Principal Agent Theory, aims at providing explanations and predictions about the use of accounting methods by particular firms (*Watts/Zimmerman* (1986), p. 7). It deals with various relationships between parties involved in providing resources to an organization, many of which are agency relationships. The firm itself is then defined as a **nexus of different contracts** between these parties (*Smith/Watts* (1983), p. 3, as cited in *Deegan/Unerman* (2011), p. 265). As in Principal Agent Theory, the central assumption of PAT is that all **individuals are driven by self-interest** and therefore act opportunistically as long as it increases their personal wealth (*Deegan/Unerman* (2011), p. 256). Work within PAT mainly relies on three essential hypotheses, the bonus hypothesis, the debt hypothesis and the political cost hypothesis (Figure 4-3).

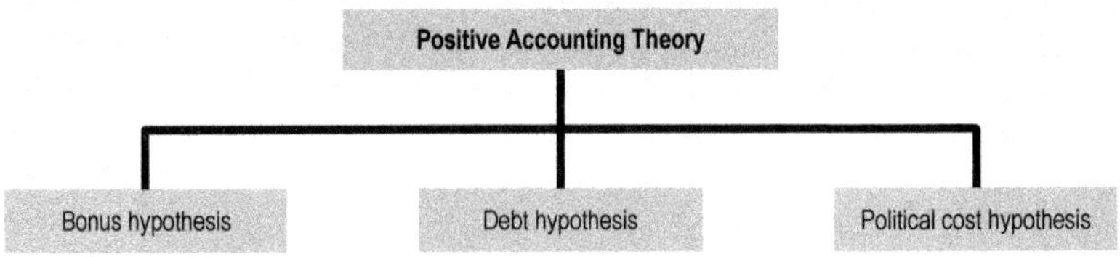

Figure 4-3: Three hypotheses of Positive Accounting Theory

The **bonus hypothesis** predicts that – consistent with the concept of bonding to reduce agency costs – firms remunerate their managers with variable compensation that aligns their interests with the owners' interests, i.e. bonuses that are typically tied to the firm's performance (*Deegan/Unerman* (2011), p. 277). This results in an incentive for managers to present the firm's performance in an optimistic way in order to increase their personal remuneration (*Healy* (1985)). Moreover, changes in accounting or reporting methods, like the introduction of new accounting standards or new reporting guidance like the IIRC Framework, may also influence the managers' bonuses if they affect the underlying presentation of performance. The direction of the change may thus be a predictor of whether or not a firm implements a new method (*Deegan/Unerman* (2011), p. 279).

According to the **debt hypothesis**, debt contracting may influence a firm's accounting and reporting in two ways. Considering the link between managers (agents) and providers of debt capital (principals) as an agency relationship, the principals put in place a mechanism to align the interests of the two parties in order to reduce agency costs. Facing the one-sided risk[123] of credit default, lenders want the firm not to undertake risky activities or pay excessive dividends. As an alternative to an explicit agreement on such behavior, the use of covenants on accounting and reporting methods may lead to their desired results. For instance, they could require the firm to use conservative accounting methods to reach their objectives (*Zhang* (2008), pp. 29-31). There is also an effect in the opposite direction. If managers

123 While lenders are exposed to the risk of non-payment of their receivable in case of a weak firm performance, they do not participate in increasing profits when the performance is good.

face the threat of covenant violation, they have an incentive to present the firm's performance in the most positive light possible to avoid technical default.

The **political cost hypothesis** refers to the relationship between a firm and outside parties like governments, unions or other interest groups. Even without a direct contractual connection to the firm, these groups may influence the distribution of wealth for managers and firm owners by changes in taxes, subsidies, regulations or by other political costs, e.g. wage increases (*Watts/Zimmerman* (1978), pp. 115-116). *Watts/Zimmerman* (1978) argue that large firms (p. 115) and firms from politically sensitive industries like the oil industry (p. 121) are particularly exposed to such influences. Firms may react to these political intrusions by using accounting methods that reduce earnings or by presenting themselves in a way that prevents political interference and the associated costs (*Watts/Zimmerman* (1978), pp. 115-121). Showing awareness for the ESG impacts of the firm's activities and demonstrating the consideration of this issue in managing the firm can be such a way of presentation. Hence, exposure to political pressures may predict the use of IR.

4.2.3 Systems-oriented theories

Similar to PAT, the purpose of systems-oriented theories is to explain why a firm provides certain information. These theories take the view that an **organization and the society** in which it operates constitute a **system of mutual influences** (*Deegan/Unerman* (2011), p. 321). A systems-oriented perspective analyzes the role of information and disclosures between the firm and society (or particular groups in society) (*Gray et al.* (1996), p. 45). Systems-oriented theories comprise Legitimacy Theory, Stakeholder Theory and Institutional Theory (Figure 4-4).

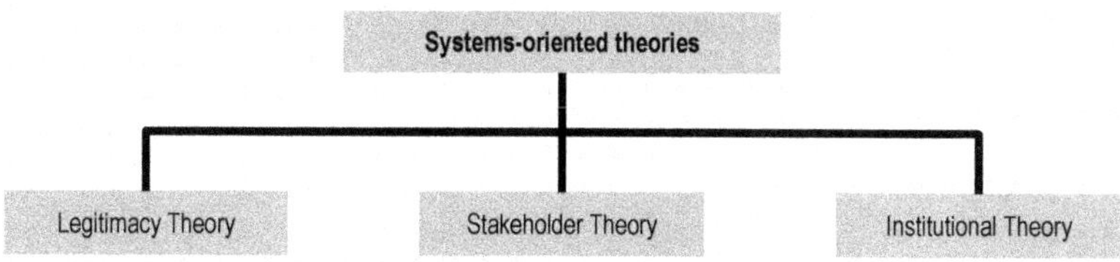

Figure 4-4: Overview of systems-oriented theories

Legitimacy Theory assumes that there is a "*social contract*" between the organization and the society (*Shocker/Sethi* (1973), p. 97), which represents the implicit and explicit expectations of society to the organization's conduct of operations (*Deegan/Unerman* (2011), p. 325). While these expectations traditionally merely comprised profit maximization (e.g., *Ramanathan* (1976), p. 516), they changed over time so that organizations nowadays are also expected to take into account the environmental, human and other social consequences of their business activities (*Heard/Bolce* (1981)). To be considered legitimate, the organization has to act within these societal bounds and norms (*Deegan/Unerman* (2011), p. 323). Therefore, legitimacy is thus a resource that the firm depends on if it wants to survive (*Dowling/Pfeffer* (1975); *O'Donovan* (2002)). It is the perception of the firm's legitimacy by society that is of particular importance, though (*Suchman* (1995), p. 574). The organization can influence this resource, e.g. by disclosure-related strategies (*Woodward et al.* (1996)). Using IR, which connects – among other aspects – the different capitals and thus integrates the financial, social and environmental perspective, may be such a strategy.

Although different in particular aspects (e.g., *Näsi et al.* (1997), p. 296), **Stakeholder Theory**[124] is closely related to and somewhat overlapping with Legitimacy Theory (*Gray et al.* (1995), p. 52). Due to the different views that the diverse groups of stakeholders have, it considers an organization to have various social contracts with each of these stakeholder groups rather than one contract with society as such (*Deegan/Unerman* (2011), p. 348). The ethical or moral ("normative") branch of Stakeholder Theory states that all stakeholders have certain minimum rights that the organization must grant them, based on the fact that the organization influences their lives (*Deegan/Unerman* (2011), p. 349). These rights include being informed about how they are impacted by the firm (*O'Dwyer* (2005)), which is also in line with the concept of a firm's accountability (*Gray et al.* (1996), p. 38). Thus, a firm is responsible to report on its activities and their impacts on stakeholders. As opposed to this, the managerial branch of Stakeholder Theory is more organization-centered (*Gray et al.* (1996), p. 46). The firm manages its stakeholders (*Deegan/Unerman* (2011), p. 353) so that the power of a stakeholder group (*Ullmann* (1985), p. 2) determines in how far the firm addresses the group's demands (*Näsi et al.* (1997)). Disclosures in annual (integrated) reports or other communications are thus an element for the firm to manage its stakeholders, e.g. to influence their support or approval.

Institutional Theory to a certain degree also relates to Legitimacy Theory and Stakeholder Theory. It provides explanations why organizations in comparable environments take on similar characteristics (*Larrinaga-González* (2007)). Conforming to institutional pressures for change may reward the organizations with an increase in legitimacy (*Meyer/Rowan* (1977)). *DiMaggio/Powell* ((1983), p. 149) define the "*constraining process that forces a unit in a population to resemble other units that face the same set of environmental conditions*" as "*isomorphism*". They distinguish between three different forms. "Coercive isomorphism" is induced by powerful stakeholders on which the firm depends, as they put formal or informal pressure on the company to change its practices according to the manner they desire (*DiMaggio/Powell* (1983), p. 150). Instead, "mimetic isomorphism" results from the organization's uncertainty about the institutional practices of competing organizations, which may encourage the firm to imitate or improve the practice of its contestants to gain a competitive advantage or avoid a disadvantage (*DiMaggio/Powell* (1983), p. 151). The third form is "normative isomorphism". It refers to the pressures that group norms – in particular, professionalization – impose on an individual or an organization to adopt certain practices (*DiMaggio/Powell* (1983), p. 152), e.g. the preparation of reports that comply with reporting standards or guidance like the International <IR> Framework.

[124] The term "Stakeholder Theory" may be misleading, as it refers to different theories from various fields (*Hasnas* (1998), pp. 25-26). Instead, it can rather be considered an umbrella term for a variety of theories on different aspects of the relationship between a firm and its stakeholders, e.g. stakeholders' rights or their power (*Deegan/Unerman* (2011), p. 348).

4.2.4 Hypotheses development

Building on this theoretical basis and on the differences between the South African and the US reporting environment described in chapter 3, a set of hypotheses regarding the reporting practice in the two countries ($H_{1.1}$-$H_{1.4}$) can be derived. The hypotheses deal with the **degree of IR in firms' reports** in both countries, interpreting this degree not in terms of compliance with IR guidance, but in terms of the alignment with the Guiding Principles from the International <IR> Framework, irrespective of whether the reports actually abide by IIRC guidance materials[125] or not.[126] This allows an assessment of the question in how far the idea of IR is implemented in the reports. While the first two hypotheses ($H_{1.1}$ and $H_{1.2}$) deal with comparisons between the two countries at two different points in time, the other two ($H_{1.3}$ and $H_{1.4}$) deal with comparisons between the situations at these two points in time for each country.

South African firms that are listed on the JSE are required to report on their extent of application of the King Code and need to explain every instance of non-application in their annual report (Paragraph 8.63(a) of the JSE Listings Requirements). In 2012, this provision related to King III, which was applicable starting from March 2010. King III, in turn, requires firms to **apply IR or explain why they do not** (King III Report, Introduction and background, recital 13 (pp. 17-18)). As the International <IR> Framework had not been issued at that time, guidance on IR was provided by the Consultation Draft (or prior versions) of the IIRC Framework or from the IRCSA discussion paper. Both are similar to the IIRC's final Framework to a remarkable degree, though. In the US, there was no requirement to use IR.

Even though the use of IR is not a mandatory requirement (e.g., JSE LR, Annexure 2, No. 3), the apply-or-explain principle can be expected to put pressure on South African firms. According to the theoretical approaches outlined in the previous sections, there can be several **drivers for firms to use IR**. In line with Principal Agent Theory, firms can use IR to reduce information asymmetries with investors and thus reduce agency costs. Firms may also use IR if it allows them to present the company's condition according to management's preferences, following the bonus and debt hypothesis of PAT. Moreover, applying IR can be a means to prevent more serious political intrusions like a mandatory reporting requirement or laws that intervene the firm's actual operations, in line with the political cost hypothesis of PAT. Various aspects of IR, including future orientation, the connectivity of quantitative and qualitative information or the broad definition of capitals, allow managers discretion in presenting the firm's situation. Arguing that the society or certain stakeholder groups (in particular investors) may expect the firm to issue an integrated report would also explain an application from a Legitimacy and Stakeholder Theory point of view. In terms of Institutional Theory, expectations from stakeholders would lead to coercive isomorphism and thus to an application of IR, too. Arguing with pressure created by competitors that apply IR or by IR being a professional norm, firms may also apply IR as a form

---

[125] When the sample firms released the reports under examination, the final International <IR> Framework had not been issued, yet. So the firms may have used guidance from previous versions of the Framework. Cf. *Eccles et al.* (2015), p. 192, for a similar approach.

[126] Section 4.3 describes the measure in detail.

of mimetic or normative isomorphism, respectively. While these arguments may also be valid for US firms, the apply-or-explain principle can be expected to strongly promote them for South African firms. The pressure on US firms will probably be substantially weaker. Therefore, a country comparison for the year 2012 presumably yields a clear difference in reporting practice in such a way that South African reports have a higher degree of IR than US reports:

$H_{1.1}$	*South African firms practice IR to a higher degree than US firms in financial year 2012.*

In 2006, King III had not yet been released. Instead, King II was applicable for JSE-listed companies on a comply-or-explain basis at that point in time (King II Code, par. 1.1.1; JSE LR, par. 8.63 (a)). Various principles in **King II** relate to requirements that are also covered by IR.[127] Like in 2012, there was no comparable reporting framework with a similar compliance requirement in the USA. In a similar vein as outlined above, the arguments from Principal Agent Theory, from the three PAT hypotheses and from the three systems-oriented theories can therefore also be used for the application of the King II principles in 2006. However, the reasoning as regards IR holds to a somewhat lower degree, since the overlap of the International <IR> Framework with its own draft version and with the IRCSA Framework is larger than the overlap with the King II principles. Nonetheless, South African firms can be expected to have a higher degree of IR in their 2006 reports than US firms:

$H_{1.2}$	*South African firms practice IR to a higher degree than US firms in financial year 2006.*

Turning to a comparison over time in each country, the respective anticipations base on a similar reasoning as mentioned above. Between 2006 and 2012, both King III, which introduced the requirements for South African firms to release integrated reports, and various **guidance documents for IR** were published. The latter included the IRCSA Framework (in 2011) and the IIRC guidance documents from the Discussion Paper (in 2011) to the Consultation Draft of the Framework (in 2012). Hence, compared with the reporting guidance existing in 2006, guidance in 2012 was closer to the final IIRC Framework.[128] The incentives and the pressure to apply the respective King Code for each year, as argued by the theoretical reasoning above, were presumably similar at both points in time, since both codes required an explanation for non-compliance or deviation from the requirements.[129]

[127] For instance, like the International <IR> Framework, King II uses the concept of different capitals that drive value creation (King II Report, section 4, chapter 1, recital 12 (p. 95)) or puts focus on stakeholder relations (section 4, chapter 2 (pp. 97-101)). King II uses the term "*Integrated Sustainability Reporting*" (section 4 (p. 91-124)) in this regard.

[128] In addition, the required form of reporting was explicitly named IR in 2012. The name is of minor relevance for the purpose of this study, however, since the examination aims at the adherence to the spirit of IR (*Eccles/Krzus* (2015), p. 11) rather than at compliance with the actual concept and name, as mentioned before.

[129] *Clayton et al.* ((2015), p. 13) also document that the drivers of the firms' reporting under King II and King III were similar.

Besides, by practicing IR (since 2010) or related reporting (before 2010) for several years, the firms may have gained experience and proficiency in using IR or may even have embedded integrated thinking, possibly resulting in an increased degree of IR in the firms' reports (in line with professional isomorphism). In summary, the already high likelihood of using King guidance is unchanged but the guidance is closer to the final IR Framework and thus to this study's IR measure and firms are probably more proficient in terms of IR. Therefore, it is plausible to expect a higher degree of IR in South African reports in 2012 compared with 2006:

$H_{1.3}$	*South African firms practice IR to a higher degree in financial year 2012 than in financial year 2006.*

In the USA, there was no apply-or-explain principle for any reporting guidance similar to IR in either of the two years under examination. US firms were not exposed to each of the South African King Codes, which in turn could have approximated them to IIRC guidance. However, some regulations and guidance emerged between 2006 and 2012 that affected US reports in terms of IR features. In particular, the requirements for reporting on mine safety and on license payments by oil and gas industries, introduced by the Dodd-Frank reforms in 2009 (Public Law 111-203), as well as SEC guidance on reporting on climate change from 2010 (SEC Release 33-9106 (2010)) include contents that IR covers, too. The former two requirements only affect very specific aspects in particular industries, though, and observers find that the vast majority of public US firms ignore the SEC requirements to report on climate change (*Hirji* (2013)). Moreover, due to fear of litigation, many US firms still avoid making voluntary disclosures, such as those required by the International <IR> Framework ((e.g., *AICPA* (2014), p. 3). Thus, despite emerging guidance that aligned the recommended reporting closer to this study's IR measure, the **low exposure to this guidance** arguably remains largely unchanged and does not lead to a substantial increase in the small probability of IR usage. Hence, as opposed to the South African situation, no change in the use of IR is anticipated for US firms:

$H_{1.4}$	*US firms practice IR to an unchanged degree in financial year 2012 compared with financial year 2006.*

Figure 4-5 summarizes and illustrates the four hypotheses. They are tested in the descriptive analysis of this study, as described in the following sections.

4.3 Methodology

This section presents the methodology of the descriptive study, including the sample and the data collection. The variable of interest represents the degree of IR in a firm's report, measured by the adherence to the seven IR Guiding Principles.

In line with the IIRC's definition of an integrated report and with the idea of "*an organization's primary reporting vehicle*" (DP IR, p. 2), this **analysis draws on the firms' principal report** to analyze in how far it adheres to the idea of IR. All three options how the report can relate to the firms' other communications outlined in section 2.3.1, namely the embedment in an existing report, the (narrow form of the) One Report approach and the Octopus Model, consider the integrated report as (a part of) a single report. So rather than looking at the entire spectrum of a firm's communications, including sustainability reports, governance reports, website disclosures etc., this study focuses on the company's principal document.[130] Usually this communication is the firm's annual report, integrated report or a document with a similar title.[131] For comparability purposes, all reports are required to include a letter from the chairman and/or CEO, the accounts and a management report or similar narrative review.

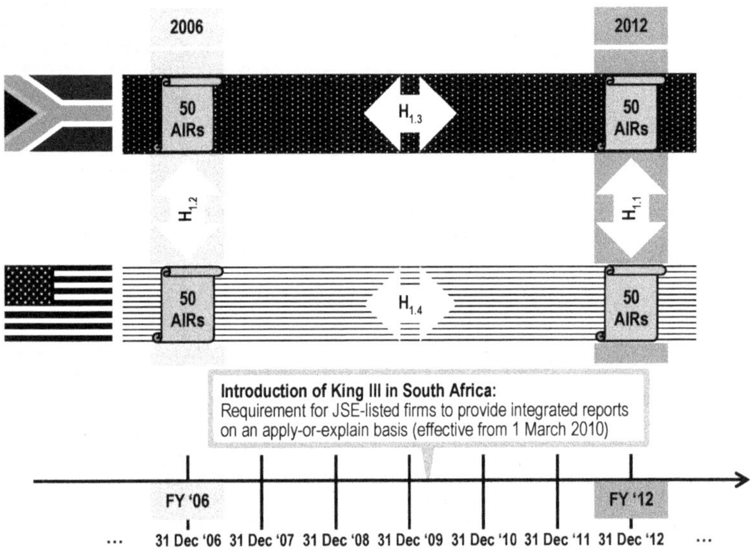

Figure 4-5: Setting of the study

4.3.1 Sample

The sample covers 50 South African and 50 US firms. For each company, the reports for two financial years are examined, resulting in a **balanced panel** with 200 firm-year observations (n=200) in total.

---

[130] Cf. *Churet/Eccles* ((2014), p. 10) for a similar approach. Looking at the entire spectrum of reports would probably yield more disclosures, e.g. on sustainability issues (*IRRCI/Si2* (2013), p. 52). However, it is not the aim of the study to assess the overall level of disclosures that the firm presents, but the degree of IR of the firm's communication. In analyzing this report, links and references to other communications are considered, though (see section 4.3.2).

[131] US firms' annual reports often include the Form 10-K. Cf. also *IRRCI/Si2* (2013), p. 52.

The two financial **years** analyzed are 2012 and 2006.[132] Taking into regard that data on the price reactions for up to one year[133] after the release of the respective reports had to be available for further analysis, 2012 was the year with the most current data available at the time the study began. In 2012, South African companies had to apply the principles of King III and thus IR[134] – or explain why they would not – and had guidance documents that were close to the final IIRC framework. Instead, the reporting requirements in 2006 did not explicitly use the term IR and had less overlap with this final Framework, although already showing some similarities with the idea of IR (see section 3.1.3). Thus, the selection of these two years allows a comparison of pre- and post-IR reports for South African companies.[135] In the USA, there were no requirements to apply IR or a comparable reporting format in either of the two years. Therefore, no structural change occurred for the reporting firms in that country.

In addition to the comparisons over time, the sample allows cross-country comparisons between South Africa and the USA. In 2006, the comparison draws on a situation with no IR regulations in either **country** whereas the comparison for 2012 includes firms factually required to apply IR in South Africa and firms without a particular exposure to IR in the USA. Taken together, the four comparisons across countries and over time address the hypotheses stated in section 4.2.4. The research design also makes it possible to compare the differences over time between these countries and to examine the difference in these differences. This second-level comparison could support the notion that potential disparities in the findings are a result of the IR introduction in South Africa through King III.[136]

The South African companies were part of the FTSE/JSE All-Share **index**, which covers 99% of the market capitalization of all ordinary securities listed on the JSE main board[137] (*FTSE* (2016), p. 1). The US firms formed part of the S&P 500, an index including 500 top companies in leading US industries and covering approximately 80% of the

[132] For comparability reasons this study defines financial year 2012 (2006) as a firm's financial year ending between 1 July 2012 (2006) and 30 June 2013 (2007), except minor overlaps due to the firm's financial year being bound to the end of a week rather than a month. Thus, e.g. financial year 2012 according to this study may be what the respective firm calls "year 2013", if it ends on 31 March 2013.

[133] While the explanatory analysis reported in chapter 5 focuses on a period of 90 days after the report release, data for up to one year was analyzed, e.g. for comparability with existing studies. The tables in the web appendix include the respective data.

[134] However, IR in 2012 did not follow the International <IR> Framework by the IIRC, which had not been released then. Instead, the 2011 Framework for integrated reporting and the Integrated Report by the IRCSA existed as guidance at that time.

[135] The selection also takes into account the financial crisis beginning in 2008/2009, which would have created a lot of noise in the data on the share price reactions. Therefore the study does not use the reports directly before and after the date that the IR requirement came into effect (financial years beginning in or after March 2010).

[136] A difference-in-differences design addresses a potential bias induced by omitted variables by capturing the omitted variables that occur on group level by group-level fixed effects (*Angrist/Pischke* (2009), pp. 227-243, with further references and examples). Changes within the groups may occur while the group-level fixed effects remain. So comparing these changes for different groups allows conclusions that are unaffected of the omitted influences.

[137] Together with the AltX for small and medium-sized companies, the JSE main board constitutes the JSE's equity market; more than 400 firms are listed on the main board (*JSE* (n.d.a; n.d.b.; n.d.c.)).

US market capitalization (*S&P* (2016), p. 1; *S&P* (n.d.), p. 1). As of 31 December 2012, the FTSE/JSE All-Share index had 164 constituents, while the S&P 500 – in line with its name – had 500. A couple of reductions decrease this initial sample. Table 4-2 presents the reduction process and provides the number of firms omitted.

Selection process of the final sample				
	Sample size			
	RSA Firms	USA Firms	Total sample Firms	Total sample Firm years
Initial sample of FTSE/JSE All-Share and S&P 500 (as of 31 December 2012)	**164**	**500**	**664**	**1,328**
less firms not listed on the same index on 31 December 2006	-49	-133	-182	-364
less firms from the financial services sector	-33	-66	-99	-198
less with no data available in Datastream	-13	-90	-103	-206
Remaining firms	69	211	280	560
Random selection of 50 firms per country	50	50	100	200
less firms with not all necessary reports (i.e. Integrated or Annual Reports including a letter from the chairman/CEO, the accounts and a management's discussion for financial years 2005, 2006, 2011 and 2012) available	-19	-76	-95	-190
Random selection of further companies in case the necessary reports were not available (Iteration of these two steps until 50 companies from each country index were found for which the necessary reports were available)	19	76	95	190
Final sample	**50**	**50**	**100**	**200**

Table 4-2: Sample selection process

For the time comparison it was necessary to have the reports of the same companies for 2012 as for 2006. Thus, all firms that were not part of the same index on 31 December 2006 were **excluded from the sample.**[138] Like in the majority of accounting studies[139] firms from the financial sector[140] were also left out. Moreover, companies with missing data in Datastream[141] were omitted. After these reductions of the initial sample, an iterative process of randomly selecting 50 firms per country, excluding the selected companies that did not

138 This gives rise to a potential survivorship bias (cf. *Wald* (1980), *Mangel/Samaniego* (1984) and *Elton et al.* (1996)), which is acknowledged but inevitable here due to the panel data setting described above.

139 Cf. e.g. *Nienhaus* (2015), *Maury/Pajuste* (2005) or *Faulkender/Petersen* (2006).

140 This covers all industries belonging to sector 40 according to the Global Industry Classification Standard (GICS), which is used by the S&P 500, or all industries/sectors under code 8000 (codes between 8000 and 8999) of the Industry Classification Benchmark (ICB), which is used by the FTSE/JSE All-Share index, respectively. Both systems are comparable and translatable, with only minor differences that do not impact large-cap companies (*Vermorken* (2011)).

141 Datastream data was required for the explanatory analysis (see chapter 5), which uses the same sample.

provide the necessary reports[142] for financial years 2012, 2011, 2006 and 2005[143] and randomly selecting new firms to replace the omitted ones eventually led to a final sample of 50 firms per year and country. The overall sample therefore includes 200 firm-year observations.

Industry distribution

The firms in the sample belong to various sectors.[144] Figure 4-6 presents the industry distribution. The largest four sectors Materials, Industrials, Consumer Discretionary and Consumer Staples represent more than 70% of the sample firms, Consumer Discretionary being the largest (including 20% of the companies). Telecommunication Services is the smallest sector (2% of the firms). Generally, the distribution is similar between the two countries, despite differences occurring in five particular **sectors:** Materials (24%) and Consumer Staples (20%) represent a clearly greater percentage of the South African sub-sample than of the US sub-sample (14% and 10%, respectively). Instead, Energy, Information Technology and Utilities play a larger role in the US sample than in the South African one, with 10%, 14% and 6% compared to 4%, 6% and 0%, respectively. The explanatory analyses in the following chapter include controls for industry fixed effects.

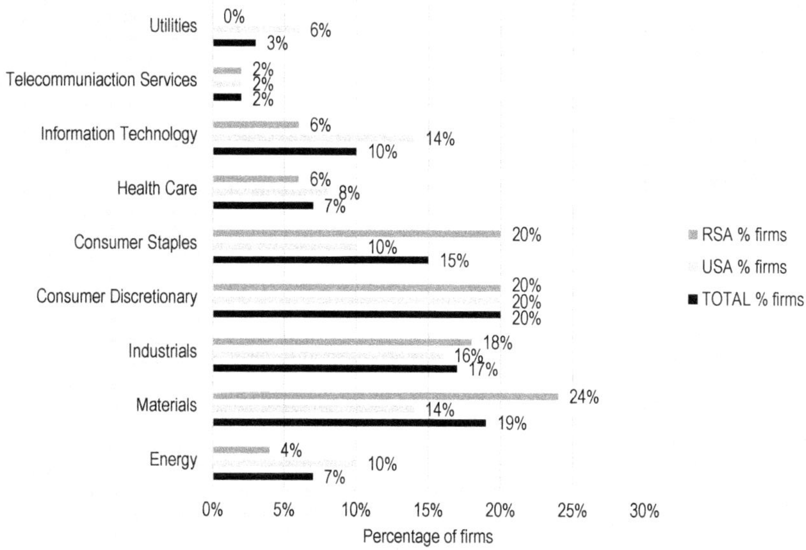

Figure 4-6: Industry distribution of the sample firms

[142] The reports were required to include the aforementioned parts: a letter from the chairman and/or CEO, the accounts and a management report or similar narrative review.

[143] Several items of the disclosure index require a comparison with the previous year's report.

[144] The industry distribution follows the GICS on sector level (cf. *MSCI* (2014)).

Fundamental firm characteristics

Table 4-3 shows basic descriptive statistics characterizing the final sample. It reports the mean, median and standard deviation (std. dev.), the 25% (Q25) and 75% (Q75) quartile and the number of observations (N) for each year-country sub-sample separately.

Return on assets (ROA) is an indicator of the firms' profitability. For both countries, the mean ROA is higher in 2006 than in 2012, especially for South African firms. The companies from South Africa show a higher mean profitability than their US counterparts in both years, but also more variation as a comparison of both the standard deviations and interquartile ranges (Q75-Q25) indicates. Thus, this measure yields substantial differences between the sub-samples.

For **sales,** a measure of the company's size, there is also considerable variation across the four sub-samples. However, the picture is different in terms of the country comparison. US firms have the higher mean value and variation measures in both years, here. Further indicators of size are **market capitalization** and **total assets.** Similar to the sales values, both of these measures are higher on average in the USA than in South Africa and higher in 2012 compared with 2006, albeit with high standard deviations in all sub-samples. The differences in these measures again signal material sub-sample differences.

With higher **equity ratios**, South African firms show a more solid financial structure on average than their US counterparts, especially in 2012. The interquartile ranges and standard deviations imply within- and between-sub-sample differences, here, too. The next three measures stand for the market view on the firms and represent their risk characteristics. The mean **book to market ratio** is substantially higher in both 2012 sub-samples than in their 2006 equivalents (both values <1), indicating that the firms' valuation according to their statement of financial condition is closer to the market value in 2012. The South African mean is clearly higher than the US mean in 2012, but they are similar in 2006.

In 2006, South African sample firms show a higher **stock return momentum** than US firms on average. Both sub-samples have almost the same mean momentum in 2012 (on the level of the USA 2006 sub-sample), though. In the USA, the mean **betas** in both years are close to 1, meaning that on average firm stocks fluctuate almost like the S&P 500 index. The South African means are both close to 0.5, demonstrating that on average the stock prices move in the same direction as the FTSE/JSE All-Share index, but are less volatile than the index. There is great variation within and between the sub-samples for these measures, indicated by the standard deviations and interquartile ranges and their differences between the sub-samples.

In summary, Table 4-3 shows the **variation within and between the sub-samples** in terms of the listed characteristics. While such variation is partially also expected in terms of IR and is thus an essential part of the descriptive analysis in this chapter, the explanatory analysis in the following chapter also takes it into regard. It uses some of the measures listed here (or related measures) to control for the respective influences. Moreover, the analyses are run both on total sample and on country level, acknowledging these differences.

Fundamental firm characteristics for each country/year sub-sample							
Variables[a]		mean	std. dev.	Q25	median	Q75	N
Return on assets	RSA 2006	24.04%	19.66%	14.32%	20.55%	26.94%	50
	RSA 2012	12.29%	11.18%	4.48%	10.89%	17.68%	50
	USA 2006	15.82%	7.90%	9.93%	14.13%	20.85%	50
	USA 2012	11.98%	6.70%	6.88%	10.73%	14.12%	50
	Total sample	**16.04%**	**13.27%**	**8.89%**	**13.94%**	**21.10%**	**200**
Sales	RSA 2006	2,314.77	3,977.28	570.88	957.93	2.189.66	50
	RSA 2012	3,628.02	6,900.32	890.30	1,458.76	3,050.97	50
	USA 2006	25,800.00	56,100.00	5,174.00	9,969.50	15,900.00	50
	USA 2012	35,300.00	74,000.00	8,012.00	12,900.00	22,400.00	50
	Total sample	**16,800.00**	**48,400.00**	**1,126.84**	**4,850.37**	**12,100.00**	**200**
Market capitalization	RSA 2006	2,930.62	4,567.65	598.28	1,219.91	2,715.35	50
	RSA 2012	3,831.29	5,633.15	781.61	1,778.81	4,535.27	50
	USA 2006	32,776.10	52,198.65	9,133.65	14,317.19	30,360.25	50
	USA 2012	36,332.41	58,375.77	8,799.71	16,625.81	30,303.39	50
	Total sample	**18,967.61**	**42,057.12**	**1,448.05**	**6,443.31**	**17,665.30**	**200**
Total assets	RSA 2006	2,090.49	3,140.93	454.60	830.91	1,648.74	50
	RSA 2012	3,561.33	5,426.56	723.47	1,338.50	3,807.12	50
	USA 2006	22,600.00	37,200.00	4,243.18	10,100.00	23,000.00	50
	USA 2012	35,900.00	53,300.00	6,795.00	16,700.00	35,700.00	50
	Total sample	**16,000.00**	**35,300.00**	**1,058.11**	**4,436.77**	**14,900.00**	**200**
Equity ratio	RSA 2006	46.56%	20.33%	31.66%	47.14%	62.36%	50
	RSA 2012	46.11%	18.92%	30.74%	46.37%	60.53%	50
	USA 2006	41.38%	17.30%	28.96%	41.63%	50.33%	50
	USA 2012	34.84%	21.83%	25.25%	35.79%	47.52%	50
	Total sample	**42.22%**	**20.08%**	**28.96%**	**42.52%**	**56.16%**	**200**
Book to market ratio	RSA 2006	26.43%	37.27%	14.54%	26.06%	42.86%	50
	RSA 2012	49.76%	48.66%	18.11%	33.85%	76.72%	50
	USA 2006	28.22%	15.30%	18.98%	24.33%	39.99%	50
	USA 2012	41.09%	31.72%	20.82%	34.34%	60.01%	50
	Total sample	**36.37%**	**36.37%**	**17.86%**	**30.15%**	**47.56%**	**200**
Stock return momentum	RSA 2006	18.33%	27.69%	1.35%	15.73%	27.43%	50
	RSA 2012	9.37%	19.84%	-3.19%	7.25%	20.91%	50
	USA 2006	9.86%	13.70%	2.53%	9.10%	16.47%	50
	USA 2012	8.13%	11.15%	-0.74%	7.37%	10.44%	50
	Total sample	**11.42%**	**19.47%**	**0.55%**	**9.10%**	**19.66%**	**200**
Beta	RSA 2006	0.53	0.29	0.30	0.49	0.66	50
	RSA 2012	0.57	0.37	0.28	0.49	0.88	50
	USA 2006	1.05	0.37	0.80	1.02	1.20	50
	USA 2012	1.01	0.37	0.73	0.94	1.31	50
	Total sample	**0.79**	**0.43**	**0.47**	**0.75**	**1.06**	**200**

[a] Return on assets is calculated as the quotient of net income to total assets. Sales are presented in USD million. Market capitalization (in USD million) is calculated as the number of shares outstanding in million shares times share price in USD, translated from ZAR if necessary with the currency rate at the firm's financial year end. Total assets (at the firm's financial year end) is presented in USD million. Equity ratio is calculated as the quotient of total equity to total assets. Book to market ratio is calculated as the quotient of the book value of equity to the market value of equity. Stock return momentum is the cumulated stock returns for the six months ending at the beginning of the annual report release month. Beta is the firm's beta factor, calculated as the quotient of the covariance of the firm's returns with the respective market index returns to the variance of the respective market index returns, estimated based on the firm's stock returns of 1080 days (three years) before the annual report release date.

Table 4-3: Fundamental characteristics of the sample firms

4.3.2 Content analysis catalogue

The variable of interest for the study at hand is the **degree of IR in firms' reports**. This study uses an IR score as described below to measure this degree. Speaking of a "degree" is a neutral way to interpret the reporting measure, avoiding terms like "quality" instead. While disclosures are partly seen as an abstract concept that is totally immeasurable (*Cooke/Wallace* (1989), p. 51), it is particularly the quality of reporting that is hard to capture (*Botosan* (2004), p. 290). To assess this quality, a content analysis catalogue that includes a weighting of the items would be necessary (*Beretta/Bozzolan* (2008), pp. 337-338), e.g. according to the users' perception of importance (*Barth* (2009), pp. 121-122). Such a weighting includes subjectivity, however (*Cooke/Wallace* (1989), p. 51; *Barth* (2009), p. 122) and may therefore bias the results. The study at hand refrains from explicitly weighting the items and considers the measure merely as a depiction of how integrated the reports are in terms of their adherence to the International <IR> Framework. Impact studies on the usefulness of IR may then evaluate whether or not a high degree of IR is a sign of quality. The capital market study in chapter 5 represents one step in this regard.

This section introduces the **content analysis catalogue** that the study employs to measure the degree of IR. After briefly presenting general characteristics of the content analysis technique and assessing its criteria for this study, the section explains the catalogue in detail, both in terms of its elements and in terms of the scoring.

4.3.2.1 Content analysis

To collect the data on the degree of IR, the study employed a **content analysis**. This research technique provides a structured way to describe the content of communication (*Berelson* (1952), p. 14-18). According to *Berelson's* definition, this structure becomes manifest in the three **criteria** objectivity, systemization and quantification.[145]

The analysis is **objective** if the definition of the categories of analysis is so precise that different researchers would find the same results (*Berelson* (1952), p. 16). **Systemization** requires a consistent set of rules to determine the inclusion or exclusion of items in the catalogue (*Holsti* (1969), p. 4). Furthermore, it is necessary that the items are **quantifiable** to ensure the use of statistical methods to analyze the data (*Kassarjian* (1977), pp. 9-10).

With IR following a principles-based approach (IR F. 1D), this study bases the measurement of the degree of IR upon the application of the **Guiding Principles** from the IR Framework. As section 2.3 and chapter 3 have elaborated, the Guiding Principles contain the main distinguishing marks of IR compared with other reporting approaches, while the Content Elements requirements are largely in line with contents considered by other regulations. A focus on the principles is thus more suitable to elaborate the distinctiveness of IR from other reporting formats. Nevertheless, the Guiding Principles requirements and the Content Elements requirements overlap to some degree, as the provisions on the principles often base upon particular contents. However, the Guiding Principles requirements also

[145] Cf. *Kassarjian* (1977) for different definitions of content analysis. They commonly use these three criteria to assess the quality of the analysis, though.

take other aspects into account, e.g. the format of the report. Hence, the catalogue to collect the data draws on the Guiding Principles rather than on the Content Elements.

The design of **this study** reflects the three mentioned **criteria** for content analysis. As the data to a great extent was hand-collected by one person[146], there is an inherent risk of subjectivity (e.g., *Kromrey* (2016), pp. 321-322). Thus, to ensure the **objectivity** of the data collection, the catalogue includes a detailed description of the requirements for all items, accompanied by examples and – in some cases – the underlying definitions of the terms in question. In addition, a pre-test with single randomly selected reports of sample and non-sample companies and a post-test in the form of a re-collection of data from the first examined reports helped to strengthen consistency. The use of software[147] supported the data collection to further enhance objectivity. Regarding **systemization**, the selection of items for the index was closely aligned with the Guiding Principles requirements in the IR Framework. So was the wording of the items. The catalogue includes references to the respective Framework paragraphs for each item to document this systematic selection. As all items are category (mostly binary) variables, the study also meets the **quantification** criterion.

4.3.2.2 Elements of the catalogue

Table 4-4 presents the **general structure** of the content analysis catalogue.[148] The catalogue contains eight categories: seven for the different Guiding Principles and an additional one for items that capture further characteristics of the reports. Each category contains various items, which are aggregated in different item groups.

The category Strategic Focus and Future Orientation (**STRAT**) includes eight items that deal with the firm's significant opportunities, risks and dependencies (item group STRAT1), with management's views on the firm's interests and performance (STRAT2) and with the role of the capitals for the achievement of strategic objectives (STRAT3).

Connectivity of Information (**CONX**) is the category with the highest number of items (29), which once more underlines the aforementioned importance of this Guiding Principle. The items cover several of the different dimensions of connectivity listed in the Framework, i.e. connectivity between Content Elements (CONX1), time dimensions (CONX2), capitals (CONX3), financial and other information (CONX4), quantitative and qualitative information (CONX5) and also between different sources of information (CONX6). In addition, one group of items from this category deals with the structure, presentation and language of the report (CONX7).

---

146 The data has been collected by the author and research assistants. However, to strengthen consistency in the interpretation of the items, data on one item has been collected by the same person for all reports.

147 Data on several items stems from software entirely. Moreover, the hand-collection of content-related data made use of the search function of the pdf reader both to facilitate the collection and to generate more comparable results.

148 The general structure of the catalogue shown in Table 4-4 summarizes the different categories and the groups of items. Appendix 1 provides a more detailed version of the catalogue, including the individual items. A third, extended version of the catalogue in web appendix 1 shows the in depth definitions, explanations and examples for each item.

General structure of the content analysis catalogue based on the International <IR> Framework				
Category/group of items		**International <IR> Framework reference**	**# items**	**Max. # points**
Strategic Focus and Future Orientation (STRAT)		**IR F. 3A**	**8**	**8**
STRAT1	Significant opportunities, risks and dependencies	IR F. 3.4	4	4
STRAT2	Views of those charged with governance	IR F. 3.4	3	3
STRAT3	Contribution of the capitals to achievement of strategic objectives	IR F. 3.5	1	1
Connectivity of Information (CONX)		**IR F. 3B**	**29**	**33**
CONX1	Connectivity between the Content Elements	IR F. 3.8	6	6
CONX2	Connectivity between time dimensions	IR F. 3.8	3	3
CONX3	Connectivity between different capitals	IR F. 3.8	2	2
CONX4	Connectivity of financial information and other information	IR F. 3.8	10	10
CONX5	Connectivity of quantitative and qualitative information	IR F. 3.8; 4.53	3	3
CONX6	Connectivity between different sources of information	IR F. 3.8	2	4
CONX7	Structure, presentation and language of report	IR F. 3.9	3	5
Stakeholder Relationships (STAKE)		**IR F. 3C**	**12**	**12**
STAKE1	The stakeholders' (legitimate) needs and interests	IR F. 3.14; 1.7-8	4	4
STAKE2	Communication with stakeholders in response to their needs and interests	IR F. 3.14; 1.7-8	4	4
STAKE3	Decision and actions in response to stakeholders' needs and interests	IR F. 3.14; 1.7-8	4	4
Materiality (MAT)		**IR F. 3D**	**8**	**8**
MAT1	The materiality determination process	IR F. 3.18-3.29; 4.42	3	3
MAT2	The reporting boundary	IR F. 3.30-3.35; 4.43-4.45	4	4
MAT3	Limitations of ability to disclose material information	IR F. 3.30-3.35; 4.46	1	1
Conciseness (CONC)		**IR F. 3E**	**7**	**14**
CONC1	Use of links and references	IR F. 3.38	4	8
CONC2	Report length ("as few words as possible")	IR F. 3.38	1	2
CONC3	Use of plain language and avoidance of highly generic disclosures	IR F. 3.38	2	4
Reliability and Completeness (REL)		**IR F. 3F**	**12**	**12**
REL1	Statement about responsibility for the report	IR F. 3.41; 1.20	1	1
REL2	Mechanisms employed to ensure reliability of the report	IR F. 3.42	1	1
REL3	Omitted information and unavailable data	IR F. 3.43; 1.18	3	3
REL4	Balanced consideration of disclosures	IR F. 3.45	3	3
REL5	Reporting against previous and future expectations	IR F. 3.45	2	2
REL6	Information on the use of estimates	IR F. 3.46	2	2
Consistency and Comparability (COMP)		**IR F. 3F**	**8**	**8**
COMP1	Consistent use of KPIs	IR F. 3.55	2	2
COMP2	Use of benchmark data	IR F. 3.57	2	2
COMP3	Presentation of data in the form of ratios	IR F. 3.57	1	1
COMP4	Reporting of commonly used indicators	IR F. 3.57	3	3
Additional items (ADD)[a]		**NA**	**5**	**NA**
ADD1	Basic report characteristics	IR F. 1.20; 3.41	3	NA
ADD2	Readability of the document	(IR F. 3.9)	2	NA
TOTAL			**89**	**95**

[a] Items in the ADD category are not awarded points and are thus not considered for the IR score. Instead, they provide additional information on the respective report. This information is used in the further course of this study.

Table 4-4: General structure of the content analysis catalogue

The Guiding Principle Stakeholder Relationships (**STAKE**) represents the next category, which comprises twelve items in total. They deal with the needs and interests of different stakeholders (STAKE1) on the one hand and with the firm's response to them in form of communication (STAKE2) and actions (STAKE3) on the other.

The categories Materiality (MAT) and Conciseness (CONC) are related, they even constituted one joint Guiding Principle in the CD IR. However, **MAT** contains eight items that aim for information on the determination of materiality (MAT1), the reporting boundary (MAT2) and potential limitations to disclose material information (MAT3).

The seven **CONC** items instead deal with rather formal or technical issues like links or references in the report (CONC1), the length of the report (CONC2) or the language that the report uses (CONC3).

Twelve items stem from the Guiding Principle Reliability and Completeness (**REL**). They deal with disclosures on the persons responsible for the report (REL1), on the mechanisms to ensure the reliability of the report (REL2) and on omitted information (REL3). Another group of items (REL4) examines whether the information in the report is balanced, e.g. if it includes positive and negative performance aspects. Moreover, two groups of REL items aim at the way to present e.g. performance data: Does it come with comparative data on previous and future expectations for the respective indicator (REL5) and does the report clarify if and how it uses estimates (REL6)?

Consistency and Comparability (**COMP**) is the last Guiding Principle in the Framework. The respective category in the catalogue contains eight items, checking whether the firm provides data consistent with previous reports (COMP1), whether the report contains benchmark data for the indicators it discloses (COMP2) and whether it presents data in the form of ratios (COMP3). Moreover, one group of items aims at the disclosure of data that is common in reports from the firm's industry (COMP4).

On top of these elements derived from the Guiding Principles requirements, the catalogue contains five additional items (**ADD**). They are not considered for the IR score, though, as they either do not directly stem from the Guiding Principles requirements or are not applicable to all reports in the sample. However, the results from these items supplement and help to interpret the other findings. This category includes items that deal with the type of the report, reference to IIRC regulations and the addressees of the report (ADD1). Besides, the category contains items on the readability of the report (ADD2).

4.3.2.3 Data collection and scoring

There are three different **types of items** in terms of data collection and score. While most items were hand-collected, the collection of some items required the use of software. Regarding their score, most items are binary, while others are categorical. The categories and scores of the latter items derive from an underlying of an integer or continuous format. Building on these distinctions, type A, B and C items are defined.

Type A represents the vast majority of items.[149] Items of this type were hand-collected in a two-step approach. In a first step, the researcher thoroughly looked through the entire report. If this yielded no information on a particular item, a set of keywords[150] was searched for with the search function in a second step, to avoid overlooking information and to strengthen the comparability and objectivity of the collection. In terms of quantification, **type A** items are binary variables: A point is awarded for an item if the disclosures in the report[151] satisfy the requirements of the respective item, no point is awarded otherwise (*Marston/Shrives* (1991), p. 198).

As opposed to this, **type B** items[152] are not binary variables. They are categorical, instead, with five categories of 0.0, 0.5, 1.0, 1.5 and 2.0 points, respectively. The respective categories derive from the number of links and references in the report. A researcher single-handedly counted various kinds of references.[153] According to the quintiles of the relative number of references (i.e., the quotient of the number of references in the report to the number of words in the report), the item in question falls into one of the five categories and thus gets a score of 0.0 points for the first quintile and up to 2.0 for the fifth.

Similarly, **type C** items[154] are also categorical, with five categories of 0.0 to 2.0 points. They are different from type B, however, as the entire underlying data is collected with the help of software. The different type C items aim at the number of words in the report, the use of boilerplate disclosures and the use of jargon. According to the IR Framework, firms are required to keep these measures low (IR F 3.38). Therefore, the respective item gets 2.0 points if the underlying score falls into the first quintile and 0.0 if into the last, which represents another difference to type B items.

---

149 The detailed version of the catalogue in Appendix 1 includes the type of each individual item.

150 An individual set of keywords relates to each item. For instance, the following keywords pertains to item REL3.3 "Steps to obtain unavailable data": "availab" (covering "available", but also "unavailable", "not available", availability" etc.), "informati" (covering "information", "informative" etc.), "data", "obtain" (covering "obtain", "obtainable", "obtaining" etc.), "collect" (covering "collect", but also "collection", "collecting" etc.) and "collat" (covering "collate", "collating", "collation" etc.). Generally, the same set of words was used for a particular item in every report. Minor adaptions applied, however, if particular properties of the report or the firm required so (e.g., while the list of keywords for item CONX4.3.1 "The implications of long term customer relationships for revenue growth and profit growth" included the terms "customer", "client" etc., the word "guest" was added to this list for Target Corporation (Target), as the firm refers to its customers with this term, cf. *Target* (2013), p. 2 of Form 10-K).

151 In line with the IR Framework (IR F. 1.16, 3.38, 4.42), points were awarded if the report under investigation only described in so far as its nature and effect was clear and referenced other documents for further information. For instance, item MAT1.3 "A link to a more detailed description of the materiality determination process" explicitly considers this approach. Refer to web appendix 1 for the detailed requirements.

152 In particular, type B items include CONX6.1, CONX6.2, CONX7.2.2, CONC1.1, CONC1.2, CONC1.3 and CONC1.4.

153 Various items in the CONX and CONC categories aim for different kinds of references, e.g. item CONX6.1 "Connectivity of information in the integrated report and the organization's other communications" or item CONC1.1 "Internal cross-references in the report".

154 Type C comprises items CONX7.1, CONC2, CONC3.1 and CONC3.2.

Besides influencing the calculation of type B items as described above, the **number of words** in the report also directly underlies the calculation of the score for item CONC2 "As few words as possible". The Microsoft Word word count provides the number of words for the txt file of the report. For the sake of comparability, all numbers, currency symbols and other symbols that typically relate to numbers (such as decimal separators or brackets) were deleted. Otherwise, a different format of numbers could result in a substantial difference between two reports. For instance, "5 342 265" would count as three words, whereas "5342265" or "5,322,265" would only count as one. Since annual reports typically contain a lot of quantitative data, this could lead to a material difference overall. The reports then get a score between 0.0 and 2.0 in steps of 0.5, according to the quintiles of the underlying word count.

To approximate the use of **boilerplate disclosures**, this study uses the degree of similarity between two reports (*Nelson/Pritchard* (2016)). The software Ferret Copy Detector[155] calculates the similarity between the txt files of a firm's entire report for the current financial year and the one for the previous year, based on the number of matching trigrams of words in the texts.[156] A value of 0 means no similarity, whereas a value of 1 indicates total identity. The score for item CONC3.2, which requires the avoidance of boilerplate, then derives from the quintiles of the similarity measure as for the word count described above.

For the analysis of **jargon use**, this study has examined the letters to the stakeholders[157] in the firms' reports. The decision to draw on the letter is in line with common practice in the related readability literature (e.g., *Courtis* (1986a); *Courtis* (1986b); *Subramanian et al.* (1993); *Schroeder/Gibson* (1990); *Smith/Taffler* (1995); *Smith/Taffler* (2000)). *Subramanian et al.* ((1993), p. 53, with further references) present various reasons for using the letter. Providing a summary of the firm's performance and a review of other topics, this section of the report gives a holistic view from management's perspective. It is the most widely read part of the annual report, often serving as a basis for investors' decisions. The letter can thus be seen as a calling card for the report.[158] However, since other sections of the report may be of a more technical nature (*Subramanian et al.* (1993), p. 53) and since the letter is usually only a small part of the report, this text can only give an indication of the jargon use in the entire report, rather than allowing robust inferences about this issue.

Grammar and writing analysis **software** RightWriter™[159] (*Schroeder/Gibson* (1988)) shows a **list of jargon words** (i.e., entirely new words, abbreviations, acronyms, buzz words, and nouns created from common verbs or verbs created from common nouns) (*Schroeder/Gibson* (1988), p. 13). The quotient of the total number of these jargon words to the total number of words in the letter represents the use of jargon. While a value of 0.0 means that

[155] Cf. https://github.com/petercrlane/ferret (last accessed on 29 August 2016).

[156] Cf. *Nelson/Pritchard* ((2007), pp. 17-18) for a detailed description of the procedure and interpretation.

[157] The term "Letter to the Stakeholders" may refer to the letter from the Chairman and/or CEO to the shareholders and/or other stakeholders, since both author and addressees slightly vary among the different reports in the sample.

[158] For instance, *Bhana* (2009) documents that South African firms use the chairman's letter to emphasize good news.

[159] Cf. http://right-writer.com/ (last accessed on 29 August 2016).

the usage is acceptable, a rate above 0.5 indicates a very heavy use of jargon (*Schroeder/Gibson* (1988), p. 13). The measure underlies the calculation of the score for items CONX7.1 and CONC3.1. In line with the quintiles of this similarity, the reports are awarded between 0.0 and 2.0 points according to the scoring mechanism described above.

The scoring procedure of type B and type C items and the fact that items in the ADD category are merely qualitative leads to a difference between the number of items in the catalogue and the maximum **number of points achievable** for the IR score. Type B and C items appear in categories CONX and CONC only. Thus, the maximum number of points achievable for the CONX (CONC) sub-score is 33 (14), while the number of items in this category is 29 (7). The maximum achievable points for all other sub-scores equal the number of items in the respective category, which results in a total of 95 achievable points for the IR score (see Table 4-4). To inform about the particular number of points that a report received, the scores may be reported on an absolute basis. Besides, to enhance the comparability with other studies and to generalize the interpretation, they are also reported as a percentage of the maximum number of points. The same holds for the sub-scores.

Supplementary measures

Various measures that underlie the calculation of items in the disclosure catalogue represent constructs that extant literature has also used on a standalone basis, in particular the three measures underlying the type C items. They include the number of words, representing the length of the report (e.g., *Lee* (2012)), the similarity of reports, standing for the use of boilerplate disclosures (*Nelson/Pritchard* (2016)) and the percentage of words that indicate the use of jargon (*Schroeder/Gibson* (1988)). Besides, the ADD category of the catalogue includes items on report readability (e.g., *Li* (2008)). The literature has employed these **four constructs** to depict several of the **shortcomings of corporate reporting** described in section 1.1 (Figure 4-7). As IR intends to tackle these shortcomings, the constructs may help to interpret the results on the IR score and its sub-scores and may put them into context. Moreover, they may also provide alternative explanations of the capital market consequences examined in chapter 5 of this study.

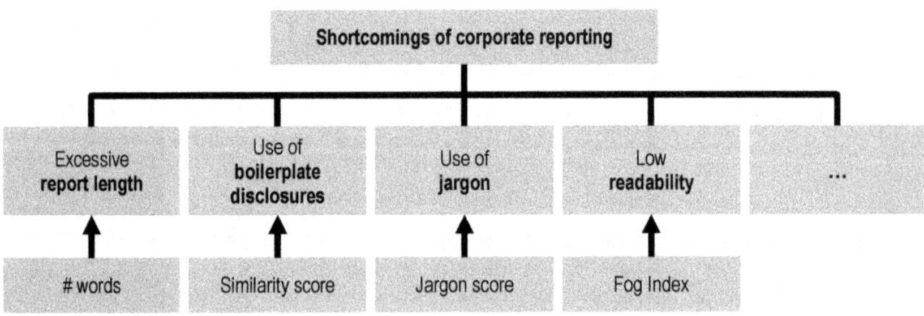

Figure 4-7: Supplementary measures

The number of words in a report is a typical measure of report **length** (e.g., *Miller* (2010)). Excessive report length is one shortcoming of corporate reporting. Hence, the literature commonly uses the number of words to approximate the difficulty in processing report information (e.g., *You/Zhang* (2009); *Miller* (2010)). This study also employs report length in this regard. Therefore, word count, as described above under type C items, is also considered as a separate measure.[160]

A few studies have already used the similarity of reports as a standalone measure, representing the use of **boilerplate disclosures** in a report, or in turn the degree of news that the document includes. To foster the informative value of the report, the IR Framework requires firms to avoid boilerplate (IR F. 3.38). *Brown/Tucker* (2011) and *Nelson/Pritchard* (2016) are examples from extant literature that employ a similarity measure. This study uses the similarity measure described above under type C items to supplement the IR findings.[161]

Brown et al. (1978), *Thompson et al.* (1981), *Subramanian et al.* (1993), *Joiner et al.* (2002) or *Tan et al.* (2015) and other studies examine the **use of jargon**, another shortcoming in corporate communications. Drawing on the percentage of jargon words in the Letter to the Stakeholders,[162] which underlies the scoring mechanism of type C items from the disclosure catalogue, this analysis also employs jargon use as a standalone measure.[163]

There is also a great array of studies that analyzes the **readability** of a report (*Courtis* (1998), p. 459). Examples include *Courtis* (1986a), *Phillips et al.* (2007), *Li* (2008) or *Nelson/Pritchard* (2016)). The study at hand uses the Fog Index (*Gunning* (1952)) to measure readability.[164] It calculates the reading level as the sum of the average number of words per sentence and the percentage of words of three or more syllables, multiplied by 0.4 (*Gunning* (1952), pp. 35-37). The index value expresses the school grade (i.e., the number of years of education) necessary to fully comprehend the text. Along with the data on the use of jargon, the software RightWriter™ delivered this score for the text of the Letter to the Stakeholders in the respective report.[165] As the legibility of firms' communications represents another problem of corporate reporting, this study employs the Fog Index as an additional measure to supplement the findings on IR.

---

160 To further test for robustness, the study also used the number of pages in the pdf version of the report as an alternative measure of report length (unreported). The results were qualitatively unchanged.

161 Alternatively, the study used the mean similarity between a firm's report and the reports of all other firms in the sample on the same year. The same was done with the reports of all other firms from the firm's country on the same year (both unreported). Neither measure yielded qualitatively different results.

162 As described above under type C items, using the Letter to the Stakeholders implies that the results on this measure need to be interpreted with caution.

163 As an alternative measure, this study also used the quotient of unique jargon words to the number of total unique words in the letter (unreported). The results were qualitatively unchanged.

164 However, there has been controversy in the readability literature about different measurement methods of readability (*Smith/Taffler* (1992)). This study therefore also used the Flesch-Kincaid Grade Level Index (*Kincaid et al.* (1975), p. 14) as a second measure of readability (unreported). The interpretation of this index is the same as for the Fog Index. This did not yield qualitatively different results.

165 The same caution for inferences as described above for the use of jargon needs to be exercised in interpreting the results on readability.

To **sum up**, the content analysis catalogue captures the use of IR from the IIRC's principles-based view, drawing on the IR Guiding Principles. Sub-scores for each principle add up to the total score to depict the degree of IR in a firm's report. Besides binary hand-collected items, the catalogue comprises items whose scores base upon underlying measures that address special aspects from the requirements of the Framework, including the number of different kinds of links and references, the length of the report, the use of boilerplate disclosures and the use of jargon. These latter three measures, in addition to the readability of the report, are used as separate measures to put the findings on IR into context, as they depict the shortcomings of corporate reporting.

4.4 Results

This section provides evidence on the reporting practice of the sample firms. It begins with a presentation of some general characteristics of the examined reports. Next, the section describes the statistics on the degree of IR in the reports, which bases upon the Guiding Principles, and on the different sub-scores and selected distinctive items. The focus lies with comparisons of the year-country sub-samples. Contrasting these sub-samples particularly allows to evaluate the novelty of several IR features against what was already part of traditional annual reports. Examples from the analyzed reports supplement the aggregate descriptive data to provide a more illustrative picture of the findings. Eventually, the section summarizes the descriptive statistics on the supplementary measures described in section 4.3.2.3.

4.4.1 Basic characteristics of the reports

Table 4-5 presents an overview of the basic characteristics of the sample reports, including their labels, their potential abidance by IIRC regulations and their intended primary addressees. The table shows the results for each year-country sub-sample separately, as well as the total sample score.

General characteristics of the reports					
Variables[a]	Report label "integrated"	IIRC abidance	Addressees		N
			stakeholders	shareholders	
RSA 2006	0%	0%	16%	34%	50
RSA 2012	96%	46%	60%	6%	50
USA 2006	0%	0%	12%	86%	50
USA 2012	2%	2%	18%	78%	50
Total sample	**25%**	**12%**	**27%**	**51%**	**200**

[a] The values depict the percentage of companies that satisfy the mentioned criteria. The label "integrated" refers to all reports that explicitly include the expression "integrat" in their names. This may be "integrated report", "integrated annual report", "annual integrated report", but also other potential names including "integration" or "integrating". Data on IIRC abidance refers to guidance documents released by the IIRC This includes the DP IR or preliminary versions of the Framework, up until the CD IR, which was released in March 2013. As the IIRC was founded in 2010, no report could reference IIRC guidance in 2006. Data on the addressees stems either from an explicit statement at some point in the report defining the addressees or from the chairman's or CEO's letter. It is only categorized into one of the two groups if the letter explicitly addresses the members of the respective group. In various cases, the addressees remain unclear. The reports may take into account various groups, however, even if only addressing shareholders in the letter from the chairman.

Table 4-5: Basic characteristics of the sample reports

As described in the previous sections, the disclosure catalogue measures the alignment of a report with the Guiding Principles of the International <IR> Framework, irrespective of whether the report is labelled "integrated report" and whether it abides by IIRC guidance. This approach permits a conclusion on the presence of IR in traditional annual reports, even before the IIRC's project emerged. Nonetheless, data on the label of the report and on IIRC abidance was collected under the ADD category in the disclosure catalogue for **information purposes.**

The findings on these features are hardly surprising. 48 of 50 (96%) South African firms[166] and one US firm use the **label "integrated"** in 2012, whereas no report in either country has "integrated" in its title[167] in 2006. The result for South Africa 2012 is clearly higher than the 38% of firms that *Makiwane/Padia* (2013) find to use the label "integrated report" in the 2010/2011 period for their sample of 92 listed firms from South Africa. As opposed to this, the finding is in line with the 88% of the top 100 JSE-listed firms that use the label in financial year 2013, as *Nkonki Inc.* (2014) documents. However, the comparability with these studies may be limited due to differences in sample size and firm selection, although the timeframe and various selected companies of *Nkonki Inc.'s* (2014) sample and the sample used in the study at hand overlap to some degree.

As regards the firms' **abidance by IIRC guidance**, the results are in line with the findings on the title of the report. 23 (46%) South African firms plus the one (2%) aforementioned US firm state to have used IIRC guidance documents for the preparation of their 2012 reports. This may refer to the DP IR or preliminary versions of the Framework, up until the CD IR, which was released in November 2012. As the IIRC was founded in 2010, obviously no report references an IIRC guidance document in 2006.

Another characteristic of the reports is their intended audience. On total sample level, 53 reports (27%) explicitly name all stakeholders as their addressees, while 102 (51%) have a shareholder focus.[168] However, there are differences across countries and years. While 30 (60%) of the South African firms address stakeholders and 3 (6%) address shareholders in 2012, only 9 firms (18%) focus on stakeholders in the USA in the same year.

---

166 The only South African firms with an "annual report" in 2012 are African Oxygen Ltd. (Afrox) and Datatec Limited (Datatec). Their IR scores of 64 and 62.5 points out of 95, respectively, are above the mean for South African firms in 2012 (60.7). This underlines that the IR Framework (and with that the IR score) draws on various features of traditional reporting. In turn, the idea of IR may be present in a report even though it is not explicitly named "integrated". The only US firm to use an "integrated annual report" is The Clorox Company (Clorox).

167 This refers to all reports that explicitly include the expression "integrat" in their names. This may be "integrated report", "integrated annual report", "annual integrated report", but also other potential names including "integration" or "integrating".

168 Data on this issue stems from an explicit statement at some point in the report identifying the addressees or from the chairman's or CEO's letter. A report is only categorized into one of the two groups if the letter explicitly addresses the members of the respective group. In 45 cases, the addressees are unclear. For instance, the letters are just labeled "Letter from the Chairman" (e.g., *PPG* (2013), front matter) instead of e.g. "Dear fellow shareowners" (e.g., *UPS* (2013), p. 1). The reports may take into account various groups, however, even if only addressing shareholders in the letter from the chairman. For instance, the CEO and chairman of *Baker Hughes Incorporated* ((2013), p. 5) honor their employees and other stakeholders, but explicitly address their letter (and thus, the report) to their shareholders (p. 2).

39 (78%) US firms have a shareholder focus, instead. In 2006, 8 (16%) South African reports explicitly consider stakeholders as their **addressees**, with 17 (34%) reports considering shareholders. In contrast, only 6 firms (12%) address stakeholders in the USA, while 43 (86%) focus on shareholders in 2006. The country differences can be explained by two factors. On the one hand, the South African results are explicable by the more stakeholder-oriented reporting approach in South Africa, in particular in the IRCSA Framework, which influenced many of the examined reports. On the other hand, the findings for the US reports are probably driven by the traditional investor orientation of reporting in the USA, as outlined in section 3.2.

4.4.2 The degree of Integrated Reporting

Turning to the degree of IR, Table 4-6 presents the descriptive statistics on both the total IR score from the disclosure catalogue (highlighted) and the sub-scores relating to the seven Guiding Principles from the International <IR> Framework. Like the tables on the sample characteristics, it reports the mean, median and standard deviation (std. dev.), the 25% (Q25) and 75% (Q75) quartile and the number of observations (N) for each year-country sub-sample separately.

4.4.2.1 Total Integrated Reporting score

The average IR score for the **total sample** is 58%, equaling 55.3 out of a possible 95 points. With 57% (54.5 points), the median is only slightly lower than this mean. With an interquartile range (Q75-Q25) of 8 percentage points and a standard deviation of 6 percentage points (equaling 11% of the mean), there is only little variation in the data. The minimum value of 42% (39.5 points) and the maximum value of 78% (74 points) differ considerably, though.

South African mining chemicals provider Omnia Holdings Limited reaches the **highest IR score** of 78% (74 points) with its 2012 report. The South Africa 2012 sub-sample also includes the reports that place second (chemical group AECI Limited (AECI) with 76% (72 points)), and third (retail company Mr. Price Group Limited and cement supplier PPC with 75% (71 points) each) overall. Instead, the USA 2012 sub-sample contains the three reports with the **lowest IR scores**. These findings are somewhat in line with the results from the EY, CSSA and Nkonki rankings. Gold Fields, winner of the EY ranking in 2012, is among the top quarter firms of this study. Sasol, winner of the 2006 and 2007 EY ranking and the 2007 CSSA Award, and Group Five, CSSA winner in 2012, are in the top half of the study at hand. Nkonki's 2012 winner PPC places third, here.

The **differences between the year-country sub-samples** indicated by these reports are also visible in the mean and median scores, as Table 4-6 shows. With both a mean and median of 64%, the South Africa 2012 sub-sample exceeds the US sub-sample from the same year (mean and median of 55%) by almost 10 percentage points. Table 4-7 provides the results of (two-tailed) t-tests and non-parametric Wilcoxon-Mann-Whitney tests[169] that examine differences in the means between the sub-samples.[170] Panel A of the latter table reveals that the difference in the IR score between the countries is highly significant (1% level) in 2012. For 2006, South African firms show a mean and median IR score of 58%, scarcely exceeding the USA 2006 sub-sample, which yields a mean and median score of 56%. This difference in the means is significant at the 5% level (Panel B). The numbers for the South African sub-samples are clearly higher than the mean IR score of 20% that *Zhou et al.* (2016) find for their sample of JSE-listed firms. However, differences in sample size and selection and in the collection of the data hamper the comparability of the findings. The same holds when comparing the data from the two US sub-samples with *Serafeim's* (2015) findings, as the mean of 39% in *Serafeim's* US sample is also clearly lower than the mean IR scores for US firms from the study at hand. Variation in the data is similar throughout the four sub-samples, with a standard deviation that equals 9% of the mean, i.e. 6 (South Africa 2012) or 5 (all other sub-samples) percentage points in absolute terms. The interquartile ranges are 6 percentage points for both US samples as well as 7 and 8 percentage points for the South African 2006 and 2012 sub-sample, respectively, which underlines this resemblance in variation. Boxplots for the four sub-samples illustrate this similarity, but at the same time show the differences in the medians (Figure 4-8[171]).

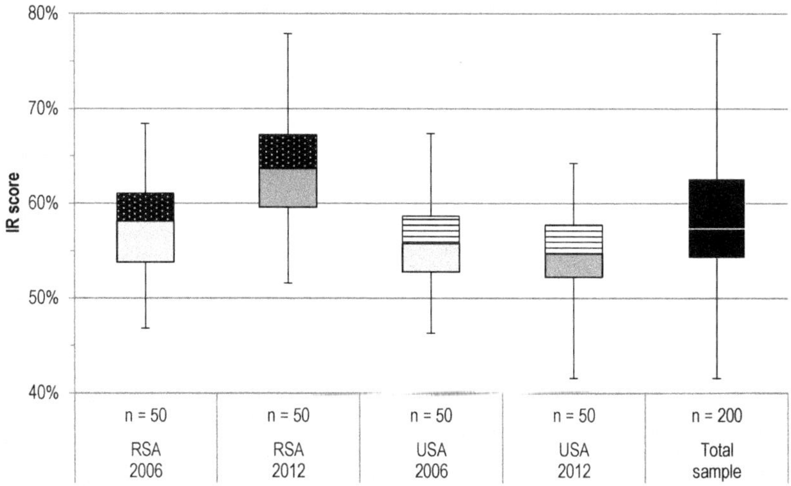

Figure 4-8: Boxplots of the IR score and sub-scores

[169] While t-tests base on the assumption that the underlying data follows a normal distribution, Wilcoxon-Mann-Whitney tests require no assumption on the distribution of the data. Although a normal distribution seems plausible for almost all variables judging from the histograms of the respective data, the non-parametric alternative is applied for robustness.

[170] Both tests use the null hypothesis that the difference of mean scores between the South African and the US firms equals 0 and the alternative hypothesis that this difference does not equal 0.

[171] Note that the y-axis of the figure is truncated at 40% for better visibility.

IR score and sub-scores for each country/year sub-sample							
Variables[a]		mean	std. dev.	Q25	median	Q75	N
IR score	RSA 2006	58.04%	5.06%	53.68%	58.16%	61.05%	50
	RSA 2012	63.93%	6.05%	59.47%	63.68%	67.37%	50
	USA 2006	55.96%	5.05%	52.63%	55.79%	58.95%	50
	USA 2012	55.04%	5.12%	52.11%	54.74%	57.89%	50
	Total sample	**58.24%**	**6.33%**	**54.21%**	**57.37%**	**62.63%**	**200**
Sub-score STRAT	RSA 2006	72.25%	19.93%	62.50%	75.00%	87.50%	50
	RSA 2012	78.75%	13.89%	75.00%	87.50%	87.50%	50
	USA 2006	75.25%	14.83%	75.00%	75.00%	87.50%	50
	USA 2012	73.25%	11.85%	62.50%	75.00%	75.00%	50
	Total sample	**74.88%**	**15.50%**	**62.50%**	**75.00%**	**87.50%**	**200**
Sub-score CONX	RSA 2006	63.73%	7.39%	59.09%	62.88%	68.18%	50
	RSA 2012	69.39%	6.33%	66.67%	69.70%	74.24%	50
	USA 2006	66.52%	5.61%	62.12%	68.18%	71.21%	50
	USA 2012	66.48%	6.30%	62.12%	66.67%	71.21%	50
	Total sample	**66.53%**	**6.70%**	**62.12%**	**66.67%**	**71.21%**	**200**
Sub-score STAKE	RSA 2006	31.33%	18.49%	16.67%	25.00%	41.67%	50
	RSA 2012	55.00%	29.21%	25.00%	50.00%	83.33%	50
	USA 2006	19.67%	9.18%	16.67%	16.67%	25.00%	50
	USA 2012	21.50%	8.09%	16.67%	16.67%	25.00%	50
	Total sample	**31.88%**	**23.02%**	**16.67%**	**25.00%**	**41.67%**	**200**
Sub-score MAT	RSA 2006	39.75%	4.85%	37.50%	37.50%	37.50%	50
	RSA 2012	53.50%	13.13%	50.00%	50.00%	62.50%	50
	USA 2006	35.00%	13.36%	25.00%	25.00%	50.00%	50
	USA 2012	38.75%	11.91%	25.00%	37.50%	50.00%	50
	Total sample	**41.75%**	**13.29%**	**37.50%**	**37.50%**	**50.00%**	**200**
Sub-score CONC	RSA 2006	68.93%	11.07%	60.71%	67.86%	78.57%	50
	RSA 2012	55.79%	7.97%	50.00%	57.14%	60.71%	50
	USA 2006	55.29%	10.39%	50.00%	57.14%	60.71%	50
	USA 2012	43.43%	11.48%	35.71%	42.86%	53.57%	50
	Total sample	**55.86%**	**13.66%**	**46.43%**	**57.14%**	**64.29%**	**200**
Sub-score REL	RSA 2006	72.33%	11.96%	66.67%	75.00%	75.00%	50
	RSA 2012	79.50%	12.05%	75.00%	75.00%	91.67%	50
	USA 2006	72.83%	8.88%	66.67%	75.00%	75.00%	50
	USA 2012	74.83%	10.71%	66.67%	75.00%	83.33%	50
	Total sample	**74.88%**	**11.25%**	**66.67%**	**75.00%**	**83.33%**	**200**
Sub-score COMP	RSA 2006	38.25%	15.45%	25.00%	37.50%	50.00%	50
	RSA 2012	41.25%	22.48%	25.00%	37.50%	50.00%	50
	USA 2006	44.38%	12.26%	37.50%	50.00%	50.00%	50
	USA 2012	46.88%	12.26%	37.50%	50.00%	50.00%	50
	Total sample	**42.69%**	**16.36%**	**37.50%**	**37.50%**	**50.00%**	**200**

[a] The variables are the relative IR score from the disclosure catalogue and sub-scores, representing the Guiding Principles of the International <IR> Framework: STRAT is Strategic Focus and Future Orientation, CONX is Connectivity of Information, STAKE is Stakeholder Relationships, MAT is Materiality, CONC is Conciseness, REL is Reliability and Completeness and COMP is Consistency and Comparability, respectively.

Table 4-6: Descriptive statistics of the IR score and sub-scores

Comparison of the mean IR score and sub-scores for the different sub-samples

Panel A: RSA 2012 vs. USA 2012

Variables[a]	**Sub-sample 1: RSA 2012**		**Sub-sample 2: USA 2012**		**Difference in means**	**Tests of comparison**[b]	
	mean	**N**	**mean**	**N**		**t-test: t-statistics**	**Wilcoxon-Mann-Whitney test: z-statistics**
IR score	**63.93%**	50	**55.04%**	50	**8.88%**	**7.9316 *****	**6.4500 *****
Sub-score STRAT	78.75%	50	73.25%	50	5.50%	2.1303 **	2.4220 **
Sub-score CONX	69.39%	50	66.48%	50	2.91%	2.3027 **	2.3760 **
Sub-score STAKE	55.00%	50	21.50%	50	33.50%	7.8156 ***	6.1250 ***
Sub-score MAT	53.50%	50	38.75%	50	14.75%	5.8826 ***	4.9760 ***
Sub-score CONC	55.79%	50	43.43%	50	12.36%	6.2515 ***	5.2520 ***
Sub-score REL	79.50%	50	74.83%	50	4.67%	2.0468 **	2.0990 **
Sub-score COMP	41.25%	50	46.88%	50	-5.63%	-1.5533	-2.5120 **

Panel B: RSA 2006 vs. USA 2006

Variables[a]	**Sub-sample 1: RSA 2006**		**Sub-sample 2: USA 2006**		**Difference in means**	**Tests of comparison**[b]	
	mean	**N**	**mean**	**N**		**t-test: t-statistics**	**Wilcoxon-Mann-Whitney test: z-statistics**
IR score	**58.04%**	50	**55.96%**	50	**2.08%**	**2.0614 ****	**2.2010 ****
Sub-score STRAT	72.25%	50	75.25%	50	-3.00%	-0.8539	-0.7010
Sub-score CONX	63.73%	50	66.52%	50	-2.79%	-2.1236 **	-2.1340 **
Sub-score STAKE	31.33%	50	19.67%	50	11.67%	3.9966 ***	3.4390 ***
Sub-score MAT	39.75%	50	35.00%	50	4.75%	2.3626 **	2.4040 **
Sub-score CONC	68.93%	50	55.29%	50	13.64%	6.3559 ***	5.6210 ***
Sub-score REL	72.33%	50	72.83%	50	-0.50%	-0.2374	-0.3330
Sub-score COMP	38.25%	50	44.38%	50	-6.13%	-2.1963 **	-2.3280 **

Panel C: RSA 2012 vs. RSA 2006

Variables[a]	**Sub-sample 1: RSA 2012**		**Sub-sample 2: RSA 2006**		**Difference in means**	**Tests of comparison**[b]	
	mean	**N**	**mean**	**N**		**t-test: t-statistics**	**Wilcoxon-Mann-Whitney test: z-statistics**
IR score	**63.93%**	50	**58.04%**	50	**5.88%**	**5.2781 *****	**4.6520 *****
Sub-score STRAT	78.75%	50	72.25%	50	6.50%	1.8919 *	1.6530 *
Sub-score CONX	69.39%	50	63.73%	50	5.67%	4.1160 ***	3.8530 ***
Sub-score STAKE	55.00%	50	31.33%	50	23.67%	4.8412 ***	4.0610 ***
Sub-score MAT	53.50%	50	39.75%	50	13.75%	6.9451 ***	5.9580 ***
Sub-score CONC	55.79%	50	68.93%	50	-13.14%	-6.8155 ***	-5.8440 ***
Sub-score REL	79.50%	50	72.33%	50	7.17%	2.9855 ***	3.0350 ***
Sub-score COMP	41.25%	50	38.25%	50	3.00%	0.7777	0.0530

Continued...

Panel D: USA 2012 vs. USA 2006							
Variables[a]	Sub-sample 1: USA 2012		Sub-sample 2: USA 2006		Difference in means	Tests of comparison[b]	
	mean	N	mean	N		t-test: t-statistics	Wilcoxon-Mann-Whitney test: z-statistics
IR score	**55.04%**	50	**55.96%**	50	**-0.92%**	**-0.9006**	**-0.7690**
Sub-score STRAT	73.25%	50	75.25%	50	-2.00%	-0.7450	-1.1150
Sub-score CONX	66.48%	50	66.52%	50	-0.03%	-0.0254	-0.0240
Sub-score STAKE	21.50%	50	19.67%	50	1.83%	1.0592	1.1280
Sub-score MAT	38.75%	50	35.00%	50	3.75%	1.4812	1.4890
Sub-score CONC	43.43%	50	55.29%	50	-11.86%	-5.4143 ***	-4.7600 ***
Sub-score REL	74.83%	50	72.83%	50	2.00%	1.0164	1.0310
Sub-score COMP	46.88%	50	44.38%	50	2.50%	1.0197	1.1550

[a] The variables are the relative IR score from the disclosure catalogue and sub-scores, representing the Guiding Principles of the International <IR> Framework: STRAT is Strategic Focus and Future Orientation, CONX is Connectivity of Information, STAKE is Stakeholder Relationships, MAT is Materiality, CONC is Conciseness, REL is Reliability and Completeness and COMP is Consistency and Comparability, respectively.

[b] Two-tailed t-test and Wilcoxon-Mann-Whitney test that test the following hypothesis:
H_0: Mean sub-sample 1 – Mean sub-sample 2 = 0;
H_a: Mean sub-sample 1 – Mean sub-sample 2 ≠ 0.
*, **, and *** indicate statistical significance at the 10%, 5% and 1% levels, respectively.

Table 4-7: Comparison of the IR score and sub-scores

Table 4-8 presents the descriptive statistics on the **changes in IR scores over time** (deltas). The deltas depict the difference between a firm's score in 2012 and the company's respective score in 2006. On total sample level, there is a mean and median increase of IR scores of approximately 2 percentage points between 2006 and 2012. This positive change seems to be driven by the South African firms. The South African sub-sample shows a mean increase of 6 percentage points (with a median of 5 percentage points). South African food and agricultural company AFGRI Limited (AFGRI) is the firm with the strongest increase of the IR score in the sample. AFGRI's score rises by 21 percentage points (20 points) from 2006 to 2012. For US firms instead, the IR score decreases by 1 percentage point on average (median of 1 percentage point). The test results in Table 4-7 reveal that while the difference over time is highly significant for South African firms (Panel C), the change is insignificant in the USA (Panel D).

A comparison of the deltas for both countries shows that the **difference-in-differences** is significant at the 1% level (Table 4-9). Comparing only the pre- and post-King III situation in South Africa ignores a potential general time trend, while a simple comparison of the two countries in 2012 or 2006 ignores pre-existing country differences. As opposed to that, the documented significant difference-in-differences suggests that the introduction of King III, which required the application of IR for the South African sample firms from 2010 on, is likely to actually be the driver of the observed increase in the IR scores in South Africa.[172]

[172] Cf. *Angrist/Pischke* ((2009), pp. 227-233) for an explanation and further examples of difference-in-differences research designs.

Differences over time in the mean IR score and sub-scores for each country/year sub-sample							
Variables[a]		mean	std. dev.	Q25	Median	Q75	N
DELTA IR score	RSA 2012-2006	5.88%	6.92%	1.05%	5.26%	11.05%	50
	USA 2012-2006	-0.92%	5.60%	-4.74%	-1.05%	2.63%	50
	Total sample 2012-2006	**2.48%**	**7.13%**	**-2.63%**	**1.84%**	**6.84%**	**100**
DELTA sub-score STRAT	RSA 2012-2006	6.50%	22.05%	-12.50%	0.00%	25.00%	50
	USA 2012-2006	-2.00%	17.92%	-12.50%	0.00%	12.50%	50
	Total sample 2012-2006	**2.25%**	**20.44%**	**-12.50%**	**0.00%**	**12.50%**	**100**
DELTA sub-score CONX	RSA 2012-2006	5.67%	6.62%	0.00%	6.06%	9.09%	50
	USA 2012-2006	-0.03%	6.96%	-4.55%	0.00%	3.03%	50
	Total sample 2012-2006	**2.82%**	**7.34%**	**-3.03%**	**3.03%**	**9.09%**	**100**
DELTA sub-score STAKE	RSA 2012-2006	23.67%	33.60%	0.00%	29.17%	50.00%	50
	USA 2012-2006	1.83%	9.57%	-8.33%	0.00%	8.33%	50
	Total sample 2012-2006	**12.75%**	**26.92%**	**0.00%**	**4.17%**	**29.17%**	**100**
DELTA sub-score MAT	RSA 2012-2006	13.75%	13.66%	0.00%	12.50%	25.00%	50
	USA 2012-2006	3.75%	12.18%	0.00%	0.00%	12.50%	50
	Total sample 2012-2006	**8.75%**	**13.82%**	**0.00%**	**0.00%**	**12.50%**	**100**
DELTA sub-score CONC	RSA 2012-2006	-13.14%	12.65%	-17.86%	-14.29%	-7.14%	50
	USA 2012-2006	-11.86%	12.49%	-21.43%	-10.71%	0.00%	50
	Total sample 2012-2006	**-12.50%**	**12.52%**	**-21.43%**	**-14.29%**	**-3.57%**	**100**
DELTA sub-score REL	RSA 2012-2006	7.17%	16.24%	0.00%	8.33%	16.67%	50
	USA 2012-2006	2.00%	11.24%	0.00%	0.00%	8.33%	50
	Total sample 2012-2006	**4.58%**	**14.13%**	**0.00%**	**4.17%**	**16.67%**	**100**
DELTA sub-score COMP	RSA 2012-2006	3.00%	20.45%	-12.50%	0.00%	12.50%	50
	USA 2012-2006	2.50%	16.12%	0.00%	0.00%	12.50%	50
	Total sample 2012-2006	**2.75%**	**18.32%**	**-12.50%**	**0.00%**	**12.50%**	**100**

[a] The variables are differences over times (DELTA) between financial year 2012 and financial year 2006 in the relative IR score and the sub-scores from the disclosure catalogue, representing the Guiding Principles of the International <IR> Framework: STRAT is Strategic Focus and Future Orientation, CONX is Connectivity of Information, STAKE is Stakeholder Relationships, MAT is Materiality, CONC is Conciseness, REL is Reliability and Completeness and COMP is Consistency and Comparability, respectively.

Table 4-8: Descriptive statistics of the differences in the IR score and sub-scores over time

An economic interpretation of the results shows that there is substantial room for improvement in terms of IR, as both mean and median of the score are only slightly higher than 50%. Even the highest score of 78% is not close to 100%.[173] Nevertheless, the facts that all year-country sub-samples show mean and median scores above 50% and that the lowest score overall is 42% indicate that an essential part of what constitutes the IR score is also present in traditional annual reports, as in those from the USA or from South Africa in 2006. This finding is in line with the conceptual reasoning in chapter 2, which – among other things – revealed that many features of IR draw on elements that were already present in traditional reporting. The comparison of the reporting regulations with the IR Framework in chapter 3 supports this assertion. A detailed analysis of the sub-scores sheds light on where traditional reporting already covers aspects of IR and where the new format is distinct. However, the substantial differences between South Africa 2012 and 2006 as well

[173] This interpretation needs to consider the fact that the reports were only measured against the IR Framework requirements, but were published before it was actually released. Firms could thus not be compliant with the Framework. While some requirements of the Framework are somewhat general in nature, others are rather specific. Expecting scores close to 100% would thus not be realistic.

as South Africa 2012 and USA 2012 suggest that IR brought remarkable changes to the disclosures.

Comparison of the differences over time in the mean IR score and sub-scores for the different sub-samples										
Variables[a]	**RSA 2012-2006**		**USA 2012-2006**		**Difference**	**Tests of comparison**[b]				
	mean	**N**	**mean**	**N**	**in means**	**t-test: t-statistics**		**Wilcoxon-Mann-Whitney test: z-statistics**		
DELTA IR score	**5.88%**	50	**-0.92%**	50	**6.80%**	**5.4019**	***	**4.7140**	***	
DELTA sub-score STRAT	6.50%	50	-2.00%	50	8.50%	2.1152	**	2.0400	**	
DELTA sub-score CONX	5.67%	50	-0.03%	50	5.70%	4.1925	***	3.8460	***	
DELTA sub-score STAKE	23.67%	50	1.83%	50	21.83%	4.4188	***	3.7450	***	
DELTA sub-score MAT	13.75%	50	3.75%	50	10.00%	3.8644	***	3.5520	***	
DELTA sub-score CONC	-13.14%	50	-11.86%	50	-1.29%	-0.5115		-0.4710		
DELTA sub-score REL	7.17%	50	2.00%	50	5.17%	1.8501	*	2.2460	**	
DELTA sub-score COMP	3.00%	50	2.50%	50	0.50%	0.1358		-0.0920		

[a] The variables are differences over times (DELTA) between financial year 2012 and financial year 2006 in the relative IR score and the sub-scores from the disclosure catalogue, representing the Guiding Principles of the International <IR> Framework: STRAT is Strategic Focus and Future Orientation, CONX is Connectivity of Information, STAKE is Stakeholder Relationships, MAT is Materiality, CONC is Conciseness, REL is Reliability and Completeness and COMP is Consistency and Comparability, respectively.

[b] Two-tailed t-test and Wilcoxon-Mann-Whitney test that test the following hypothesis:
H_0: Mean sub-sample 1 – Mean sub-sample 2 = 0;
H_a: Mean sub-sample 1 – Mean sub-sample 2 ≠ 0.
*, **, and *** indicate statistical significance at the 10%, 5% and 1% levels, respectively.

Table 4-9: Comparison of the differences in the IR score and sub-scores

4.4.2.2 Sub-scores on the Guiding Principles

The observed pattern of differences in the mean (and median) scores between the sub-samples is also reflected in most of the **sub-scores** that represent the IR Guiding Principles.

Strategic Focus and Future Orientation (STRAT)

The **STRAT** sub-score – together with REL – is the sub-score with the highest mean score on total sample level (75%). It shows comparably little variation (yet higher than the overall score), with a standard deviation that equals 21% of the mean. In addition, there is at least one report in each sub-sample that scored 100% for the STRAT sub-score. With the exception of REL, there is no other Guiding Principle sub-score for which companies in more than one sub-sample reach the maximum number of points. Hence, it is not surprising that the mean scores for STRAT are also relatively high (between 72% and 79%) across all four sub-samples.

Some (groups of) items in this sub-score require disclosures that many firms make irrespective of IR so that almost all firms get the points for the respective items. One of these **item groups** is STRAT1. The underlying items draw on the disclosure of opportunities and risks from the market position and the firm's business model, which are representative of the future orientation principle. This group of items makes up four[174] out of eight maximum

[174] A point is awarded for each an opportunity and a risk from the market position and each an opportunity and a risk from the business model.

points for STRAT. However, both market position and business model imply a multitude of aspects that risks and opportunities can be connected with so that many firms end up scoring these four points. For instance, South African hotel and casino operator Sun International Limited (Sun) writes in their 2012 Integrated Annual Report:

> *"A relatively new factor in the South African gaming industry (which currently still represents 80% of our business) is the growth in alternate forms of gaming outside the traditional casinos. To counter this increasing competition for discretionary income, we have an absolutely unique portfolio of properties in which we have invested heavily and which deliver experiences to our guests that cannot be replicated by these alternative gaming products. We also have a large database of our highly loyal Most Valued Guests built up over decades, which gives us a distinct competitive advantage.*
>
> *We are still managing to – and should continue to – improve casino revenues, but it is definitely getting tougher to grow aggressively in our relatively mature and saturated local markets."*
>
> (*Sun* (2013), pp. 18-19)

With this short statement, the report addresses both the risks (saturated markets) and opportunities (large database of guests due to their established market position) resulting from the firm's market position, but at the same time also the risks (competition through new alternate forms of gaming the company has not in their portfolio) and opportunities (large variety of offerings) from their business model. Hence, this statement covers the entire item group **STRAT1**. At the same time, this example shows that there is an overlap between risk and opportunities from the business model on the one hand and from the market position on the other.

Although many reports from all sub-samples score high, **differences occur between years and countries**. The mean sub-score of 79% from South Africa 2012 is higher than the 2012 US mean of 73%. This difference is significant at the 5% level. In 2006, there was no significant difference. The deltas show a marginally significant (10% level) increase of 7 percentage points for the South African mean, whereas there is only a scarce and insignificant decrease of 2 percentage points in the US. Hence, there is a difference of these changes between the countries, which is significant at the 5% level.

An economic interpretation of these changes reveals that IR seems to promote the Strategy principle, telling from the comparisons between South Africa 2012 and 2006 and between South Africa and USA 2012. The high overall scores throughout all sub-samples are surprising at first sight, though, considering that national regulations do not or only partially cover this principle. However, as the aforementioned example reveals, the items in the STRAT category also reflect aspects like risks and opportunities to a high degree. This may explain the scores, as these aspects are covered by national regulations (see chapter 3).

Connectivity of Information (CONX)

CONX yields only slightly lower scores on average than STRAT throughout all sub-samples. The mean sub-score ranges between 64% and 69%, while the standard deviations of around 10% of the mean as well as the interquartile ranges of around 10 percentage points indicate little variation. The average score is substantially higher than *Zhou et al.'s* (2016) mean of 5%, but the comparability of these values is debatable due to differences in data collection. Given the various dimensions of connectivity, this sub-score is the one with the highest number of points achievable (33). However, this variety includes dimensions that were already established in corporate reporting before IR, such as the connectivity between time dimensions (item group CONX2, yielding 3 points) or between quantitative and qualitative information (CONX5, 3 points). In both of these and other groups of items, many firms reach the maximum number of points. US retailing firm Target provides an example of presenting quantitative indicators alongside qualitative explanatory information on how the indicators are computed in their 2006 annual report:

> "*Gross margin rate represents gross margin (sales less cost of sales) as a percentage of sales. See Note 3 for a description of expenses included in cost of sales.*
>
> *In 2006, our consolidated gross margin rate was 31.9 percent compared to 31.9 percent in 2005.*"
>
> (*Target* (2007), p. 12 of Form 10-K)

Another issue in this regard is the presentation of quantitative indicators with a quantitative and/or qualitative **explanation for changes from previous values.** One of many examples stems from US coating supplier PPG Industries, Inc.'s (PPG) 2012 report:

> "*Net sales in 2012 totaled $15,200 million compared to $14,885 million in 2011, an increase of 2%. Higher selling prices increased sales 2%, higher volumes increased sales 1% and acquisitions contributed 2% to sales. These increases were partially offset by 3% from negative foreign currency impact. Sales volumes varied significantly by region, with volume growth in North America of nearly 5% and modest growth in emerging regions. European volumes declined 4% versus the prior year period with every coatings business except aerospace experiencing sluggish end-use market conditions. Improved selling prices were achieved in each of the three coatings segments and Optical and Specialty Materials. In our coatings segments, higher selling prices were in response to persistent raw material and other cost inflation. The unfavorable currency impact was primarily driven by the U.S. dollar strengthening against the Euro and Latin American currencies.*"
>
> (*PPG* (2013), p. 18)

Yet, other groups of CONX items yield more variation. In particular, item group CONX4, which makes up 10 points dealing with the **connectivity of financial information and other information**, shows remarkable differences among the sub-samples. South African firms score 4.7 and 3.3 points on average in 2012 and 2006 respectively in this item group, whereas US firms have mean scores of 3.4 and 2.9. The underlying requirements from the Framework are rather specific here, which may explain the relatively low scores. For instance, the Framework requires firms to disclose the implications of environmental policies for cost reduction or new business opportunities (IR F. 3.8). South African sugar producer Illovo Sugar Limited's (Illovo) 2012 report fulfils this requirement by explaining both the environmental and the connected financial benefits of their cogeneration approach (i.e., generating energy from remainders of the sugar production):

> "*Dry, fibrous bagasse, remaining after the extraction of juice from the crushed stalks of sugar cane, provides us with a substantial renewable energy opportunity for cogeneration, replacing fossil fuel sources such as coal and electricity generated from coal, thereby reducing GHG. In addition to bagasse, certain of our operations, Ubombo in Swaziland, Nchalo in Malawi and Noodsberg in South Africa, are able to supplement their cogeneration capacity by utilising additional green cane biomass and wood as boiler feedstock. During the year under review, these operations utilised approximately 150 000 tons of biomass and wood as renewable fuel sources to produce heat and energy in their dual-fired boilers. We are continuing to assess opportunities to increase the cogeneration capabilities of all our operations.*
>
> *In addition to the environmental and cost benefits, cogeneration provides a potential source of additional revenue through the export of energy into national grids. With its integrated cogeneration facility, it is anticipated that our Ubombo mill in Swaziland will export 55 GWh to the national grid over a 48-week period by 2015. During the year under review, a total of 36.95 GWh was exported to the grid. The sale of this renewable energy directly enables the SEC to reduce its Scope 1 emissions and consequently its customers' Scope 2 emissions. Based on the Swaziland grid emissions factor published by the GHG Protocol, (a purchased electricity calculation tool – 480kg CO_2 per MWh) the sale of this electricity enabled SEC to avoid 18 068 tCO_2e in 2012/13. During the year, and on a test basis, Zambia Sugar also exported a small amount of power into the national grid.*"
>
> (*Illovo* (2013), pp. 96-97)

With the variation in this item group, CONX4 is presumably a driver of the **year and country differences** in the CONX sub-score. The South Africa 2012 mean (69%) is higher than its US counterpart for that year (66%). As opposed to this, the average US sub-sample score (67%) was significantly (5% level) higher than the South African one (64%) in 2006. This reversal draws on a highly significant increase of 6 percentage points in the South African scores, while no significant change occurs in the USA. Hence, there is a highly significant difference-in-differences for this sub-score. This supports the view of chapters 2 and 3 that connectivity is a key aspect and major novelty of IR, although some dimensions of connectivity are also present in traditional reporting, as reasoned above. The latter notion is backed by the relatively high scores throughout all four sub-samples.

Stakeholder Relationships (STAKE)

South African energy and chemical company Sasol shows a **best practice example** for disclosures on the **STAKE** sub-score in their 2012 report. It illustrates how a report can provide information on stakeholders' needs and interests as well as the firm's response in form of both communication and actions in a concise and well-arranged way, using a tabular format. The depicted page yields all 12 points awarded for this sub-score (Figure 4-9[175]).

[175] Note that in Sasol's report, the table is continued on the following page. It also includes disclosures about customers, business partners, suppliers, organized business, communities and the media.

our key relationships

how we manage the expectations of our stakeholders

Understanding and being responsive to our stakeholders' expectations is critical to our ability to create value. Building and maintaining trust and respect among our stakeholders impacts positively on our reputation, and is essential to proactively address risks and opportunities.
Our Global Stakeholder Management Strategy recognises that our engagement with stakeholders should develop sustainable healthy relationships, and directs our organisation's stakeholder management, irrespective of geographic location or stakeholder category.

In line with global best practices and the King III Code, Sasol has adopted an inclusive approach to stakeholder relations. An overview of our principal stakeholders, how we engage with them and the general nature of their expectations, is provided in the table below.

Stake-holder	How we engage with our stakeholders	Stakeholder's expectations	How we respond to stakeholder's expectations	Stakeholder's contribution to value creation	Page
Employees	• Induction programme. • Ongoing safety training. • Personal development and training needs assessment. • Internal newsletter, posters and billboards. • Regular communications from chief executive officer. • Sasol intranet and internet. • Active and continuing shop floor briefings. • Management engagement and road shows. • Performance reviews and development discussions. • Employee surveys. • Transparency in communication.	• A safe, stimulating and rewarding work environment. • Fair remuneration and benefits. • Open communication with management. • Opportunities for personal and career development. • Progress on transformation in South Africa. • Recognition of job well done. • Collaboration and teamwork across business units. • Access to employee wellness programmes and counselling.	• Provide benchmarked competitive remuneration and benefits packages. • Enforce stringent safety measures. • Provide ongoing training and education options. • Encourage open communication between employees and managers. • Offer employee wellness programmes and HIV counselling. • Interventions to address outcomes of employee surveys.	• Form the foundation of our business. Through their effort, commitment and integrity, Sasol can produce, deliver and succeed.	6 7 72
Unions	• Partnership forums with unions at business unit and group level, including two-way discussions on issues and the company's strategy. • Shop floor briefings. • Safety meetings. • Engagement with the group executive committee and chief executive officer.	• A safe working environment. • Fair remuneration and benefits. • Open communication with management. • Skills development, training, and career development. • Progress on transformation in South Africa.	• Enforce stringent safety measures. • Provide benchmarked competitive remuneration and benefits packages. • Partner with unions to address employee issues. • Consult with unions on decisions affecting their members. • Provide effective programmes and initiatives to facilitate safety performance. • Provide effective programmes and initiatives to facilitate employee relations.	• Through engagement and discussion regarding labour issues, we gain a better understanding of employee needs, and we develop and build relationships and grow trust.	6 7 72
Shareholders	• Regular engagements and road shows. • Investor newsletters. • Interim and annual reports. • SENS and media releases. • Results published in media. • Site visits. • Sasol internet.	• Sustained returns on investment through strategic and organic growth, sound risk management and exemplary governance practices.	• Strong leadership who provide strategic direction and who lead by example. • Focus on good corporate governance and ethics. • Progress with project pipeline and future growth projects.	• Provide financial capital required to sustain and grow the business.	14 28 42 56 74
Government, regulators and political role players	• Personal meetings at all levels. • Written communication. • Workshops and presentations. • Government engagement through organised business and industry. • Participation in government-initiated platforms. • Participation in government's bilateral engagements with other countries.	• Job creation. • Alleviation of poverty. • Contribute to the eradication of inequality. • Demonstrate business growth. • Transparent and responsible behaviour. • Consistency in messages. • Compliance with relevant legislation such as broad-based black economic empowerment (BBBEE) codes and environmental regulations. • Demonstrate commitment to transformation. • Innovative solutions for energy security.	• Engage constructively on new policies and regulations affecting Sasol's operations. • Comply with and report transparently on existing regulations. • Contribute to the economies of countries in which we operate by paying taxes and royalties as well as creating jobs. • Support priorities of the countries in which we operate by participating in government initiatives, for example, reducing energy consumption, and disclosing and managing carbon emissions. • Develop community projects that impact areas of regional and national importance such as education and health.	• Give us our licence to operate and provide the enabling regulatory framework in which we operate.	34 35 41 48 72

Sasol annual integrated report 2013 IR

38

Figure 4-9: Example STAKE: Sasol (RSA 2012)
(*Sasol* (2013), p. 38)

The sub-score shows clear differences between the two countries in both years, though. South African firms surpass their US counterparts with a mean of 55% compared to 22% in 2012 and 32% compared to 20% in 2006. In both years, these country **differences** are highly significant. This result is consistent with the aforementioned finding that US firms rather address shareholders only, whereas South African companies address stakeholders to a higher extent. Both these findings are plausible, given that stakeholder orientation in reporting has already been established in South Africa for a considerable period of time.[176] It seems to have increased further after the introduction of IR, as the highly significant mean delta of 24% indicates.[177] For US firms, disclosures on stakeholders do not change significantly between the two years in question. Hence, the changes over time in the two countries differ significantly (1% level).

Materiality (MAT)

The **MAT** sub-score comprises eight out of the 95 points for the complete disclosure catalogue. This category includes items that deal with the materiality determination process, the reporting boundary and limitations to provide information. While firms score relatively high on average for the reporting boundary items (MAT2), the mean scores for the materiality determination disclosures (MAT1) are very low. In 2012, South African reports score 1 out of 3 points on average for the latter **item group**. Although this score is rather low, it still exceeds the mean scores of the reports from the other sub-samples (ranging between 0.1 and 0.3 on average). This outcome underlines that the requirement to describe the determination of materiality is in fact a novelty to corporate reporting. City Lodge Hotels Limited (City Lodge) presents an example in their 2012 report by describing their identification of material issues as follows:

> "*Following an internal workshop, inputs gathered from these key sources were assessed and summarised prior to being presented to the board for their approval of the most material issues for inclusion in this IR.*
>
> *The issues identified were mapped according to their materiality as shown in the diagram below.*
>
> *As the final step in the process, this information fed directly into the articulation of our current business strategy.*"
>
> (*City Lodge* (2013), p. 11)

The fact that only the South Africa 2012 sub-sample, the only setting in which firms faced a requirement to release integrated reports, reaches an average MAT sub-score that exceeds 50% is consistent with the notion that Materiality is a **key principle of IR** and that IR in turn promotes this principle. At first sight, the overall low scores are surprising, given that Materiality principles are also present in other regulations on corporate reporting (see chapter 3). However, the requirements on the Materiality principle from the IR Framework

---

176 A complete chapter (chapter 12) in the King I Report from 1994 deals with stakeholder communications and reporting.

177 South African firms have to a considerable extent used guidance from the IRCSA DP for their 2012 reports. The finding is thus plausible as this framework promotes addressing stakeholders (see chapter 3).

(and thus the items of the content analysis catalogue) particularly address disclosures on materiality, such as the materiality determination process. As these disclosures do represent a novelty compared with other regulations, the finding of low mean scores overall is comprehensible.

As the mentioned results regarding the score indicate, MAT yields **differences** between the countries and over time. There is a large difference between South Africa (54%) and the USA (39%) in 2012, which is significant at the 1% level. In addition, South African firms on average already exhibited a significantly (5% level) higher degree of MAT in their reports than US firms in 2006 (40% as opposed to 35%). However, while the increase in South Africa from 2006 to 2012 is highly significant, the change in the US score over time is insignificant. Therefore, the difference-in-differences of 10 percentage points is highly significant (1% level).

Conciseness (CONC)

CONC and COMP are the only two sub-scores for which the mean for South Africa 2012 is not the highest of the four year-country sub-samples. On average, South African firms (56%) have a significantly (1% level) higher **CONC** score than their US counterparts (43%) in 2012. The difference was similar in 2006 (and also significant at the 1% level), but with slightly higher values (69% compared to 55%). The negative deltas for both countries reflect this lower level in 2012. Both deltas are highly significant (1% level), while there is no significant difference between these changes over time in the two countries.

The total sample mean of 56% for CONC is on the same level as the mean for the total IR score. These **results can be explained** by the fact that in the South African 2006 sub-sample the reports were both the shortest on average in terms of word count[178] and the highest on average (for three out of four items) in using links and references compared with the other sub-samples. Figure 4-10[179] illustrates the number of links and references that companies throughout the different sub-samples use in their reports. The items that base upon these numbers constitute 10 out of the 14 points that are awarded for CONC so that they substantially impact the sub-score. Not only the comparable level of the CONC sub-score and the total IR score, but also the negative changes of the CONC sub-score over time show that there is much room for improvement in terms of conciseness, despite the introduction of IR. The phenomena of lengthy reports and potential information overload are not eliminated for the examined reports. However, an observer's statement reveals that after the introduction of IR in South Africa, firms needed to overcome an initial phase of increasing report length to get used to the Conciseness principle (*Orton-Jones* (2015), p. 38). The data from this study may therefore provide insight into this initial increase rather than into a sustainable trend.

---

178 A detailed analysis of report length follows in the further course of this section.

179 While the figure shows the absolute number of links and references, the number of references in relation to the word count is relevant the CONC sub-score. This intensifies the effect, however, since the South Africa 2006 sub-sample has the shortest reports on average.

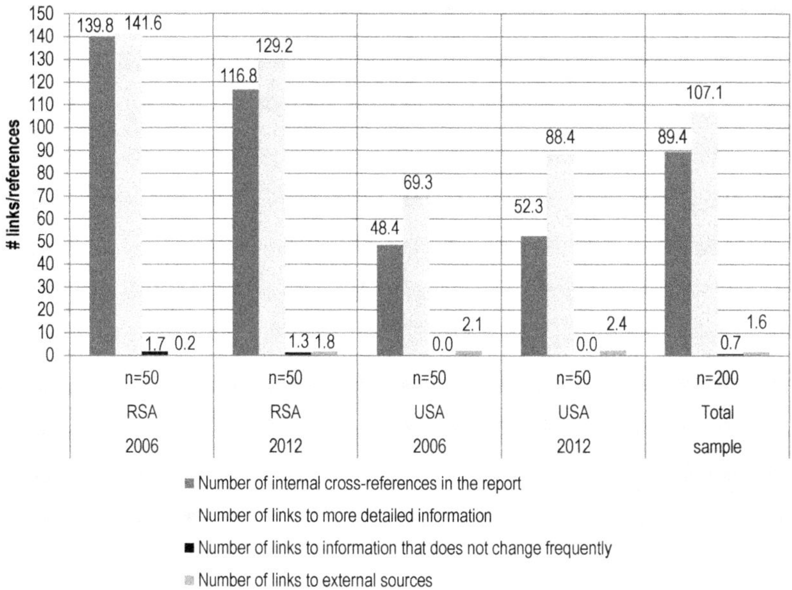

Figure 4-10: Mean number of links and references in the report

Reliability and Completeness (REL)

The **REL** sub-score shows a similar pattern as the STRAT score discussed above. It also yields a very high total sample mean of 75%. With a standard deviation that equals 15% of the mean, the variation is very low, instead. Except in the USA 2006 sub-sample (with a maximum of 92%), there was at least one report in each sub-sample to reach all points of the REL sub-score. The mean scores for the four sub-samples range between 73% and 80%. Similar to STRAT, some item groups in the REL sub-score require disclosures that are not specific for IR. Hence, almost all firms score the points for these items.

REL4 is such an **item group**. Making up 3 out of 12 points, it requires balanced disclosures, in particular the consideration of both capital increases and decreases, both strengths and weaknesses and both positive and negative performance. Again, the underlying concepts leave room for interpretation. Moreover, these items refer to classical contents of annual reports[180] and the sample firms, being rather large-sized, can be expected to experience

[180] However, although the concept of different Capitals is a somewhat innovative issue introduced by IR, firms implicitly or explicitly have made disclosures about various capitals irrespective of IR. For instance, a classical investment in non-current assets can be interpreted as an increase in manufactured (for a tangible asset) or intellectual capital (for an intangible asset like a patent) in exchange with a decrease in financial capital.

both various good and bad results with their manifold subsidiaries and their mostly international presence. Thus, it appears plausible that many firms yield high REL sub-scores. For instance, AECI reviews the year of its subsidiary Chemical Services Limited (Chemserve) in its 2006 report:

> "*The first acquisition in the Brazil country step-out strategy was completed in May with the Resitec investment. This acquisition delivered a pleasing performance notwithstanding a strong Brazilian currency. Expansions are under way to increase capacity for existing products and to broaden the company's base. Chemserve is actively seeking further acquisitions in Brazil.*"
>
> (*AECI* (2007), p. 18)

However, reviewing the year of SANS Fibre, another subsidiary of the group, the same report provides the following disclosures:

> "*Internal problems also affected the company. Some poor plant performances in the first seven months resulted in low raw material to finished goods conversion efficiencies and reduced productivity. The implementation of appropriate corrective measures was severely hampered by the power outages. It is pleasing, however, that a substantial improvement has since been sustained.*"
>
> (*AECI* (2007), p. 20)

Despite already high scores in 2006, there is a mean **increase in both countries** for the REL sub-score. The increase is higher for South Africa (7 percentage points) than for the USA (2 percentage points), though. This difference-in-differences is marginally significant at the 10% level (5% level for the Wilcoxon test). While the mean sub-score is not significantly different for the two countries in 2006 (72% and 73%, respectively), the stronger increase leads to a higher mean sub-score in South Africa (80%) than the USA (75%) for the year 2012 (significant difference at the 5% level). The economic interpretation yields that, judging from the high mean scores throughout all sub-samples, reliability is also high in traditional reports and does not provide a novelty of IR. This notion underlines the conceptual reasoning from chapter 2 and the likeness of IR and other reporting regulations in this regard, as outlined in chapter 3. Nonetheless, the comparisons between South Africa 2012 with the US sub-sample of the same year and the 2006 sub-sample from the same country again indicate that the introduction of IR may enhance this principle.

Consistency and Comparability (COMP)

Finally, the mean **COMP** sub-score of 43% for the total sample is clearly lower than the mean overall IR score (58%), indicating particular room for improvement of the reports in terms of comparability. In addition, this sub-score shows an unexpected pattern of sub-sample differences. US firms have higher mean scores than their South African counterparts in both years (44% compared to 38% in 2006 and 47% compared to 41% in 2012). The differences are significant at the 5% level.[181] None of the countries shows a significant change over time, though. The difference-in-differences is not significant, either. As the

[181] For 2012, only the Wilcoxon test shows a significant (5% level) difference, however.

conceptual analysis (see chapter 2) revealed, there is a trade-off in IR between the flexibility for firms to tailor their reporting to their business model on the one hand and the comparability of the disclosures on the other. According to the reasoning of this analysis, various aspects of the Framework are rather in line with the former perspective, at the expense of comparability. The empirical findings indicate support for this view.

US firms score higher than South African firms in two **particular groups of items**, which together make up 4 out of 8 points in this sub-score. One of them is the consistent use of KPIs (COMP1). This finding is in line with a high degree of standardization that can be expected from US reports due to the influence of the highly structured Form 10-K (see chapter 3). Moreover, US firms showed higher scores in the use of industry or regional benchmark data (COMP2). For instance, *DIRECTV* presents a chart in their 2012 annual report that graphically compares the firm's cumulative total return with that of the S&P 500 Index and that of an industry peer group (Figure 4-11). Hence, readers get an impression of both regional and industry benchmarks.

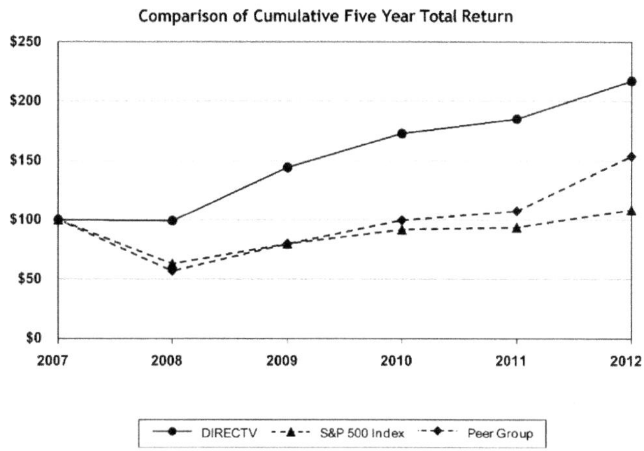

Company Name / Index	12/31/07	12/31/08	12/31/09	12/31/10	12/31/11	12/31/12
DIRECTV	100	99.1	144.3	172.7	185.0	217.0
S&P 500 Index	100	63.0	79.7	91.7	93.6	108.6
Peer Group	100	56.9	79.6	99.6	107.5	153.8

Figure 4-11: Example COMP2: DIRECTV (USA 2012)
(*DIRECTV* (2013), p. 131)

4.4.3 Supplementary measures

Table 4-10 presents the descriptive statistics for the four supplementary measures outlined in section 4.3.2, namely report length, the use of boilerplate disclosures, the use of jargon and readability. These measures depict different shortcomings of corporate reporting.

		Supplementary measures for each country/year sub-sample					
Variables[a]		**mean**	**std. dev.**	**Q25**	**median**	**Q75**	**N**
# words	RSA 2006	44,485.84	18,306.14	31,673.00	39,774.50	50,879.00	50
	RSA 2012	54,361.82	16,671.03	40,947.00	52,112.00	61,864.00	50
	USA 2006	45,920.46	17,933.62	31,378.00	45,757.00	54,167.00	50
	USA 2012	53,958.88	18,655.98	39,951.00	52,372.00	61,159.00	50
	Total sample	**49,681.75**	**18,337.88**	**36,286.50**	**47,363.50**	**59,351.00**	**200**
Similarity score	RSA 2006	0.3368	0.0906	0.2732	0.3454	0.3857	50
	RSA 2012	0.3276	0.1461	0.2120	0.3088	0.4329	50
	USA 2006	0.4409	0.0889	0.3856	0.4470	0.4933	50
	USA 2012	0.5443	0.1099	0.4729	0.5550	0.6138	50
	Total sample	**0.4124**	**0.1415**	**0.3114**	**0.4196**	**0.5103**	**200**
Jargon score	RSA 2006	0.0115	0.0033	0.0091	0.0113	0.0134	50
	RSA 2012	0.0132	0.0032	0.0108	0.0127	0.0159	50
	USA 2006	0.0091	0.0051	0.0056	0.0077	0.0110	50
	USA 2012	0.0111	0.0045	0.0084	0.0106	0.0135	50
	Total sample	**0.0112**	**0.0043**	**0.0081**	**0.0109**	**0.0136**	**200**
Fog Index	RSA 2006	16.1792	1.4875	14.9840	16.1350	17.2520	50
	RSA 2012	16.4858	1.4021	15.6000	16.4735	17.6170	50
	USA 2006	15.3634	1.9224	13.7060	15.2855	16.7880	50
	USA 2012	16.3503	1.7800	15.2300	16.5050	17.4880	50
	Total sample	**16.0947**	**1.7059**	**14.9280**	**16.1735**	**17.2765**	**200**

[a] # words is the number of words in the report. Similarity score is the degree of similarity or resemblance with the firm's report from the previous financial year (ranging from 0 to 1). Jargon score is the quotient of the number of jargon words to the number of total words in the letter from the chairman/CEO (ranging from 0 to 1). Fog Index is the Fog Index of readability for the letter from the chairman/CEO, which can be interpreted as the years of education necessary to understand a text.

Table 4-10: Descriptive statistics of the supplementary measures

The mean **report length** (# words) of the country sub-samples is similar, both in 2012 (about 54,400 words in South Africa compared with 54,000 in the USA) and 2006 (about 44,500 and 45,900, respectively). Table 4-11 presents the results of the tests of comparisons between the sub-sample means for the supplementary measures. Neither of the outlined country differences is significant, as Panels A and B reveal. The medians are similar to each other in 2012, too, after differing by about 6,000 words in 2006. Likewise, the standard deviation is comparable in both countries. In 2012, the in-sample variation is about 16,700 words in South Africa and about 18,700 words in the USA. These values equal 31% of the mean in South Africa and 35% in the USA. In 2006, the standard deviation is close to 18,000 words for both countries, equaling about 40% of the respective means.[182] The delta values in Table 4-12 show an increase in report length over time by almost 10,000 words on average in South Africa, whereas US reports increase in length by 8,000 on average between 2006 and 2012. Both increases are significant, at the 1% and 5% level, respectively (Panels C and D of Table 4-11). As firms from both countries increase their report length, there is no significant difference between these deltas (Table 4-13). These findings show that the introduction of IR did not (yet) lead to a decrease in report length, contrary to the

[182] Note that the country-level comparisons may be driven by the country-specific size or industry distribution of the firms. In comparing the differences-in-differences over time, these influences can be neglected. For the explanatory analysis in chapter 5, a separate test takes the industry influence on report length/conciseness into regard.

IIRC's intention. Instead, the trend that reports get even longer (see section 1.1) seems to continue. However, as mentioned for the conciseness of the reports (see section 4.4.2.2), IR might lead to shorter reports in the long term after surpassing a time of increasing volume that firms need to adapt to the new approach.

Firms from the US sub-samples clearly and significantly (1% level for both years) use more **boilerplate disclosures**, measured as the similarity of a firm's report with the same firm's report from the previous year (similarity score), than their South African counterparts. The standard deviation is lower in the USA, though. South African firms show an average degree of 0.33 (out of a maximum score of 1) in 2012 and a standard deviation of 0.15, which equals 45% of the mean. US firms have an average similarity score of 0.54, instead, with a standard deviation of 20% of the mean (0.11 in absolute terms). The mean value of South African firms for 2006 is 0.34, while the standard deviation equals 27% of this mean or 0.09 in absolute terms. In the USA, the average similarity score for 2006 is 0.44, the standard deviation being 20% of the mean in relative terms and 0.09 in absolute terms. Mean deltas show that while there was a very slight, yet insignificant decrease of 0.01 in South Africa between 2006 and 2012, the similarity has significantly (1% level) increased by 0.10 on average in the USA. The latter development is in line with the rather standardized US reporting format, impacted by the highly structured Form 10-K and by the role of the aforementioned fear of litigation for disclosure practice (*Nelson/Pritchard* (2016), p. 267). In South Africa instead, the insignificant decrease does not allow valid inferences about a reduction of boilerplate disclosures resulting from the introduction of IR. However, if there was an increase in the score before the observed period, one could possibly argue that IR has stopped this trend. Data from prior periods is not known, though. Nonetheless, comparing these opposing trends in the two countries yields a highly significant difference-in-differences.

The **jargon** score (ranging between 0 and 1) is relatively low throughout all four sub-samples, but shows some degree of variation. Standard deviations of 0.003 (24% of the mean) and 0.005 (41% of the mean), respectively, go along with mean values of 0.013 for South African firms and 0.011 for US firms in 2012. This country difference is significant at the 1% level. A similar pattern on a slightly lower level is visible for the 2006 average values, which are 0.012 for South Africa and 0.009 for the USA, the difference also being highly significant. The corresponding standard deviations of 0.003 (29% of the mean) and 0.005 (56% of the mean), respectively, again indicate considerable variation in these scores. With values of 0.002, the deltas between 2012 and 2006 are almost equal in the two countries. Both deltas are significant, at the 1% (South Africa) and 5% level (USA), respectively, whereas the difference-in-differences between the countries is insignificant. While the overall low scores may indicate support for a clear language in corporate reports (e.g., as found by *Marx/Mohammadali-Haji* (2014) for South Africa), they are not in line with evidence for more complex reporting language (as indicated by studies such as *Subramanian et al.* (1993) or *Loughran/McDonald* (2014) for the USA). However, differences in the selection of the samples leave doubt about the comparability with earlier studies. Moreover, the scores do not necessarily represent the use of jargon in the entire report, as they stem from the Letter to the Stakeholders (see section 4.3.2).

Comparison of the mean supplementary measures for the different sub-samples

Panel A: RSA 2012 vs. USA 2012

Variables[a]	Sub-sample 1: RSA 2012		Sub-sample 2: USA 2012		Difference in means	Tests of comparison[b]	
	mean	N	mean	N		t-test: t-statistics	Wilcoxon-Mann-Whitney test: z-statistics
# words	54,361.82	50	53,958.88	50	402.94	0.1139	0.3170
Similarity score	0.3276	50	0.5443	50	-0.2168	-8.3822 ***	-6.4940 ***
Jargon score	0.0132	50	0.0111	50	0.0021	2.7536 ***	2.9850 ***
Fog Index	16.4858	50	16.3503	50	0.1356	0.4230	0.7030

Panel B: RSA 2006 vs. USA 2006

Variables[a]	Sub-sample 1: RSA 2006		Sub-sample 2: USA 2006		Difference in means	Tests of comparison[b]	
	mean	N	mean	N		t-test: t-statistics	Wilcoxon-Mann-Whitney test: z-statistics
# words	44,485.84	50	45,920.46	50	-1,434.62	-0.3958	-0.7790
Similarity score	0.3368	50	0.4409	50	-0.1040	-5.7943 ***	-5.3700 ***
Jargon score	0.0115	50	0.0091	50	0.0024	2.8015 ***	3.5710 ***
Fog Index	16.1792	50	15.3634	50	0.8157	2.3730 **	2.3270 **

Panel C: RSA 2012 vs. RSA 2006

Variables[a]	Sub-sample 1: RSA 2012		Sub-sample 2: RSA 2006		Difference in means	Tests of comparison[b]	
	mean	N	mean	N		t-test: t-statistics	Wilcoxon-Mann-Whitney test: z-statistics
# words	54,361.82	50	44,485.84	50	9,875.98	2.8205 ***	3.2950 ***
Similarity score	0.3276	50	0.3368	50	-0.0093	-0.3814	-0.5380
Jargon score	0.0132	50	0.0115	50	0.0018	2.7539 ***	2.6270 ***
Fog Index	16.4858	50	16.1792	50	0.3067	1.0608	1.1370

Panel D: USA 2012 vs. USA 2006

Variables[a]	Sub-sample 1: USA 2012		Sub-sample 2: USA 2006		Difference in means	Tests of comparison[b]	
	mean	N	mean	N		t-test: t-statistics	Wilcoxon-Mann-Whitney test: z-statistics
# words	53,958.88	50	45,920.46	50	8,038.42	2.1965 **	2.2750 **
Similarity score	0.5443	50	0.4409	50	0.1035	5.1744 ***	5.0120 ***
Jargon score	0.0111	50	0.0091	50	0.0020	2.1197 **	2.8260 ***
Fog Index	16.3503	50	15.3634	50	0.9868	2.6634 ***	2.5650 **

[a] # words is the number of words in the report. Similarity score is the degree of similarity or resemblance with the firm's report from the previous financial year (ranging from 0 to 1). Jargon score is the quotient of the number of jargon words to the number of total words in the letter from the chairman/CEO (ranging from 0 to 1). Fog Index is the Fog Index of readability for the letter from the chairman/CEO, which can be interpreted as the years of education necessary to understand a text.

[b] Two-tailed t-test and Wilcoxon-Mann-Whitney test that test the following hypothesis:
H_0: Mean sub-sample 1 – Mean sub-sample 2 = 0;
H_a: Mean sub-sample 1 – Mean sub-sample 2 ≠ 0.

*, **, and *** indicate statistical significance at the ten per cent, five per cent and one per cent levels, respectively.

Table 4-11: Comparison of the supplementary measures

Differences over time in the supplementary measures							
Variables[a]		mean	std. dev.	Q25	median	Q75	N
DELTA # words	RSA 2012-2006	9,875.98	22,260.19	-7,077.00	12,599.50	27,677.00	50
	USA 2012-2006	8,038.42	14,036.39	1,095.00	6,850.00	14,211.00	50
	Total sample 2012-2006	**8,957.20**	**18,537.07**	**-2,408.00**	**8,438.00**	**18,197.00**	**100**
DELTA Similarity score	RSA 2012-2006	-0.0093	0.1221	-0.1035	0.0033	0.0733	50
	USA 2012-2006	0.1035	0.1061	0.0402	0.0973	0.1771	50
	Total sample 2012-2006	**0.0471**	**0.1271**	**-0.0311**	**0.0583**	**0.1213**	**100**
DELTA Jargon score	RSA 2012-2006	0.0018	0.0036	-0.0001	0.0015	0.0040	50
	USA 2012-2006	0.0020	0.0052	-0.0021	0.0022	0.0042	50
	Total sample 2012-2006	**0.0019**	**0.0044**	**-0.0005**	**0.0022**	**0.0042**	**100**
DELTA Fog Index	RSA 2012-2006	0.3067	1.6177	-0.9950	0.1090	1.0590	50
	USA 2012-2006	0.9868	1.9996	-0.1670	1.1795	2.2150	50
	Total sample 2012-2006	**0.6467**	**1.8415**	**-0.5385**	**0.5385**	**1.8580**	**100**

[a] The variables are differences over times (DELTA) between financial year 2012 and financial year 2006 in the supplementary measures. # words is the number of words in the report. Similarity score is the degree of similarity or resemblance with the firm's report from the previous financial year (ranging from 0 to 1). Jargon score is the quotient of the number of jargon words to the number of total words in the letter from the chairman/CEO (ranging from 0 to 1). Fog Index is the Fog Index of readability for the letter from the chairman/CEO, which can be interpreted as the years of education necessary to understand a text.

Table 4-12: Descriptive statistics of the differences over time in the supplementary measures

There is less within-sample variation for report **readability** (Fog Index) than for the other three measures. Standard deviations range between 9% and 13% of the mean for the four sub-samples. In line with the low within-sample variation, there is also hardly any difference between the countries in 2012, with mean (median) values of 16.5 (16.5) for South Africa and 16.4 (16.5) for the USA, respectively. The small difference in the means is insignificant. As opposed to this, the means and medians do differ between the 2006 sub-samples. In South Africa, the mean (median) Fog Index is 16.2 (16.1), which is significantly (5% level) higher than the US value of 15.4 (15.3). While the difference over time is insignificant for South Africa, US firms show a significant increase (1% level) of the Fog Index, meaning a decline in readability. As a result, the difference in the deltas between the countries is marginally significant (10% level). The index values can be interpreted as the years of education necessary to understand the text. All four sub-sample means are higher than 12, which is the "*danger line of difficulty*" (*Gunning* (1952), p. 20), and thus indicate that the examined texts are on average too difficult to read.[183] The patterns over time are similar to those for the similarity scores. While the significant increase in the USA is in line with research that finds high and increasing Fog values in US corporate reports (e.g., *Li* (2008), *Loughran/McDonald* (2014)), interpreting the unchanged values over time for South Africa would require more data from previous periods. The latter data could reflect a stabilization of the development of readability over the introduction of IR or could also suggest that IR had no impact at all. However, as for the aforementioned measures, the comparability of the findings with the literature is questionable due to differences in the samples. Moreover, this study uses the chairman's letter, only. Hence, similar to the jargon score, it is after all debatable whether the index values are representative of the entire report.

[183] As *Gunning's* threshold of twelve refers to magazines, a higher threshold may be more appropriate. *Li* ((2008), p. 225) characterizes annual reports with a Fog Index between 14 and 18 as difficult. The mean values for the samples of the study at hand also meet this definition of difficulty.

Comparison of the differences in the mean supplementary measures for the different sub-samples									
Variables[a]	RSA 2012-2006		USA 2012-2006		Difference	Tests of comparison[b]			
	mean	N	mean	N	in means	t-test: t-statistics		Wilcoxon-Mann-Whitney test: z-statistics	
DELTA # words	9,875.98	50	8,038.42	50	1,837.56	0.4937		0.4360	
DELTA Similarity score	-0.0093	50	0.1035	50	-0.1127	-4.9296	***	-4.3710	***
DELTA Jargon score	0.0018	50	0.0020	50	-0.0002	-0.2774		-0.0970	
DELTA Fog Index	0.3067	50	0.9868	50	-0.6802	-1.8699	*	-1.9920	**

[a] The variables are differences over times (DELTA) between financial year 2012 and financial year 2006 in the supplementary measures. # words is the number of words in the report. Similarity score is the degree of similarity or resemblance with the firm's report from the previous financial year (ranging from 0 to 1). Jargon score is the quotient of the number of jargon words to the number of total words in the letter from the chairman/CEO (ranging from 0 to 1). Fog Index is the Fog Index of readability for the letter from the chairman/CEO, which can be interpreted as the years of education necessary to understand a text.

[b] Two-tailed t-test and Wilcoxon-Mann-Whitney test that test the following hypothesis:
H_0: Mean delta RSA – Mean delta USA = 0;
H_a: Mean delta RSA – Mean delta USA ≠ 0.
*, **, and *** indicate statistical significance at the 10%, 5% and 1% levels, respectively.

Table 4-13: Comparison of the differences in the supplementary measures

4.4.4 Summary of the results

Overall, the **basic characteristics** of the reports reflect the respective institutional and regulatory environments. The term "integrated" as well as references to IIRC guidance materials almost only occur in reports from South African firms in year 2012, the only setting that requires firms to use IR on an apply-or-explain basis. While US reports mainly address shareholders in both years, their counterparts have more of a stakeholder focus, in particular in 2012. This result is in line with the more stakeholder- and ESG-oriented guidance that South African companies follow, in particular the different King Codes, as well as with the traditional investor orientation of US reporting.

The **degree of IR** is significantly higher in South African reports than in US reports, both in 2006 and 2012. Over the introduction of King III the degree increases significantly in South Africa, while remaining basically unchanged in the USA so that the difference is even greater in 2012. Both the average and maximum values of the scores reveal that there is room left for improvement in applying the Guiding Principles.

A similar pattern is visible for most of the **sub-scores.** Only the CONC and COMP sub-scores show different results, which is particularly observable in the differences-in-differences for the sub-scores (Table 4-9). CONC shows high average values throughout the sub-samples, irrespective of report length. There seems to be a negative trend for South Africa, though, in spite of the introduction of IR. This may ground in an initial deterioration before users fully understand the idea of conciseness within IR. The COMP sub-score is higher in the USA on average than in South Africa in both years, but is also among the categories with substantial room for improvement for all sub-samples. It is questionable if IR can yield such improvement, since the IIRC acknowledges the trade-off between report comparability and reporting flexibility, but appears to favor and promote the latter in the IR Framework. STAKE and MAT also show relatively low scores, which is in line with traditional reporting focusing on shareholders and financial aspects rather than all stakeholders. Moreover, this finding reflects that IR adds new disclosure requirements for materiality over financial reporting. The categories with the highest scores on average are REL and STRAT, but also CONX shows high mean scores. While Reliability is an established principle of corporate reporting, Strategic Focus and in particular Connectivity are rather new aspects of IR. Under these principles, the Framework holds various classical disclosure requirements, which explains the high scores.

Results from the **supplementary measures** show that in terms of report length, there are no significant differences between the countries in either year. Boilerplate disclosures are used more frequently in US reports in both years and show a significant difference of deltas between the countries, whereas jargon is more frequent in South African reports in both 2012 and 2006. In 2012, reports are equally readable in both countries, whereas in 2006, the Fog Index is higher in South Africa on average (i.e., reports are less readable there). Between 2006 and 2012, report length and jargon use increase significantly on average for the South African firms, while the use of boilerplate and report readability show no significant changes. As opposed to this, all four supplementary measures increase significantly for the US firms between 2006 and 2012, indicating a growing presence of the respective shortcomings of reporting practice.

These **mixed findings** on the supplementary measures contrast the simple expectation that their trends might strictly oppose the developments of the IR score, as they represent the shortcomings of corporate reporting that IR intends to tackle. Rather than showing improvement, boilerplate use and readability remain unchanged in South Africa over the introduction of IR. Nevertheless, the difference in deltas between South Africa and the USA is significant in favor of South African firms. This finding originates in a significant deterioration in the US values, though, rather than in an improvement of South African reports. Increases in jargon use and report length over time are observable in both countries. These findings also contradict the aforementioned expectation. However, they are in line with the reduction in the CONC sub-score, which includes items that derive from three of the supplementary measures. As outlined above, it remains to be seen if the increasing volume of the reports is a sustaining trend or if firms in South Africa learn to implement more conciseness after an initial phase of deterioration. Moreover, for jargon and readability it is debatable whether the proxies, which base on the Letter to the Stakeholders, are representative of the entire report. Arguing that the letter is a calling card for the report, the remaining parts of the document could even be less readable and use more jargon.

4.5 Discussion

This section aims at discussing the findings on the IR score and its differences across the four year-country sub-samples. The outlined results are analyzed against the expectations from theoretical reasoning as set out in the hypotheses. Table 4-14 summarizes the comparisons of the average IR scores between the sub-samples. It presents the absolute differences in means, along with their significance level from the two-tailed t-test (Wilcoxon-Mann-Whitney test).

Overview of the differences in the mean IR scores between the different sub-samples				
Sub-sample[a]	RSA 2012	RSA 2006	USA 2012	USA 2006
RSA 2012	---	---	---	---
RSA 2006	5.88% *** (***)	---	---	---
USA 2012	8.88% *** (***)	NA	---	---
USA 2006	NA	2.08% ** (**)	-0.92%	---

[a] The table shows the differences in the mean IR score between different combinations of sub-samples, including RSA 2012 – RSA 2006, RSA 2012 – USA 2012, RSA 2006 – USA 2006, and USA 2012 – USA 2006. The differences labelled "NA" are left out due to their missing informative value.
*, **, and *** indicate statistical significance at the 10%, 5% and 1% levels, respectively, based on a two-tailed t-test (two-tailed Wilcoxon-Mann-Whitney test).

Table 4-14: Overview of the differences in the mean IR scores

The difference of almost 9 percentage points between **South Africa and the USA in 2012** is the highest of all four differences. It is highly significant (1% level) as shown by both the t-test and the Wilcoxon test. Almost all sub-scores present a similar picture. These results are in line with the theoretical reasoning. Even though it is not compulsory to use the principles of IR in either country, firms could do so to reduce information asymmetries and thus agency costs, as Principal Agent Theory argues. Moreover, employing the reporting principles that IR entails may help managers to present the firm's situation according to their personal preferences. Following the reasoning of the different hypotheses of PAT, managers may want to show the firm in a positive light to generate higher bonus payments or to comply with covenants. Alternatively, firms may want to present themselves as rather small or unprofitable to avoid political intrusions and costs. The future orientation, the connectivity of quantitative and qualitative information or the concept of different capitals are only some aspects of IR that give managers discretion to present the firm's status quo according to their respective needs. In addition to managers' incentives, perceived pressures from society (following Legitimacy Theory), from particular stakeholder groups (Stakeholder Theory) or from competitors (Institutional Theory) may drive firms into using IR. The apply-or-explain principle from the South African King III regulations intensifies these motivations for South African companies compared to US firms. Hence, the empirical findings support the hypothesis of a higher IR presence in South African reports than in US reports in 2012 ($H_{1.1}$), as Figure 4-12 shows:

$H_{1.1}$: *South African firms practice IR to a higher degree than US firms in financial year 2012.* supported

Figure 4-12: Results for $H_{1.1}$

In **2006, the country difference** in mean IR scores of around 2 percentage points between South Africa and the USA is also significant (at the 5% level for both tests), albeit smaller in value than in 2012. This result is also consistent with the arguments from the different aforementioned theories. In general, firms can employ the reporting principles under examination to reduce information asymmetries in line with Principal Agent Theory. Furthermore, using future-oriented disclosures or a conception of firm value that bases upon multiple capitals gives managers discretion to present the firm's situation according to their respective preferences, as argued in the different hypotheses of PAT. Pressures from stakeholders, the society or from competitors may also be drivers of the application of reporting according to the respective principles, in line with the reasoning of the systems-oriented theories. However, as opposed to the situation in 2012, South African firms did not face the King III regulations in 2006 and were thus not explicitly required to apply IR or explain why they do not. King II was valid at that time, which used a comply-or-explain principle. Although not explicitly including a requirement for IR, the King II Report contained guidance resembling various IR principles. Thus, the empirical finding of a significant but smaller country difference compared with 2012 is consistent with the expectations. The mixed findings on the sub-scores in 2006 underline this notion. Overall, as Figure 4-13 shows, the results support the hypothesis that the idea of IR is already more present in South African reports than in their US counterparts in 2006 ($H_{1.2}$):

$H_{1.2}$: South African firms practice IR to a higher degree than US firms in financial year 2006. **supported**

Figure 4-13: Results for $H_{1.2}$

The **difference in mean IR scores for South African firms between 2006 and 2012** of almost 6 percentage points is highly significant (1% level in both tests). All sub-scores except CONC and COMP also show significant increases. These results are consistent both with *Makiwane/Padia's* (2013) findings, who report an increase in the IR disclosures in a comparison of pre- and post-King III annual (integrated) reports, and with the theoretical arguments. While the drivers for the application of King III in 2012 were presumably not stronger than for King II in 2006, since both codes were to be used on a comply-or-explain or apply-or-explain basis, respectively, it was the content of King III that made a difference here. Although King II already contained various requirements that referred to aspects that IR would employ later on, King III explicitly requires firms to use IR. In addition to that, the IRCSA's and IIRC's guidance on IR as available in 2012 was to a remarkable degree consistent with the yet to be released IIRC Framework, from which the score in the study at hand derives. Furthermore, over the years, the firms could gain experience and proficiency in reporting according to the principles in question and thereby improve the application of these principles (professional isomorphism). South African scores could thus be expected to be higher in 2012 than in 2006 ($H_{1.3}$). The outlined empirical results support this expectation (Figure 4-14):

$H_{1.3}$: South African firms practice IR to a higher degree in financial year 2012 than in financial year 2006. **supported**

Figure 4-14: Results for $H_{1.3}$

US firms show a slight reduction of approximately 1 percentage point in the mean IR score from **2006 to 2012**. However, this decrease is insignificant, as well as the changes in almost all sub-scores. Given the aforementioned releases of different guidance materials on IR between 2006 and 2012, in particular the IIRC's materials, US firms also had the opportunity to voluntarily employ the IR Guiding Principles, which are applicable for organizations from any country. Unlike South African companies, US firms had no apply-or-explain rule or similar regulatory driver for an application, though. Due to this lack of pressure and thus of exposure to IR, US firms were unlikely to change their reporting in terms of IR principles over the period from 2006 to 2012. The empirical findings support this expectation. Except CONC, which decreases significantly, no sub-score shows a significant change between 2006 and 2012 for the US sub-sample. Neither does the total IR score. As Figure 4-15 reveals, these results provide support for ($H_{1.4}$):

$H_{1.4}$: US firms practice IR to an unchanged degree in financial year 2012 compared with financial year 2006. **supported**

Figure 4-15: Results for $H_{1.4}$

All in all, the results on the four hypotheses show that after the introduction of the apply-or-explain approach in South Africa, there was a significant increase in the degree of IR in the reports from this country. The additional analysis of the country difference between the changes over time (difference-in-differences) suggests that the introduction of King III could be the driver of this increase. Findings on the sub-scores, i.e. the particular IR Guiding Principles, are mostly in line with these findings on the total score, adding further support. These results thus back the assertion from the conceptual analysis that IR goes beyond traditional reporting in various regards, although the descriptive data reveals that also reports in non-IR settings adhere to various IR Guiding Principles to a notable degree.

5 Capital market consequences of Integrated Reporting

Building on the descriptive analysis in the previous chapter, this chapter deals with investors' informed decision making. An explanatory study examines the capital market consequences of IR. Like in the descriptive study, an analysis of the related extant literature in the first section allows to derive the research gap that the explanatory study addresses. Drawing on theoretical reasoning, the second section formulates a hypothesis. After an outline of the methodology the results are presented and discussed.

5.1 State of research

Three **different streams in empirical literature** are relevant for this part of the study. The first stream includes research on the economic consequences of IR in general. As the previous chapters have elaborated, some of the most distinctive features of IR, in particular connectivity of information and conciseness, relate to the format of the report rather than the mere contents. Thus, the second stream of interest for this study contains literature on the market impact of different reporting formats. This stream also includes various studies that deal with the impacts of different shortcomings of corporate reporting. As outlined in chapter 4, some measures that reflect these shortcomings also determine the degree of IR. The third stream of literature deals with a particular market phenomenon, the investor underreaction effect. This effect describes market participants' slow and/or insufficient reaction to news (*Dreman/Lufkin* (2000), p. 63; *Hong et al.* (2000), p. 266) suggesting that investors' information processing may be a potential driver. Hence, the underreaction phenomenon may relate to the format of report information and to IR.

Stream 1: Studies on the impact of IR on the capital market

Due to the novelty of the topic, empirical studies on IR and its impact on the capital market (stream 1) have only been released in recent years, mostly in the status of a working paper. Two studies deal with the effect of IR on **analysts' forecasts**. *Bernardi/Stark* (2015) examine the impact of the IR introduction on forecast quality. For a sample of 40 South African firms in the period of 2008 to 2012 (200 firm-years) they find a positive association of the Bloomberg ESG score with analysts' forecast accuracy after the introduction of IR, but not for the period before the introduction. There is no such effect for financial firms, though. *Zhou et al.* (2016) use a sample of 132 South African companies in the period between 2009 and 2012 (443 firm-years), for which they find a negative association of IR with analysts' forecasts error and dispersion. As opposed to *Bernardi/Stark* they measure IR directly, using content analysis based on a self-constructed disclosure catalogue, which they derive from the PF IR. So the latter measure is more likely to actually reflect IR than the Bloomberg database measure. The focus of both studies on analysts as intermediaries, however, could not be representative of the direct effect on investors.

Other studies analyze the direct **impact of IR on investors**. *Serafeim* (2015) is the only study to use a **US sample** (5,762 firm-year observations from 1,114 firms and a period from 2008 to 2012). He finds that firms which practice IR have an **investor base** that is more long-term oriented and less transient than the investor base of non-IR firms. The study does not examine investors' reaction to IR information, though, but focuses on a characterization of a firm's investor base. It approximates IR with data from the Thomson Reuters Asset 4 database, which provides scores for the different capitals that IR uses. Hence, it is debatable if the measure actually depicts IR adequately (see section 4.1).

As with the descriptive studies, many papers use **South African samples**. *Barth et al.* (2015) analyze **various economic impacts** of IR. They base their IR measure upon EY's Excellence in Reporting rankings (e.g., *EY* (2014)), while using bid-ask spreads as a proxy for stock liquidity and Tobin's Q to approximate firm value. For both of the latter constructs the study finds a positive association with IR, using a sample of 224 firm-years from 92 firms. To examine the firm value relationship in more detail, the study distinguishes between an expected future cash flow component (numerator of firm value) and a cost of capital component (denominator).[184] The results show a positive association of IR with expected future cash flows and a negative one between IR and the cost of capital (although with weak evidence for the latter). As outlined in section 4.1, the explanatory variable leaves room for doubt. Drawing on EY rating data, the IR measure – like other data from surveys conducted by accounting firms – may suffer from a data collection that could be inconsistent between researchers and driven by business interests.

The aforementioned study by *Zhou et al.* (2016) also analyzes the association of IR with a firm's **cost of capital**. For this part of the study, the authors use 430 firm-year observations from 130 firms and find a negative association between IR and the cost of capital (which is stronger for firms with low analyst following). The study explains this negative association between IR and the cost of capital – among other things – with a decrease of information asymmetry through IR. However, *Zhou et al.* neither provide empirical evidence for the decrease of the information asymmetry nor for a lower asymmetry leading to a decrease in the cost of capital. In particular the relation of IR with the cost of capital requires further investigation (*Martinez* (2016), p. 5). Moreover, the IR measure bases on the PF IR so that minor differences with the final interpretation of IR may occur.

Lee/Yeo (2016) is another study about the impact of IR on a firm's **market valuation**, using Tobin's Q and abnormal returns as dependent variables. The study finds a firm's market value, as well as its subsequent-year profitability (ROA) to be positively associated with the degree of IR, in particular for firms with high organizational complexity and those with high external financing needs. In addition, the results show that in firms with higher needs for external financing, those with a higher degree of IR have higher firm valuations. *Lee/Yeo* argue that these results suggest an improvement of the firm's information environment and a mitigation of information asymmetries. The IR measure is a score from a content analysis catalogue building on the Content Elements of the International <IR> Framework, while the sample comprises 822 firm-year observations from firms listed on the JSE between 2010 and 2013. Regarding the dependent variables, it is unclear if there actually is a direct impact of IR on a firm's market value. Many different aspects influence market valuation and interdependencies may exist among various indicators of the firm's performance. Hence, it is hard to tell if a potential change in market valuation occurs due to the firm's reporting or if it is a reflection of interdependencies with other factors.

---

[184] The sample size reduces to 164 firm-years from 67 firms for these two sub-studies.

Martinez (2016) investigates the relationship of IR with **information asymmetry**. The study also bases the IR score upon the EY ratings. Using a sample of 192 firm-years from 64 unique firms that were listed on the JSE between 2013 and 2015, *Martinez* finds a negative association between IR and information asymmetry (measured by bid-ask spreads). However, rather than providing evidence for a reduction of information asymmetry in response to IR, these results and further findings on the development of the information asymmetries over time and their relation with institutional ownership rather suggest that firms with a better information environment are more closely following IR. Besides, as with *Barth et al.* (2015), the explanatory variable that the study uses is debatable due to its usage of the EY data, which carries the risk of inconsistencies and biases.

Turning to studies that use an **international sample**, *Arguelles et al.* (2016) employ a sample of early IR adopters, comprising firms from the IIRC's Pilot Programme as well as self-declared adopters (960 firm-year observations from 357 unique firms) and a control group of the same size. The study finds a stronger association of the adherence to the IR reporting principles (like *Serafeim* (2015), the study measures this by Asset 4 data) with a firm's **market valuation** (measured by the market value of equity) for IR early adopters than for non-adopters. Moreover, the value relevance of the early moving firms' level of integrativeness increases over time compared to firms that are not early movers. Again, as the measurement of the adherence to the IR principles draws on database data, it is debatable whether the variable actually reflects IR.

With a somewhat similar approach *Mervelskemper/Streit* (2016) analyze whether **IR moderates the value relevance of firms' ESG performance**. The study uses a sample that comprises 812 firm-year observations from 215 unique firms domiciled in 19 different countries. According to the findings, the value relevance of a firm's ESG performance is higher for firms that publish integrated reports than for those that publish separate sustainability reports. Instead, the study finds no evidence that the participation in the IIRC's Pilot Programme may moderate the value relevance of the firms' ESG performance. Assessing the usage of IR merely by the question whether firms publish a report that is labelled as "integrated report" or whether they participate in the Pilot Programme is unlikely to capture the idea of IR adequately, though. Moreover, there are various factors that affect a firm's market value so that it is hard to isolate the impact of the ESG performance and thus draw inferences about a potential moderation of the latter.

In another international setting, *Ott* (2016) employs an event study to analyze the stock market reaction to 54 IR-related events, such as the development of the IR Framework or the IIRC's Pilot Programme. The author considers 268,974 firm-event observations of 4,981 unique firms across Europe, finding a positive **market reaction to IR events** in general. For firms that already engaged in non-financial reporting before the occurrence of IR (REP firms), the returns are significantly higher than for firms that did not. Also for REP firms, the returns that relate to IR-events are significantly higher than those for non-IR events. In terms of regulation, *Ott* finds more negative reactions to IR-related events for firms domiciled in countries with stronger regulation. This finding indicates investors' fear of too much regulation in these countries, whereas investors from countries with lower regulatory quality seem to aspire for better reporting. While this study allows inferences about investors' reactions to events concerning the regulation and institutional setting of IR, inferences about the firms' actual reporting are not possible from this research.

These studies cover remarkable results on the impacts of IR, despite the novelty of the topic and the short period for which data has been available. Nevertheless, there are several **issues to discuss** about the extant empirical IR literature. The studies use various **dependent variables**, which represent different impacts of IR and whose interdependencies are not clear. For instance, while *Zhou et al.* (2016) explain their hypothesis of a negative association between IR and the cost of capital – among other things – with a decrease of information asymmetry through IR, they neither provide evidence for the decrease of information asymmetry nor for lower asymmetry leading to a decrease in the cost of capital. *Lee/Yeo* (2016) argue that they find results that suggest a decrease in information asymmetry through IR, whereas *Martinez* (2016) finds a significant association between these two constructs, but argues that the causality is reverse to *Lee/Yeo's* suggestion. The interdependencies among these and other used measures are not always evident. E.g., a firm's cost of capital is also driven by factors beyond information asymmetry (*Lambert et al.* (2012)). This study draws on the association between the immediate and the long-term market response to a firm's report release as an indicator of investor underreaction. This straightforward approach to depict market reaction does not rely on the aforementioned dependent variables. Furthermore, with a focus on the firm-specific report release dates, this indicator of underreaction relates more directly to the reports and is less susceptible to alternative explanations and an omitted variables bias than the other measures.

Different measures of IR, e.g. alignment with the Framework (*Martinez* (2016); *Zhou et al.* (2016)) or the "*quality*" of IR (*Barth et al.* (2015)), represent the **explanatory variables**. The use of the variable names seems to be somewhat interchangeable,[185] although the different measurement methods for the scores entail some consequences. Various studies (*Bernardi/Stark* (2015); *Serafeim* (2015) and *Arguelles et al.* (2016)) use IR proxies from databases. While this approach conveys objective and comparable data and allows the use of large samples, it remains questionable in how far this data represents the character of IR.[186] Using data from studies by accounting firms, like the EY rankings (as in *Barth et al.* (2015) and *Martinez* (2016)), may provide inconsistent and potentially biased data, instead. Both data collection methods may thus be of limited validity (*Velte/Stawinoga* (2016), p. 19). Manual data collection with regard to official IIRC guidance (as employed by *Zhou et al.* (2016) and *Lee/Yeo* (2016)) is more adequate in this regard. Moreover, both *Zhou et al.* (2016) and the versions of the EY rankings used by *Barth et al.* (2015) and *Martinez* (2016) employ measures that base upon pre-final versions of the IR Framework[187] so that minor differences in the interpretation of IR may occur. The study at hand uses the IR score as described in section 4.3.2, which bases upon the final Framework.

---

[185] E.g., while *Barth et al.* (2015) and *Martinez* (2016) use the same proxy for their IR measure (scores from the *EY* rating), they refer to the measure with different terms ("quality" and "alignment with the Framework", respectively). This study avoids the term "quality" for the IR measure (see section 4.3.2).

[186] Cf. *Barth et al.* ((2015), p. 9) for similar criticism on the use of databases to depict IR.

[187] Until the 2014 edition, the EY rating bases upon preliminary versions of the Framework (cf. *EY* (2014), p. 25), including all editions used by the two studies. See section 4.1 for a discussion of the EY scores.

Another issue is the selection of the samples. **Samples that comprise voluntary adopters of IR**, like the one used by *Arguelles et al.* (2016) may suffer from a self-selection bias. Their results are likely to be biased in favor of IR benefits (*Barth et al.* (2015), p. 9). The study at hand does not primarily examine the adoption of IR (as the status of adopting the entire concept or its name), but the use of the Guiding Principles that IR promotes. For the explanatory analysis, it uses the same sample as in the descriptive examination detailed in the previous chapter, due to the reasons explained there. Thus, speaking in terms of the IR concept, it includes voluntary adopters, mandatory adopters and non-adopters. However, the main results of the economic consequences study remain qualitatively unchanged when using only observations from a mandatory setting.

Stream 2: Studies on the impact of report format and shortcomings of corporate reporting on the capital market

Supplementing the literature on the economic consequences of IR outlined in stream 1, the second stream of literature (stream 2) somewhat extends the focus as it deals with the **impact of the (annual) report format** in general. Moreover, it particularly concentrates on some of the aforementioned **shortcomings of corporate reporting and the respective market reaction**. Earlier studies examine how the reporting format affects analysts. *Hirst/Hopkins* (1998) find that a clear format of presenting comprehensive income and its components (i.e., using a separate statement of income rather than the statement of changes in equity) results in a better **detection of earnings management by analysts** and therefore in better stock price judgments. *McEwen/Hunton* (1999) identify financial statement items whose use is associated with **accurate analysts' forecasts** (e.g., income information with a long-term focus) and items that are associated with less accurate forecasts. The study's finding that analysts ignore certain items may be a function of information complexity[188] or relevance, according to the authors' speculation. Thus, they suggest this question as a topic for further research. *Lehavy et al.* (2011) find that low readability of Form 10-Ks is associated with greater dispersion, lower accuracy and greater overall uncertainty in analyst earnings forecasts. As mentioned above, by focusing on analysts these studies might not be representative of the direct effect on investors, the primary users of integrated reports.

Other studies concentrate on the **impact of the shortcomings of reporting on investors** as direct market participants. Most importantly, *You/Zhang* (2009) examine the moderating effect of report length on investor underreaction, using a sample of 24,269 US firm-year observations from electronic Form 10-K filings between 1 January 1995 and 31 December 2005. They find a significantly **stronger market underreaction for firms with relatively longer reports** than for firms with shorter reports. However, for the time horizon of one year that the study uses, the return measure may be particularly noisy due to confounding events, e.g. quarterly information that the firms provide. In addition, while lengthy reports represent one of the shortcomings of reporting in the literature, this measure may also be representative of other aspects, like the informative value of the document.

188 In line with the *SEC* ((2008), p. 18), this study considers the complexity of information simply as the difficulty to understand the substance of the underlying transaction or event.

Lee (2012) finds that for longer and less readable reports, relatively more market response takes place in the post-filing drift window beginning two days after the report filing and ending 60 days after the filing, while relatively less response takes place in the filing window starting one day before and ending one day after the filing. These results from a sample of over 60,000 Form 10-Q reports of US firms filed with the SEC between 2001 and 2007 indicate that length and low readability, as common **shortcomings of reporting, impair the market's ability to assimilate earnings-related information** from quarterly reports. As mentioned for *You/Zhang* (2009), report length may stand for the informative value on the one hand and for the difficulty to process the report on the other. This ambiguity hampers the interpretation of these results.

Some recent studies also provide evidence for **other market effects** induced by shortcomings of corporate reports. *Miller* (2010) shows that report length and low readability are associated with lower **trading activity** in the market. Also drawing on (inverted) measures of report length and low readability, *Lawrence* (2013) shows that individual traders **invest** more in firms with clear and concise financial disclosures and that returns increase when the disclosures are clear and concise. *Callen et al.* (2013) use report readability as a proxy for accounting quality.[189] They find **higher delays** in stock price adjustment[190] for firms with lower report readability, but lower delay for those with longer reports. The aforementioned ambiguity of report length as a measure also applies for these studies, requiring caution in the interpretation of the results. Moreover, a variety of aspects may influence market transactions, in particular investments and returns. It is more straightforward to argue an association of reporting properties with the reaction time of the market (as *Callen et al.* (2013) do) than with the degree of the reaction.

As outlined in section 4.3, the similarity of two consecutive reports can approximate the use of boilerplate disclosures[191], representing another common shortcoming of corporate reporting. *Brown/Tucker* (2011) provide evidence that investors' response (i.e., cumulative abnormal returns) to 10-K filings is stronger for filings in which the MD&A shows a higher degree of modification compared with the previous year, relative to filings with less modifications. Instead, there is no significant association of analysts' forecast revisions with MD&A modification scores. In turn this means that reports with a high degree of boilerplate disclosures are associated with a **weaker reaction of the market**. As mentioned before, due to various potential interdependent impacts on stock prices, an influence of report properties on the degree of the market reaction is hard to argue, however.

An **analysis** of this research reveals that there are various studies that examine properties of corporate reports and their market consequences, including reactions by analysts and different reactions by investors. Only *You/Zhang* (2009) and *Lee* (2012) use event study designs that deal with the development of the market reaction (price drift) over time and that

[189] The study uses it as a robustness test while mainly using measures that base on financial statement data as proxies for accounting quality, namely accrual quality, special items and earnings surprises.

[190] *Callen et al.* (2013) derive their delay measure from the firm's stock response to market information (*Hou/Moskowitz* (2005)).

[191] Boilerplate disclosures show no substantial changes to the prior year's report, but repeat meaningless sample sentences, instead.

relate it to the publication of corporate report information, though. While *Lee* uses quarterly reports and focuses on the amount of earnings-related information impounded into the market prices during different time windows, *You/Zhang* use Form 10-Ks, US firms' primary reports, and concentrate on the predictive power of the filing date returns on the longer-term market returns to show underreaction. **The study at hand** bases upon the latter research design, but alters and extends it. *You/Zhang* use report length, which is common in the literature to represent a shortcoming of corporate reporting. However, the measure may also depict information value.[192] This study mainly examines the impact of the degree of IR, which aims at assisting investors' decision making. Furthermore, different supplementary measures (including the Fog Index, that *Lee* (2012) uses, too) are employed to extend the analysis and put the results on IR into context. Moreover, the study adds an international dimension by using a sample that includes both US and South African firms. Finally, while *You/Zhang* use the 12-months returns as the dependent variable, the study at hand employs a shorter time frame of 90 days after the report release. This is supposed to preclude confounding effects from quarterly earnings announcements and quarterly reports from subsequent periods.

Stream 3: Studies on investor underreaction

The described study by *You/Zhang* (2009) connects the second stream with the third stream of literature, which deals with investor underreaction (stream 3). In general terms, the **investor underreaction** effect describes market participants' slow and/or insufficient reaction to news (*Dreman/Lufkin* (2000), p. 63; *Hong et al.* (2000), p. 266). Figure 5-1 illustrates the effect graphically.

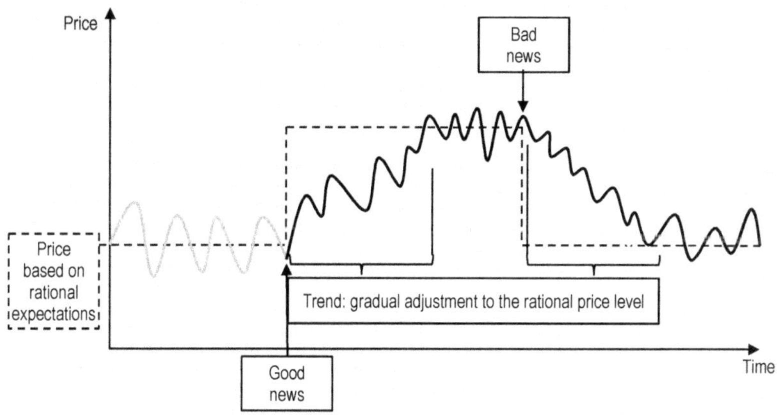

Figure 5-1: Underreaction to good and bad news at the stock market (based on *Grigaliuniene* (2013), p. 34)

[192] E.g. *Callen et al.'s* (2013) results show that firms with longer reports have lower price delay, a finding the authors interpret to be the result of more information in the reports (*Callen et al.* (2013), pp. 285-286).

After a positive reaction to good news, **prices keep trending** up, whereas a downward trend follows a negative reaction to bad news (*Shleifer* (2000), p. 112). Instead, an efficient market would suggest an immediate (or quick) incorporation of new information into the prices (*Dreman/Lufkin* (2000), p. 63). In more specific terms, investor underreaction is indicated by positive (negative) cumulative abnormal returns following large positive (negative) price changes, which are induced by good (bad) news (*Madura/Richie* (2004), p. 92). Thus, current news have predictive power not only for the immediate returns after the news announcement, but also for later returns (*Shleifer* (2000), p. 112). A classic example is the post-earnings announcement drift (PEAD), which is well documented in the literature (*Bernard/Thomas* (1989; 1990)). *Bernard/Thomas* (1990) provide evidence for a price drift lasting for about one year after earnings announcements. Investor underreaction provides the prevalent explanation for this drift (*Chen/Jiang* (2013), p. 176). However, underreaction may occur also in response to other information, in particular to firms' reports.

Since there is plenty of literature on the underreaction effect, it is useful to subdivide the studies for a clear focus on the work with relevance to the examination at hand. While some studies examine the underreaction by analysts (e.g., *Abarbanell/Bernard* (1992); *Amir/Ganzach* (1998)), most studies focus on investor underreaction as outlined above (e.g., *Hirshleifer et al.* (2009); *Hung et al.* (2015)). However, investor underreaction may occur in response to **different sources and types of information**. Some papers document investors' underreaction to information from sources outside the firm, such as analysts (e.g., *Givoly/Lakonishok* (1980); *Stickel* (1991); *Gleason/Lee* (2003)). Others focus on information that the firm provides itself. Mostly, the latter studies deal with the aforementioned information from earnings announcements (e.g., *Bernard/Thomas* (1989; 1990); *Hirshleifer et al.* (2009); *Jung et al.* (2016)).[193] But there is also other firm information that may trigger an underreaction. Since the study at hand analyzes the market consequences of (integrated) annual report information, this study focuses on research that documents the underreaction effect for the latter type of information.

Only two studies deal with investor **underreaction to annual report information** so far. *You/Zhang* (2007) compare underreaction to earnings information with underreaction to annual report (Form 10-K) information. Drawing on 23,738 firm-year observations (**US firms'** 10-K filings from 1 January 1995 to 31 December 2005), the authors find that investors' underreaction to 10-K information is more pronounced than to earnings information. They report that 10-K underreaction appears to be the main driver of the overall underreaction to financial information. In their aforementioned study from 2009, the same authors employ a similar sample (24,269 firm-year observations from US firms' 10-K filings from 1 January 1995 to 31 December 2005). *You/Zhang* (2009) provide further evidence for the existence of underreaction to 10-K information. As in the former study, several tests document the distinction between price drifts occurring in response to earnings information on the one hand and in response to 10-K information on the other. Furthermore, the 2009 study includes the outlined examination of a moderating effect of report length on investor underreaction. Both studies focus on a single country, however.

193 *Grigaliuniene* ((2013), p. 35) provides a list of studies that deal with events other than earnings announcements.

Besides these two studies, there is some earlier evidence on **market reaction to annual report information** in general terms. *Foster et al.* (1983), *Stice* (1991) and *Easton/Zmijewski* (1993) found no or only little market reaction to information from 10-K or 10-Q information for time periods before the introduction of the SEC's EDGAR database, which made the reports easily accessible for the public. *Qi et al.* (2000) provide evidence that reports from the EDGAR period provide incremental information to investors (abnormal returns in the release window are positively related with future changes in earnings), whereas 10-K reports from the pre-EDGAR period do not. *Griffin* (2003) also uses a sample from EDGAR filings, showing the value relevance of the reports and a short response lag of two days. However, these studies do not explicitly document the investor underreaction effect in terms of a price drift.

While the aforementioned studies use US data only, evidence from other countries, in particular **South Africa**, is scarce. No studies are known to the author that document an underreaction effect to annual report information for South African firms. On a more general level, there is only evidence on inefficiencies in the South African Market, including the PEAD. *Mlonzi et al.* (2011) find the weak form of market efficiency for the JSE AltX[194]. Moreover, *Frisch et al.* (2014) also document that the South African Stock Market is not fully efficient. One phenomenon that is considered as such an inefficiency is the accrual anomaly (*Fan/Yu* (2013)), another is the PEAD. *Griffin et al.* (2010) show that the PEAD occurs across many countries all over the world, including South Africa. Consistent with this, *Funke Busayo* (2013) documents the PEAD and examines its determinants in South Africa, France and the USA. *Hung et al.* (2015) also provide evidence for the PEAD in various countries including South Africa, while also showing that the introduction of IFRS decreases the effect. This indicates that a more sophisticated form of financial reporting may reduce investor underreaction. There is no direct evidence for a market reaction to the release of the reports, though.

Analyzing this literature on investor underreaction as such shows a broad coverage of this topic, in particular by studies that use US settings. Research that deals with the area of underreaction to annual report information is scarce, though, while empirical work with a focus on South Africa (or other countries) is also rare. For the cross-section of these two aspects, there is no study at all that is known to the author. **The study at hand** uses a sample that comprises annual (integrated) reports of both US and South African companies and thus aims at reducing this research gap.

Summary

In **summary**, some extant literature already deals with the economic consequences of IR (stream 1), although IR is still a young topic. Another stream of research shows in how far the format of reports and some shortcomings of corporate reporting impact the capital market (stream 2). Finally, there is also evidence for the existence of investor underreaction (stream 3), but hardly for information from the firms' annual reports, and hardly for non-

[194] The JSE AltX is an alternative index for small and medium-sized companies.

US samples. At the cross-section of streams 2 and 3, there is only scarce evidence for a potential moderation of the underreaction by report format or particular properties of the reports. Moreover, the only studies that deal with such a topic use US settings. By linking all three outlined streams of research, the study at hand aims at reducing the research gap at the cross-section of the streams while contributing to each of them. However, this study employs a more direct measure of market response than previous research, which is also less susceptible to alternative explanations. Hence, this analysis may assist in a better understanding of the capital market effects for both the users and preparers of corporate reports. Besides, the findings may also yield helpful insights for reporting regulators. Figure 5-2 summarizes the different streams and the research gap that this study aims at.

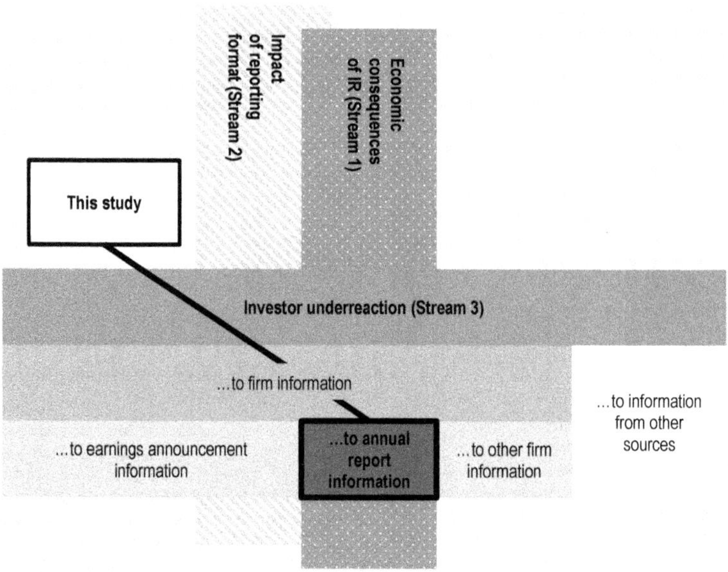

Figure 5-2: The relationship of the study at hand to extant empirical literature on economic consequences of IR and other market impacts

5.2 Theory and hypothesis development

This section lays the theoretical foundation and derives the central hypothesis for the capital market study. After providing theoretical arguments for the existence of investor underreaction, reasoning from different theories argues a moderation of this effect by the format of the report, in particular by IR.

5.2.1 The investor underreaction effect

For a long time, the EMH of asset prices (*Fama* (1965; 1970; 1991)) and other theories that base upon the **concept of rational expectations** (*Muth* (1961)) were predominant in capital market research. These theories ground on two main assumptions (*Brav/Heaton* (2002), pp. 575-579): Investors are assumed to have complete knowledge of the fundamental structure of their economy (rational expectations assumption 1, the "*information availability assumption*" (*Friedman* (1979), p. 26)) and to be completely rational information processors who make optimal statistical decisions (rational expectations assumption 2, the "*information exploitation assumption*" (*Friedman* (1979), p. 25)). As a consequence, the EMH considers market prices to always fully reflect available information (*Fama* (1970), p. 383).

However, in practice anomalies occur in markets that controvert this assertion. To explain existing market anomalies, such as over- or underreaction, more modern approaches relax either or both of the aforementioned assumptions. **Rational structural uncertainty** explanations object the information availability assumption (rational expectations assumption 1). These explanations see investors as incompletely informed and lacking critical structural knowledge. Nevertheless, the second assumption remains unchanged: investors still make optimal statistical decisions (*Brav/Heaton* (2002), p. 576). **Behavioral** explanations loosen the information exploitation assumption (rational expectations assumption 2), instead. Even if investors still have considerable knowledge about the fundamental structure of the economy, they suffer from cognitive biases, such as conservatism (*Edwards* (1968)), thus being unable to process available information rationally (*Brav/Heaton* (2002), pp. 576-577). While theoretically distinct, these two approaches of relaxing the rational expectations assumptions are hard to distinguish in practice (*Brav/Heaton* (2002), pp. 589-592). Figure 5-3 gives an overview of the rational expectations assumptions and the explanations that relax these assumptions.

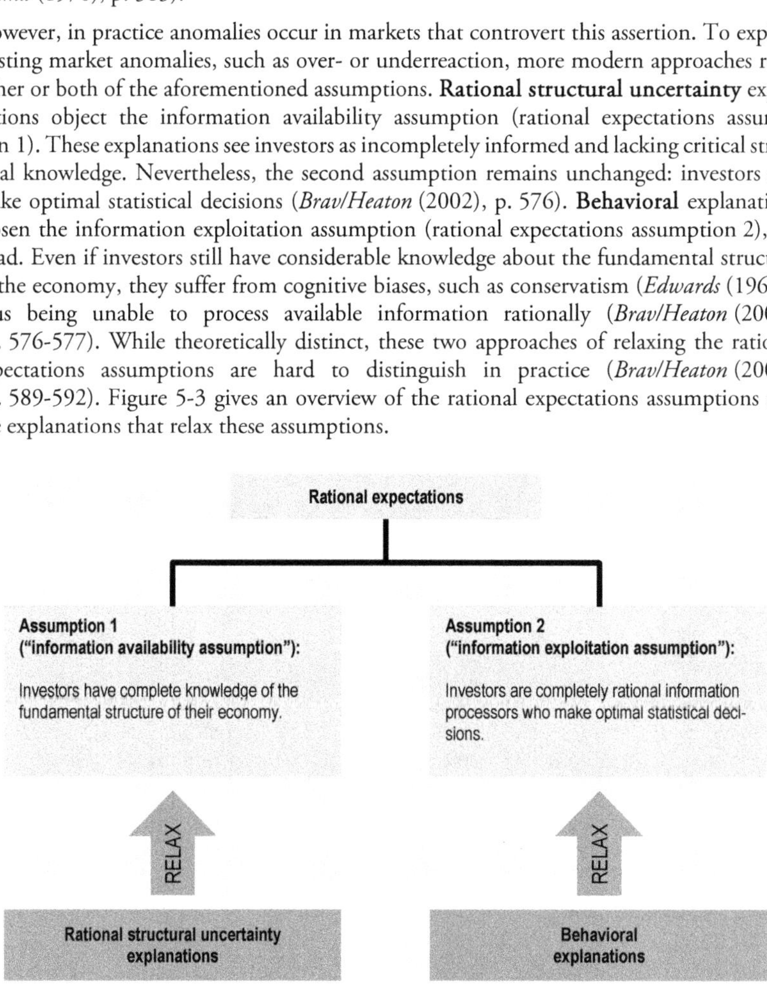

Figure 5-3: Rational expectations assumptions and explanations that relax these assumptions

There are several **reasons for the existence of investor underreaction**, including arguments from either of the two explanatory branches presented. Market participants are able to **correct prior estimation errors** (made based on irrationality or incomplete information) over time (*Brav/Heaton* (2002), pp. 576-578). These corrections base upon rational learning – updating beliefs based on own observations (*Levy* (2015), p. 1). Hence, the stock price slowly approaches the level that it would have with rational expectations.

Further explanations of investor underreaction can be found in cognitive behavioral aspects. *Daniel et al.* (1998) argue that investor **overconfidence** leads to an overestimation of their private information (and therefore a price overreaction to this private information) so that new public information (e.g., earnings figures or information from corporate reports) is in turn underestimated and only leads to a deferred price adjustment. Moreover, **conservatism** could prevent market participants from directly adjusting their valuation of share prices when facing new information, since they assume the news to include a temporary component and stick at least partially with prior beliefs (*Barberis et al.* (1998), p. 315).[195] This delays the full adjustment of the stock price. *Hong/Stein* (1999) build a model that grounds on two groups of **boundedly rational traders** and their interaction. "Newswatchers" base their forecasts on signals about future fundamentals that they observe privately, without taking current or past prices into regard. They cannot extract other newswatchers' information from the prices. "Momentum traders" instead do consider these past price movements, but base their forecasts solely on them (without considering new information). The model further assumes private firm-specific information to diffuse gradually among the newswatchers. Combining this gradual information diffusion with the presumption that newswatchers cannot rely on price movements but only refer to their private information, yields an underreaction pattern in the market prices.[196]

5.2.2 Moderation of investor underreaction by Integrated Reporting

IR may **impact the underreaction effect**. Following the reasoning of chapter 2, IR links to both the rational structural uncertainty approach and the behavioral approach. The enhanced information basis for investors aims at the available information (rational expectations assumption 1) and/or to the processing of this information by the investor (rational expectations assumption 2).

It seems plausible that IR information weakens the aforementioned arguments that explain the underreaction effect. Regarding rational expectations assumption 1, integrated reports provide more information than traditional financial reports. Through the Fundamental Concept of six capitals and through the Guiding Principles Strategic Focus and Future Orientation as well as Stakeholder Relationships, IR provides a broader information basis. Thereby the likelihood of **estimation errors** is reduced in the first place, and therefore also the necessity for correction through rational learning.

---

195 The reasoning of the Anchoring effect (*Tversky/Kahneman* (1974), pp. 1128-1130) appears in the same vein (*Shefrin* (2002), pp. 19-20).

196 Momentum traders then react to the information that they draw from the price changes. They profit from the underreaction pattern by chasing the trend. As the model presumes that they only follow simple (univariate) trading strategies, this trend-chasing behavior leads to overreaction in the longer-term.

In terms of rational expectations assumption 2, various arguments support the notion that IR also enhances information processing. Turning to the behavioral reasoning, *Hirshleifer* ((2001), p. 1546) argues that while easily processable information (e.g., concrete examples) may cause overreactions, people weigh cognitively costly information less. As integrated reports can be argued to provide information in a more processable way than traditional financial reporting formats, both the speed of **conservative** market participants updating their beliefs and the speed of information diffusion in the *Hong/Stein* (1999) model of **bounded rationality** are increased by IR, which accelerates market reaction.

Bloomfield (2002) provides another theoretical approach to explain a potential impact of IR on investor underreaction: the **Incomplete Revelation Hypothesis** (IRH). It states that data that is more costly to extract from public information drives less trading interest[197] and is in consequence less completely revealed by market prices (*Bloomfield* (2002), p. 235). Therefore, the IRH also predicts larger underreaction for information that is more difficult to find (*Bloomfield* (2002), p. 237). In turn, underreaction should be weaker for IR information, as it enhances the understandability of the information.

The Guiding Principles Connectivity of Information, Materiality and Conciseness are important principles of IR that add innovative and distinctive value to integrated reports over traditional annual reports. Readers ideally get a connected view of how the different dimensions of a business interact, but in a concise document that does not distract them with unnecessary information. Thus, these principles can be anticipated to drive a potential reduction of the underreaction effect by IR. **Theoretical arguments from other disciplines than finance and accounting** support this expectation. In particular, the Connectivity of Information principle includes some disclosure requirements that are subject of Cognitive Load Theory (CLT) from cognitive psychology, whereas the Pragmatic Theory of Language (Pragmatics) from philosophy and linguistics offers some arguments about the effectiveness and efficiency of material and concise disclosures.

As the aforementioned arguments from behavioral theories allude, the question how "costly" information is in cognitive terms plays an important role for its processing (*Hirshleifer* (2001), p. 1546). Concerning the cognitive side of processing information, one has to distinguish short-term (or "working") and long-term memory. While people have limited capacity of working memory (*Miller* (1956); *Simon* (1974)), long-term memory is immeasurably large (*Sweller* (1993), p. 1). **CLT** deals with excessive cognitive load for working memory and draws instructional implications[198] (*Sweller et al.* (2011), p. 201). *Hewitt* (2007) has applied this theory as a framework for his research on the accrual anomaly. The theory differs between two basic types of cognitive load, intrinsic and extraneous cognitive load, which add up to the total cognitive load for the working memory (*Sweller et al.* (2011), p. 58). Intrinsic cognitive load refers to the basic characteristics of the information itself rather than to the design of the information material (*Sweller* (1993), p. 6).

---

197 Trading interest is the additional number of shares that traders are willing to trade for given deviations of the market price from the value that the trader assigns to the share based on his information.

198 The original purpose of the theory is to derive instructional implications for learning material. This does not need to be reduced to classical educational settings, however. Generally speaking, all information material that intends to present news can be interpreted as learning material for its readers.

The primary determinant of intrinsic cognitive load is the number of interacting elements in the presented information, with a high level of element interactivity imposing a high intrinsic cognitive load (*Sweller* (1994), p. 307). Instead, extraneous cognitive load depends on the way that the information is structured (*Sweller* (1994), p. 303). As opposed to intrinsic cognitive load, it is thus reducible by manipulating the presentation format of the information (*Sweller et al.* (1998), p. 259). Figure 5-4 summarizes the two categories of cognitive load.

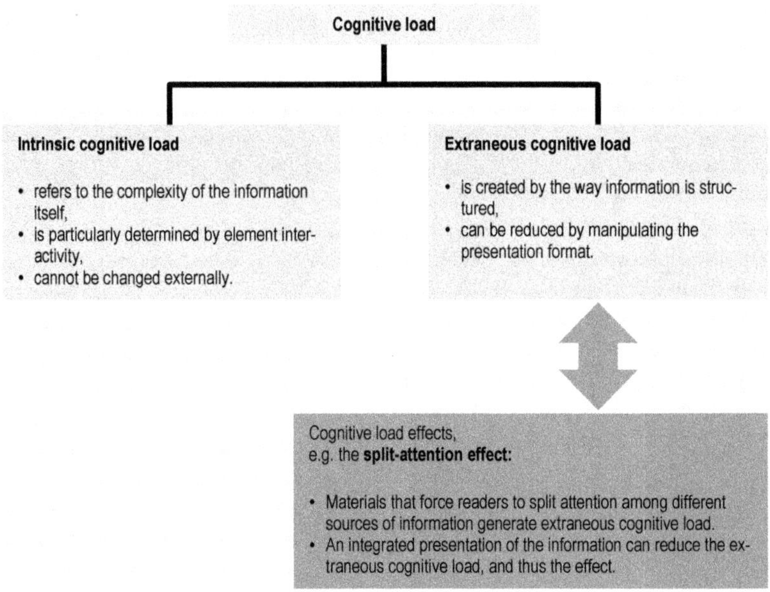

Figure 5-4: Cognitive Load Theory

Over more than 30 years, CLT – with the overarching goal to generate new instructional procedures to facilitate learning and problem solving – has derived different cognitive load effects from broad experimental research and has generated instructional implications on this basis (*Sweller et al.* (2011), p. 87).[199] One of the central cognitive load effects is the **split-attention effect** (Figure 5-4). It occurs when instructional material requires readers to split their attention among different sources of information (*Sweller* (1993), p. 5) and thus represents a source of extraneous cognitive load for the readers (*Sweller/Chandler* (1994), p. 226), who need to mentally integrate the different pieces of information (*Sweller et al.* (2011), p. 111). There is evidence from numerous experimental studies that use a setting of worked examples (e.g., *Tarmizi/Sweller* (1988)), combinations of diagrams

[199] *Sweller et al.* (2011), pp. 87-201, provide a comprehensive and detailed overview of the cognitive load effects.

and written explanations (e.g., *Rose/Wolfe* (2000); *Rose* (2002); *Ayres/Youssef* (2008)), multiple sources of text (e.g., *Chandler/Sweller* (1992)) or computer usage (e.g., *Chandler/Sweller* (1996); *Cerpa et al.* (1996)). While many of these studies employ learning/instruction contexts like machine programming or language learning, some also use a business/economics context (e.g., *Rose/Wolfe* (2000)). The main corrective to overcome the split-attention effect is the (physical) integration of information (*Sweller et al.* (2011), p. 124). Thus, IR, particularly through the Connectivity of Information principle, can be assumed to reduce cognitive load of the information presented – compared with a traditional reporting format. This in turn fosters the speed of information processing and reduces investor underreaction.

Furthermore, *Bloomfield* (2012) suggests to apply **Pragmatics**[200] to corporate reporting. This field of linguistics deals with the transmission of meaning in language via other channels than the "coded" contents (i.e., the spoken words or the written text itself), which in turn are subject of Semantics (*Huang* (2007), pp. 209-244). The goal of Pragmatics is to understand the efficiency of this way to convey information (*Bloomfield* (2012), p. 359). The theory makes three substantial distinctions (Figure 5-5): (1) "speech" – the actual content of what is said – needs to be distinguished from "speech acts" – the speakers decision to make a certain statement instead of another one or none at all (*Austin* (1975)). Basing upon this, (2) "explicature" – inferences drawn from the content of the speech, known facts or logic – is different from "implicature" – inferences drawn from the speaker's choice of the speech act (*Grice* (1975)). Furthermore, (3) "news" – new information in speech or speech acts – have to be segregated from "common ground" – knowledge that speaker and listener already have in common (*Stalnaker* (2002), p. 701).

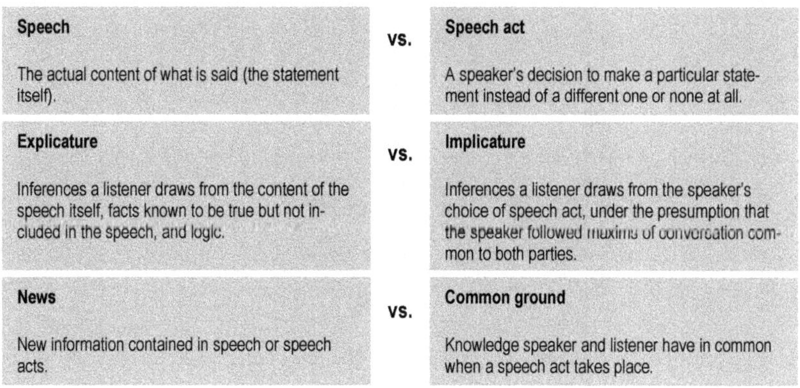

Figure 5-5: Pragmatics – Basic definitions

[200] *Huang* (2007) provides a comprehensive overview of this theory. Originally, the field goes back to the work of the philosophers Charles Morris, Rudolf Carnap and Charles Peirce in the 1930s (*Huang* (2007), p. 2). Significant work in this area stems from Herbert P. Grice, Laurence R. Horn and John L. Austin.

For a recipient to be able to draw new conclusions from the choice of speech act through implicature, it is necessary that the respective speaker followed *Grice's* maxims of conversation (*Grice* (1975), pp. 45-46). Together with the Cooperative Principle[201], these maxims ensure that the exchange of communication occurs in a truthful, relevant and perspicuous manner and that the right amount of information is provided (*Huang* (2007), p. 25). *Horn* (1984) summarized the assertion of *Grice's* maxims more briefly in his Bipartite System of Antithetical Principles of Conversation. Basically, both approaches aim for a **trade-off between the necessary and the sufficient length of a contribution to a conversation** (given that the contribution as such is true). They claim that as long as it is necessary, one should say as much as one can, but one should not say more than one has to, given that the contribution is sufficient. Figure 5-6 presents both approaches and the underlying Cooperative Principle.

Cooperative Principle (Grice):
Make your conversational contribution such as is required, at the state at which it occurs, by the accepted purpose or direction of the talk exchange in which you are engaged.

Maxims of Conversation (Grice):

I. Quality: Try to make your contribution one that is true.
   a. Do not say what you believe to be false.
   b. Do not say that for which you lack adequate evidence.

II. Quantity:
   a. Make your contribution as informative as is required (for the current purposes of exchange).
   b. Do not make your contribution more informative than is required.

III. Relation: Be relevant.

IV. Manner: Be perspicuous.
   a. Avoid obscurity of expression.
   b. Avoid ambiguity.
   c. Be brief (avoid unnecessary prolixity).
   d. Be orderly.

Bipartite System of Antithetical Principles of Conversation (Horn):

I. The Q[uantity]-Principle
   Make your contribution sufficient: Say as much as you can (given the R-Principle).

II. The R[elation]-Principle
   Make your contribution necessary: Say no more than you must (given the Q-Principle).

Figure 5-6: Pragmatics – Principles and Maxims of Conversation (as consolidated in *Huang* (2007)) (based on *Bloomfield* (2012), p. 360)

If a conversation sticks to these rules, speaker and addressee will – through cooperation – exchange information effectively and efficiently. *Bloomfield* applies this theory to the context of corporate disclosures, stating that to be efficient, **disclosures need to elevate information**, while still providing redundant prior information (*Bloomfield* (2012), p. 364). Interpreting an integrated report according to the Octopus Model, as a high level report underpinned by more detailed reports on special fields (section 2.3.1), the question which

[201] "*Make your conversational contribution such as is required, at the stage at which it occurs, by the accepted purpose or direction of the talk exchange in which you are engaged.*" (*Grice* (1975), p. 45).

information has to be elevated precisely displays the question of materiality – in terms of which information has to be included in an integrated report. Hence, with IR promoting the Guiding Principles of Materiality and Conciseness, an integrated report supports an effective and efficient communication according to Pragmatics. This adds further support to the argument that IR reduces the underreaction effect.

5.2.3 Hypothesis development

In summary, the **different theoretical approaches** outlined in the previous section argue a negative relation of IR with investor underreaction. The broader information basis that integrated reports provide over traditional financial reports may reduce investors' estimation errors (rational structural uncertainty) and therefore the need to correct these errors through rational learning. Furthermore, IR delivers a more accessible reporting format. In terms of the behavioral approaches, IR can thus be argued to speed up the updates of beliefs for conservative market participants, as well as the diffusion of information across newswatchers in *Hong/Stein's* (1999) model of bounded rationality. The IRH yields an additional argument: As integrated reports deliver less costly information than other reporting formats, the information that the reports provide presumably attracts more trading interest and is thus revealed in the market prices to a higher degree than more costly information from other reporting formats. Reasoning from psychology and linguistics supplements these approaches. Similar to IRH, CLT argues that IR, in particular through the Connectivity of Information principle, reduces the cognitive load that the report imposes on its readers when they try to process the delivered information. This reduction in turn accelerates their information processing, which reduces market underreaction. Eventually, Pragmatics states that efficient communication yields meaning not only through particular explicit contents, but also through the implicit choice to use or elevate these contents. Hence, as it promotes materiality and conciseness, IR can be argued to support effective and efficient communication.

In conjunction, these arguments allow to posit the following directional **hypothesis** on investor underreaction and its moderation by IR:

H_2	*As the degree of IR in an annual report increases, the degree of investor underreaction decreases.*

5.3 Methodology

This section presents the methodology for the capital market analysis. The study builds on the descriptive analysis outlined in chapter 4, using the same sample and employing the IR score, some sub-scores and the supplementary measures as independent variables for regressions. After an outline of the general structure of the used ordinary least squares (OLS) regression models in the first part, the second part of this section explains the aforementioned and other variables in detail. A third part of the section presents the assumptions for the use of OLS regressions and tests whether the study at hand fulfils the respective requirements.

5.3.1 Regression models

Central to this capital market consequences study is the examination of a potential moderating effect of the degree of IR on investor underreaction to annual report information. Drawing on the sample from the descriptive analysis of IR practice (see chapter 4), the study uses a research design that bases upon *You/Zhang* (2009). It employs an **event study method.**[202] Apart from the hand-collected data mentioned in the previous chapter, the data for the variables stems from Datastream.

The **event** is the release of the annual report. Market reaction to this event is measured by the abnormal returns accumulated for a period starting on the release date and ending at least five and up to 90 calendar days afterwards.[203] Since firms also release quarterly reports, a larger **event window** would be particularly exposed to noisy results due to these confounding events.[204]

The study follows a two-step organization. First, a basic model examines the mere underreaction, before a second step analyzes a potential moderation of the underreaction.

Basic model: the investor underreaction effect

While the abnormal returns accumulated for the event window represent a (medium- to) long-term (or "delayed") market response to the annual report release, the same measure accumulated for the three-day period starting on the release date and ending two days later captures the short-term (or "immediate") response. With the delayed response being the dependent variable in the regression models of this study, the immediate response represents the main independent variable. Hence, the basic OLS regression model examines a potential association of the two variables, which could show that the immediate returns have predictive power over the delayed returns (indicating **investor underreaction**). The basic model in the subsequent analyses is as follows:

$$(5.1) \quad Delayed\ response_{i;t;\tau} = \alpha + \beta_1\ Immediate\ response_{i;t} + \sum_{k=1}^{K} \beta_{k+1}\ Control_{i;t}^{k} + \varepsilon_{i;t}$$

where,

$Delayed\ response_{i;t;\tau}$ = measure used to gauge the (medium to) long-term market response to the release of the annual report. Abnormal returns for firm i and period t, accumulated over a window of τ days;

[202] Event studies are common in accounting research, going back to *Dolley* (1933), whereas the methodology as used today was introduced by *Ball/Brown* (1968), *Beaver* (1968) and *Fama et al.* (1969). For a discussion of the event study technique, cf. *MacKinlay* (1997) or *McWilliams/Siegel* (1997).

[203] The study analyzes the effect for different event windows, starting with a five day event window (τ=5) and ending with a 90 day window (τ=90), in steps of five days.

[204] However, this study also uses larger windows of up to 360 days (largely unreported) to generate results comparable to *You/Zhang* (2009), who used a 360 days window.

$Immediate\ response_{i;t}$ = measure used to gauge the short-term market response to the release of the annual report. Abnormal returns for firm i and period t, accumulated over a three day window; and

$Control_{i;t}^{k}$ = one of K control variables.

The coefficient β_1 describes the **alignment of the long-term market reactions with the short-term returns.** For instance, a β_1 with a positive sign means that the long-term returns follow the direction of the short-term returns (*You/Zhang* (2009), pp. 570-575). A significance of this coefficient means that the short-term returns have predictive power over future returns: The information from the report does not only have the power to predict the returns shortly after the report release, but also the returns over a longer term (*Shleifer* (2000), p. 112).

Moderation of the investor underreaction effect by IR

This study, however, examines if the **degree of IR of the released report can moderate the underreaction effect.** Supposedly, the higher the degree of IR and thus the more understandable and informative the report, the better investors are able to process the news from the report. Hence, the information is incorporated into the prices faster and the long-term returns are less associated with the release date returns (see H_2). Figure 5-7 depicts this relationship.

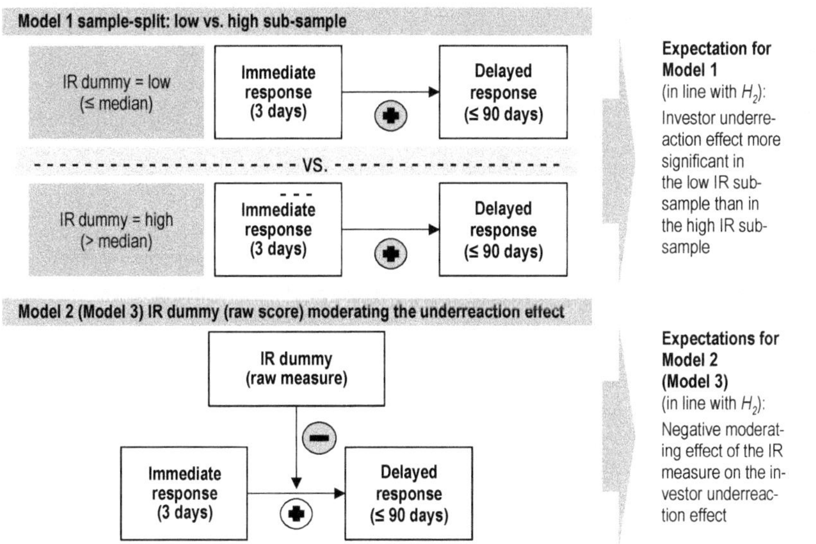

Figure 5-7: Three models to analyze the moderation of investor underreaction by IR

The study employs **three different models**, to examine the potential moderation by the degree of IR. Model 1 splits the sample at the median of the IR measure and runs regression (5.1) for both sub-samples to compare β_1 between them. Model 2 introduces a dummy variable that is 1 for an observation of the IR measure higher than the median and 0 otherwise. This dummy variable is interacted with the immediate response variable in the regression so that the coefficient of the interaction term depicts the potential moderation.[205] Model 3 uses the same technique as Model 2, the only difference being that the regression interacts the raw IR measure with the immediate response variable instead of interacting a dummy variable with the immediate response. The regression including the interaction terms (Model 2 and Model 3) is as follows:

$$(5.2) \quad Delayed\ response_{i;t;\tau} = \alpha + \beta_1\ Immediate\ response_{i;t} + \beta_2\ Degree\ of\ IR_{i;t} + \beta_3\ Immediate\ response_{i;t} \times Degree\ of\ IR_{i;t} + \sum_{k=1}^{K} \beta_{k+3}\ Control_{i;t}^{k} + \varepsilon_{i;t}$$

where,

$Degree\ of\ IR_{i;t}$ = measure used to gauge the degree of IR in the report of firm i for period t, derived from the IR score as explained in chapter 5. Raw measure in Model 3, dummy variable that is 1 if the value is higher than the median and 0 otherwise in Model 2; and

all other variables as defined above.

In line with H_2, the following **expectations** are stated: For Model 1, the coefficient of the immediate market returns (β_1) is anticipated to be positive, signaling the underreaction. However, this positive coefficient should be less significant for the sub-sample with a high degree of IR than for the one with the low degree, as there is presumably less underreaction in response to reports with high IR. Accordingly, a negative coefficient for the interaction term of immediate responses and IR (β_3) is anticipated for Model 2 and Model 3 (β_1 is again expected to be positive).

Different results across the three models may occur. On the one hand, models using dichotomized variables have less variation in these variables and less power than models with continuous variables (*Cohen* (1983)). On the other hand, models using sample splits or dichotomized variables may create apparent, but spurious effects (*Maxwell/Delaney* (1993)), especially moderating effects (*Bissonnette et al.* (1990)). Thus, interpreting the findings requires the consideration of the results from all three models.

---

[205] For firms with a low degree of IR (IR dummy = 0), $\beta_1\ Immediate\ response_{i;t}$ depicts the association of immediate and delayed market response. For high IR firms (IR dummy = 1), $\beta_1\ Immediate\ response_{i;t} + \beta_3\ Immediate\ response_{i;t} \times Degree\ of\ IR_{i;t}$ shows this association. The coefficient of the interaction term (β_3) thus describes the additional underreaction effect for high IR firms compared with low IR firms.

You/Zhang (2009) (pp. 578-580) employ a comparable setting. They analyze a moderating effect of report length on investor underreaction. Drawing on their results and putting the findings on the degree of IR into context, the study at hand also investigates potential moderating effects of report length and the other **supplementary measures** presented in the previous chapter, analyzing the three mentioned models for each of these variables separately. These measures represent **shortcomings of corporate reporting**, which IR intends to overcome by providing a broader information basis and by fostering the understandability of the reports. The expectations for the supplementary measures are thus reverse to those for the degree of IR. While a positive sign for β_1 is expected again for the underreaction, a lower significance of this coefficient is presumed for the low value sub-sample than the high value sample in Model 1. For Model 2 and Model 3 β_3 is expected to be positive in case of the supplementary measures.

5.3.2 Variables

The depicted models employ **three types of variables.** (1) To capture the underreaction effect, firms' stock returns are used. (2) The IR score from the descriptive study, some modifications of this score and the aforementioned supplementary measures are employed as potential moderators of investor underreaction. (3) Data on several firm characteristics serve as controls for other potential influences on the cumulated abnormal returns.

(3) Investor underreaction

Central to this examination is investor underreaction, the **relationship between the immediate and the delayed market response** to the release of the annual report. The variables to represent these constructs are basically the same: abnormal returns accumulated over a period starting on the report release date. They only differ in the period for which the returns are accumulated.

To calculate the daily abnormal returns, this study uses the **OLS market model**, which has been shown to provide a basis for "*well-specified*" methodologies (*Brown/Warner* (1985), p. 25). The formula is as follows:

$$ar_{i;t;\tau} = r_{i;t;\tau} - (\hat{\alpha}_{i;t} + \hat{\beta}_{i,t} * r_{m;t;\tau}) \quad (5.3)$$

where,

$ar_{i;t;\tau}$	=	abnormal return for firm i and period t on day τ;
$r_{i;t;\tau}$	=	actual return for firm i and period t on day τ;
$r_{m;t;\tau}$	=	return for market index m and period t on day τ; and
$\hat{\alpha}_{i;t}$ and $\hat{\beta}_{i;t}$	=	market model parameters, estimated in an OLS regression of the form $r_{i;t;\tau} = \hat{\alpha}_{i;t} + \hat{\beta}_{i;t} * r_{m;t;\tau} + ar_{i;t;\tau}$ with data from the estimation window, which started 1080 days before the report release and ended one day before the report release.

In terms of the aggregation of the abnormal returns over the event window, this study uses cumulative abnormal returns (i.e., daily abnormal returns added together over the event window), which is useful to depict a gradual flow of information in the market (*Goerke* (2009), p. 476). There are, however, different methods commonly used in the literature **to accumulate the abnormal returns** and there is an argument on which method is preferable (*Barber/Lyon* (1997)). For instance, *You/Zhang* (2009) use the buy-and-hold method (i.e., daily abnormal returns accumulated by a multiplicative method[206]), which has some conceptual advantages and facilitates a cross-sectional analysis of how the abnormal returns vary with report characteristics (*You/Zhang* (2009), p. 575), but also enables testing the stability of the abnormal returns (*Goerke* (2009) p. 482). At the same time, there are several shortcomings of the buy-and-hold method, including e.g. an exaggeration of short-term abnormal returns.[207] Large sample sizes mitigate many of these shortcomings (*Mitchell/Stafford* (2000), p. 288). Due to its rather small sample, the study at hand does not primarily employ the buy-and-hold method. Nevertheless, the study re-calculated all analyses with buy-and-hold abnormal returns, finding no material changes in the results.[208]

Thus, the **formulae** to calculate the cumulative abnormal returns, which depict the delayed market response (5.4), and the release date returns, which depict the immediate response (5.5), are as follows:

(5.4) $car\_aird_{i;t;\tau} = \sum_{\tau=0}^{\tau} ar_{i;t;\tau}$

and

(5.5) $rdr\_car_{i;t} = \sum_{\tau=0}^{2} ar_{i;t;\tau}$

where,

$car\_aird_{i;t;\tau}$ = cumulated abnormal returns for firm i and period t on day τ;

$rdr\_car_{i;t}$ = release date returns for firm i and period t; and

all other variables as defined above.

(2) IR and supplementary measures

To examine a potential moderation of the investor underreaction by IR, this study uses the IR score from the descriptive study, representing the **degree of IR** in the respective firm's report. The variables differ slightly across the three aforementioned models that examine this association (see section 5.3.1). In Model 1 and Model 2, a dummy variable (equaling 1 if the degree of IR is higher than the median and 0 otherwise) separates the high and low

206 For the exact formula, cf. *Barber/Lyon* (1997), p. 344.

207 Cf. *Mitchell/Stafford (2000)*, with further references, for a discussion of the buy-and-hold returns.

208 In addition, all models have further been re-calculated with a third measure that accumulates the daily abnormal returns by a simple multiplication. Again, the results remain essentially unchanged.

IR sub-samples (Model 1) or is interacted with the immediate return variable (Model 2). Model 3 interacts the raw degree of IR with the release date returns, instead. Since IR intends to enhance the informative value of the report in general (see chapter 2) and the understandability of a report in particular (e.g., IR F. 3.9; DP IR, pp. 4-5, 6-7), IR can be expected to weaken the investor underreaction effect. The better information basis for investors presumably comes with a quicker market reaction and less orientation at the immediate returns.

Taking into account the importance and innovative character of the Guiding Principles Connectivity of Information and Conciseness outlined in section 2.3 and chapter 3, the market consequences study gives particular consideration to these principles. The three models are recalculated, checking for a moderation of the underreaction by the **degree of connectivity of information.** The variable used here is the (relative) CONX sub-score.[209] Even though it is possible to argue that the degree of connectivity increases the difficulty to process the information in a report, the expectation for this specification draws on the theoretical reasoning outlined in section 5.2. CLT argues that integrated information may reduce the cognitive load of information processing (split-attention effect). This view is in line with the IIRC's assertion that more connected information enhances decision making by enabling users to assess the combined impact of different factors (DP IR, p. 22). Thus, the anticipations are the same as for the aforementioned specification.

Another particularly innovative trait of IR is the specific accentuation of conciseness for the report (see section 2.3.2). Both the definition of "concise" in the Merriam-Webster dictionary[210] and the one in the Oxford English Dictionary[211] point out the use of few words as a main characteristic of conciseness. The Framework also lists this as a necessary feature of this Guiding Principle (IR F. 3.38). Hence, instead of merely considering the points for the different requirements of the CONC category as direct summands for the IR score, the study also uses an **indirect consideration of conciseness** as an alternative interpretation. An alternative IR score (#1) is calculated as the difference between the total absolute IR score and the CONC sub-score[212], scaled by the number of words in the report.

However, as the length of a report may vary considerably in response to factors that the reporting firm cannot change for reporting purposes (e.g., and most notably the firm's industry or business model), scaling by the mere number of words introduces some degree of bias.[213] Thus, the study **recalculates the aforementioned measure** using the expected report length instead of the actual length. The second version (#2) of the alternative IR score is therefore defined as the difference between the total absolute IR score and the CONC sub-score, scaled by the mean number of words of sample company reports from the firm's

---

209 For the alternative IR measures as well as for the supplementary measures, a dummy variable (Model 1 and Model 2) and the respective raw measure (Model 3) are used across the three examination models in accordance with the use of these variables in the case of the degree of IR.

210 Cf. http://www.merriam-webster.com/dictionary/concise (last accessed on 29 August 2016).

211 Cf. http://www.oed.com/view/Entry/38276?rskey=qEo74Y&result=1#eid (last accessed on 29 August 2016).

212 Subtracting the CONC sub-score from the total IR score prevents from considering conciseness twice.

213 Corresponding with this notion, *Mio/Fasan* (2014) find that firms' disclosures on materiality are induced by the firms' industry.

industry (GICS industry level). Both alternative IR scores are considered in additional specifications of the underreaction moderation study, with expectations being the same as for the original IR score.

Further specifications of the study examine a potential moderation of the underreaction by different shortcomings of corporate reporting. The variables comprise the **supplementary measures** explained in section 4.3.2, namely the number of words (report length), the similarity score (use of boilerplate disclosures), the jargon score (use of jargon) and the Fog Index (report readability). In line with extant literature and with the Framework, which lists these measures as parameters that are to be minimized (see section 4.3.2), the anticipations for these measures are reverse to the expectations for the IR measures above.[214]

(3) Control variables

A firm's abnormal returns may reflect a multitude of different phenomena. To isolate a potential underreaction effect, this analysis needs to consider other potential impacts on the dependent variable separately. Therefore, common drivers of a firm's abnormal returns are considered in the regressions as **control variables**. Building on prior literature (e.g., *You/Zhang* (2007; 2009)), the study at hand controls for market risk, the firm's size, the firm's growth opportunities and stock return momentum. In additional tests, controls for the information effect of the preceding earnings announcement (PEAD) as well as for *Sloan's* (1996) accrual anomaly are employed.

The risk of an investment determines stock returns, as investors demand a higher return to compensate for higher **risk**. Thus, this study uses a firm's beta factor, which depicts the firm's risk compared to the market portfolio[215], as a control variable in the regressions. Betas are estimated by an OLS regression for a period of 1080 days (3 years) before the annual report release.

A firm's **size** can serve as a proxy for its general information environment. Larger firms tend to provide more information, thus reducing the risk of adverse selection (*Gode/Mohanram* (2003), p. 405), as more public disclosures decrease the information advantage of insiders (*Leuz/Wysocki* (2015), pp. 24). Furthermore, this lowers liquidity risk for larger firms (e.g., *Diamond/Verrecchia* (1991)). Both effects can eventually lead to higher stock returns.

---

214 Some variables arguably allow different interpretations, however. For instance, while report length – in line with *You/Zhang* (2009) – stands for the difficulty to process the information in the report on the one hand (a longer report is harder to consider in its entirety), it could also be a proxy for the information content of the report on the other hand (more available information can lead to a more complete knowledge of the investors), possibly resulting in a reduction of underreaction instead of an increase. Furthermore, the use of boilerplate disclosures reduces the informative value of a report, thus possibly increases the underreaction effect, but may also foster comparability, since it is stereotyped or standardized text (cf. the definitions in the Oxford English Dictionary (http://www.oed.com/view/Entry/21014?redirectedFrom=boilerplate#eid17056928, last accessed on 29 August 2016) or the Merriam-Webster dictionary (http://www.merriam-webster.com/dictionary/boiler%20plate, last accessed on 29 August 2016)). This in turn might help readers to quickly digest report information and might therefore reduce underreaction.

215 The FTSE/JSE All Share (S&P 500) serves as the reference market index for South African (US) firms.

Size is measured by the natural logarithm of the market capitalization (in USD) at the financial year end.

Extant literature (e.g., *Fama/French* (1992; 1993)) provides evidence that a firm's book-to-market ratio, defined as the quotient of the book value of equity to the market value of equity, represents its **growth opportunities**. A low value of the ratio indicates that the market expects future benefits that are not yet reflected in the book value of equity. As the stock prices reflect these expectations, the book-to-market ratio has a negative association with stock returns. This study uses the ratio as a control variable in the regressions.

In addition, the study at hand introduces the six months raw returns ending on the filing month as a control. These returns depict the **stock return momentum**. There is evidence that recently successful stocks outperform unsuccessful stocks in the intermediate term (three to twelve months), as investors tend to exploit this momentum (*Jegadeesh/Titman* (1993); *Chan et al.* (1996)). This also provides an explanation for a drift in market reactions to new information (*Chan et al.* (1996), p. 1693) so that it is helpful to control for this variable in this study.

The **post-earnings announcement drift** (PEAD) is a market anomaly. It states that instead of quickly digesting new earnings information, investors tend to underreact to the news. A drift of the abnormal returns occurs in the (positive or negative) direction of the earnings for a substantial period after the news release so that the underreaction is corrected only gradually (*Swart/Hoffmann* (2013), p. 17). There is broad empirical evidence for this phenomenon (e.g., *Ball/Brown* (1968); *Bernard/Thomas* (1989; 1990); *Swart/Hoffmann* (2013)). When analyzing the capital market consequences of IR, underreaction to the firm's previous earnings announcement rather than to the report release could be the driver of an occurring price drift. To take this issue into account, the study at hand includes standardized unexpected earnings as a control variable in a separate test. It can be interpreted as a measure of the information content of the precedent (quarterly) earnings announcement (*Latané/Jones* (1977), p. 1457). Following *Bernard/Thomas* (1989), the measure is calculated as the unexpected earnings in quarter q scaled by the standard deviation of the unexpected earnings in the estimation period (fourth quarter of the examined financial year and the eleven previous quarters). The unexpected earnings are the difference between the actual earnings and the expected earnings, which are estimated by the earnings from the respective quarter in the previous year and a trend component. Only the earnings for the fourth quarter of the financial year in question are considered for the regressions.

A firm's accruals also have predictive power both for its future earnings and for future stock returns (*Sloan* (1996)) so that the study also needs to control for a potential reflection of the accruals information in the abnormal returns. As opposed to the PEAD, in which underreaction to the publication of earnings information is observable, investors seem to overreact to earnings information in case of the so-called "**accrual anomaly**" (*Zach* (2003), p. 1). The persistence of the accrual component of earnings is lower than that of the cash portion, since the respective firms do not realize all future benefits anticipated by the accruals (*Allen et al.* (2013), p. 113). However, investors overestimate the persistence of the accrual component so that they are surprised when high (low) accrual firms fall short of (exceed) prior expectations (*Wu et al.* (2010), p. 178). Similar to *Pincus et al.* (2007) and other studies, the study at hand calculates this measure as the difference of the firm's net income before extraordinary items and its cash flow from operating activities, scaled by the average total assets for the year.

In addition to the aforementioned list of control variables, all models also control for **fixed effects** for year, country and industry. Therefore, they include dummy variables that are 1 for financial year 2006 or for South Africa, respectively, and 0 otherwise. Moreover, they include dummies for all but one industries (GICS sector level) that are 1 if the firm is in the respective sector and 0 otherwise.[216] Appendix 2 provides a list of the detailed definitions and calculations of all control variables.

5.3.3 Assumptions of the OLS regressions

Using OLS regressions requires different assumptions.[217] The first assumption deals with the **selection of the variables.** It states that no relevant exogenous variables are missing and that all exogenous variables used in the model are relevant. The variables in this study are well established in extant literature that deals with market returns. *Fama/French* (1992; 1993) show that the set of variables is useful to explain the variation in stock returns. The selection is therefore likely to satisfy this assumption.

Second, OLS regressions require (pairwise) **linear relations between the dependent and the independent variables.** In line with previous studies (e.g., *Hung et al.* (2015), *Miller* (2010)), the models use the natural logarithm of market capitalization and of report length in the respective settings instead of the raw measures to transform multiplicative relations into linear relations. Furthermore, RESET tests (*Ramsey* (1969)) show that with minor exceptions in single combinations of model and time frame, all independent variables have a linear relation to the dependent variable.

Moreover, the inclusion of dummy variables to control for year and country fixed effects deals with potential structural interruptions, which can be an issue with **panel data** if economic relationships between parameters change over time or between countries.

There are various requirements regarding the **error terms.** OLS regressions base upon the assumption that the expected value of the error terms is 0 for all observations. A violation may occur through systematic errors in data collection and analysis. Although mistakes cannot be completely precluded, a thorough collection and editing of the data (see sections 4.3.2 and 5.3.2) intends to ensure the satisfaction of this assumption. An inconstant variance of the error terms (heteroscedasticity) or a correlation of the error terms with each other (autocorrelation) could also hamper the testing of hypotheses. This is not an issue in this study, since all models use robust *White* (1980) and *Newey/West* (1987) standard errors. Besides, for a certain minimum number of observations (30-50), the error term can be presumed to asymptotically follow a normal distribution, according to the central limit theorem. The regressions in this study use at least this minimum number of observations.

---

216 To avoid perfect multicollinearity, one industry dummy needs to be left out of the calculation. This study leaves GICS sector 15 (Materials) out of all regressions.

217 Cf. *Von Auer* ((2016), pp. 19-54, 155-167) and *Wooldridge* ((2014), pp. 71-89)) for the discussion of the OLS assumptions.

A further assumption is that there is no perfect **multicollinearity** among the independent variables, i.e. none of them is constant or is an exact linear combination of another. A violation of this assumption would make it impossible to calculate the respective model. However, tests for variance inflation factors (VIFs) reveal that there is imperfect multicollinearity (VIF > 5) between single variables in Model 3. This means no violation of the assumption, but it causes an inflation of standard errors. Hence, it is more difficult to find significant coefficients. This is not an issue, though, as it counteracts the findings. Attained results persist despite this imperfect multicollinearity.

The final presumption states that exogenous variables are not correlated with the error term. A violation of this assumption is called "endogeneity". Inter alia, causes of **endogeneity** can be reverse causality or simultaneity, self-selection or omitted correlated variables (*Antonakis et al.* (2010), pp. 1090-1099). For this study, it is necessary to distinguish between the basic underreaction setting, which regresses delayed market returns on the immediate returns, and between the models that include the IR score (or alternative IR scores or supplementary measures, respectively) to examine a moderation of the underreaction. A direct **reverse causality**, i.e. the dependent variable in the regression actually causing the independent variable, can be neglected, here, for both types of models. Due to the time sequence of the report release, the immediate stock returns and the delayed returns, it is implicitly clear that the medium-term stock returns cannot drive the short-term returns, nor can the price drift after the release cause the degree of IR in the report published before.

Nonetheless, the measures might jointly be driven by **omitted factors**, in particular self-selection issues. For the basic setting, two tests intend to rule out possible alternative drivers of the underreaction. First, a test considers earnings information released before the report and accruals information, to exclude that the price drift stems from the earnings announcement or that the drift is a reflection of the accruals anomaly rather than a reaction to the report information. A second test compares the association of the long-term abnormal returns with the release date returns on the one hand and the association of the long-term returns with the returns around a pseudo-release date (ten days before the actual report release) on the other hand, checking whether the price drift is a phenomenon that may generally occur after any date rather than the report release only. For the moderation setting, variations of the analysis also address certain other factors potentially influencing investor underreaction, to check for alternative approaches that might explain the moderation of the underreaction effect other than the degree of IR in the firm's annual report. These factors primarily comprise IR sub-scores and alternative measures of IR as well as examinations with the aforementioned supplementary measures as alternatives for or in combination with the IR score.

5.4 Results

This section presents the results of the capital market study. First, the descriptive statistics are shown. An analysis of the correlations between these measures supplements this depiction. The second part provides the results of the multivariate analysis.

5.4.1 Univariate and bivariate analyses

Descriptive statistics

Table 5-1 presents the descriptive statistics for the continuous variables used in the basic underreaction model (equation (5.1)). For brevity, the table includes the cumulative abnormal return only for $\tau = 30$. The mean, median, standard deviation (std. dev.) and the 25% (Q25) and 75% quartiles (Q75) are reported separately for each year-country sub-sample for a better understanding of the data.

Figure 5-8 plots the development of the mean **cumulative abnormal returns** over the 90 days after the annual report release for the four sub-samples.

Figure 5-8: Cumulative abnormal returns relative to the release of the annual (integrated) report

Descriptive statistics of the cumulative abnormal returns, release date returns and control variables							
Variables[a]		mean	std. dev.	Q25	median	Q75	N
Cumulated abnormal return (30th day after AIR release)	RSA 2006	1.33%	9.37%	-5.32%	0.18%	4.87%	50
	RSA 2012	-0.61%	6.57%	-4.92%	0.09%	2.78%	50
	USA 2006	-0.30%	6.30%	-3.76%	-0.50%	3.67%	50
	USA 2012	0.07%	6.02%	-3.17%	-0.35%	3.96%	50
	Total sample	**0.12%**	**7.18%**	**-3.99%**	**-0.14%**	**3.93%**	**200**
Release date return	RSA 2006	0.46%	2.46%	-1.10%	0.88%	1.96%	50
	RSA 2012	-0.05%	2.41%	-1.43%	-0.36%	0.58%	50
	USA 2006	0.14%	1.82%	-0.52%	0.26%	0.94%	50
	USA 2012	0.24%	1.54%	-0.83%	0.21%	1.19%	50
	Total sample	**0.20%**	**2.09%**	**-1.04%**	**0.14%**	**1.34%**	**200**
Beta	RSA 2006	0.53	0.29	0.30	0.49	0.66	50
	RSA 2012	0.57	0.37	0.28	0.49	0.88	50
	USA 2006	1.05	0.37	0.80	1.02	1.20	50
	USA 2012	1.01	0.37	0.73	0.94	1.31	50
	Total sample	**0.79**	**0.43**	**0.47**	**0.75**	**1.06**	**200**
Market capitalization	RSA 2006	2,930.62	4,567.65	598.28	1,219.91	2,715.35	50
	RSA 2012	3,831.29	5,633.15	781.61	1,778.81	4,535.27	50
	USA 2006	32,776.10	52,198.65	9,133.65	14,317.19	30,360.25	50
	USA 2012	36,332.41	58,375.77	8,799.71	16,625.81	30,303.39	50
	Total sample	**18,967.61**	**42,057.12**	**1,448.05**	**6,443.31**	**17,665.30**	**200**
Book to market ratio	RSA 2006	26.43%	37.27%	14.54%	26.06%	42.86%	50
	RSA 2012	49.76%	48.66%	18.11%	33.85%	76.72%	50
	USA 2006	28.22%	15.30%	18.98%	24.33%	39.99%	50
	USA 2012	41.09%	31.72%	20.82%	34.34%	60.01%	50
	Total sample	**36.37%**	**36.37%**	**17.86%**	**30.15%**	**47.56%**	**200**
Stock return momentum	RSA 2006	18.33%	27.69%	1.35%	15.73%	27.43%	50
	RSA 2012	9.37%	19.84%	-3.19%	7.25%	20.91%	50
	USA 2006	9.86%	13.70%	2.53%	9.10%	16.47%	50
	USA 2012	8.13%	11.15%	-0.74%	7.37%	16.44%	50
	Total sample	**11.42%**	**19.47%**	**0.55%**	**9.10%**	**19.66%**	**200**
Standardized unexpected earnings	RSA 2006	0.16	0.98	-0.74	0.37	1.03	49
	RSA 2012	-0.24	0.90	-1.09	-0.40	0.55	50
	USA 2006	0.30	0.87	-0.31	0.35	0.95	49
	USA 2012	-0.51	0.91	-1.10	-0.68	0.15	50
	Total sample	**-0.07**	**0.96**	**-0.90**	**-0.07**	**0.83**	**198**
Operating accrual	RSA 2006	0.02	0.19	-0.06	0.00	0.05	50
	RSA 2012	-0.03	0.09	-0.07	-0.03	0.02	50
	USA 2006	-0.04	0.06	-0.06	-0.05	-0.02	50
	USA 2012	-0.05	0.04	-0.06	-0.05	-0.03	50
	Total sample	**-0.03**	**0.11**	**-0.06**	**-0.04**	**0.00**	**200**

[a] The cumulated abnormal return on the 30th day after the release of the firm's annual (integrated) report is calculated as the sum of the daily abnormal stock returns from the release date up to the 30th day. The release date return is calculated as the sum of the daily abnormal returns for the release date of the firm's annual (integrated) report and the two following days. Beta is the firm's beta factor, calculated as the quotient of the covariance of the firm's returns with the respective market index returns to the variance of the respective market index returns, estimated based on the firm's stock returns of 1080 days (three years) before the annual report release date. Market capitalization (in USD million) is calculated as the number of shares outstanding times share price in USD, translated from ZAR if necessary with the currency rate at the firm's financial year end. Book to market ratio is calculated as the quotient of the book value of equity to the market value of equity. Stock return momentum is the cumulated stock returns for the six months ending at the beginning of the annual report release month. The standardized unexpected earnings is calculated as the unexpected earnings in quarter q scaled by the standard deviation of the unexpected earnings in the estimation period (fourth quarter of the examined financial year and the eleven previous quarters). The unexpected earnings are the difference between the actual earnings and the expected earnings, which are estimated by the earnings from the respective quarter in the previous year and a trend component. Only the earnings for the fourth quarter of the financial year in question are considered for the regressions. The operating accrual is calculated as the difference of the firm's net income before extraordinary items and its cash flow from operating activities, scaled by the average total assets for the year.

Table 5-1: Descriptive statistics of the returns and the control variables

For an examplary time **interval of 30 days** after the report release date, the mean of the cumulative abnormal returns is 0.12% for the full sample. While the means vary without a clear pattern across the four sub-samples, the picture is different for the medians. The South African sub-samples for both 2006 and 2012 have positive median values, whereas both US sub-samples have negative medians. This seems to be in line with other international data, which provides evidence for higher returns in South Africa than in the USA (e.g., *Credit Suisse* (2015)). Since the South African firms are on average also much smaller than their US counterparts, this data seems also consistent with the notion that smaller firms usually have higher returns (the so-called "size effect" documented by *Banz* (1981) and others). However, the lack of a clear pattern across the sub-sample in terms of their means in this data[218] is also plausible, due to the aggregation of the data and the calculation of the mean. Computing a single firm's cumulative abnormal returns for a given day already requires to add up the firm's daily abnormal returns up to that day, each day value being the result of manifold influences. Moreover, as the report release dates vary across firms, the time interval of 30 days relative to the release date includes different calendar dates for each firm. So the measure represents a large variety of different day values of different firms, condensed in one number.

The mean of the **release date returns** in 2006 is higher in the South African sub-sample than in the US, whereas 2012 shows a reverse picture. In the South African sub-sample the 2012 mean returns are even negative. The relationships of the medians are similar. As the release date returns are calculated the same way as the cumulative abnormal returns, only for a shorter interval, the same argumentation as outlined before holds here, too. The lack of a pattern between the sub-samples is therefore plausible.

Stock return momentum is the six months (180 days) nominal return on the firm's stock. The mean of 11.4% for the total sample is within in the range of values from previous studies (e.g., *Huddart et al.* (2007); *You/Zhang* (2009)). The average momentum for the South Africa 2006 sub-sample is 18% and is thus substantially higher than in the other three sub-samples, which are all between 8% and 10%. This is plausible, however, seeing that the South African economy was in a very good state at that time, as data from the *World Bank* database shows. For instance, in terms of household consumption, net national per capita income and industry value added, South Africa had large growth rates in and

[218] For other time intervals, the data does not show clear patterns between the sub-samples either.

around 2006, both in time comparison and compared with the USA.[219] Hence, it seems reasonable that firms also showed a good performance at that time, which was honored by investors with exceptionally high stock returns following the report release.

While the medians for the **standardized unexpected earnings** in the two countries in 2006 are both positive and almost identical, both values are negative in 2012. For the means, the signs show the same pattern. The 2006 values are in line with extant literature (e.g., *Feldman et al.* (2010); *Lerman et al.* (2007)). For the 2012 values, there are no directly comparable studies known to the author. *Chung et al.'s* (2014) data support the trend in the findings from this study, though, albeit with a measure that uses a slightly different method of standardization for the unexpected earnings. The fact that the negative sign for 2012 in the study at hand appears in both countries, together with decreasing business confidence indices for this time in both countries[220], indicates plausibility for these values, too.

Mean (and median) **beta factors** for the US sub-sample are close to 1 in both years. The South African sub-samples both show a mean (and median) close to 0.5. Both values seem plausible with regard to previous studies. For instance, *You/Zhang* (2009) present beta factors for several sub-samples of US firms that are also close to 1. *Hung et al.* (2015) provide two sub-samples with firms from various countries, one of which includes US firms, while the other includes South African firms. While the mean for the former is close to 1, the latter sub-sample mean of 0.8 falls between 0 and 1, indicating that the investment moves in the same direction as the market, but to a weaker degree – in line with the South African means from the study at hand.

In terms of firm size, there is a large difference between the two countries in both years. While the mean **market capitalization** is USD 2.9 billion (USD 3.8 billion) for South African firms in 2006 (2012), their US counterparts have a mean market capitalization of USD 32.7 billion (USD 36.3 billion). This difference is not surprising as it is consistent with historic data on the market capitalization of firms in these two countries.[221]

The **book to market ratio** represents a firm's growth opportunities (e.g., *Fama/French* (1992; 1993)). The market perceives smaller values of the ratio as indicators of more potential opportunities for growth (*Fama/French* (1992), p. 444). In the study at hand, the mean book to market ratios in both countries are between 0.25 and 0.30 for 2006 and between 0.40 and 0.50 for 2012. Given the aforementioned good business confidence

---

219 Cf. http://data.worldbank.org/indicator/NE.CON.PETC.KD.ZG?page=1, http://data.worldbank.org/indicator/NY.ADJ.NNTY.PC.KD.ZG?page=1 and http://data.worldbank.org/indicator/NV.IND.TOTL.KD.ZG, respectively (all last accessed on 29 August 2016).

220 For South Africa, cf. the indices provided by the Bureau for Economic Research (research institute): https://www.ber.ac.za/home/#indicators. For the USA, cf. e.g. the Purchasing Managers Index: http://www.tradingeconomics.com/united-states/business-confidence (both last accessed on 29 August 2016).

221 Cf. e.g. data from the *World Bank* database on the market capitalization in different countries: http://data.worldbank.org/indicator/CM.MKT.LCAP.GD.ZS/countries?display=default in combination with http://data.worldbank.org/indicator/NY.GDP.MKTP.CD/countries (both last accessed on 29 August 2016).

in 2006, the lower values for this year are reasonable. The ratios for 2012, a less extraordinary year in terms of business outlook, are in line with values from extant literature for the same and former years (e.g., *You/Zhang* (2009); *Barth et al.* (2015); *Hung et al.* (2015)).

A firm's **accruals** supposedly have predictive power for stock returns due to the difference in persistence of the cash and the accrual component of earnings. The accrual measure shows a median (mean) of -0.04 (-0.03) for the sample. The values for the sub-samples range between 0.00 and -0.05 (0.02 and -0.05). This is largely in line with results from previous studies (e.g., *Hirshleifer et al.* (2011); *Wu et al.* (2010); *Barth et al.* (2015)). The South Africa 2006 values are somewhat higher than those from the other three sub-samples, but these values are still in the range of values provided by other literature (e.g., *Allen et al.* (2013)) and are thus reasonable.[222]

Overall, the descriptive statistics of the return data and the control variables are largely in line with expectations and prior literature.[223] Through the consideration of year and country control dummies as well as additional examinations on country level, the multivariate analysis further ensures that the differences existing among the sub-samples for some variables do not drive the results.

Correlations

Table 5-2 and Table 5-3 show the pairwise Pearson (below the diagonal) and Spearman[224] (above the diagonal) **correlations** of the measures from the explanatory analysis. While the descriptive statistics include the more readily interpretable raw data on the market capitalization and the report length (number of words), the correlation table includes the natural logarithm of the respective data instead. This strengthens consistency with the multivariate analysis, which also uses the latter measures.

Table 5-2 reveals a weak[225], yet highly significant[226] positive **correlation between the release date returns and the (30 days) cumulative abnormal returns.** The Pearson (Spearman) correlation coefficient is 0.33 (0.37). The delayed market response thus generally has the same direction as the immediate response. Both Pearson and Spearman correlations are significant at the 1% level. This is a potential indicator of the investor underreaction effect.

---

[222] The cited literature, however, does not use US or international samples. No study is known to the author that presents descriptive results of accruals measures for South African firms, though.

[223] Recall that section 4.4 presents the descriptive statistics for the degree of IR and the supplementary measures.

[224] As opposed to Pearson correlations, Spearman correlation coefficients are non-parametric. They do not assume normally distributed data. Their calculation bases upon the ranks of the underlying values of the variable.

[225] Various classifications exist in the literature to assess the strength of correlations, e.g. *Cohen* (1988) or *Evans* (1996). All classifications necessarily base upon subjectivity. This study follows *Evans'* (1996) interpretation of correlations, considering (the absolute value of) a correlation coefficient between 0.00 and 0.19 as very weak, between 0.20 and 0.39 as weak, between 0.40 and 0.59 as moderate, between 0.60 and 0.79 as strong and between 0.80 and 1.00 as very strong.

[226] The correlations of the release date returns with all examined cumulative abnormal return values for the different time periods are significant, both on total sample and country level (unreported).

In addition, beta and the return momentum show weak or very weak negative Pearson (Spearman) coefficients of -0.22 (-0.14) and -0.16 (-0.10) with the delayed response measure. Except for the Spearman coefficient of the return momentum, these correlations are at least marginally significant, indicating an association of these controls with the long-term returns. The IR score shows only very weak negative or positive linear relationships with the cumulated abnormal returns on the 30th day after the report release and with the release date returns, respectively. Neither of these correlations is significantly different from 0. However, since the analysis of a moderation of the underreaction effect, as intended by this study, requires a multivariate examination (see section 5.3), the bivariate correlations cannot yield expectations for this moderation.

Correlation matrix for the market response variables, IR score and control variables

Variables	Cumulated abnormal return (30th day)	Release date return	IR score	Beta	Ln market capitalization	Book to market ratio	Stock return momentum
Cumulated abnormal return (30th day)	1.0000	0.3681 ***	-0.0859	-0.1378 *	-0.0423	-0.0043	-0.0967
Release date return	0.3296 ***	1.0000	0.0773	-0.0541	-0.0386	0.0547	-0.0839
IR score	-0.0969	0.0396	1.0000	-0.2292 ***	-0.2617 ***	0.0562	-0.0341
Beta	-0.2170 ***	-0.1096	-0.2380 ***	1.0000	0.6052 ***	0.1013	-0.1155
Ln market capitalization	-0.0853	-0.1092	-0.2639 ***	0.5451 ***	1.0000	-0.0641	-0.1008
Book to market ratio	0.0180	0.0967	0.1700 **	0.0379	-0.1421 **	1.0000	0.0406
Stock return momentum	-0.1639 **	-0.0351	-0.0104	-0.0785	-0.1682 **	-0.0314	1.0000

Pearson (Spearman) pairwise correlation coefficients are reported below (above) the diagonal.
*, **, and *** indicate statistical significance at the 10%, 5% and 1% levels, respectively.

Table 5-2: Matrix of pairwise Pearson and Spearman correlations for the market response variables, IR score and control variables

The pairwise correlations between the **IR score, the alternative IR scores and the supplementary measures** give some insight into the relatedness between these variables.[227] The findings may give indications of how the respective measures could moderate the underreaction effect, compared with the IR score. Table 5-3 presents the respective coefficients.

[227] Again, it is not possible to draw direct conclusions for the examination of a potential moderating effect of IR on the underreaction effect, however, since correlations are only bivariate and the moderating effect includes the interaction of three variables.

Correlation matrix for the market response variables, IR scores and the supplementary measures

Variables	Cumulated abnormal return (30th day)	Release date return	IR score	CONX sub-score	Alternative IR score 1	Alternative IR score 2	Report length (ln # words)	Use of boilerplate disclosures	Use of jargon	Readability (Fog Index)
Cumulated abn.return (30th day)	1.0000	0.3681 ***	-0.0859	-0.1698 **	0.0067	0.0123	-0.0122	0.0000	-0.0222	-0.0173
Release date return	0.3296 ***	1.0000	0.0773	0.0717	0.0685	0.0450	-0.0331	-0.0213	-0.1096	-0.1189 *
IR score	-0.0969	0.0396	1.0000	0.6827 ***	-0.0050	0.4992 ***	0.2956 ***	-0.3315 ***	0.0433	0.0357
CONX sub-score	-0.1585 **	0.0344	0.6793 ***	1.0000	-0.1381 *	0.3221 ***	0.3443 ***	-0.0672	-0.1017	0.0017
Alternative IR score 1	-0.0463	0.0407	-0.0501	-0.0969	1.0000	0.3610 ***	-0.9383 ***	-0.1566 **	-0.1676 **	-0.0917
Alternative IR score 2	-0.0296	0.0382	0.3171 ***	0.2244 ***	0.5949 ***	1.0000	-0.1705 **	-0.1203 *	-0.1119	-0.0422
Report length (ln # words)	0.0056	-0.0324	0.3119 ***	0.3384 ***	-0.8755 ***	-0.3670 ***	1.0000	0.0827	0.1717 **	0.0946
Use of boilerplate disclosures	-0.0401	-0.0289	-0.3314 ***	-0.0575	-0.2205 ***	-0.1896 ***	0.1137	1.0000	-0.1847 ***	-0.1088
Use of jargon	-0.0472	-0.1759 **	0.0108	-0.1195 *	-0.1111	-0.1057	0.1319 *	-0.2103 ***	1.0000	0.2958 ***
Readability (Fog Index)	0.0351	-0.1446 **	0.0434	0.0030	-0.0736	-0.0347	0.0780	-0.1006	0.2991 ***	1.0000

Pearson (Spearman) pairwise correlation coefficients are reported below (above) the diagonal.
*, **, and *** indicate statistical significance at the 10%, 5% and 1% levels, respectively.

Table 5-3: Matrix of pairwise Pearson and Spearman correlations for the market response variables, IR scores and the supplementary measures

There is a strong positive correlation between the IR score and the **connectivity sub-score**, with Pearson and Spearman correlation coefficients of almost 0.7. Both coefficients are highly significant. This finding is plausible from a technical perspective, as CONX constitutes a high percentage of the total IR score. Moreover, from a conceptual perspective, these values reflect the importance of the Connectivity of Information principle for IR, which both the literature and the Framework underline.

Two alternative IR scores employ a different reflection of the Conciseness principle, considering the IR score (without the CONC sub-score) relative to the report length or the expected report length rather than treating conciseness as an additive component of the IR score (see section 5.3.2). Not surprisingly, the original IR score shows a (weak to moderate) positive correlation with **alternative IR score 2**, with a highly significant Pearson (Spearman) coefficient of 0.32 (0.50). At the same time, there is only a very weak negative correlation between the IR score and the **alternative IR score 1**, with insignificant correlation coefficients of -0.05. For the multivariate analysis of the underreaction effect and its moderation, these unalike linear relationships between the original IR score and the two respective alternative specifications may suggest differing directions of moderation on the underreaction effect through the two alternative scores. While the alternative IR score 2 and the original IR score seem to work in the same direction, alternative score 1 might show a different picture.

In comparison with the original IR score, the **supplementary measures** provide mixed results. The report length shows a weak positive correlation with the total IR score. Pearson (0.31) and Spearman (0.30) coefficients are both highly significant. Analyzing the impacts of IR and report length on a third measure, such as market returns, might therefore lead to similar conclusions for these variables. Report length is used to approximate either the information content of a report or the difficulty to process the information in the report. The outlined finding of a positive correlation between report length and the IR score supports the former interpretation, as the latter would rather suggest a converse relationship of report length with IR, which stands for easily processable reports. Instead, the use of boilerplate disclosures probably has the opposite impact of IR on a third variable, as the similarity score shows a weak, but highly significant negative correlation with the degree of IR. Pearson and Spearman coefficients of -0.33, respectively, demonstrate these linear relationships. This negative correlation may suggest that in terms of moderating investor underreaction, the IR score and the use of boilerplate disclosures work in opposing directions – in line with the IIRC's assertion that IR needs to tackle the use of boilerplate. As opposed to the first two supplementary measures, the jargon score and the Fog Index for readability are not significantly correlated with the IR score. The very weakly positive Pearson (Spearman) coefficients of 0.01 (0.04) and 0.04 (0.04) between the IR score and the two respective measures are close to 0. This might be due to the fact that both the jargon score and the Fog Index values base upon the Letter to the Stakeholders only, which constitutes only a small part of the entire report. Overall, these findings are also consistent with the mixed results on the supplementary measures from the descriptive analysis (see section 4.4) in so far as they are not interpretable as measures that simply oppose the results on IR.

To **sum up**, the pairwise correlations between the variables from the basic underreaction model are in line with the expectations to a large degree. In particular, this holds for the association of short-term and long-term market response, supporting the expectation that there is investor underreaction in this setting. Direct indications for a potential moderation of this effect by the degree of IR or by other report characteristics are not inferable from the bivariate statistics. However, the results show that the IR score, the alternative IR scores and the supplementary measures do not necessarily relate to each other in the presumed way, which raises questions on the interpretation of some of the latter variables.

5.4.2 Regression analysis

This section presents the results of the multivariate analysis, using **OLS regressions**. First, the basic underreaction setting (irrespective of the degree of IR) is presented. Afterwards, the results on a potential moderating effect of IR are reported. Third, various robustness tests check for probable alternative explanations of the results on the moderation.

The output tables present the t-statistics in parentheses below the coefficients and attach asterisks to signal statistical significance at the 10% (*), 5% (**) or 1% level (***). However, due to the magnitude of different regressions, the presentation mostly uses summary tables that show aggregate results for the three different models and the different time intervals. These tables provide a conclusion on whether the results for the moderation effect are in line with expectations and present the adjusted R-squared for each regression.[228]

5.4.2.1 Basic model: the investor underreaction effect

Table 5-4 shows the results of the basic underreaction model (equation (5.1)) for the cumulative abnormal returns in a 30-day interval after the report release (τ=30). In addition, it presents three modifications of this model that include controls for the standardized unexpected earnings, the operating accruals and both of these measures, respectively.

Along with the expectations, the coefficient of the immediate market response is positive and highly significant. Cumulative abnormal returns 30 days after the report release therefore align with the immediate market response to the release. The value of 0.996 indicates that there is about 0.996% of delayed market response for each 1% of immediate response (*You/Zhang* (2009), p. 579). This finding supports the **notion of an underreaction effect** to the information presented in the annual reports. However, rather than on the report itself, this outcome could base on earnings information, which firms typically announce shortly before the report release.[229] Furthermore, the finding could relate to the accrual anomaly, with the operating accrual also being derivable from the earnings announcement.[230] To preclude these potential alternative reasons of the effect, the first modification of the model controls for standardized unexpected earnings, the second for operating accruals and the third for both of these measures (*You/Zhang* (2009), pp. 575-578). In all of these models, the coefficient of the immediate returns stays highly significant, although the operating accruals also show a significant (negative) coefficient, which is consistent with

[228] The tables in web appendices 2 and 3 include the detailed results for all values of τ in steps of five days.

[229] The documented price drift would thus represent or overlap with the PEAD, which is subject of many studies (e.g., *Bernard/Thomas* (1989); *Abarbanell/Bernard* (1992)).

[230] Cf. *Ball Corporation* (2013) for an example of information provided with an earnings announcement.

prior literature (*Sloan* (1996)). Similar results occur for all examined timeframes up to 90 days; results on country level show an almost unchanged picture to the total sample results.[231] The underreaction thus seems to be related to the annual report.

Regressions investor underreaction to AIR information					
Variables	Predicted sign	**Basic model**	**Controlling for the PEAD**	**Controlling for the accrual anomaly**	**Controlling for the PEAD and the accrual anomaly**
Dependent variable		Cumulated abnormal return (30th day after AIR release)	Cumulated abnormal return (30th day after AIR release)	Cumulated abnormal return (30th day after AIR release)	Cumulated abnormal return (30th day after AIR release)
Release date return	(+)	0.996 ***	1.000 ***	1.002 ***	1.010 ***
		(4.125)	(4.070)	(4.110)	(4.075)
Standardized unexpected earnings			-0.001		0.000
			(-0.175)		(-0.010)
Operating accrual				-0.102 ***	-0.107 ***
				(-3.156)	(-3.317)
Beta		-0.043 ***	-0.045 ***	-0.042 **	-0.043 **
		(-2.609)	(-2.626)	(-2.502)	(-2.474)
Natural logarithm of market capitalization		-0.002	-0.002	-0.002	-0.002
		(-0.306)	(-0.320)	(-0.292)	(-0.299)
Book to market ratio		0.001	0.004	0.004	0.006
		(0.054)	(0.176)	(0.194)	(0.315)
Stock return momentum		-0.069 *	-0.062	-0.056	-0.048
		(-1.773)	(-1.496)	(-1.474)	(-1.198)
Constant		0.084	0.085	0.069	0.067
		(0.637)	(0.642)	(0.537)	(0.528)
Year fixed effects		YES	YES	YES	YES
Country fixed effects		YES	YES	YES	YES
Industry fixed effects		YES	YES	YES	YES
N		200	198	200	198
Adjusted R^2		0.132	0.127	0.151	0.148

The table reports OLS coefficient estimates and t-statistics in parentheses below the coefficients. The predicted signs are presented next to the variables in parentheses.
*, **, and *** indicate statistical significance at the 10%, 5%, and 1% levels, respectively.

Table 5-4: Regressions investor underreaction – Testing for the PEAD and the accrual anomaly

An additional test (*You/Zhang* (2009), pp. 576-577) examines the conclusion that annual report information rather than information from other sources or mere random effects drives the market movement. Table 5-5 provides the aforementioned basic model next to an alternative model and a combination of both. The alternative setting replaces the immediate returns variable with a **pseudo measure** of the immediate market response. This variable captures the three-day cumulative abnormal returns starting ten days before the release of the report (whereas the original immediate response variable depicts the three-day cumulated abnormal returns starting on the release date itself). If this measure turns out to be a

[231] Web appendix 2.1 provides the detailed results for the test for PEAD and accrual anomaly on total-sample and country level.

predictor of future stock returns just like the regular release date returns, the price drift may be driven by other influences than the report information. The results show no significance for the coefficient of the pseudo measure, though, neither in the alternative setting (pseudo measure only), nor in the combined setting (pseudo and original response), whereas the coefficient of the original immediate market response is highly significant and positive, even after including the pseudo variable. Again, this holds true for the other day intervals, as well, and is supported by country-level results.[232]

In **summary**, the results from the basic regression provide evidence for the existence of investor underreaction to annual report information. The two tests substantiate that these results actually relate to the information in the report rather than to different kinds of information or to other influences. Having documented the existence of the underreaction effect itself, the following part of the study examines a potential moderation of this effect by the degree of IR in the firms' reports.

Regressions investor underreaction to AIR information							
Variables	Predicted sign	**Basic model (real release date returns)**		**Pseudo release date returns**		**Real and pseudo release date returns**	
Dependent variable		Cumulated abnormal return (30th day after AIR release)		Cumulated abnormal return (30th day after AIR release)		Cumulated abnormal return (30th day after AIR release)	
Release date return	(+)	0.996 (4.125)	***			1.000 (4.100)	***
Pseudo release date return				-0.029 (-0.095)		0.056 (0.201)	
Beta		-0.043 (-2.609)	***	-0.052 (-3.018)	***	-0.043 (-2.509)	**
Natural logarithm of market capitalization		-0.002 (-0.306)		-0.004 (-0.630)		-0.002 (-0.308)	
Book to market ratio		0.001 (0.054)		0.007 (0.364)		0.001 (0.069)	
Stock return momentum		-0.069 (-1.773)	*	-0.074 (-1.829)	*	-0.069 (-1.786)	*
Constant		0.084 (0.637)		0.138 (1.030)		0.083 (0.633)	
Year fixed effects		YES		YES		YES	
Country fixed effects		YES		YES		YES	
Industry fixed effects		YES		YES		YES	
N		200		200		200	
Adjusted R^2		0.132		0.047		0.128	

The table reports OLS coefficient estimates and t-statistics in parentheses below the coefficients. The predicted signs are presented next to the variables in parentheses.
*, **, and *** indicate statistical significance at the 10%, 5%, and 1% levels, respectively.

Table 5-5: Regressions underreaction – Testing for a pseudo release date

232 Web appendix 2.2 provides the detailed results for the test with the pseudo release date on total-sample and country level.

5.4.2.2 Moderation of the investor underreaction effect by IR

The three models described in section 5.3.1 examine whether the **degree of IR moderates the underreaction** effect. According to H_2, the degree of investor underreaction is expected to be lower for a higher degree of IR. In Model 1, the (positive) coefficient for the immediate market returns is thus presumably more significant in the "low" than in the "high" sub-sample. In Model 2 and Model 3 the coefficients of the interaction term of the IR (dummy) variable and the immediate returns is expected to be negative. The regressions have been calculated for different estimation windows, starting with a window of five days up to a window of 90 days. After exemplarily presenting the results for two windows in detail (30 and 60 days, respectively), aggregated tables show the results for all windows.

Table 5-6 presents the results for the three models for the abnormal returns cumulated over an exemplary **time interval of 30 days.**

Regressions moderation of investor underreaction by IR (estimation window of 30 days)									
Variables	Predicted sign	**Model 1**				**Model 2**		**Model 3**	
		low		**high**					
Dependent variable		Cumulated abnormal return (30th day after AIR release)		Cumulated abnormal return (30th day after AIR release)		Cumulated abnormal return (30th day after AIR release)		Cumulated abnormal return (30th day after AIR release)	
Release date return	(+)	**1.299**	***	**0.746**	*	**1.297**	***	**3.665**	
		(3.936)		**(1.782)**		**(4.408)**		**(1.478)**	
IR dummy						-0.021	*		
						(-1.885)			
Release date return x IR dummy	(-)					**-0.481**			
						(-1.027)			
IR score								-0.206	**
								(-2.027)	
Release date return x IR score	(-)							**-4.496**	
								(-1.040)	
Beta		-0.066	**	-0.035		-0.044	***	-0.046	***
		(-2.394)		(-1.448)		(-2.622)		(-2.681)	
Natural logarithm of market capitalization		-0.002		0.000		-0.001		0.000	
		(-0.251)		(0.025)		(-0.095)		(-0.047)	
Book to market ratio		-0.010		0.025		0.002		0.005	
		(-0.466)		(0.741)		(0.088)		(0.234)	
Stock return momentum		-0.012		-0.088	*	-0.068	*	-0.071	*
		(-0.254)		(-1.731)		(-1.728)		(-1.789)	
Constant		0.135		0.003		0.067		0.175	
		(0.720)		(0.019)		(0.514)		(1.291)	
Year fixed effects		YES		YES		YES		YES	
Country fixed effects		YES		YES		YES		YES	
Industry fixed effects		YES		YES		YES		YES	
N		101		99		200		200	
Adjusted R^2		0.177		0.038		0.146		0.153	

The table reports OLS coefficient estimates and t-statistics in parentheses below the coefficients. The predicted signs are presented next to the variables in parentheses.
*, **, and *** indicate statistical significance at the 10%, 5%, and 1% levels, respectively.

Table 5-6: Regressions moderation of the underreaction by IR (estimation window of 30 days)

The **findings** are partly in line with the expectations, but do not meet all of them. In Model 1, there is a positive coefficient for the immediate returns in both the "low" and "high" sub-sample. While the "low" coefficient is highly significant (at the 1% level), the coefficient in the "high" sub-sample is only marginally significant (10% level)[233]. This finding aligns with the expectation from H_2. It indicates that although underreaction is present for firms both with a high and low degree of IR, it is more clearly visible for the "low" IR firms. The values of the coefficients underline this conclusion to some degree. The "low" coefficient (1.30) is substantially higher than the "high" coefficient (0.75), indicating stronger underreaction for "low" IR firms. According to a Wald test of simple and composite linear hypotheses about the parameters (*Wald* (1943)), this difference is not statistically significant (one-tailed p-value of 0.13), however. Similarly, the coefficients of the interaction terms between the IR dummy and raw variable and the release date returns in Model 2 and Model 3 both show the expected negative sign, but without statistical significance. Hence, there is only some evidence of the expected effect for a time frame of 30 days.

The picture changes with the time frame, though. For instance, an **interval of 60 days** yields results more clearly in line with the expectation from H_2 (Table 5-7). The coefficients for the release date returns in Model 1 show the same pattern as for the 30-day interval: a highly significant coefficient in the "low" sub-sample and a marginally significant one in the "high" sub-sample. In terms of the values, the "low" coefficient (1.71) more than doubles the "high" coefficient (0.83). A one-tailed Wald test shows that this difference is marginally significant in statistical terms (p-value of 0.06). The interaction terms in Model 2 and Model 3 are negative, again. In this case, both are also marginally significant.

The **differences in the results across the models** may have different reasons. Since models with dichotomized variables, like Model 1 and Model 2, have considerably less variation and power than those with continuous variables (*Cohen* (1983)), models with continuous variables, like Model 3, would presumably be more likely to show significant results. However, sample splits and dichotomized variables may also create apparent, but spurious effects (*Maxwell/Delaney* (1993)), especially in moderation settings (*Bissonnette et al.* (1990)). This phenomenon may explain that the occurrence of significant associations is more frequent in Model 1 (and Model 2) than in Model 3. For an unbiased interpretation, it is thus necessary to consider the results of all three models, as significant results only in Model 1 (and Model 2) may be spurious.

Table 5-8 **aggregates the regression results** for the three models for values of τ from five to 90 days (in steps of five). The table presents a conclusion regarding the expectations from the regressions for each model and each value of τ. For intervals of five to 50 days, only Model 1 provides statistically significant evidence for a moderation of the underreaction effect by the degree of IR. One-tailed Wald tests support this evidence further by showing significant differences in the values of the coefficients of the release date returns between the low and high IR sub-sample in the expected direction (unreported). Model 2 presents evidence for the expected effect for time frames of 55 days and higher, while Model 3 yields supportive results for time frames between 60 and 75 days.

[233] All reported results refer to the two-tailed test, if not indicated differently.

Regressions moderation of investor underreaction by IR (estimation window of 60 days)									
Variables	Predicted sign	**Model 1**				**Model 2**		**Model 3**	
		low		**high**					
Dependent variable		Cumulated abnormal return (60th day after AIR release)		Cumulated abnormal return (60th day after AIR release)		Cumulated abnormal return (60th day after AIR release)		Cumulated abnormal return (60th day after AIR release)	
Release date return	(+)	**1.708**	***	**0.826**	*	**1.895**	***	**6.509**	**
		(4.076)		**(1.746)**		**(4.585)**		**(2.244)**	
IR dummy						-0.029	**		
						(-2.081)			
Release date return x IR dummy	(-)					**-1.047**	*		
						(-1.856)			
IR score								-0.264	**
								(-2.192)	
Release date return x IR score	(-)							**-8.832**	*
								(-1.797)	
Beta		-0.107	***	-0.019		-0.053	**	-0.055	**
		(-3.569)		(-0.632)		(-2.508)		(-2.578)	
Natural logarithm of market capitalization		0.000		0.008		0.006		0.006	
		(-0.032)		(0.856)		(0.836)		-0.882	
Book to market ratio		-0.016		0.046		0.012		0.016	
		(-0.648)		(1.050)		(0.492)		-0.649	
Stock return momentum		-0.008		-0.051		-0.043		-0.046	
		(-0.157)		(-0.717)		(-0.801)		(-0.858)	
Constant		0.145		-0.205		-0.066		0.071	
		(0.668)		(-0.915)		(-0.413)		(0.433)	
Year fixed effects		YES		YES		YES		YES	
Country fixed effects		YES		YES		YES		YES	
Industry fixed effects		YES		YES		YES		YES	
N		101		99		200		200	
Adjusted R^2		0.236		0.051		0.156		0.158	

The table reports OLS coefficient estimates and t-statistics in parentheses below the coefficients. The predicted signs are presented next to the variables in parentheses.
*, **, and *** indicate statistical significance at the 10%, 5%, and 1% levels, respectively.

Table 5-7: Regressions moderation of the underreaction by IR (estimation window of 60 days)

The **adjusted R-squares** expectedly decrease with increasing time intervals. For a time frame of five days (which is very close to the three-day time frame used for the calculation of the release date returns), the adjusted R-squares are close to 0.5 for the different (sub-)models, demonstrating that the respective model explains about half of the variation in the dependent variable. For higher values of τ, the R-squares range between 0.13 and 0.28 (-0.02 and 0.10) for the "low" ("high") sub-sample in Model 1 and between 0.07 and 0.20 for Model 2 and Model 3. This is largely in line with the R-squares from *You/Zhang* (2009), who use a comparable setting. For Model 1, the values are almost unanimously higher for the "low" sub-sample than the "high" sub-sample. These values indicate that for firms with a low degree of IR, the underreaction model can explain the movement in the cumulative abnormal returns comparably well. However, for firms with a high degree of IR, the model is less adequate to explain the return movement. This supports the expectations.

Investor underreaction and its moderation over time: Three regression models – Aggregate results							
(Sub-) Sample[a] used:	Total sample (n=200)						
Explained variable:	Cumulative abnormal returns – calculated by addition of daily abnormal returns						
Primary explanatory variable:	Release date returns – cumulative abnormal returns for the 3 days [0; 2] following the report release						
High vs low sample split criteria/moderating variable:	Relative IR score (proportion of points in the disclosure catalogue)						
Days (τ):		**Model 1**			**Model 2**		**Model 3**
	Conclusion[b]	Adjusted R^2 ("low" sub-sample)	Adjusted R^2 ("high" sub-sample)	Conclusion[b]	Adjusted R^2	Conclusion[b]	Adjusted R^2
5	IND	0.467	0.504	IND	0.502	IND	0.506
10	**SUPP**	0.284	0.086	IND	0.159	IND	0.169
15	**SUPP**	0.282	0.092	IND	0.182	IND	0.192
20	**SUPP**	0.179	0.037	IND	0.127	IND	0.141
25	**SUPP**	0.238	0.078	IND	0.176	IND	0.193
30	**SUPP**	0.177	0.038	IND	0.146	IND	0.153
35	**SUPP**	0.186	0.038	IND	0.141	IND	0.143
40	**SUPP**	0.210	-0.011	IND	0.137	IND	0.138
45	**SUPP**	0.205	0.010	IND	0.124	IND	0.115
50	**SUPP**	0.234	-0.022	IND	0.118	IND	0.109
55	**SUPP**	0.256	0.034	**SUPP**	0.154	IND	0.146
60	**SUPP**	0.236	0.051	**SUPP**	0.156	**SUPP**	0.158
65	**SUPP**	0.179	0.040	**SUPP**	0.138	**SUPP**	0.144
70	**SUPP**	0.146	0.012	**SUPP**	0.116	**SUPP**	0.113
75	**SUPP**	0.131	0.011	**SUPP**	0.103	**SUPP**	0.099
80	**SUPP**	0.145	0.006	**SUPP**	0.094	IND	0.082
85	**SUPP**	0.145	0.043	**SUPP**	0.097	IND	0.093
90	**SUPP**	0.130	0.043	**SUPP**	0.084	IND	0.075

[a] The size of the (sub-)samples (n) may vary slightly due to unavailable data. In case of the high vs. low sample split, the sizes of the sub-samples are not necessarily identical due to some values of the split criteria variable being equal to the median.

[b] CON: Contrary to expectations; SUPP: Supportive of expectations; IND: Indifferent (includes cases in which the coefficient of the primary explanatory variable is negative and/or insignificant).

Table 5-8: Aggregated regression results for the moderation of the underreaction (IR score, total sample)

5.4.2.3 Robustness tests

To check for alternative explanations of the found associations and therefore mitigate endogeneity issues due to omitted influences, the study employs different robustness tests. After an examination of the moderation on country level for both considered countries, the connectivity sub-score and two alternative IR scores respectively are employed in the moderation setting (on full-sample level) instead of the total IR score. Afterwards, the aforementioned supplementary measures replace the IR score in the moderation setting in the same vein. Finally, a setting that considers interactions of the release date returns with both the IR score and report length compares these two potential moderators of underreaction directly.

Regressions on country level

The regressions on **country level** provide largely comparable results to the total sample results. In South Africa (Table 5-9), the regressions show results that support the expectations for $\tau \geq 10$ in Model 1, $\tau \geq 40$ in Model 2 and $\tau \geq 55$ in Model 3. For US firms (Table 5-10), there is evidence supportive of the expectations for $20 \leq \tau \geq 75$ in Model 1, $\tau \geq 55$ in Model 2 and $\tau = 90$ in Model 3. Thus, in both countries the degree of IR seems to moderate an existing investor underreaction, although the evidence is slightly differently distributed over the time frames, and stronger for South Africa in terms of the dispersion over the three models. Overall, however, these findings underline the meaning of the results on full sample level.

Investor underreaction and its moderation over time: Three regression models – Aggregate results

(Sub-) Sample[a] used:	South African sub-sample (n=100)
Explained variable:	Cumulative abnormal returns – calculated by addition of daily abnormal returns
Primary explanatory variable:	Release date returns – cumulative abnormal returns for the 3 days [0; 2] following the report release
High vs low sample split criteria/moderating variable:	Relative IR score (proportion of points in the disclosure catalogue)

Days (τ):	**Model 1**			**Model 2**		**Model 3**	
	Conclusion[b]	Adjusted R^2 ("low" sub-sample)	Adjusted R^2 ("high" sub-sample)	Conclusion[b]	Adjusted R^2	Conclusion[b]	Adjusted R^2
5	IND	0.540	0.513	IND	0.521	IND	0.524
10	**SUPP**	0.021	0.072	IND	-0.014	IND	-0.017
15	**SUPP**	0.013	0.135	IND	0.055	IND	0.041
20	**SUPP**	0.018	-0.029	IND	0.002	IND	0.000
25	**SUPP**	0.060	0.023	IND	0.050	IND	0.060
30	**SUPP**	0.003	-0.032	IND	0.022	IND	0.015
35	**SUPP**	0.010	0.059	IND	0.023	IND	0.019
40	**SUPP**	-0.007	0.139	**SUPP**	0.036	IND	0.037
45	**SUPP**	-0.030	0.223	**SUPP**	0.064	IND	0.070
50	**SUPP**	-0.057	0.135	**SUPP**	0.021	IND	0.023
55	**SUPP**	-0.075	0.121	**SUPP**	0.047	**SUPP**	0.046
60	**SUPP**	-0.097	0.169	**SUPP**	0.045	**SUPP**	0.054
65	**SUPP**	-0.004	0.169	**SUPP**	0.100	**SUPP**	0.112
70	**SUPP**	-0.046	0.160	**SUPP**	0.080	**SUPP**	0.097
75	**SUPP**	0.017	0.133	**SUPP**	0.086	**SUPP**	0.095
80	**SUPP**	-0.001	0.122	**SUPP**	0.076	**SUPP**	0.074
85	**SUPP**	0.090	0.203	**SUPP**	0.128	**SUPP**	0.121
90	**SUPP**	0.060	0.254	**SUPP**	0.122	**SUPP**	0.116

[a] The size of the (sub-)samples (n) may vary slightly due to unavailable data. In case of the high vs. low sample split, the sizes of the sub-samples are not necessarily identical due to some values of the split criteria variable being equal to the median.

[b] CON: Contrary to expectations; SUPP: Supportive of expectations; IND: Indifferent (includes cases in which the coefficient of the primary explanatory variable is negative and/or insignificant).

Table 5-9: Aggregated regression results for the moderation of the underreaction (IR score, South Africa)

For further robustness of the results, the study also examines the **South African firms for the year 2012** only, generating a setting in which all firms were (factually) obliged to apply IR, albeit not under the International <IR> Framework. As Model 1 splits the sample in half, the already small sample size of 50 firms in this test is further reduced to 25 for each group. Due to a lack of power in these sub-samples and due a potential violation of the assumption of normally distributed error terms, the results for Model 1 are neglected for this test. However, in particular the results from Model 3 are consistent with the total sample results and support the expectations, although supportive evidence starts at higher values of τ than for the aforementioned settings.[234] All in all, the results on country level are thus supportive of the expectations and in line with the main setting (full-sample level).

Investor underreaction and its moderation over time: Three regression models – Aggregate results

(Sub-) Sample[a] used:	USA sub-sample (n=100)
Explained variable:	Cumulative abnormal returns – calculated by addition of daily abnormal returns
Primary explanatory variable:	Release date returns – cumulative abnormal returns for the 3 days [0; 2] following the report release
High vs low sample split criteria/moderating variable:	Relative IR score (proportion of points in the disclosure catalogue)

Days (τ):	**Model 1**			**Model 2**		**Model 3**	
	Conclusion[b]	Adjusted R^2 ("low" sub-sample)	Adjusted R^2 ("high" sub-sample)	Conclusion[b]	Adjusted R^2	Conclusion[b]	Adjusted R^2
5	**CON**	0.390	0.675	IND	0.443	IND	0.450
10	IND	0.562	0.454	**SUPP**	0.497	IND	0.484
15	IND	0.352	0.294	IND	0.328	IND	0.337
20	**SUPP**	0.372	0.164	IND	0.274	IND	0.290
25	**SUPP**	0.414	0.259	IND	0.322	IND	0.341
30	**SUPP**	0.272	0.255	IND	0.236	IND	0.249
35	**SUPP**	0.242	0.199	IND	0.202	IND	0.214
40	**SUPP**	0.286	0.239	IND	0.243	IND	0.252
45	**SUPP**	0.230	0.246	IND	0.245	IND	0.242
50	**SUPP**	0.253	0.253	IND	0.231	IND	0.234
55	**SUPP**	0.266	0.263	**SUPP**	0.251	IND	0.243
60	**SUPP**	0.273	0.302	**SUPP**	0.268	IND	0.257
65	**SUPP**	0.181	0.247	**SUPP**	0.243	IND	0.233
70	**SUPP**	0.242	0.251	**SUPP**	0.272	IND	0.265
75	**SUPP**	0.237	0.152	**SUPP**	0.225	IND	0.224
80	IND	0.301	0.182	**SUPP**	0.259	IND	0.249
85	IND	0.251	0.298	**SUPP**	0.274	IND	0.266
90	IND	0.229	0.336	**SUPP**	0.267	**SUPP**	0.255

[a] The size of the (sub-)samples (n) may vary slightly due to unavailable data. In case of the high vs. low sample split, the sizes of the sub-samples are not necessarily identical due to some values of the split criteria variable being equal to the median.

[b] CON: Contrary to expectations; SUPP: Supportive of expectations; IND: Indifferent (includes cases in which the coefficient of the primary explanatory variable is negative and/or insignificant).

Table 5-10: Aggregated regression results for the moderation of the underreaction (IR score, USA)

[234] Web appendix 3.1 includes the detailed and aggregate results for the South Africa 2012 setting.

Alternative measures of IR

The study further examines some of the particularly distinctive features of IR, including the connectivity of information and materiality/conciseness. Regressions are re-run with the relative CONX sub-score and with two alternative IR scores. The latter two scores relate the total IR score from the catalogue to the number of words in the report and the expected number of words for the firm's industry, respectively. These measures underline the importance of conciseness by considering report length as a relativizing factor to the content instead of an additive input to the IR score.

Table 5-11 presents the findings for the setting that uses the **CONX sub-score.** The regressions produce mixed results.

Investor underreaction and its moderation over time: Three regression models – Aggregate results

(Sub-) Sample[a] used:	Total sample (n=200)
Explained variable:	Cumulative abnormal returns – calculated by addition of daily abnormal returns
Primary explanatory variable:	Release date returns – cumulative abnormal returns for the 3 days [0; 2] following the report release
High vs. low sample split criteria/moderating variable:	Relative CONX sub-score (proportion of points in the disclosure catalogue)

Days (τ):	**Model 1**			**Model 2**		**Model 3**	
	Conclusion[b]	Adjusted R^2 ("low" sub-sample)	Adjusted R^2 ("high" sub-sample)	Conclusion[b]	Adjusted R^2	Conclusion[b]	Adjusted R^2
5	IND	0.502	0.479	IND	0.505	IND	0.506
10	**CON**	0.098	0.271	IND	0.195	IND	0.181
15	IND	0.158	0.198	IND	0.202	IND	0.195
20	**CON**	0.114	0.117	IND	0.142	IND	0.141
25	**CON**	0.173	0.244	IND	0.193	IND	0.196
30	**CON**	0.130	0.149	IND	0.160	IND	0.157
35	**CON**	0.111	0.163	IND	0.158	IND	0.152
40	**CON**	0.113	0.098	IND	0.138	IND	0.136
45	**CON**	0.107	0.093	IND	0.110	IND	0.112
50	**CON**	0.092	0.089	IND	0.103	IND	0.108
55	**CON**	0.123	0.131	IND	0.140	IND	0.147
60	**CON**	0.111	0.143	IND	0.152	IND	0.159
65	**CON**	0.001	0.114	IND	0.123	**SUPP**	0.142
70	**CON**	0.046	0.112	IND	0.083	IND	0.103
75	**CON**	0.045	0.054	IND	0.074	IND	0.092
80	**CON**	0.075	0.042	IND	0.068	IND	0.075
85	**CON**	0.052	0.101	IND	0.075	IND	0.084
90	**CON**	0.025	0.093	IND	0.054	IND	0.065

[a] The size of the (sub-)samples (n) may vary slightly due to unavailable data. In case of the high vs. low sample split, the sizes of the sub-samples are not necessarily identical due to some values of the split criteria variable being equal to the median.

[b] CON: Contrary to expectations; SUPP: Supportive of expectations; IND: Indifferent (includes cases in which the coefficient of the primary explanatory variable is negative and/or insignificant).

Table 5-11: Aggregated regression results for the moderation of the underreaction (CONX sub-score, total sample)

Model 1, the comparison of the sub-samples with low and high CONX scores, yields findings that contrast the expectations for almost all time horizons, meaning that the positive coefficients of the immediate market returns are more significant in the high CONX sub-sample than in the low one. Meanwhile, the findings for Model 2 and Model 3 are mostly indifferent, i.e. the coefficient of the interaction term between the immediate returns and the CONX score is insignificant[235], even though it shows the expected negative sign in many cases. These mixed results are also visible in the country-level findings (unreported). While the South African sub-sample mostly shows results that support the expectations for several time frames in all three models (especially for $\tau \geq 50$), the outcomes for the US firms are similar to the full-sample results: the findings for Model 1 are mostly contrary to the expectations despite some supportive evidence for $\tau \geq 75$, whereas Model 2 and Model 3 provide indifferent results. There is thus **no definite tendency** for a positive or negative moderation of the underreaction effect by the connectivity of information. Moreover, the occurrence of significant results almost solely in Model 1 (on total-sample and US level) leaves doubt about whether the significances are spurious.

For the alternative IR scores, the results are mixed. The total sample results for **alternative IR score 1** (Table 5-12), i.e. the total IR score divided by the number of words in the report, are mostly contrary to the expectations in Model 1, but indifferent for Model 2 and Model 3. Similar results occur on country level, with only the US sub-sample producing results as expected for very few values of τ. The overall picture of the findings therefore presents a moderation of investor underreaction that contrasts anticipations: When considering the IR score relative to the length of the report, the underreaction effect is stronger for firms with a high alternative IR score. This conclusion might be misleading, though. The one-sided occurrence of significant results in Model 1 puts the existence of actual associations into doubt for this alternative IR setting, as the found significances might be spurious.

Furthermore, an interpretation of the aforementioned results for alternative IR score 1 needs to consider that the number of words in a firm's report arguably is substantially driven by the firm's activities, i.e. by its business model. **Alternative IR score 2** takes this into account. Rather than by the actual length of a firm's report, the IR score is divided by an expected report length (i.e., the mean number of words of all reports from the firm's industry in the sample). Table 5-13 presents the aggregate results: Model 1 yields findings that are clearly supportive of the expectations for almost all time frames, Model 2 and Model 3 also produce such results for some time frames. Both the South African and the US sub-sample underline these results when running the regressions on country level. This setting, which controls for the variation in report length that occurs due to differences in the firm's activities, thus shows results that are in line with of the main setting. In this regard this setting opposes alternative IR setting 1, which did not include the mentioned control. Under these circumstances, the relative consideration of conciseness therefore supports the results of the setting that employs the main IR score (which considers conciseness as an additive sub-score).

[235] The "indifferent" category in the aggregate table also includes cases of an insignificant underreaction effect in the first place, however, which is the case for single values of τ.

Investor underreaction and its moderation over time: Three regression models – Aggregate results							
(Sub-) Sample[a] used:	Total sample (n=200)						
Explained variable:	Cumulative abnormal returns – calculated by addition of daily abnormal returns						
Primary explanatory variable:	Release date returns – cumulative abnormal returns for the 3 days [0; 2] following the report release						
High vs. low sample split criteria/moderating variable:	Alternative IR score 1 – quotient of the total IR score without the Conciseness (CONC) sub-score to the number of words in the report, multiplied by 10,000						
Days (τ):		**Model 1**			**Model 2**		**Model 3**
	Conclusion[b]	Adjusted R^2 ("low" sub-sample)	Adjusted R^2 ("high" sub-sample)	Conclusion[b]	Adjusted R^2	Conclusion[b]	Adjusted R^2
5	IND	0.407	0.597	IND	0.503	IND	0.502
10	IND	0.143	0.147	IND	0.152	IND	0.153
15	IND	0.259	0.103	IND	0.180	IND	0.181
20	**CON**	0.112	0.084	IND	0.122	IND	0.123
25	**CON**	0.176	0.154	IND	0.167	IND	0.169
30	**CON**	0.140	0.147	IND	0.131	IND	0.133
35	**CON**	0.100	0.140	IND	0.123	IND	0.128
40	**CON**	0.060	0.105	IND	0.112	IND	0.119
45	**CON**	0.055	0.080	IND	0.102	IND	0.112
50	**CON**	0.015	0.106	IND	0.101	IND	0.109
55	**CON**	0.089	0.107	IND	0.124	IND	0.132
60	**CON**	0.127	0.092	IND	0.129	IND	0.136
65	**CON**	0.129	0.073	IND	0.114	IND	0.119
70	**CON**	0.109	0.037	IND	0.076	IND	0.083
75	**CON**	0.110	0.016	IND	0.060	IND	0.069
80	**CON**	0.076	0.017	IND	0.059	IND	0.065
85	**CON**	0.103	0.021	IND	0.071	IND	0.076
90	**CON**	0.057	-0.001	IND	0.051	IND	0.052

[a] The size of the (sub-)samples (n) may vary slightly due to unavailable data. In case of the high vs. low sample split, the sizes of the sub-samples are not necessarily identical due to some values of the split criteria variable being equal to the median.

[b] CON: Contrary to expectations; SUPP: Supportive of expectations; IND: Indifferent (includes cases in which the coefficient of the primary explanatory variable is negative and/or insignificant).

Table 5-12: Aggregated regression results for the moderation of the underreaction (alternative IR score 1, total sample)

To sum up, the alternative IR measures partly yield support for the results from the main setting. Considering the CONX score only, the total picture is mixed, including some supportive results, but also findings that contrast the expectations. This mixed picture particularly becomes apparent when taking also the results on country level into account. The regressions that use alternative IR score 1 present an overall conclusion that contrasts with the anticipations. However, this outcome might be misleading, as the evidence bases almost entirely upon Model 1 so that the significances may be spurious. Moreover, the alternative score does not control for the notion that a firm's business model presumably drives the report length to a large extent. Alternative IR score 2 controls for this issue. As opposed to alternative IR setting 1, the results from this setting allow a conclusion in line with the forecasted interaction and with the main setting. The evidence in this setting draws on all three models, here.

Investor underreaction and its moderation over time: Three regression models – Aggregate results							
(Sub-) Sample[a] used:	Total sample (n=200)						
Explained variable:	Cumulative abnormal returns – calculated by addition of daily abnormal returns						
Primary explanatory variable:	Release date returns – cumulative abnormal returns for the 3 days [0; 2] following the report release						
High vs. low sample split criteria/moderating variable:	Alternative IR score 2 – quotient of the total IR score without the Conciseness (CONC) sub-score to the mean number of words in the reports of all firms in the same GICS industry, multiplied by 10,000						
Days (τ):		**Model 1**		**Model 2**		**Model 3**	
	Conclusion[b]	Adjusted R^2 ("low" sub-sample)	Adjusted R^2 ("high" sub-sample)	Conclusion[b]	Adjusted R^2	Conclusion[b]	Adjusted R^2
5	IND	0.506	0.492	IND	0.503	IND	0.503
10	IND	0.271	0.138	IND	0.152	IND	0.152
15	IND	0.320	0.183	IND	0.180	IND	0.184
20	**SUPP**	0.254	0.105	IND	0.116	IND	0.120
25	**SUPP**	0.310	0.092	IND	0.163	**SUPP**	0.173
30	**SUPP**	0.261	0.071	IND	0.127	IND	0.133
35	**SUPP**	0.294	0.061	IND	0.123	IND	0.126
40	**SUPP**	0.305	0.104	IND	0.109	IND	0.116
45	**SUPP**	0.293	0.144	IND	0.099	IND	0.106
50	**SUPP**	0.310	0.120	IND	0.088	IND	0.093
55	**SUPP**	0.346	0.081	IND	0.124	**SUPP**	0.128
60	**SUPP**	0.345	0.083	**SUPP**	0.134	**SUPP**	0.134
65	**SUPP**	0.315	0.098	**SUPP**	0.119	**SUPP**	0.120
70	**SUPP**	0.233	0.126	IND	0.075	IND	0.078
75	**SUPP**	0.222	0.151	IND	0.063	IND	0.064
80	**SUPP**	0.257	0.150	IND	0.061	IND	0.063
85	**SUPP**	0.199	0.170	IND	0.068	IND	0.069
90	**SUPP**	0.180	0.162	IND	0.050	IND	0.050

[a] The size of the (sub-)samples (n) may vary slightly due to unavailable data. In case of the high vs. low sample split, the sizes of the sub-samples are not necessarily identical due to some values of the split criteria variable being equal to the median.

[b] CON: Contrary to expectations; SUPP: Supportive of expectations; IND: Indifferent (includes cases in which the coefficient of the primary explanatory variable is negative and/or insignificant).

Table 5-13: Aggregated regression results for the moderation of the underreaction (alternative IR score 2, total sample)

Supplementary measures

IR intends to tackle different shortcomings of corporate reporting. Among other things, the IR Framework requires firms to keep the length of their report, the use of boilerplate disclosures and the use of jargon low. In addition, IR promotes a high readability of the reports. This study analyzes a potential moderating influence of these four parameters on investor underreaction, as these particular report characteristics, rather than the IR score, could explain the observed moderation of the underreaction effect. The expectations for these settings are contrary to the settings that use the IR score, sub-scores or alternative IR scores. While a high IR score was expected to decrease investor underreaction, a low[236] score in the

[236] With readability approximated by the Fog Index, a high readability is depicted by a low Fog Index score.

supplementary measures is in line with IR. Therefore, high scores in the latter measures should increase the underreaction effect.

However, the results of the regressions are hardly in line with the expectations. The regressions using **report length** as the sample-split criteria or moderating variable produce results contrary to the anticipations for all three models (Table 5-14). Thus, longer reports seem to decrease investor underreaction instead of increasing it. On country level, the South African results strongly back this notion, with findings contrasting the expectations in almost every time frame in each of the three models. The US results also underline this, but mainly in Model 1, whereas Model 2 and Model 3 show mostly indifferent findings. These results are in line with the aforementioned interpretation of report length as a measure of the information value of the report rather than as an indicator of the difficulty to process the information.

Investor underreaction and its moderation over time: Three regression models – Aggregate results

(Sub-) Sample[a] used:	Total sample (n=200)
Explained variable:	Cumulative abnormal returns – calculated by addition of daily abnormal returns
Primary explanatory variable:	Release date returns – cumulative abnormal returns for the 3 days [0; 2] following the report release
High vs. low sample split criteria/moderating variable:	Report length (ln of # words)

Days (τ):	Model 1			Model 2		Model 3	
	Conclusion[b]	Adjusted R^2 ("low" sub-sample)	Adjusted R^2 ("high" sub-sample)	Conclusion[b]	Adjusted R^2	Conclusion[b]	Adjusted R^2
5	IND	0.583	0.446	IND	0.503	IND	0.502
10	IND	0.186	0.233	IND	0.154	IND	0.151
15	IND	0.124	0.294	IND	0.183	IND	0.182
20	IND	0.097	0.162	IND	0.117	IND	0.120
25	IND	0.150	0.198	IND	0.166	IND	0.168
30	**CON**	0.143	0.145	IND	0.127	IND	0.129
35	IND	0.139	0.136	IND	0.123	IND	0.124
40	**CON**	0.104	0.105	IND	0.112	IND	0.116
45	**CON**	0.075	0.074	IND	0.100	IND	0.109
50	**CON**	0.107	0.018	**CON**	0.097	**CON**	0.106
55	**CON**	0.123	0.074	IND	0.126	**CON**	0.133
60	**CON**	0.090	0.119	IND	0.127	**CON**	0.137
65	**CON**	0.091	0.102	**CON**	0.119	**CON**	0.126
70	**CON**	0.043	0.081	IND	0.078	IND	0.089
75	**CON**	0.031	0.074	IND	0.066	IND	0.077
80	**CON**	0.049	0.060	IND	0.068	IND	0.071
85	**CON**	0.038	0.109	IND	0.077	IND	0.083
90	**CON**	0.027	0.052	IND	0.053	IND	0.058

[a] The size of the (sub-)samples (n) may vary slightly due to unavailable data. In case of the high vs. low sample split, the sizes of the sub-samples are not necessarily identical due to some values of the split criteria variable being equal to the median.

[b] CON: Contrary to expectations; SUPP: Supportive of expectations; IND: Indifferent (includes cases in which the coefficient of the primary explanatory variable is negative and/or insignificant).

Table 5-14: Aggregated regression results for the moderation of the underreaction (report length, total sample)

The results on the similarity of the reports, which represents the **use of boilerplate disclosures**, are mixed. Table 5-15 shows the aggregate findings for this setting. Seven time frames in Model 1 produce findings in support of the anticipation that higher similarity of the reports is associated with increased investor underreaction. Instead, only three time frames show results that contrast this anticipation. The outcomes of Model 2 and Model 3 are mostly indifferent, once more. Country-level results from the USA underline this mixed overall picture, whereas the South African sub-sample yields findings that contradict the expectations unanimously. In both countries this evidence also bases merely upon Model 1, though. Hence, the significant associations from Model 1 could be spurious so that any conclusion about a potential moderation of investor underreaction might be misleading, here.

Investor underreaction and its moderation over time: Three regression models – Aggregate results							
(Sub-) Sample[a] used:	Total sample (n=200)						
Explained variable:	Cumulative abnormal returns – calculated by addition of daily abnormal returns						
Primary explanatory variable:	Release date returns – cumulative abnormal returns for the 3 days [0; 2] following the report release						
High vs. low sample split criteria/moderating variable:	Use of boilerplate disclosures (Percentage of similarity with the firm's report on the previous financial year)						
Days (τ):		**Model 1**		**Model 2**		**Model 3**	
	Conclusion[b]	Adjusted R^2 ("low" sub-sample)	Adjusted R^2 ("high" sub-sample)	Conclusion[b]	Adjusted R^2	Conclusion[b]	Adjusted R^2
5	IND	0.436	0.601	IND	0.508	IND	0.507
10	**SUPP**	0.029	0.490	**SUPP**	0.177	IND	0.158
15	**SUPP**	0.072	0.347	IND	0.188	IND	0.181
20	**SUPP**	0.024	0.256	IND	0.122	IND	0.114
25	**SUPP**	0.098	0.309	IND	0.167	IND	0.163
30	**SUPP**	0.135	0.198	IND	0.125	IND	0.125
35	**SUPP**	0.119	0.217	IND	0.118	IND	0.116
40	IND	0.125	0.203	IND	0.107	IND	0.103
45	IND	0.081	0.198	IND	0.105	IND	0.094
50	IND	0.063	0.173	IND	0.089	IND	0.080
55	IND	0.109	0.213	IND	0.121	IND	0.113
60	IND	0.132	0.207	IND	0.127	IND	0.121
65	IND	0.127	0.230	IND	0.118	IND	0.109
70	IND	0.089	0.211	IND	0.083	IND	0.075
75	**SUPP**	0.090	0.211	IND	0.072	IND	0.063
80	**CON**	0.069	0.216	IND	0.072	IND	0.063
85	**CON**	0.078	0.271	IND	0.079	IND	0.073
90	**CON**	0.072	0.251	IND	0.056	IND	0.052

[a] The size of the (sub-)samples (n) may vary slightly due to unavailable data. In case of the high vs. low sample split, the sizes of the sub-samples are not necessarily identical due to some values of the split criteria variable being equal to the median.

[b] CON: Contrary to expectations; SUPP: Supportive of expectations; IND: Indifferent (includes cases in which the coefficient of the primary explanatory variable is negative and/or insignificant).

Table 5-15: Aggregated regression results for the moderation of the underreaction (use of boilerplate disclosures, total sample)

For the **use of jargon**, the findings also contradict the expectations (Table 5-16). The evidence only bases upon results from Model 1, though, as almost all results from Model 2 and Model 3 are indifferent. This holds for both the total sample and the country sub-samples. The significant associations from Model 1, which suggest that a higher degree of jargon in the Letter to the Stakeholders might be associated with a decreased underreaction effect, could therefore be spurious.

Investor underreaction and its moderation over time: Three regression models – Aggregate results

(Sub-) Sample[a] used:	Total sample (n=200)
Explained variable:	Cumulative abnormal returns – calculated by addition of daily abnormal returns
Primary explanatory variable:	Release date returns – cumulative abnormal returns for the 3 days [0; 2] following the report release
High vs. low sample split criteria/moderating variable:	Use of jargon (Percentage of jargon words in the Letter to the Stakeholders (based on total words))

Days (τ):	Model 1			Model 2		Model 3	
	Conclusion[b]	Adjusted R^2 ("low" sub-sample)	Adjusted R^2 ("high" sub-sample)	Conclusion[b]	Adjusted R^2	Conclusion[b]	Adjusted R^2
5	IND	0.489	0.521	IND	0.502	IND	0.506
10	IND	0.344	0.029	**CON**	0.163	**CON**	0.164
15	IND	0.310	0.103	IND	0.184	IND	0.182
20	IND	0.239	0.071	IND	0.119	IND	0.116
25	IND	0.299	0.099	IND	0.170	IND	0.165
30	**CON**	0.237	0.064	IND	0.130	IND	0.126
35	IND	0.208	0.076	IND	0.118	IND	0.115
40	**CON**	0.223	0.013	IND	0.109	IND	0.104
45	**CON**	0.276	-0.010	IND	0.100	IND	0.096
50	**CON**	0.243	-0.028	IND	0.089	IND	0.083
55	**CON**	0.233	0.032	IND	0.117	IND	0.112
60	**CON**	0.233	0.032	IND	0.125	IND	0.120
65	**CON**	0.235	0.024	IND	0.108	IND	0.103
70	**CON**	0.240	0.020	IND	0.076	IND	0.071
75	**CON**	0.251	0.001	IND	0.062	IND	0.059
80	**CON**	0.246	-0.011	IND	0.056	IND	0.055
85	**CON**	0.225	0.004	IND	0.063	IND	0.065
90	IND	0.194	-0.003	IND	0.043	IND	0.044

[a] The size of the (sub-)samples (n) may vary slightly due to unavailable data. In case of the high vs. low sample split, the sizes of the sub-samples are not necessarily identical due to some values of the split criteria variable being equal to the median.

[b] CON: Contrary to expectations; SUPP: Supportive of expectations; IND: Indifferent (includes cases in which the coefficient of the primary explanatory variable is negative and/or insignificant).

Table 5-16: Aggregated regression results for the moderation of the underreaction (use of jargon, total sample)

Finally, the results on report **readability** are contrary to the expectations, with evidence from all three models (Table 5-17). Country-level results back these findings to some degree. While there are such findings in all three models in South Africa, US findings only underline the total sample findings in Model 1, whereas Model 2 and Model 3 yield indifferent results. Moreover, Model 1 in the US sub-sample even provides results that support the expectations (i.e., a higher Fog Index for the Letter to the Stakeholders increases investor underreaction) for time frames roughly between 15 and 35 days. The overall picture is still in contrast with the anticipations, though.

Investor underreaction and its moderation over time: Three regression models – Aggregate results

(Sub-) Sample[a] used:	Total sample (n=200)
Explained variable:	Cumulative abnormal returns – calculated by addition of daily abnormal returns
Primary explanatory variable:	Release date returns – cumulative abnormal returns for the 3 days [0; 2] following the report release
High vs. low sample split criteria/moderating variable:	Readability of the Letter to the Stakeholders (Fog Index)

Days (τ):	Model 1			Model 2		Model 3	
	Conclusion[b]	Adjusted R^2 ("low" sub-sample)	Adjusted R^2 ("high" sub-sample)	Conclusion[b]	Adjusted R^2	Conclusion[b]	Adjusted R^2
5	IND	0.577	0.483	IND	0.508	**CON**	0.509
10	**CON**	0.149	0.183	IND	0.153	IND	0.164
15	IND	0.140	0.194	IND	0.180	IND	0.180
20	**SUPP**	0.083	0.136	IND	0.115	IND	0.115
25	IND	0.111	0.207	IND	0.163	IND	0.163
30	**CON**	0.143	0.104	IND	0.125	IND	0.123
35	IND	0.147	0.114	IND	0.119	IND	0.119
40	**CON**	0.140	0.047	IND	0.109	IND	0.103
45	**CON**	0.169	-0.013	IND	0.107	IND	0.098
50	**CON**	0.157	-0.029	IND	0.092	IND	0.083
55	**CON**	0.197	0.002	**CON**	0.129	IND	0.118
60	**CON**	0.190	0.024	**CON**	0.141	**CON**	0.132
65	**CON**	0.159	0.019	**CON**	0.123	IND	0.110
70	**CON**	0.107	-0.007	IND	0.085	IND	0.076
75	**CON**	0.119	-0.017	**CON**	0.076	**CON**	0.069
80	**CON**	0.125	-0.029	**CON**	0.070	IND	0.064
85	**CON**	0.121	0.029	IND	0.077	IND	0.072
90	**CON**	0.073	0.004	IND	0.052	IND	0.051

[a] The size of the (sub-)samples (n) may vary slightly due to unavailable data. In case of the high vs. low sample split, the sizes of the sub-samples are not necessarily identical due to some values of the split criteria variable being equal to the median.

[b] CON: Contrary to expectations; SUPP: Supportive of expectations; IND: Indifferent (includes cases in which the coefficient of the primary explanatory variable is negative and/or insignificant).

Table 5-17: Aggregated regression results for the moderation of the underreaction (readability, total sample)

In **summary**, the four supplementary measures mostly contrast the expectation that a higher value of these variables is associated with increased investor underreaction. For the use of boilerplate disclosures and the use of jargon, the evidence almost entirely stems from Model 1 only, though, both on full-sample and country level. Hence, the significant findings in these cases are likely to be spurious. For the report length and the readability of the Letter to the Stakeholders, there is evidence from all three models. The latter results are somewhat counterintuitive, as well as contradictory to the results from the IR variables, which in turn led to the conclusion that a higher degree of IR is related to a decrease in underreaction.

Joint consideration of the IR score and report length

The results from the supplementary measures do not provide clear evidence for an association of the measures with increased underreaction, which was the expectation due to their representation of shortcomings in the corporate reporting practice. Instead, particularly report length and the readability of the Letter to the Stakeholders appear to be associated with decreased underreaction, just like the IR score. A further robustness test therefore uses both the IR score and report length in a **joint regression model** and interacts each measure with the release date returns. Again, this happens both in the form of dummies (Model 2) and raw scores (Model 3). In addition to an interpretation as a driver of the difficulty to read the report, report length can also be seen as an indicator of the informative value of the document. According to this interpretation, it has a similar connotation as the degree of IR, since IR also serves an information purpose. Moreover, the results from the correlation analysis show a significant positive correlation between IR and report length (see section 5.4.1), which underlines their similar impact. The joint regression model (Model 2 and Model 3) including the interaction terms is as follows:

$$(5.6) \quad Delayed\ response_{i;t;\tau} = \alpha + \beta_1\ Immediate\ response_{i;t} + \beta_2\ Degree\ of\ IR_{i;t} + \beta_3\ Immediate\ response_{i;t} \times Degree\ of\ IR_{i;t} + \beta_4\ Report\ length_{i;t} + \beta_5\ Immediate\ response_{i;t} \times Report\ length_{i;t} + \sum_{k=1}^{K} \beta_{k+3}\ Control_{i;t}^{k} + \varepsilon_{i;t}$$

where,

$Report\ length_{i;t}$ = measure used to gauge the length of the report of firm i for period t, natural logarithm of the number of words in the report. Raw measure in Model 3, dummy variable that is 1 if the value is higher than the median and 0 otherwise in Model 2; and

all other variables as defined above.

Table 5-18 presents the **findings** of this test. Due to the results of the aforementioned settings and for the reasons outlined above, both the IR score and the report length can be expected to be associated with a decrease in underreaction, here. In six different time frames for $\tau \geq 55$, the results of Model 2 show the expected significant negative coefficient of the interaction term between the IR dummy and the release date returns, whereas report length does not yield significant results. For Model 3 instead, all time frames provide indifferent findings except one, which shows results supportive of the expectations for report length, but not for the IR score. However, in particular the (unreported) results of one-tailed test for the coefficients instead of the reported two-tailed results provide strong support for the expectation that both the IR score and report length are associated with a decrease in underreaction.[237] Overall, the test shows that the significant negative association of the long term returns with the interaction term between the IR score and the release date returns also occurs in various settings when a measure for report length is included in the model. Thus, the observed (negative) moderation of the underreaction by the degree of IR holds when additionally considering an alternative measure of information value.

Investor underreaction and its moderation over time: Two regression models – Aggregate results						
(Sub-) Sample[a] used:	Total sample (n=200)					
Explained variable:	Cumulative abnormal returns – calculated by addition of daily abnormal returns					
Primary explanatory variable:	Release date returns – cumulative abnormal returns for the 3 days [0; 2] following the report release					
Moderating variables:	Relative IR score (proportion of points in the disclosure catalogue), report length (ln of # words)					
Days (τ):	**Model 2**			**Model 3**		
	Conclusion[b] IR score	Conclusion[b] report length	Adjusted R^2	Conclusion[b] IR score	Conclusion[b] report length	Adjusted R^2
5	IND	IND	0.498	IND	IND	0.502
10	IND	IND	0.152	IND	IND	0.161
15	IND	IND	0.176	IND	IND	0.184
20	IND	IND	0.118	IND	IND	0.134
25	IND	IND	0.169	IND	IND	0.185
30	IND	IND	0.138	IND	IND	0.146
35	IND	IND	0.135	IND	IND	0.139
40	IND	IND	0.132	IND	IND	0.136
45	IND	IND	0.117	IND	IND	0.116
50	IND	IND	0.120	IND	**SUPP**	0.122
55	**SUPP**	IND	0.153	IND	IND	0.150
60	**SUPP**	IND	0.152	IND	IND	0.160
65	**SUPP**	IND	0.139	IND	IND	0.147
70	**SUPP**	IND	0.111	IND	IND	0.111
75	**SUPP**	IND	0.097	IND	IND	0.094
80	IND	IND	0.091	IND	IND	0.076
85	IND	IND	0.094	IND	IND	0.089
90	**SUPP**	IND	0.078	IND	IND	0.067

[a] The size of the (sub-)samples (n) may vary slightly due to unavailable data.
[b] CON: Contrary to expectations; SUPP: Supportive of expectations; IND: Indifferent (includes cases in which the coefficient of the primary explanatory variable is negative and/or insignificant).

Table 5-18: Aggregated regression results for the moderation of the underreaction (IR score vs. report length, total sample)

[237] Results drawing on one-tailed tests for the significance of the coefficients (unreported) yield supportive findings for the IR score in nine time frames ($\tau \geq 50$), and for report length in three time frames (τ = 50, 55 and 65) in Model 2. In Model 3, three time frames ($65 \leq \tau \geq 75$) produce supportive results for the IR score, with also three time frames (τ = 50, 55 and 65) showing findings in line with the expectations for report length. The occurrence of significant supportive results in Model 3 for both variables may mitigate doubt about the reliability of the results due to a potential spuriousness of the findings from Model 2. Web appendix 3.9 includes the results of the one-tailed tests.

5.5 Discussion

Chapter 5 analyzes the impact of IR on the capital market, in particular on the investor underreaction effect. As reported, the results show that the **degree of IR in a firm's annual report is associated with investor underreaction** to the information in this report. The IR score bases upon the Guiding Principles that IR promotes, but does not require compliance with the International <IR> Framework (from which the Guiding Principles stem). Therefore, the disclosure catalogue has been applied to both annual reports that are considered and/or named "integrated" and to those that are not. It is thus not the intention of the study to provide evidence for the label of IR being the driver behind the found impact, but the substance behind the principles that the concept promotes.[238] Figure 5-9 summarizes the results.

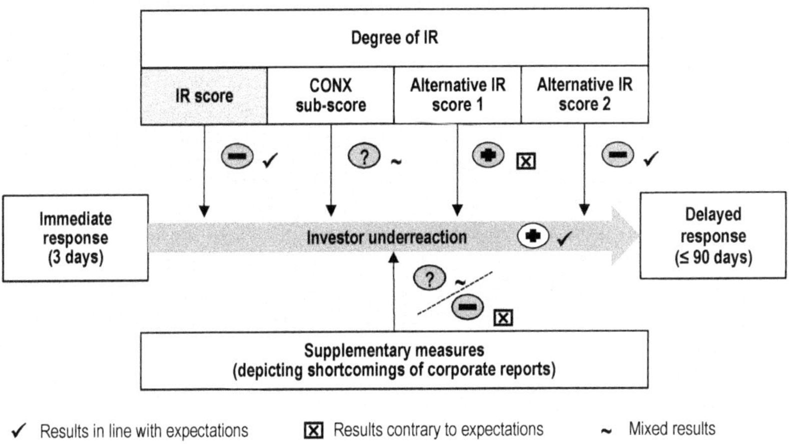

Figure 5-9: Overview of the results

A basic setting provided evidence for the existence of underreaction to the information in the examined reports. This is in line with the results from previous studies (*You/Zhang* (2007; 2009)). Building on this finding, the results from the main (moderation) setting show that for firms **with a higher degree of IR in their reports, investor underreaction is weaker.** The respective evidence stems from three different models as well as from different time frames and is consistent with the expectations outlined in section 5.3.1. These expectations were derived from different theoretical arguments. The findings thus underline the assertions from theory.

[238] As mentioned before, the results are qualitatively unchanged – yet lagged – for a South African subsample with only the 2012 reports, i.e. a setting with only "mandatory" reporters. Moreover, an additional analysis (unreported) shows that using a dummy that is 1 if the report name includes "integrated" and 0 if not yields similar findings.

Several robustness tests supplement the main moderation setting. The outcomes of the same setting on **country level** back the main evidence. Both the South African and the US sub-sample yield results similar to the full-sample setting.

Additional tests with alternative measures that focus on particular features of IR partly provide further support. Results for the **CONX sub-score** are mixed (mixed findings on the full-sample basis and for the USA sub-sample as opposed to results in line with expectations for the South African sub-sample). The interpretation of these findings needs to consider that the conclusions from the full-sample and the US setting, which are contradictory to the initial expectations, base upon evidence from Model 1 only. The found significant associations may therefore be spurious. However, the twofold nature of the connectivity of information may provide an explanation for mixed outcomes. On the one hand, connectivity drives the difficulty to understand the reports may, given the higher number of connections that the reader has to process. This effect could also root in the complex nature of the underlying business and the firm's transactions itself, rather than in the report, though. On the other hand, the connections in the report are supposed to provide a more cohesive picture of the firm's situation and may thus eventually facilitate understanding. With connectivity allowing arguments in opposite directions, the occurrence of mixed results appears plausible.

To some degree, this explanation is also applicable to the results on the two **alternative IR scores**. To better consider the Conciseness principle, the first alternative IR score relates the absolute IR score (adapted by excluding the CONC sub-score) to the number of words in the firm's report. The regressions with this measure yield results that contrast the expectations, while the evidence bases upon one model, only, though. Again, these results are thus potentially spurious. To control for the complex nature of the business itself, the second alternative IR score then uses the expected number of words for the report (i.e., the mean number of words in the reports from the firm's industry) to deflate the (adapted) absolute IR score, which produces findings that are in line with expectations. For this conclusion, there is evidence from all three models. After the inclusion of this control, the results are in line with the findings from the principal setting and therefore also with the theoretical expectations and extant literature.

To put the IR results into context and check for potential alternative explanations of the found association with the underreaction, the study also examined the **supplemental measures** presented in chapter 4. They represent report characteristics that have been connected with shortcomings of corporate reporting. Thus, the measures were expected to yield results in opposite to those from the IR measures, i.e. increasing underreaction with higher values of the measures. The findings mostly contrast these expectations, though. Two measures, namely report length, and the readability of the Letter to the Stakeholders, produce results that are in contrast to theoretical expectations. The other two measures – the use of boilerplate disclosures in the report and the use of jargon in the Letter to the Stakeholders – also provide findings opposing the anticipations. However, as the respective evidence only stems from Model 1, it may be spurious.

In case of **report length**, the findings also contradict the results of *You/Zhang* (2009), who find the expected increase of the underreaction effect with increased report length. It needs to be mentioned that they use a time frame of one year for the dependent variable, though, whereas the study at hand uses 90 days. For a timeframe of 360 days, the report length variable also shows results as expected for Model 1 (unreported), which somewhat dissipates this contradiction. Yet, as discussed before, report length is also interpretable in different ways: in addition to being a proxy for the difficulty to read the report – as longer reports hamper information processing – it may also stand for the informative value of the report. The results on the moderation of the underreaction effect are in line with the latter interpretation. Additional test results show that the moderation of the underreaction through IR persists when considering **both IR and report length** as measures of the informative value of the report in the same model.

To measure the **use of boilerplate disclosures**, the study uses the similarity of reports. The results on this variable indicate a negative association with underreaction, although the findings might be spurious, as outlined before. However, there may also be an explanation for these potentially counterintuitive findings. Again, two different interpretations of the measure are possible. Besides standing for the use of boilerplate and thus for an uninformative reporting practice, similar reports may also be a sign of a high comparability between the reports, which in turn fosters the usefulness of a report (e.g., IR F. 3.56-3.57). According to this interpretation, the result that reports with a higher degree of similarity decrease investor underreaction, which is found in several settings, seems more plausible.

Both the **use of jargon** and the **readability** yield results that contrast anticipations, too. Arguably, the use of jargon may also signal competence and therefore foster the investors' trust in the report. Similarly, a high Fog Index could possibly be interpreted as a signal for good disclosure quality since it may indicate a sophisticated description of details, such as litigation issues. Yet, these interpretations do not seem plausible as they assume that this rather indirect effect exceeded the direct effect of decreased understandability. These findings therefore not only disagree with theoretical reasoning, but also with the results on IR. In the case of the jargon score, potential spuriousness of the results needs to be considered, as the evidence only stems from Model 1. Furthermore, it has to be taken into account that both the jargon and the readability measure base on the Letter to the Stakeholders, only. Although this section of the report is considered to be relevant for investors' capital allocation decisions (e.g., *Abrahamson/Amir* (1996); *Keusch et al.* (2012), with further references), it remains questionable in how far the results are representative of the entire document, since they may convey a somewhat more positive message than the rest of the report (*Bhana* (2009)).

In **summary**, the results from the main analysis on IR are largely consistent with the expectations from theory and prior studies on related topics. Robustness tests on country level and with alternative IR variables that focus on particular Guiding Principles from the Framework partially back these results. However, additional findings on supplementary measures representing certain report characteristics and shortcomings of corporate reporting practice are not in line with the anticipations and extant literature. The evidence on two of these measures is weaker than the main results, though, as it mostly bases upon one model only, and may therefore be spurious. Instead, the IR results appear in different settings for all three models. Furthermore, various supplementary measures arguably allow contradicting interpretations or base on a small fraction of the annual report, only. Moreover, the results of an analysis of IR in conjunction with report length as an alternative explanation of the underreaction show that the associations of IR are persistent. Hence, despite contradictory evidence in some additional tests, the overall conclusion aligns with the main results, supporting the expectation from H_2 (Figure 5-10).

H_2: As the degree of IR in an annual report increases, the degree of investor underreaction decreases. → **supported**

Figure 5-10: Results for H_2

6 Summary and conclusions

The previous chapters have investigated IR from both a conceptual and an empirical perspective. This final chapter summarizes these analyses and puts their findings into the overall context of this study, as outlined in chapter 1. The implications for investors, preparers and regulators are elaborated, as well as the contributions of the findings. This chapter ends with a consideration of the limitations, from which it derives opportunities for future research.

6.1 Summary of the conceptual and the empirical analysis

With the release of the International <IR> Framework in December 2013, the IIRC has reached its first goal to develop a framework for IR. This guidance document constitutes the centerpiece of regulation on this new reporting approach. Against the background of various shortcomings in traditional reporting, the framework establishes Fundamental Concepts, Guiding Principles and Content Elements that govern an integrated report. The objective of such a report is to explain investors how the firm creates value and thus to assist them in making investment decisions. **IR shall overcome the shortcomings in corporate reporting**, such as excessive length and difficulty of firms' reports, a too narrow focus on financial aspects and past events as well as the silo structures in the reports.

This study examined IR from an investor perspective. It analyzed whether IR is useful for investors. In particular, it investigated the following two **research questions**:

- Research question 1: Do the IIRC regulations improve the usefulness of corporate reports?
- Research question 2: Do integrated reports improve their users' decision making?

A **conceptual analysis of the International <IR> Framework** (chapter 2) dealt with research question 1. This part of the study revealed that the Framework coherently composes its different dimensions – the Fundamental Concepts, the Guiding Principles and the Content Elements – to specify the requirements for reporting in line with the overall purpose of an integrated report.

This purpose requires the report to inform investors about the firm's value creation. It is thus closely related to the purpose of financial reporting, which requires firms to provide decision-useful information. IR takes a more value-oriented perspective, though. By defining value in accordance with the concept of six capitals – financial, manufactured, intellectual, human, natural and social and relationship capital – the Framework offers a way to present investors a more **holistic picture of what constitutes the firm's value** and gives them a wider basis of information for investment decisions. This information includes the capitals that the firm does not own itself, in so far as they have implicit or explicit impacts on the value for the firm (i.e., the value for investors) in the short or long term. While reporting on the different capitals and their interdependencies provides useful information for investors, doubt persists about whether and how to assess potential trade-offs between the capitals and about how to quantify the capitals.

Given that the origins of IR partly lie in sustainability reporting, the **investor primacy of IR** was subject to controversy. However, since providing financial capital eventually influences the allocation of all capitals, and due to changes in the structure of other stakeholders over time, a focus on investors seems reasonable and in line with the principles of Conciseness and Consistency. While also being useful for debtholders and short-term oriented shareholders, IR particularly benefits shareholders with a long-term perspective on the firm's value.

In light of the principles-based nature of the Framework, the seven **Guiding Principles play an important role for IR**. They serve as an aid to orientation in identifying useful contents for the report. While the three principles of Reliability and Completeness, Materiality as well as Consistency and Comparability draw on equal or similar principles known from financial reporting, the other four are more innovative. The consideration of Stakeholder Relationships adds to the aforementioned holistic view on a firm's value. However, unlike sustainability reporting, from which this principle is known, IR subordinates stakeholders' interests to the value creation for investors. By making Strategic Focus and Future Orientation a Guiding Principle, the IIRC strengthens the forward-looking perspective of IR, addressing the narrow focus of traditional reporting as criticized by report users. Moreover, IR puts emphasis on conciseness, intending to tackle the length of corporate reports and the difficulty in understanding them. The Connectivity of Information principle reveals trade-offs and interactions between different elements of a firm's business. It aims at providing a better understanding of the firm for investors. This principle bases upon the idea of integrated thinking, which requires the firms to consider the relationships between different units and the different capitals that affect the firm. Eventually, this way of thinking shall lead to integrated decision making, thus establishing a cycle of integrated thinking and reporting. IR also faces tensions between some of the Guiding Principles, though. In particular, there is a trade-off between the Reliability and Completeness principle on the one hand and the Materiality principle on the other, taking over the tension between relevance and reliability known from financial reporting. Furthermore, as acknowledged by the IIRC, the principles-based nature of the framework yields a trade-off between the Comparability principle and the individuality for the firms to report according to their particular business model. These tensions determine the requirements on the different contents. Nevertheless, the Guiding Principles align with the purpose of integrated reports overall.

With the exception of the broader depiction of the business model and the firm's performance due to the six capitals, the **Content Elements** yield little innovation compared to financial reporting. The other contents, provided by the Content Elements Organizational Overview and External Environment, Governance, Risks and Opportunities, Strategy and Resource Allocation, Outlook and Basis of Preparation and Presentation, are all covered by existing reporting requirements and actual reports, albeit to varying degrees and with differences across countries and regulations (in particular as regards future-, risk- and strategy-oriented information). Nevertheless, the conceptual study revealed the relevance of these contents for investors' analysis of the firm and for the resulting investment decisions. At the same time, the unauthoritative structure and the lack of concreteness in the specific requirements leave doubt about the reliability and comparability of the disclosures. Hence, the IR Framework adapts the aforementioned tension known from financial reporting.

Overall, since the Guiding Principles represent the purpose of integrated reports and serve as an aid to orientation for the contents, and since the Content Elements largely align with these principles, the International <IR> Framework provides a coherent basis for reporting. The conceptual analysis showed that an **integrated report can thus be useful** for investors' assessment of a firm's value and as a basis for capital allocation decisions. The information that investors are provided with is better tailored to their information needs than in traditional reports, both in terms of the selection and the presentation of the information. Nevertheless, it is questionable and highly dependent on the reporting firms whether or not the companies prepare integrated reports and if so, how. The IIRC has no legal power and the Framework leaves remarkable room for discretion. However, considering the benefits for investors and – through integrated thinking – arguably also for management, firms might at least adhere to single features of the concept if they do not adopt the concept in its entirety. In particular, this adherence could relate to the innovative Guiding Principles.

In the empirical analysis, the study examined the reporting practice in South Africa and the USA. Before this investigation, the reporting landscape in both countries was introduced for a better understanding of the rules and circumstances under which the reports in question had been prepared (chapter 3). Both **South Africa** and the USA have a developed reporting landscape with professional institutions, while drawing on a history of accounting and exhibiting essential importance of the capital market. In South Africa, historical developments, in particular the apartheid era and its aftermath, social and health inequality in the country as well as the importance of natural resources for the economy have raised awareness for ESG issues. The King Committee has developed three versions of the King Code, which provides guidance for good governance and in its latest version (King III) includes the requirement to apply IR. Before the release of the International <IR> Framework, the IRCSA DP provided guidance on IR, as the King Code includes the requirement to apply IR, but hardly yields specific guidelines. According to the JSE Listings Requirements, firms listed on the JSE need to apply the King Code or explain instances of non-appliance (par. 8.63 (a)). Besides the King Code, the IR guidance materials and the Listings Requirements, these listed firms also need to abide by the Companies Act and the IFRS. All of these regulations include requirements for reporting. In particular the IRCSA DP showed remarkable overlap with the IIRC Framework, both in terms of the Guiding Principles and the Content Elements.

Throughout its history, the wealthy US economy showed a focus on capital markets and investor protection. Most importantly, the SEC is responsible for protecting investors' interests. The Commission regulates firms' listing and security trading, but also their financial reporting. It deferred the job to issue particular accounting standards to the FASB, however. In conjunction with the IASB, the FASB has also developed parts of a Conceptual Framework, which set out an overall objective and Qualitative Characteristics that govern financial reporting. These Qualitative Characteristics overlap with various IR Guiding Principles, but the innovative features of IR, as mentioned above, are not fully covered. Firms listed on a securities exchange in the **USA** face reporting regulation and guidance from different sources, including statutes like the Securities Act of 1933 and the Securities Exchange Act of 1934, or regulations, such as Regulation S-K, Regulation S-X. Moreover, US listed firms need to adhere to SEC Releases on financial reporting, auditing and other issues, and to staff advice like Staff Accounting Bulletins. Form 10-K specifies the minimum level of information that registrants need to provide in their annual report as filed with the SEC. The Form provides a standardized structure for the report and references different regulations (in particular, Regulations S-K and S-X) for the specific contents. These contents largely cover those that the IR Framework prescribes for integrated reports. In addition, the NYSE listing rules, various private guidance documents on governance and governance reporting, as well as the SASB's standards on sustainability reporting draw on the reporting requirements referenced in Form 10-K. The sustainability accounting/reporting standards provide additional non-mandatory guidance on how to consider social and ecological issues in the report, thereby potentially providing a first step toward an integrated report.

Two empirical parts conjunctively dealt with research question 2. A **descriptive study** (chapter 4) investigated the question how existing reporting practice exhibits IR. **Extant literature** on IR practice covers different countries and continents to a varying degree. In line with South Africa's outlined pioneering role for IR, numerous studies provide evidence on the IR practice in South Africa. Instead, several other countries, in particular from the American continent, are hardly covered by research on this topic. Moreover, existing research suffers from various flaws. A lot of studies have been issued by accounting firms so that the data could be driven by the firms' business interests. Other studies rely on database data to depict IR, which potentially fails to portray this reporting format as intended. Research that draws on hand-collected data in turn sometimes uses pre-final versions of the International <IR> Framework or only depicts particular aspects of IR, like single capitals. While many studies focus on the Content Elements or capitals for their portrayal of IR, the Guiding Principles contain the most innovative features of the new reporting approach and are therefore probably most suitable to represent the degree of IR. Furthermore, in most cases small and/or biased (e.g. by containing only voluntary adopters of IR) samples prevent statistically valid and generalizable conclusions on the reporting practice. The studies that do allow such conclusions focus on a time comparison of the pre- and post-King III situation in South Africa or on a country comparison at a single point in time. Each of these comparisons may be driven by the singularities of the examined timeframe or country, respectively.

Supplementing this previous research and addressing the several shortcomings, the study at hand examined the reports from two countries at two points in time. To reduce the research gap regarding the IR presence in America, it examines US reports. However, reports from South Africa contrast these findings and put them into context. In financial year 2012, South African firms were supposed to employ IR in adherence to the apply-or-explain requirement from King III. No requirement on IR had been present in this country in 2006. In the USA, there was no comparable requirement in either year.[239] Hence, this **research design** allowed comparisons over time in each country as well as cross-country comparisons at two different points in time. In addition, a cross-country comparison of the changes over

[239] The SASB standards, which arguably represent a first step toward IR in US regulation, have not been available at the time that the examined reports were released, as they have been issued gradually starting on 31 July 2013.

time (difference-in-differences) strengthened the conclusions of the findings, mitigating potential biases by e.g. country fixed effects. This study developed a catalogue for content analysis to capture the degree of IR in the firms' reports. The catalogue combined manually collected items with software data to depict the requirements of the Guiding Principles from the final International <IR> Framework and aggregated all items in one IR score.

According to Agency Theory, managers can reduce information asymmetries with investors by signaling and reporting, thereby decreasing agency costs. Following the bonus and debt hypothesis of PAT, managers may want to use reporting to present the firm according to their own preferences. Firms can also use reporting to prevent political intrusions in line with the political cost hypothesis of PAT. The discretion that IR allows firms for their reporting may help to design their reports according to their preferences. Moreover, the expectations of the society or certain stakeholders may expect the firm to issue integrated reports, as Legitimacy Theory and Stakeholder Theory argue, respectively. Besides, pressures from stakeholders could lead to coercive isomorphism in line with Institutional Theory, while competitors' IR practice or the development of IR as a professional norm would trigger a firm's application of IR as mimetic or normative isomorphism, respectively. Together with the regulatory setting in the two countries in 2006 and 2012, these **theories** led to a set of four hypotheses concerning time and country comparisons of IR practice.

These **hypotheses** stated the expectations that South African firms practice IR to a higher degree than US firms in 2012 ($H_{1.1}$), but also in 2006 ($H_{1.2}$), due to the King II principles that already covered various ideas of IR. Moreover, South African reports were expected to exhibit IR to a higher degree in 2012 than in 2006 ($H_{1.3}$), provided the introduction of King III and firms' gains in experience and proficiency with the reporting format over time. Instead, US reports were not expected to change the degree to which they exhibit IR from 2006 to 2012 ($H_{1.4}$), as during that time only negligible regulatory changes for particular industries came up, which could only slightly change firms' reports toward integrated reporting.

The **results** yielded support for all hypotheses, showing that IR indeed provides innovation over traditional reports. A comparison of the deltas between the two countries gave additional support for this notion. However, the values of the scores also revealed that various features of IR were not yet covered by existing reports, leaving room for improvement in firms' reporting practice. Breaking the results down into the different Guiding Principles showed that almost all sub-scores increased in South Africa to a significantly stronger degree than in the USA from 2006 to 2012. Only the Consistency and Comparability principle and the Conciseness principle did not follow this expectation. Comparability did not change over time in either country and remained stronger in US reports than in those of South African firms. Conciseness decreased rather than increased, for both countries. The latter finding is in line with the increase of both report length and the use of jargon in both countries. As opposed to various other features of IR, the Conciseness principle and the underlying measures are thus not implemented in reporting practice. Moreover, US reports showed significant increases over time in other measures that depict several shortcomings of corporate reporting, too.

Drawing on the descriptive data, an **explanatory study** (chapter 5) analyzed whether the degree of IR in corporate reports can influence investors' informed decision making. In the **literature**, various younger studies already cover particular economic consequences of IR, including its impact on information asymmetries or on the firms' cost of capital. Moreover, there is a stream of research that deals with the capital market impacts of report format in general or the impact of different characteristics and shortcomings of (annual) reports. A particular market phenomenon in the literature is investor underreaction, a topic that many studies deal with. Instead of incorporating released news into prices immediately, the market shows a lagged reaction to the release. The immediate returns after the news release are associated with long-term returns for weeks and even months later, indicating that the market at that later point in time still draws on the information from the event. Research on particular aspects of these fields of research and on their cross-section is rare. Only few studies deal with investor underreaction to annual report information, while most analyses examine underreaction to earnings announcements (PEAD), instead. An even lower number deals with the interaction of report format and underreaction, while no study has connected all three topics and examined the interaction of IR as a reporting format with investor underreaction so far.

Therefore, the **study at hand** set in at the cross-section of all three streams of research to analyze a potential moderation of the underreaction effect by the degree of IR in firms' reports. In line with the IIRC's assertions and with conceptual reasoning, IR was assumed to be negatively associated with investor underreaction. Enhancing investors' information about the firm and making it more understandable, an integrated report was supposed to enable a better incorporation of the information into prices and thus reduce the underreaction, compared to a traditional report.

Theoretical reasoning supported this position. In a first step, the rational structural uncertainty approach and several behavioral approaches explained the existence of the underreaction effect by tackling the two main rational expectations assumptions underlying the EMH, the information availability assumption and the information exploitation assumption. A second step argued a potential association of this underreaction with IR. By providing a broader information basis than traditional reports, integrated reports may reduce investors' estimation errors (rational structural uncertainty) so that there is less need to correct these errors through rational learning. Besides, IR delivers a more accessible reporting format. According to behavioral reasoning, IR may therefore accelerate the updates of beliefs for conservative market participants and the diffusion of information across newswatchers in *Hong/Stein's* (1999) model of bounded rationality. In addition, the IRH and reasoning from other disciplines, supported the notion that IR might reduce the underreaction effect. According to the IRH, integrated reports deliver less costly information than traditional reports so that this information presumably attracts more trading interest and is better revealed in market prices than information from other formats. CLT from psychology (among other things) stated that a connected information format can reduce the cognitive load of processing the information. Pragmatics from linguistics argued that besides the content of communication, the act of communicating conveys meaning as well, e.g. through the decision to elevate or not to elevate certain information. These arguments yielded the

hypothesis that the degree of underreaction decreases with a higher degree of IR in corporate reports (H_2).

To examine this hypothesis, the analysis employed an event study design. It used the IR data from the descriptive study and added archival data on the stock price movement and on certain firm characteristics. After showing that market underreaction was present for the reports in the sample and precluding alternative explanations for the price drift (most importantly, the PEAD), the analysis used **three different models** to investigate a moderation of the effect through IR: a split-sample model that compared the underreaction effect between a sub-sample with an above-median degree of IR and a sub-sample with a below-median degree (Model 1), a setting that interacted a dummy for a high or low degree of IR with the short-term returns on total-sample level (Model 2) and a modification of the latter model that used the raw IR score in lieu of the dummy (Model 3). The three models may yield different findings, since sample-split designs can reduce the power of the regressions on the one hand, but can also present apparent, but spurious effects on the other hand. To interpret the findings, it was thus necessary to consider the outcomes of all three models in their entirety.

The **results on the IR score** were supportive of the anticipations. In different time frames, the score showed the expected negative interaction with investor underreaction, with evidence appearing throughout all the three models.

Different **robustness tests** further supported these findings. Similar results as in the main setting occurred for the same analyses on **country level** for both South Africa and the USA. The findings on **alternative IR measures** were less clear, however. Using only the CONX sub-score as a moderator yielded mixed results across the models and countries, while an alternative IR score provided findings that even contradicted the expectations. The latter score employed a different interpretation of the Conciseness principle than the original IR score. It divided the original IR score (after subtracting the CONC sub-score) by the number of words in the report, instead of using the CONC sub-score as an additive part of the total score. This alternative IR score 1 showed a positive rather than the expected negative association with investor underreaction. These findings based almost completely on Model 1, though, meaning that the observed associations could be spurious and therefore misleading. Besides, as the number of words in a firm's report is typically driven by the firm's business model and industry, a second alternative score replaced the first one to control for this sector influence. Alternative IR score 2 used the expected report length (mean report length in the company's industry) instead of the actual length to deflate the score. The results for this measure then showed strong evidence in favor of the expectations throughout all three models.

Moreover, four **supplementary measures** have been used in lieu of the IR score to check for further alternative explanations of the observed main results. Three of these measures had been calculated into the scores of particular items of the IR content analysis catalogue and were now used on their own to analyze a moderation of the underreaction effect. All four measures represent different shortcomings of corporate reporting that IR intends to tackle so that the expectations for the moderations of underreaction were reverse to the expectations used in the main setting and in the aforementioned tests: A higher value of these measures was anticipated to be associated with increased underreaction. The tests largely showed results that contradicted these expectations, however. For the use of boilerplate disclosures and the use of jargon, the evidence almost only relied on Model 1, though. These results could thus be spurious. For the Fog Index of readability, evidence based on all three models. But like the use of jargon, the respective score had drawn on the Letter to the Stakeholders only, leaving doubt whether the measure is representative of the entire report. Instead, the findings on report length, which also contradicted the expectation of increasing investor underreaction, both were consistent in all three models and referred to the entire report. This finding was in line with interpreting report length as a measure of the informative value of the document rather than as an indicator of the difficulty to process the information.

To address the concern that the results on the IR score were driven by an omitted influence from this latter supplementary measure, an additional test analyzed a moderating influence of both the (unadapted) **IR score and report length in the same model.** The supportive evidence for the significant (negative) association of the IR score with underreaction persisted despite the additional control. Hence, in their entirety, the results of the explanatory study supported H_2.

The **conclusions from the different parts of the study connect.** Conceptually speaking, IR provides investors with a potentially useful reporting format that may yield more relevant information for their decision making and tackle various shortcomings of corporate reporting that have been criticized over decades (research question 1). These notions are supported by the results of the capital market study, which provides evidence that IR is associated with less investor underreaction. Hence, the broader information basis and the better processibility of the reports seem to lead to better informed decision making by investors (research question 2). However, the descriptive analysis has revealed that existing reports already showed some coverage of the IR Guiding Principles, but left room for improvement. This finding was consistent with the conclusions from the conceptual analysis and with the comparison of the national reporting regulations with the IR Framework. These parts of the study had revealed that IR to a remarkable degree bases upon features that are already known from traditional (financial) reporting. At the same time, the descriptive analysis found that South African firms significantly increased the adherence to IR Guiding Principles compared to the time before King III and that they exhibited a significantly higher degree of adherence to IR than US firms. These findings showed that IR does yield innovative features over traditional reporting formats, in line with the conceptual reasoning. King III elicited these features in South Africa. The non-binding character of the IR Framework and the high degree of flexibility that the principles-based approach allows leave room for debate whether IR can achieve its potential benefits in environments that do not promote its application. Thus, the eventual usefulness of the approach depends on the reporting firms' will to implement IR and/or on (national) regulators to require or stimulate the application of the approach.

6.2 Implications

The results of both the conceptual analysis and the two empirical parts yield various **implications for the different parties involved in corporate reporting.** Among these parties are the users of the reports (in particular investors), the reporting firms and regulators (e.g., standard setters or enforcement institutions, including auditors). Moreover, the results might affect research on IR.

Investors represent the primary addressees of integrated reports in the IIRC's view. With the requirements of the Framework, the Council intends to shape the reports according to this group's information needs. The conceptual analysis has shown that the information which integrated reports are supposed to provide is generally relevant for **investors.** In particular, the reports may deliver information beyond a merely financial focus so that the large part of a firm's value that is not illuminated by traditional reporting may become explainable. However, in terms of usefulness, there is a trade-off between disclosures that are tailored to the firms' individual business model and disclosures that yield comparability for investors. Hence, the addressees might eventually be deprived of comparable disclosures. Moreover, the completeness and reliability of the information may be questionable, due to a high degree of potential discretion for the reporting firms. At the same time, the Guiding Principles, notably Connectivity of Information, Materiality and Conciseness, may result in reports being more accessible and understandable for investors. The results from the descriptive study back the notion that the introduction of IR is related to a better implementation of various Guiding Principles, in particular Connectivity of Information. Therefore, investors may assume that reports of firms that are required to apply IR are likely to connect information better than reports of firms that do not face a requirement to apply this reporting approach. Furthermore, as the explanatory study shows, reports that implement the IR Guiding Principles to a higher degree are associated with less underreaction of the stock price, which may indicate better capital allocation decisions. Although this study cannot provide an ultimate proof of a causal effect in this regard,[240] the evidence may signal investors that reports with adherence to the IR principles serve as a basis for better informed decision making. **Analysts** may benefit from such an improved information channel in a similar vein.

For the **reporting firms**, applying IR may be challenging at first. The broader contents beyond financial aspects and the connectivity of report information may require new solutions for reporting, including new concepts and systems (e.g., measuring natural or social capital aspects and connecting them with financial measures). Providing concise reports, that only comprise the most material information, may represent a similar challenge for the firms. This could question existing reporting structures and could eventually even have (beneficial) repercussions for management's decision making, thus leading to the cycle of IR and integrated thinking that the IIRC mentions. The findings of the descriptive study show that firms which implement IR can indeed improve their reports in terms of the Guiding Principles. Moreover, the documented association with weaker investor underreaction from the explanatory analysis indicates that integrated reports may foster better in-

[240] The following section presents the limitations of the analysis, including a discussion of causal claims.

formed decisions by investors. For the firms, this would implicate a closer and clearer connection of their reported information with their stock price and therefore better predictability of the latter.

This argument may also be relevant for regulators. Although they also need to consider other views for a sophisticated assessment of reporting standards and concepts (see section 6.3), **national regulators** may see IR as a channel that leads to a closer tie of stock market developments to corporate reporting and in turn to a more potentially realistic picture that share prices provide of firm value. Moreover, the findings from the descriptive study indicate that regulators may regard the introduction of IR as a useful step to overcome weaknesses in current reporting practice in terms of particular Guiding Principles. As the conceptual analysis has shown, the IIRC intends to avoid conflicts with existing rules and guidance by keeping the requirements of the IR Framework on a rather general level. This could support an easy endorsement on national level, e.g. as a supplement to existing reporting regulations. Nevertheless, the Framework might face conflicts with other laws and regulations or with reporting practice in some countries. For instance, the persisting fear of litigation regarding future-oriented disclosures in the USA might oppose a national endorsement. Similar issues occur in other countries, such as Australia (*Malley* (2014)). Alternatively, if not the entire IR Framework, the requirements of specific Guiding Principles, like Connectivity of Information and Conciseness as well as the broader capital definition may provide useful replenishments of national reporting regulations. In turn, this may bring remarkable challenges for assurance providers in contributing to the **enforcement** of such regulations, since the innovative features and contents of integrated reports require according methods for a reliable audit.

For the IIRC, the conceptual analysis is unlikely to yield news, as it mainly reflects interdependencies and trade-offs between elements of the Framework. As various remarks in the Framework, the Basis for Conclusions or the Summary of Significant Issues reveal, the **IIRC** has already considered these aspects during the development of the Framework. Instead, the empirical results may be of use for the Council, documenting that IR actually goes along with an improvement of reporting in terms of various principles. Moreover, the explanatory analysis provides results that are supportive of the IIRC's goal to improve the understandability of reporting and may also back the notion that IR shall foster effective decision making on capital allocation (DP IR, p. 22).

Lastly, this study represents a **contribution to research**. It reduces the research gaps identified in sections 4.1 and 5.1. The descriptive analysis adds to the literature on IR practice by providing data that – in line with the IIRC's principles-based approach – founds on the Guiding Principles of the International <IR> Framework and stems from an individual review of annual reports. This review combines manual and software-assisted data collection and considers measures that represent existing shortcomings of corporate reporting, integrating the different data into a score for the degree of IR. In addition, the study introduces an international setting that allows statistically profound comparisons between the countries, over time and also between the changes over time in the two countries. The explanatory study contributes to the field of impact studies on the young topic of IR. It uses a measure of capital market response that closely relates to the report release and that is independent of unobserved interdependencies between different economic influences. Besides, the study adds to the streams of empirical literature on the effects of the general format or certain characteristics of firms' reports on the capital markets as well as to the literature on investor underreaction. Aiming at the cross-section of these three streams of research, the study yields findings that reveal a significant association of IR with a weaker investor underreaction effect. However, future research could try to resolve remaining doubt about the causality of IR for this reduction. Furthermore, future studies could deal with adjacent issues on the new topic of IR.

6.3 Limitations and outlook

Inevitably, empirical research goes along with several limitations. This section discusses the drawbacks of the study at hand. It is questionable in how far the results are **generalizable** to other settings. In particular, the findings may be determined by peculiarities of the countries and years that the study uses, such as cultural aspects like flexibility. These characteristics may vary between the countries, impacting management's reporting behavior. For instance, while there is a perceived need for flexibility in accounting in the USA or the UK, other countries, such as France, follow a more uniform approach (*Gray* (1988), p. 9).[241] However, the use of two countries and points in time already yields some degree of generalization compared to a setting with only one particular **year** and **country**, whose cultural or other specific influences might drive the results. The design of the descriptive study addresses fixed effects by also considering a comparison over time between both countries. This allows conclusions largely independent of e.g. country fixed effects. Moreover, both the use of dummy variables for (year and country) fixed effects and analyses on country level show that the findings of the explanatory analysis hardly depend on these aspects.

Similarly, using some of the largest firms of each country might also impede generalizability. Even though the IR Framework intends to be applicable for firms of any **size** (IR F., p. 4), the reporting practice may vary substantially between smaller and larger companies, e.g. in terms of the extent of the disclosures or in terms of the sophistication or complexity of the business models and their description. However, it is in particular large firms that are likely to implement IR and report accordingly (*Frías-Aceituno et al.* (2014)) so that it makes sense for empirical research to focus on these rather than on small companies. Furthermore, the regression models control for size effects.

Not only the size of the particular firms, but also the number of firms in the sample, could hamper the generalizability of the results. Compared with large-scale archival studies (e.g., *You/Zhang* (2009)), the **sample size** of 200 firm-year observations is small and might thus not be representative of the firms in an entire country or of an even bigger population. In particular, this holds for the models and variations that split the sample into the different countries or into groups of a high and low degree of IR (or other measure), which further reduces sample size. All models satisfy the minimum number of observations for the validity of the central limit theorem (see section 5.4.2) though, which allows to presume that the data follows a normal distribution like the population in its entirety. However, the small

[241] *Gray* (1988) uses *Hofstede's* (2001) cultural dimensions and derives accounting values from them. For uniformity in accounting, he argues that higher ranks in uncertainty avoidance and power distance as well as lower ranks of individualism are related to higher uniformity (*Gray* (1988), pp. 9-10).

sample size enabled this study to employ a manual data collection. An independent personal review of annual reports made it possible to capture the idea of IR as intended by the International <IR> Framework. The study at hand therefore goes beyond several previous studies on IR practice (see section 4.1) in terms of accuracy and detail of the presented data.

In turn, this **manual data collection** for the IR variable, based on content analysis, comes with limitations itself. The involvement of human judgement inevitably includes the risk of subjectivity and error (*Kromrey* (2016), pp. 321-322; *Schnell et al.* (2013), pp. 403-404). As section 4.3.2 outlined, though, the collection method employed arrangements that aimed at avoiding these drawbacks, including the consistent collection of data for one item by the same researcher or a recollection of data from the first reports for consistency. Despite these efforts, errors or biases cannot be completely precluded. Besides, it is questionable if investors consider reports differently and process the data in different ways, e.g. through software or systems, or if they simply have a different focus when manually analyzing the reports. Future research might address this topic.

Software also assisted the data collection for certain items of the content analysis catalogue. While this strengthened the objectivity and consistency of the collection, the data on the use of jargon and on readability is questionable in so far that the scores draw on the Letter to the Stakeholders only. This letter usually only makes up a small fraction of the report. Nevertheless, the letter plays an important role as it is the most widely read part of the report and serves as a basis for investors' decisions. With the letter thus representing a calling card for the report, the index data on the use of jargon and on readability gives an indication of the respective measures for the entire report.

Not only the variable that approximates IR, but also the abnormal returns variable depicting investors' reactions is discussable. Capital market data is always **noisy**, which – unless there is a systematic one-directional bias – weakens the power of the statistical analyses. Since this works against the study, it in turn underlines the results observed in spite of the noise (*Nienhaus* (2015), pp. 206-207). Nonetheless, this study intended to rule out as much noise as possible through various research design choices. These choices include the consideration of market reactions for 90 days only, to avoid interference of the information of the subsequent quarterly report, or the selection of the financial years of the examined reports in such a way that the financial crisis would not influence the data on the market reactions. Moreover, employing stock returns data is in line with prior research from this field, as its use in numerous of the referenced studies (in particular from section 5.1) shows.

Another issue is the question whether the found statistical relationships allow causal inferences. *Kenny* ((1979), p. 3) lists three conditions that **causality** needs to satisfy: time precedence, relationship and non-spuriousness. As the event study design only considers market data from the aftermath of the report release and the results to a high degree reveal a significant negative relationship between the IR score and the underreaction effect, the study at hand satisfies the first two conditions. The third condition requires that there are no other causes that explain this relationship. It cannot be fully precluded that such explanations are the true cause of the price drift. However, by employing different variations of the analysis, the study tries to rule out possible alternative drivers. This comprises both the underreaction effect as such in the first place and its moderation by IR. Tests show that the basic underreaction effect differs from the PEAD and is not a response to other events shortly preceding the report release. Regarding the moderation, various tests that replace IR with other reporting properties show weaker results or even work against the relationship of IR and underreaction. A setting that combines IR and report length as two alternative explanations of the moderation shows persistence of the IR results despite the added length measure. Nevertheless, there may be other omitted variables that constitute endogeneity and thus preclude causal claims. Hence, this study considers its results associations rather than cause and effect relationships.

Since providers of financial capital are the primary addressees of IR, this study takes an investor perspective. However, by analyzing stock price reactions, the analysis implicitly **concentrates on shareholders** only. Although shareholders represent a substantial part of the group of investors, bondholders and other lenders – as other types of investors – also form part of the focus group of integrated reports, while differing from shareholders in terms of their interests (*Lachnit/Müller* (2015), pp. 547-548). The study at hand does not take the latter groups' views into account. As a consequence of neglecting debtholders' views, as well as analysts', preparers' or other perspectives (in particular direct and indirect costs of reporting), this study cannot claim to make recommendations for standard setters, who need to consider and balance a multitude of different objectives (*Holthausen/Watts* (2001), p. 52). Nonetheless, the results of this examination can inform regulators on an aspect of capital market reactions to IR, which – alongside other information – may contribute to their decision making. Providing empirical evidence for the impacts of IR on the other mentioned groups and their objectives may be in the scope of future research, though.

As IR is still in an early stage of its development, only a few features of this reporting format have been thoroughly examined, yet. Hence, there is room for **future studies**. Nonetheless, as sections 4.1 and in particular 5.1 have shown, several aspects have already been covered, including IR's associations with firm valuation, cost of capital and analysts' forecasts. Studies about the determinants of IR also give some insight to the factors driving the preparation of the reports. In this regard, it would be interesting to study the (direct) **costs of the preparation**. Case studies could yield such information and would thus contribute to a more complete picture of the impacts of IR to consider for e.g. future regulation.

Furthermore, with IR being an international concept, explanatory studies from a variety of **countries** could lead to IR research also taking into account the specialties of different cultural, economic or legal backgrounds. Various studies have already examined the adoption and practice of IR in different countries (see section 4.1). Studies on the impacts of IR focus on US or South African settings, instead. Research from other countries would increase the generalizability of the findings.

In addition to research in different countries, insights on **smaller firms** could be useful. The finding that firm size is positively related to the use of IR (*Frías-Aceituno et al.* (2014)) raises the question whether the reporting format also attracts small firms. This might particularly depend on these firms' cost-benefit considerations. If the firms are not listed, the benefits for external users (and in turn for the firms) could be limited, while the direct and indirect costs might be higher compared with traditional reports, especially around the time of the change. A surplus of these indirect costs over the benefits could lead to a restrictive reporting practice, which is not in line with the idea of IR (*Kajüter et al.* (2013b), p. 1687). However, if the preparers manage to realize the potential benefits of IR, in particular through integrated thinking, the outcome of these considerations might change.

With regard to the **processing of information**, it might be interesting to conduct research that uses eye-tracking (e.g., *Sirois et al.* (2014)). This could yield important insights on how readers look at the reports and how they process the information. Since IR is principles-based, the question how information is presented is of particular importance. An experimental setting would allow such a treatment.

Experimental research could also be helpful in addressing the mentioned concerns about noise in the capital market data and about omitted correlated variables. A **laboratory setting** could rule out these hampering aspects and therefore find cause and effect relationships by explicitly triggering intended changes in the setting as exclusive drivers of effects on the dependent variable. An example could be a setting that is close to experimental research in psychology (e.g., *Sweller/Chandler* (1994)), manipulating the information format and check the results on e.g. investment decisions.[242] The challenge here would be to ensure that the setting is realistic enough to derive conclusions for real reporting and investment practice, for instance by providing a representative integrated report and by simulating the effects of users' decisions realistically.

As regards the **future of IR** and its implementation in the corporate reporting landscape, it will be interesting to observe whether the IIRC's current Breakthrough Phase and the Council's cooperation with partners from its networks can lead to a more widespread use of the new reporting approach. In the end, it is up to the regulators and preparers to realize the potential benefits of integrated reports.

[242] *Hewitt* (2007) uses a comparable setting to investigate the accrual anomaly. *Arnold et al.* (2012) examine associations between investors' judgment of the firm value and the format of corporate reports, distinguishing between reports that integrate financial and sustainability information and those that do not. *Reimsbach et al.* (2016) analyze how an integrated reporting format influences investors' access to and acquisition of sustainability information. The latter two studies do not reflect IR in the sense of the IIRC, though. Instead, they draw on a mere combination of financial and sustainability reporting.

Appendix

Appendix 1: Content analysis catalogue based on the International <IR> Framework

Content analysis catalogue based on the International <IR> Framework				
Item #[a]	**Elements to be disclosed**	**Paragraphs/ sections in the IR F**	**Type[b]**	**Interdependencies between items[c]**
Strategic Focus and Future Orientation (An integrated report should provide insight into the organization's strategy, and how it relates to the organization's ability to create value in the short, medium and long term and to its use of and effects on the capitals.)		**IR F. 3.3**		
STRAT1				
STRAT1.1				
STRAT1.1.1	Significant opportunities flowing from the organization's market position	IR F. 3.4	A	
STRAT1.1.2	Significant risks/dependencies flowing from the organization's market position	IR F. 3.4	A	
STRAT1.2				
STRAT1.2.1	Significant opportunities flowing from the organization's business model	IR F. 3.4	A	
STRAT1.2.2	Significant risks/dependencies flowing from the organization's business model	IR F. 3.4	A	
STRAT2				
STRAT2.1	The views of those charged with governance about the relationship between past and future performance	IR F. 3.4	A	
STRAT2.2	The views of those charged with governance about how the organization balances short, medium and long term interests	IR F. 3.4	A	
STRAT2.3	The views of those charged with governance about how the organization has learned from past experiences in determining future strategic directions	IR F. 3.4	A	
STRAT3	How the capitals contribute to the organization's ability to achieve its strategic objectives in the future	IR F. 3.5	A	
# items STRAT:	*8*			
Connectivity of Information (An integrated report should show a holistic picture of the combination, inter-relatedness and dependencies between the factors that affect the organization's ability to create value over time.)		**IR F. 3.6**		
CONX1				
CONX1.1	Analysis of how the organization will combine resources or make further investment to achieve its targeted performance (connectivity between the Content Elements Strategy and Resource Allocation and Performance or Outlook, respectively)	IR F. 3.8	A	
CONX1.2				
CONX1.2.1	Information about how the strategy is tailored when new risks/opportunities are identified (connectivity between the Content Elements Strategy and Resource Allocation and Risks and Opportunities)	IR F. 3.8	A	
CONX1.2.2	Information about how the strategy is tailored when past performance is not as expected (connectivity between the Content Elements Strategy and Resource Allocation and Performance)	IR F. 3.8	A	

Continued...

CONX1.3				
CONX1.3.1	Link of the organization's strategy with changes in its external environment (connectivity between the Content Elements Strategy and Resource Allocation and Organizational Overview and External Environment)	IR F. 3.8	A	
CONX1.3.2	Link of the organization's business model with changes in its external environment (connectivity between the Content Elements Business Model and Organizational Overview and External Environment)	IR F. 3.8	A	
CONX1.4	Other connections between Content Elements	IR F. 3.8	A	
CONX2				
CONX2.1	Connectivity between past- and present-information (connectivity between time dimensions)	IR F. 3.8	A	(CONX2.3 (IR F. 3.8))
CONX2.2	Connectivity between present- and future-information (connectivity between time dimensions)	IR F. 3.8	A	(CONX2.3 (IR F. 3.8))
CONX2.3	Connectivity between past- and future-information (connectivity between time dimensions)	IR F. 3.8	A	
CONX3				
CONX3.1	Interdependencies/trade-offs between the capitals (connectivity between different capitals)	IR F. 3.8	A	
CONX3.2	How changes in the capitals affect the ability of the organization to create value (connectivity between different capitals)	IR F. 3.8	A	
CONX4				
CONX4.1				
CONX4.1.1	The implications of research and development policies for expected revenues/market share (connectivity of financial information and other information)	IR F. 3.8	A	
CONX4.1.2	The implications of technology/know-how for expected revenues/market share (connectivity of financial information and other information)	IR F. 3.8	A	
CONX4.1.3	The implications of investment in human resources for expected revenues/market share (connectivity of financial information and other information)	IR F. 3.8	A	
CONX4.2				
CONX4.2.1	The implications of environmental policies for cost reduction/new business opportunities (connectivity of financial information and other information)	IR F. 3.8	A	
CONX4.2.2	The implications of energy efficiency for cost reduction/new business opportunities (connectivity of financial information and other information)	IR F. 3.8	A	
CONX4.2.3	The implications of cooperation with local communities for cost reduction/new business opportunities (connectivity of financial information and other information)	IR F. 3.8	A	
CONX4.2.4	The implications of technologies to tackle social issues for cost reduction/new business opportunities (connectivity of financial information and other information)	IR F. 3.8	A	
CONX4.3				
CONX4.3.1	The implications of long term customer relationships for revenue growth and profit growth (connectivity of financial information and other information)	IR F. 3.8	A	
CONX4.3.2	The implications of customer satisfaction for revenue growth and profit growth (connectivity of financial information and other information)	IR F. 3.8	A	
CONX4.3.3	The implications of reputation for revenue growth and profit growth (connectivity of financial information and other information)	IR F. 3.8	A	

Continued...

CONX5				
CONX5.1	Presentation of quantitative indicators with an explanation of the measurement methods (connectivity of quantitative and qualitative information)	IR F. 3.8; 4.53	A	
CONX5.2	Presentation of quantitative indicators with an explanation of the underlying assumptions (connectivity of quantitative and qualitative information)	IR F. 3.8; 4.53	A	
CONX5.3	Presentation of quantitative indicators with an explanation of the reasons for significant variations (connectivity of quantitative and qualitative information)	IR F. 3.8; 4.53	A	
CONX6				
CONX6.1	Connectivity of information in the integrated report and the organization's other communications (connectivity between different sources of information)	IR F. 3.8	B	
CONX6.2	Connectivity of information in the integrated report and other (external) sources (connectivity between different sources of information)	IR F. 3.8	B	CONC1.4 (IR F. 3.38).
CONX7				
CONX7.1	Report is written in a clear, understandable and jargon-free language	IR F. 3.9	C	CONC3.1 (IR F. 3.38)
CONX7.2				
CONX7.2.1	Use of clearly-delineated sections	IR F. 3.9	A	
CONX7.2.2	Use of cross-referencing	IR F. 3.9	B	CONC1.1 (IR F. 3.38)
# items CONX:	29			
Stakeholder Relationships (An integrated report should provide insight into the nature and quality of the organization's relationships with its key stakeholders and how and to what extent the organization understands, takes into account and responds to their legitimate needs and interests.)		**IR F. 3.10**		
STAKE1				
STAKE1.1	The (legitimate) needs of the providers of financial capital	IR F. 1.7; 3.14	A	
STAKE1.2				
STAKE1.2.1	Other stakeholders' (legitimate) needs – Employees	IR F. 1.8; 3.14	A	
STAKE1.2.2	Other stakeholders' (legitimate) needs – Customers	IR F. 1.8; 3.14	A	
STAKE1.2.3	Other stakeholders' (legitimate) needs – Suppliers	IR F. 1.8; 3.14	A	
STAKE2				
STAKE2.1	Communication with the providers of financial capital in response to their (legitimate) needs and interests	IR F. 1.7; 3.14	A	
STAKE2.2				
STAKE2.2.1	Communication with other stakeholders in response to their (legitimate) needs and interests – Employees	IR F. 1.8; 3.14	A	
STAKE2.2.2	Communication with other stakeholders in response to their (legitimate) needs and interests – Customers			
STAKE2.2.3	Communication with other stakeholders in response to their (legitimate) needs and interests – Suppliers	IR F. 1.8; 3.14	A	
STAKE3				
STAKE3.1	Decisions/actions in response to the (legitimate) needs and interests of the providers of financial capital	IR F. 1.7; 3.14	A	
STAKE3.2				
STAKE3.2.1	Decisions/actions in response to other stakeholders' (legitimate) needs and interests – Employees	IR F. 1.8; 3.14	A	
STAKE3.2.2	Decisions/actions in response to other stakeholders' (legitimate) needs and interests – Customers	IR F. 1.8; 3.14	A	
STAKE3.2.3	Decisions/actions in response to other stakeholders' (legitimate) needs and interests – Suppliers	IR F. 1.8; 3.14	A	
# items STAKE:	*12*			

Continued…

Materiality (An integrated report should disclose information about matters that substantively affect the organization's ability to create value over the short, medium and long term.)		**IR F. 3.17**		
MAT1				
MAT1.1	Description of the materiality determination process	IR F. 4.42; 3.18-3.29	A	
MAT1.2	Identification of the role of key personnel (e.g., those charged with governance) in the materiality determination process	IR F. 4.42; 3.18-3.29	A	
MAT1.3	A link to a more detailed description of the materiality determination process.	IR F. 4.42; 3.18-3.29	A	
MAT2				
MAT2.1	Identification of the reporting boundary	IR F. 4.43; 3.30-3.35	A	
MAT2.2	Description of how the reporting boundary has been determined	IR F. 4.43; 3.30-3.35	A	
MAT2.3				
MAT2.3.1	Risks, opportunities and outcomes attributable to entities included in the financial reporting entity	IR F. 4.44; 3.30-3.35	A	
MAT2.3.2	Risks, opportunities and outcomes attributable to other entities/stakeholders	IR F. 4.45; 3.30-3.35	A	
MAT3	Limitations of the ability to disclose material information	IR F. 4.46; 3.30-3.35	A	
# items MAT:	*8*			
Conciseness (An integrated report should be concise.)		**IR F. 3.36**		
CONC1				
CONC1.1	Internal cross-references in the report	IR F. 3.38	B	CONX7.2.2 (IR F. 3.9)
CONC1.2	Link(s) to more detailed information	IR F. 3.38	B	
CONC1.3	Link(s) to information that does not change frequently	IR F. 3.38	B	
CONC1.4	Link(s) to external sources	IR F. 3.38	B	CONX6.2 (IR F. 3.8)
CONC2	As few words as possible	IR F. 3.38	C	
CONC3				
CONC3.1	Avoidance of jargon/technical language	IR F. 3.38	C	CONX7.1 (IR F. 3.9)
CONC3.2	Avoidance of highly generic disclosures ("boilerplate disclosures")	IR F. 3.38	C	
# items CONC:	*7*			
Reliability and Completeness (An integrated report should include all material matters, both positive and negative, in a balanced way and without material error.)		**IR F. 3.39**		
REL1	Statement of those charged with governance about their responsibility for the report (or explanation on future plans for such a statement)	IR F. 1.20; 3.41	A	-
REL2	Mechanisms employed to ensure the reliability of the report	IR F. 3.42	A	
REL3				
REL3.1	Nature of information omitted from the report	IR F. 1.18; 3.43	A	(MAT3 (IR F. 4.46; 3.30-3.35))
REL3.2	Reason why information has been omitted from the report	IR F. 1.18; 3.43	A	(MAT3 (IR F. 4.46; 3.30-3.35))
REL3.3	Steps taken to obtain unavailable data	IR F. 1.18; 3.43	A	MAT3 (IR F. 4.46; 3.30-3.35)

Continued...

REL4				
REL4.1	Consideration of both increases and decreases in the capitals	IR F. 3.45	A	
REL4.2	Consideration of both strengths and weaknesses of the organization	IR F. 3.45	A	
REL4.3	Consideration of both positive and negative performance	IR F. 3.45	A	
REL5				
REL5.1	Reporting against previously reported targets	IR F. 3.45	A	CONX2.1 (IR F. 3.8)
REL5.2	Reporting against forecasts, projections and expectations	IR F. 3.45	A	CONX2.2 (IR F. 3.8)
REL6				
REL6.1	Communication of the fact that information includes estimates	IR F. 3.46	A	
REL6.2	Explanation of the estimation process	IR F. 3.46	A	
# items REL:	*12*			
Consistency and Comparability (The information in an integrated report should be presented: • On a basis that is consistent over time • In a way that enables comparison with other organizations to the extent it is material to the organization's own ability to create value over time.)		**IR F. 3.54**		
COMP1				
COMP1.1	Use of the same KPIs across reporting periods or explaining the reason for a change	IR F. 3.55	A	
COMP1.2	Use of the same KPIs across reporting periods or describing the effect of a change	IR F. 3.55	A	
COMP2				
COMP2.1	Use of industry benchmark data	IR F. 3.57	A	
COMP2.2	Use of regional benchmark data	IR F. 3.57	A	
COMP3	Presenting information in the form of ratios	IR F. 3.57	A	
COMP4				
COMP4.1	Reporting quantitative indicators commonly used by organizations with similar activities – SD-KPI 1	IR F. 3.57	A	
COMP4.2	Reporting quantitative indicators commonly used by organizations with similar activities – SD-KPI 2	IR F. 3.57	A	
COMP4.3	Reporting quantitative indicators commonly used by organizations with similar activities – SD-KPI 3	IR F. 3.57	A	
# items COMP:	*8*			
Additional items				
ADD1				
ADD1.1	Type/label of the report	(IR F. 1.1-1.2)		
ADD1.2	Statement about abidance by IIRC regulations	IR F. 1.20; 3.41		
ADD1.3	Addressees of the report	(IR F. 1.7-1.8)		
ADD2				
ADD2.1	Readability of the document: Flesch-Kincaid Grade Level Index	(IR F. 3.9)		
ADD2.2	Readability of the document: Fog Index	(IR F. 3.9)		
# items ADD:	*5*			
# items TOTAL:	***89***			

[a] The numbering of the items obeys the following logic: First, the items are named after the Guiding Principle to which the respective Framework requirements belong, i.e. STRAT for Strategic Focus and Future Orientation, CONX for Connectivity of Information etc. Within the respective Guiding Principles, items are referred to by consecutive numbers. If an item has one or more sub-items, these sub-items are referred to by a sub-number (e.g., STRAT1.1). The same logic applies if sub-items have further sub-items (e.g., STRAT1.1.1).

[b] There are three types of items, depending on the method of data collection and on their score. Type A items are hand-collected items that have a binary score, yielding 1 point, if the requirement of the item is satisfied and 0 otherwise. Type B items are categorical items, for which the categories base on the hand-collected number of links or references that the report includes. According to the quintile that this number falls into, 0.0 (first quintile), 0.5 (second), 1.0 (third), 1.5 (fourth) or 2.0 (fifth) points are awarded as the score for the item. Type C items are also categorical with categories of 0.0 to 2.0 points. The underlying data is collected with the help of software, yielding measures for the number of words in the report, the similarity of the report with the one from the previous year or the percentage of jargon words in the Letter to the Stakeholders. The scores are also awarded according to the quintiles in which these measures fall, but in the reverse direction of type B. 0.0 points are awarded for the last quintile and 2.0 for the first.

[c] Some identified items represent a requirement that is set out more than once in the Framework (e.g., CONX7.1 (IR F. 3.9) and CONC3.1 (IR F. 3.38), both requiring the avoidance of jargon language). In most cases, these items can be distinguished in some way (see the requirements on the respective items for details). In order to allow several sub-scores to be created, such as sub-scores for the different Content Elements (e.g., a CONX-score or a CONC-score), none of the items is cancelled, even if two items might be the same. Instead, points can be awarded for both items. Potential correlations between the respective sub-scores occurring through this practice are not assumed to be material, so that subsequent analyses using the data of the sub-scores are not expected to be constrained.

Appendix 1: Content analysis catalogue based on the International <IR> Framework

Appendix 2: Control variables

Control variables and their calculations			
Construct	**Measure**	**Variable name**	**Calculation**
Risk	Market risk beta	$beta$	estimated in an OLS regression of the form $r_{i;t;\tau} = \hat{\alpha}_{i;t} + \hat{\beta}_{i;t} * r_{m;t;\tau} + \varepsilon_{i;t}$ with data from the estimation window, which started 1080 days before the AIR release and ended one day before the AIR release $r_{i;t;\tau}$ is the stock return for firm i on day τ in year t r_m is the market return for market m on day τ in year t $\varepsilon_{i;t}$ is the error term
Firm size	(Natural logarithm of) Market capitalization	$ln\_market\_cap\_usd$	$ln\_market\_cap\_usd = \ln(\# \, shares_{i;t} * p_{i;t}^{USD})$ $\# \, shares_{i;t}$ is the number of shares outstanding for firm i at the end of (financial) year t $p_{i;t}^{USD}$ is the share price for firm i at the end of (financial) year t
Growth opportunities	Book to market ratio	$book\_to\_market$	$book\_to\_market = \frac{equity_{i;t}^{bv}}{equity_{i;t}^{mv}}$ $equity_{i;t}^{bv}$ is the book value of equity for firm i in year t $equity_{i;t}^{mv}$ is the market value of equity for firm i in year t
Stock return momentum	180 days stock (raw) return	mom	$mom = \frac{p_{i;rm1} - p_{i;rm1-180}}{p_{i;rm1-180}}$ $p_{i;rm1}$ is the stock price for firm i on the first day of the month in which the annual report is released $p_{i;rm1-180}$ is the stock price for firm i 180 days (six months) before the first day of the month in which the annual report is released
Earnings surprise	Standardized unexpected earnings	sue	$sue_q = \frac{e_q - \hat{e}_q}{\sigma_{e_q - \hat{e}_q}}$ e_q is reported earnings per share for quarter q $\hat{e}_q$ is estimated earnings per share for quarter q $\sigma_{e_q - \hat{e}_q}$ is the standard error of the earnings per share estimation
Accrual anomaly	Operating accrual (or "accrual ratio")	acc	$acc = \frac{net\_income_{i;t} - operating\_cf_{i;t}}{\emptyset \, total\_assets_{i;t}}$ $net\_income_{i;t}$ is net income before extraordinary items for firm i in year t $operating\_cf_{i;t}$ is cash flow from operating activities for firm i in year t $\emptyset \, total\_assets_{i;t}$ is average total assets for firm i in year t

Continued...

Year fixed effects	Year dummy	y_2006	Dummy variable for the year, which is 1 if the company's report is on financial year 2006 and 0 otherwise.
Country fixed effects	Country dummy	c_rsa	Dummy variable for the company's country, which is 1 if the company is from South Africa and 0 otherwise.
Industry fixed effects	Industry dummy	$industry\_code\_gics = S$	Dummy variable for all but one sectors, which is 1 if the company is in the sector with (GICS sector level) code S and 0 otherwise.

Appendix 2: Control variables

Web appendix

The web appendix can be found at https://www.wiwi.uni-muenster.de/iur/dissertationen/hannen/webappendix.

It includes the following tables:

1 Content analysis catalogue

2 Regression results – Basic underreaction settings ("Regressions underreaction basic")

2.1 Regressions underreaction basic – Testing for the PEAD and the accrual anomaly

2.2 Regressions underreaction basic – Testing for a pseudo release date

3 Regression results – Moderation of underreaction settings ("Regressions underreaction moderation")

3.1 Regressions underreaction moderation – Degree of IR (original score)

3.2 Regressions underreaction moderation – Degree of Connectivity of Information (CONX sub-score)

3.3 Regressions underreaction moderation – Degree of IR (alternative IR score 1)

3.4 Regressions underreaction moderation – Degree of IR (alternative IR score 2)

3.5 Regressions underreaction moderation – Report length (# words)

3.6 Regressions underreaction moderation – Boilerplate disclosures (similarity with previous report)

3.7 Regressions underreaction moderation – Use of jargon in the Letter to the Stakeholders (jargon score)

3.8 Regressions underreaction moderation – Readability of the Letter to the Stakeholders (Fog Index)

3.9 Regression underreaction moderation – Degree of IR (original score) and report length (# words)

Bibliography

A

Abarbanell, Jeffery S./Bernard, Victor L. (1992): Tests of Analysts' Overreaction/Underreaction to Earnings Information as an Explanation for Anomalous Stock Price Behavior, in: The Journal of Finance, Vol. 47, No. 3, 1992, pp. 1181-1207.

Abeysekera, Indra (2013): A template for integrated reporting, in: Journal of Intellectual Capital, Vol. 14, No. 2, 2013, pp.227-245.

Abrahamson, Eric/Amir, Eli (1996): The Information Content of the President's Letter to Shareholders, in: Journal of Business Finance and Accounting, Vol. 23, No. 8, 1996, pp. 1157-1182.

Accounting for Sustainability (A4S) (n.d.): Project Aims and Mission Statement, URL: http://www.accountingforsustainability.org/about-us (29.08.2016).

Accounting Practices Board (APB)/Financial Reporting Standards Council (FRSC) (2012): Joint Announcement by the Accounting Practices Board (APB) and the Financial Reporting Standards Council (FRSC) Regarding SA GAAP, URL: http://www.syncbs.co.za/wp-content/uploads/2012/03/Withdrawel-of-SA-Gaap.pdf (29.08.2016).

Adams, Carol A. (2015): The International Integrated Reporting Council. A call to action, in: Critical Perspectives on Accounting, Vol. 27, 2015, pp. 23-28.

Adams, Sarah/Simnett, Roger (2011): Integrated Reporting: An Opportunity for Australia's Not-for-Profit Sector, in: Australian Accounting Review, Vol. 21, No.3, 2011, pp. 292-301.

Aebersold, Andreas/Suter, Daniel (2012): Der Nutzen einer integrierten Berichterstattung, in: Zeitschrift für Internationale Rechnungslegung, Vol. 7, No. 10, 2012, pp. 381-384.

Akerlof, George A. (1970): The Market for "Lemons": Quality, Uncertainty and the Market Mechanism, in: The Quarterly Journal of Economics, Vol. 84, No. 3, 1970, pp. 488-500.

Albert, Hans (2000): Kritischer Rationalismus, Tübingen, Germany 2000.

Allen, Eric J./Larson, Chad R./Sloan, Richard G. (2013): Accrual reversals, earnings and stock returns, in: Journal of Accounting and Economics, Vol. 56, No. 1, 2013, pp. 113-129.

Alves, Winfried (2011): Reporting nach US-GAAP, 2nd edition, Weinheim, Germany 2011.

American Institute of Certified Public Accountants (AICPA) (1973): Objectives of Financial Statements, New York, NY 1973.

American Institute of Certified Public Accountants (AICPA) (1994): Improving Business Reporting – A Customer Focus, New York, NY 1994.

American Institute of Certified Public Accountants (AICPA) (2014): AICPA Business Reporting FAQ – Changing Landscape of Corporate Reporting, URL: http://www.aicpa.org/InterestAreas/FRC/AccountingFinancialReporting/EnhancedBusinessReporting/DownloadableDocuments/AICPA%20Business%20Reporting%20FAQ.pdf (29.08.2016).

Amir, Eli/Ganzach, Yoav (1998): Overreaction and underreaction in analysts' forecasts, in: Journal of Economic Behavior & Organization, Vol. 37, No. 3, 1998, pp. 333-347.

Ammann, Manuel/Oesch, David/Schmid, Markus M. (2011): Corporate governance and firm value: International evidence, in: Journal of Empirical Finance, Vol. 18, No. 1, 2011, pp. 36-55.

Angrist, Joshua D./Pischke, Jörn-Steffen (2009): Mostly Harmless Econometrics – An Empiricist's Companion, Princeton, NJ 2009.

Antonakis, John/Bendahan, Samuel/Jacquart, Philippe/Lalive, Rafael (2010): On making causal claims: A review and recommendations, in: Leadership Quarterly Yearly Review, Vol. 21, No. 6, 2010, pp. 1086-1120.

Arbeitskreis Externe Unternehmensrechnung der Schmalenbach-Gesellschaft für Betriebswirtschaft e.V. (AKEU) (2013): Integrated Reporting – Herausforderungen für die Finanzberichterstattung, in: Betriebs-Berater, Vol. 68, No. 15, 2013, pp. 875-882.

Arbeitskreis "Immaterielle Werte im Rechnungswesen" der Schmalenbach-Gesellschaft für Betriebswirtschaft e.V. (AKIW) (2001): Kategorisierung und bilanzielle Erfassung immaterieller Werte, in: Der Betrieb, Vol. 54, No. 19, 2001, pp. 989-995.

Arbeitskreis "Immaterielle Werte im Rechnungswesen" der Schmalenbach-Gesellschaft für Betriebswirtschaft e.V. (AKIW) (2003): Freiwillige externe Berichterstattung über immaterielle Werte, in: Der Betrieb, Vol. 56, No. 23, 2003, pp. 1233-1237.

Arbeitskreis "Immaterielle Werte im Rechnungswesen" der Schmalenbach-Gesellschaft für Betriebswirtschaft e.V. (AKIW) (2004): Erfassung immaterieller Werte in der Unternehmensberichterstattung vor dem Hintergrund handelsrechtlicher Rechnungslegungsnormen, in: Horváth, Péter/Möller, Klaus (eds.), Intangibles in der Unternehmenssteuerung. Strategien und Instrumente zur Wertsteigerung des immateriellen Kapitals, Munich Germany 2004, pp. 221-250.

Arguelles, Mary P. M./Balatbat, Maria/Green, Wendy (2016): Is there an early-mover market value effect for signaling adoption of integrated reporting. Paper presented at the 39th European Accounting Association Annual Congress 2016, 11-13 May 2016, Maastricht, Netherlands, URL: http://www.eaacongress.org/r/home (29.08.2016).

Armbrester, Kyle/Clay, Tiffany/Roberts, Leigh (2011): Integrated Reporting an irreversible tipping point, in: Accountancy SA, April 2011, pp. 28-29.

Armitstead, Louise/Butterworth, Myra (2010): Barack Obama's attacks on BP hurting British pensioners, URL: http://www.telegraph.co.uk/news/worldnews/barackobama/7815713/Barack-Obamas-attacks-on-BP-hurting-British-pensioners.html (29.08.2016).

Arnold, Markus/Bassen, Alexander/Frank, Ralf (2012): Integrating Sustainability Reports into Financial Statements: An Experimental Study, URL: http://papers.ssrn.com/sol3/papers.cfm?abstract_id=2030891 (29.08.2016).

Arnold, Patricia/Hammond, Theresa (1994): The Role of Accounting in Ideological Conflict: Lessons from the South African Divestment Movement, in: Accounting, Organizations and Society, Vol. 19, No. 2, 1994, pp. 111-126.

Arrow, Kenneth J. (1985): The Economics of Agency, in: Pratt, John W./Zeckhauser, Richard J. (eds.), Principals and Agents: The Structure of Business, Boston, MA 1985, pp. 37-51.

Ashbaugh-Skaife, Hollis/Collins, Daniel W./Kinney Jr., William R./LaFond, Ryan (2008): The Effect of SOX Internal Control Deficiencies and Their Remediation on Accrual Quality, in: The Accounting Review, Vol. 83, No. 1, 2008, pp. 217-250.

Association of Chartered Certified Accountants (ACCA)/Net Balance Foundation (2011): Adoption of integrated reporting by the ASX 50, URL: http://www.accaglobal.com/content/dam/acca/global/PDF-technical/integrated-reporting/tech-tp-air2.pdf (29.08.2016).

Atkins, Paul S./Bondi, Bradley J. (2008): Evaluating the Mission: A Critical Review of the History and Evolution of the SEC Enforcement Program, in: Fordham Journal of Corporate & Financial Law, Vol. 13, No. 3, 2008, pp. 367-417.

Austin, John L. (1975): How to Do Things with Words, 2nd edition, Oxford, UK 1975.

Ayres, Paul/Youssef, Amina (2008): Investigating the Influence of Transitory Information and Motivation during Instructional Animations, in: Kirschner, Paul A./Prins, Frans J./Jonker, Vincent/Kanselaar, Gellof (eds.), Published Proceedings of the Eighth International Conference for the Learning Sciences, Utrecht, The Netherlands 2008, pp. 68-75.

B

Ball, Ray/Brown, Philip (1968): An Empirical Evaluation of Accounting Income Numbers, in: Journal of Accounting Research, Vol. 6, No. 2, 1968, pp. 159-178.

Ball Corporation (2013): Ball Reports Strong 2012 Results, URL: http://www.sec.gov/Archives/edgar/data/9389/000000938913000004/ex_991.htm (29.08.2016).

Banz, Rolf W. (1981): The Relationship Between Return and Market Value of Common Stocks, in: Journal of Financial Economics, Vol. 9, No. 1, 1981, pp. 3-18.

Barber, Brad M./Lyon, John D. (1997): Detecting long-run abnormal stock returns: The empirical power and specification of test statistics, in: Journal of Financial Economics, Vol. 43, No. 3, 1997, pp. 341-372.

Barberis, Nicholas/Shleifer, Andrei/Vishny, Robert (1998): A model of investor sentiment, in: Journal of Financial Economics, Vol. 49, No. 3, 1998, pp. 307-343.

Barnett, Andrew/Leoffler, Keith (1979): Readability of Accounting and Auditing Messages, in: Journal of Business Communication, Vol. 16, No. 3, 1979, pp. 49-59.

Barron, Orie E./Kile, Charles O./O'Keefe, Terrence B. (1999): MD&A Quality as Measured by the SEC and Analysts' Earnings Forecasts, in: Contemporary Accounting Research, Vol. 16, No. 1, 1999, pp. 75-109.

Bartel, Rainer (1990): Charakteristik, Methodik und wissenschaftsmethodische Probleme der Wirtschaftswissenschaften, in: Wirtschaftswissenschaftliches Studium, Vol. 19, No. 2, 1990, pp. 54-59.

Barth, Daniela (2009): Prognoseberichterstattung – Praxis, Determinanten und Kapitalmarktwirkungen bei deutschen börsennotierten Unternehmen, Frankfurt am Main, Germany 2009.

Barth, Mary E./Cahan, Steven F./Li, Chen/Venter, Elmar R. (2015): The Economic Consequences Associated with Integrated Reporting Quality: Early Evidence from a Mandatory Setting, URL: http://papers.ssrn.com/sol3/papers.cfm?abstract_id=2699409 (29.08.2016).

Beaver, William H. (1968): The Information Content of Annual Earnings Announcements, in: Journal of Accounting Research, Vol. 6, Supplement, 1968, pp. 67-92.

Becker, Gary S. (1964): Human Capital – A Theoretical and Empirical Analysis, with Special Reference to Education, New York, NY 1964.

Benston, George J./Bromwich, Michael/Wagenhofer, Alfred (2006): Principles-Versus Rules-Based Accounting Standards – The FASB's Standard Setting Strategy, in: ABACUS, Vol. 42, No. 2, 2006, pp. 165-188.

Berelson, Bernard (1952): Content Analysis In Communication Research, Glencoe, IL 1952.

Beretta, Sergio/Bozzolan, Saverio (2008): Quality versus Quantity: The Case of Forward-Looking Disclosure, in: Journal of Accounting, Auditing and Finance, Vol. 23, No. 3, 2008, pp. 333-375.

Bernard, Victor L./Thomas, Jacob K. (1989): Post-Earnings Announcement Drift: Delayed Price Response or Risk Premium, in: Journal of Accounting Research, Vol. 27, Supplement, 1989, pp. 1-36.

Bernard, Victor L./Thomas, Jacob K. (1990): Evidence that Stock Prices Do Not Fully Reflect the Implications of Current Earnings for Future Earnings, in: Journal of Accounting and Economics, Vol. 13, No. 4, 1990, pp. 305-340.

Bernardi, Cristiana/Stark, Andrew W. (2015): Environmental, Social and Governance Disclosure, Integrated Reporting, and the Accuracy of Analysts Forecasts, URL: http://papers.ssrn.com/sol3/papers.cfm?abstract_id=2641699 (29.08.2016).

Beyhs, Oliver/Barth, Daniela (2011a): Die Revolution des Geschäftsberichts, in: Frankfurter Allgemeine Zeitung, Vol. 63, No. 218, 2011, p. 12.

Beyhs, Oliver/Barth, Daniela (2011b): Integrated Reporting – Aktuelle Entwicklungen auf dem Weg zu einer integrierten Unternehmensberichterstattung, in: Der Betrieb, Vol. 64, No. 51/52, 2011, pp. 2857-2863.

Bhana, Narendra (2009): The chairman's statements and annual reports: Are they reporting the same company performance to investors?, in: Investment Analysts Journal, Vol. 38, No. 69, 2009, pp. 32-46.

Bissonnette, Victor/Ickes, William/Bernstein, Ira/Knowles, Eric (1990): Personality Moderating Variables: A Warning about Statistical Artifact and a Comparison of Analytic Techniques, in: Journal of Personality, Vol. 58, No. 3, 1990, pp. 567-587.

Blaesing, Daniel (2013): Nachhaltigkeitsberichterstattung in Deutschland und den USA – Berichtspraxis, Determinanten und Eigenkapitalkostenwirkungen, Frankfurt am Main, Germany 2013.

Bloomfield, Robert J. (2002): The "Incomplete Revelation Hypothesis" and Financial Reporting, in: Accounting Horizons, Vol. 16, No. 3, 2002, pp. 233-243.

Bloomfield, Robert J. (2012): A Pragmatic Approach to More Efficient Corporate Disclosure, in: Accounting Horizons, Vol. 26, No. 2, 2012, pp. 357-370.

Blue-Ribbon Panel on Standard Setting for Private Companies (Blue-Ribbon Panel) (2011): Report to the Board of Trustees of the Financial Accounting Foundation, URL: http://www.accountingfoundation.org/cs/ContentServer?site=Foundation&c=Document_C&pagename=Foundation/Document_C/FAFDocumentPage&cid=1176158181336 (29.08.2016).

Botosan Christine A. (1997): Disclosure Level and the Cost of Equity Capital, in: The Accounting Review, Vol. 72, No. 3, 1997, pp. 323-349.

Botosan, Christine A. (2004): Discussion of a framework for the analysis of firm risk communication, in: The International Journal of Accounting, Vol. 39, No. 3, 2004, pp. 289-295.

Bragg, Steven M. (2010): The Ultimate Accountants' Reference, 3rd edition, Hoboken, NJ 2010.

Brav, Alon/Heaton, James B. (2002): Competing Theories of Financial Anomalies, in: Review of Financial Studies, Vol. 15, No. 2, 2002, pp. 575-606.

Breen, Tom (2010): BP costs for oil spill response pass $3 billion, URL: http://www.washingtontimes.com/news/2010/jul/5/bp-costs-oil-spill-response-pass-3-billion/ (29.08.2016).

Brown, Robert D./Braskamp, Larry A./Newman, Dianna L. (1978): Evaluator Credibility as a Function of Report Style – Do Jargon and Data Make a Difference?, in: Evaluation Quarterly, Vol. 2, No. 2, 1978, pp. 331-341.

Brown, Stephen J./Warner, Jerold B. (1985): Using Daily Stock Returns: The Case of Event Studies, in: Journal of Financial Economics, Vol. 14, No. 1, 1985, pp. 3-31.

Brown, Stephen V./Tucker, Jennifer W. (2011): Large-Sample Evidence on Firms' Year-over-Year MD&A Modifications, in: Journal of Accounting Research, Vol. 49, No. 2, 2011, pp. 309-346.

Bruce, Harry (1987): Perfectly unclear, in: Canadian Business, Vol. 60, No. 3, 1987, pp. 84-85, 114.

C

Cahan, Steven F./Van Staden, Chris J. (2009): Black economic empowerment, legitimacy and the value added statement: evidence from post-apartheid South Africa, in: Accounting and Finance, Vol. 49, No. 1, 2009, pp. 37-58.

Callen, Jeffrey L./Khan, Mozaffar/Lu, Hai (2013): Accounting Quality, Stock Price Delay and Future Stock Returns, in: Contemporary Accounting Research, Vol. 30, No. 1, 2013, pp. 269-295.

Catchpowle, Lesley/Cooper, Christine (1999): No Escaping the Financial: The Economic Referent in South Africa, in: Critical Perspectives on Accounting, Vol. 10, No. 6, 1999, pp. 711-746.

Cerpa, Narciso/Chandler, Paul/Sweller, John (1996): Some Conditions under which Integrated Computer-Based Training Software Can Facilitate Learning, in: Journal of Educational Computing Research, Vol. 15, No. 4, 1996, pp. 345-367.

Chan, Louis K.C./Jegadeesh, Narasimhan/Lakonishok, Josef (1996): Momentum Strategies, in: The Journal of Finance, Vol. 51, No. 5, 1996, pp. 1681-1713.

Chandler, Paul/Sweller, John (1992): The Split-Attention Effect as a Factor in the Design of Instruction, in: British Journal of Educational Psychology, Vol. 62, No. 2, 1992, pp. 233-246.

Chandler, Paul/Sweller, John (1996): Cognitive Load While Learning to Use a Computer Program, in: Applied Cognitive Psychology, Vol. 10, No. 2, 1996, pp. 151-170.

Chartered Accountants Australia and New Zealand (CA ANZ)/EY (2015): Noise, Numbers and Cut-Through – What is the future of financial reporting, URL: https://charteredaccountantsanz.com/-/media/FutureInc/Pdfs/2015/041546_FutureIncNoiseNumbers.ashx (29.08.2016).

Chartered Secretaries Southern Africa (CSSA) (2013): Judging 2013, URL: http://www.chartsec.co.za/index.php?view=article&catid=7%3Aannual-report-awards&id=423%3Ajudging&format=pdf&option=com_content&Itemid=513 (29.08.2016).

Chatfield, Michael (1977): A History of Accounting Thought, 2nd edition, Huntington, NY 1977.

Chen, Linda H./Jiang, George J. (2013): Drift or Jump: What Drives Post-Earnings Announcement Stock Returns, in: Lee, Cheng-Few (ed.), Advances in Quantitative Analysis of Finance and Accounting, Vol. 11, Singapore 2013, pp. 175-206.

Cheng, Mandy/Green, Wendy/Conradie, Pieter/Konishi, Noriyuki/Romi, Andrea (2014): The International Integrated Reporting Framework: Key Issues and Future Research Opportunities, in: Journal of International Financial Management & Accounting, Vol. 25, No. 1, 2014, pp. 90-119.

Chung, Kee H./Kim, Oliver/Lim, Steve C./Yang, Sean (2014): The prediction of post-earnings announcement drift using a measure of market underreaction, URL: http://www.acsu.buffalo.edu/~keechung/MGF743/Readings/PEAD.pdf (29.08.2016).

Churet, Cecile/Eccles, Robert G. (2014): Integrated Reporting, Quality of Management, and Financial Performance, in: Journal of Applied Corporate Finance, Vol. 26, No. 1, 2014, pp. 8-16.

Clark, Nancy L./Worger, William H. (2016): South Africa – The rise and fall of apartheid, 3rd edition, London, UK/New York, NY 2016.

Clarkson, Peter M./Kao, Jennifer L./Richardson, Gordon D. (1994): The Voluntary Inclusion of Forecasts in the MD&A Section of Annual Reports, in: Contemporary Accounting Research, Vol. 11, No. 1-II, 1994, pp. 423-450.

Clayton, Alexandra F./Rogerson, Jayne M./Rampedi, Isaac (2015): Integrated reporting vs. sustainability reporting for corporate responsibility in South Africa, in: Bulletin of Geography, No. 29, 2015, pp. 7-17.

Cohen, Jacob (1983): The Cost of Dichotomization, in: Applied Psychological Measurement, Vol. 7, No. 3, 1983, pp. 249-253.

Cohen, Jacob (1988): Statistical Power Analysis for the Behavioral Sciences, 2nd edition, Hillsdale, NJ 1988.

Cole, Cathy J. (1990): MD&A Trends in Standard & Poor's Top 100 Companies, in: Journal of Corporate Accounting & Finance, Vol. 2, No. 2, 1990, pp. 127-136.

Coleman, James S (1998): Social Capital in the Creation of Human Capital, in: The American Journal of Sociology, Vol. 94, Supplement: Organizations and Institutions: Sociological and Economic Approaches to the Analysis of Social Structure, 1988, pp. S95-S120.

Collins, James C./Porras, Jerry I. (1996): Building Your Company's Vision, in: Harvard Business Review, Vol. 74, No. 5, 1996, pp. 65-77.

Cooke, Terry E./Wallace, R. S. Olusegun (1989): Global Survey of Corporate Disclosure Practices and Audit Firms: A Review Essay, in: Accounting and Business Research, Vol. 20, No. 77, 1989, pp. 47-57.

Courtis, John K. (1986a): An Investigation into Annual Report Readability and Corporate Risk-Return Relationships, in: Accounting and Business Research, Vol. 16, No. 64, 1986, pp. 285-294.

Courtis, John K. (1986b): Poor Communication Is Alive and Well: A Study of Annual Report Readability, in: Canadian Journal of Communication, Vol. 12, No. 3-4, 1986, pp. 1-17.

Courtis, John K. (1998): Annual report readability variability: test of the obfuscation hypothesis, in: Accounting, Auditing & Accountability Journal, Vol. 11, No. 4, 1998, pp. 459-472.

Cox, Christopher (2007): Closing Remarks to the Second Annual Corporate Governance Summit, URL: http://www.sec.gov/news/speech/2007/spch032307cc.htm (29.08.2016).

Crawford, Vincent P./Sobel, Joel (1982): Strategic Information Transmission, in: Econometrica, Vol. 50, No. 6, 1982, pp. 1431-1451.

Credit Suisse (2015): Credit Suisse Global Investment Returns Yearbook 2015, URL: http://publications.credit-suisse.com/tasks/render/file/index.cfm?fileid=AE924F44-E396-A4E5-11E63B09CFE37CCB (29.08.2016).

D

Daily, Robert A. (1971): The Feasibility of Reporting Forecasted Information, in: The Accounting Review, Vol. 46, No. 4, 1971, pp. 686-692.

Daniel, Kent/Hirshleifer, David/Subrahmanyam, Avanidhar (1998): Investor Psychology and Security Market Under- and Overreactions, in: The Journal of Finance, Vol. 53, No. 6, 1998, pp. 1839-1885.

De Villiers, Charl J./Rinaldi, Leonardo/Unerman, Jeffrey (2014): Integrated Reporting: Insights, gaps and an agenda for future research, in: Accounting, Auditing & Accountability Journal, Vol. 27, No. 7, 2014, pp. 1042-1067.

Decker, Rolf O. (1994): Eine Prinzipal-Agenten-theoretische Betrachtung von Eigner-Manager-Konflikten in der Kommanditgesellschaft auf Aktien und in der Aktiengesellschaft, Dissertation Freie Universität Berlin, Bergisch Gladbach, Germany 1994.

Deegan, Craig/Unerman, Jeffrey (2011): Financial Accounting Theory, 2nd edition, Maidenhead, UK 2011.

Deloitte (2014): Integrated Reporting in the Netherlands – The journey continues and is gaining traction and pace!, URL: https://web.archive.org/web/20150816030135/http://www2.deloitte.com/content/dam/Deloitte/nl/Documents/audit/deloitte-nl-audit-integrated-reporting-in-the-netherlands.pdf (29.08.2016).

Deloitte (2015): Annual report insights 2015 – The reporting landscape, URL: http://www2.deloitte.com/uk/en/pages/audit/articles/annual-report-insights.html (29.08.2016).

Deloitte/MVO Nederland (2015): Integrated Reporting as a driver for Integrated Thinking? Maturity of <IR> in the Netherlands 2015, URL: http://www2.deloitte.com/content/dam/Deloitte/nl/Documents/risk/deloitte-nl-risk-integrated-reporting-a-driver-for-integrated-thinking.pdf (29.08.2016).

Department for Business Innovation & Skills (BIS) (2010a): The Future of Narrative Reporting – A Consultation, URL: http://www.bis.gov.uk/assets/biscore/business-law/docs/n/10-1057-future-narrative-reporting-consultation.pdf (29.08.2016).

Department for Business Innovation & Skills (BIS) (2010b): A Long-Term Focus for Corporate Britain – A Call for Evidence, URL: http://www.bis.gov.uk/assets/biscore/business-law/docs/l/10-1225-long-term-focus-corporate-britain.pdf (29.08.2016).

Department for Business Innovation & Skills (BIS) (2011): The Future of Narrative Reporting – Consulting a new reporting framework, URL: http://www.bis.gov.uk/assets/biscore/business-law/docs/f/11-945-future-of-narrative-reporting-consulting-new-framework.pdf (29.08.2016).

Department for Business Innovation & Skills (BIS) (2012a): The Future of Narrative Reporting – The Government Response, URL: https://www.gov.uk/government/uploads/system/uploads/attachment_data/file/136489/12-588-future-of-narrative-reporting-government-response.pdf (29.08.2016).

Department for Business Innovation & Skills (BIS) (2012b): The Future of Narrative Reporting – A new structure for Narrative Reporting in the UK, URL: http://www.bis.gov.uk/assets/biscore/business-law/docs/f/12-979-future-of-narrative-reporting-new-structure.pdf (29.08.2016).

Diamond, Douglas W./Verrecchia, Robert E. (1991): Disclosure, Liquidity, and the Cost of Capital, in: The Journal of Finance, Vol. 46, No. 4, 1991, pp. 1325-1359.

DiMaggio, Paul J./Powell, Walter W. (1983): The Iron Cage Revisited: Institutional Isomorphism and Collective Rationality in Organizational Fields, in: American Sociological Review, Vol. 48, No. 2, 1983, pp. 147-160.

Dolley, James C. (1933): Characteristics and Procedure of Common-Stock Split-Ups, in: Harvard Business Review, Vol. 11, No. 3, 1933, pp. 316-326.

Dowling, John/Pfeffer, Jeffrey (1975): Organizational legitimacy: Social values and organizational behavior, in: Pacific Sociological Review, Vol. 18, No. 1, 1975, pp. 122-136.

Dreman, David N./Lufkin, Eric A. (2000): Investor Overreaction: Evidence That Its Basis Is Psychological, in: The Journal of Psychology and Financial Markets, Vol. 1, No. 1, 2000, pp. 61-75.

Druckman, Paul (2010): Integrierte Berichterstattung: die Zukunft der Unternehmensberichterstattung?, in: Die Wirtschaftsprüfung, Vol. 63, No. 23, 2010, p. I.

Druckman, Paul (2013): South African reflections on integrated reporting, URL: http://www.theaccountant-online.com/blog/reflections-on-integrated-reporting/ (29.08.2016).

Dubow, Saul (2014): Apartheid, 1948-1994, Oxford, UK 2014.

E

Easton, Peter D./Zmijewski, Mark E. (1993): SEC Form 10K/10Q Reports and Annual Reports to Shareholders: Reporting Lags and Squared Market Model Prediction Errors, in: Journal of Accounting Research, Vol. 31, No. 1, 1993, pp. 113-129.

Eccles, Robert G./Herz, Robert H./Keegan, E. Mary/Phillips, David M. H. (2001): The Value Reporting Revolution – Moving Beyond the Earnings Game, New York, NY 2001.

Eccles, Robert G./Krzus, Michael P. (2010): One Report – Integrated Reporting for a Sustainable Strategy, Hoboken, NJ 2010.

Eccles, Robert G./Krzus, Michael P. (2015): Meaning and Momentum in the Integrated Reporting Movement, in: Journal of Applied Corporate Finance, Vol. 27, No. 2, 2015, pp. 8-17.

Eccles, Robert G./Krzus, Michael P./Ribot, Sydney (2015): The Integrated Reporting Movement – Meaning, Momentum, Motives, and Materiality, Hoboken, NJ 2015.

Eccles, Robert G./Serafeim, George, G. (2011): Accelerating the Adoption of Integrated Reporting, in: De Leo, Francesco/Vollbracht, Matthias (eds.), CSR Index, Beirut, Lebanon et al. 2011, pp. 70-92.

Edwards, Ward (1968): Conservatism in human information processing, in Kleinmuntz, Benjamin (ed.), Formal Representation of Human Judgment, New York, NY 1968.

Eisenhardt, Kathleen M. (1989): Agency Theory: An Assessment and Review, in: The Academy of Management Review, Vol. 14, No. 1, 1989, pp. 57-74.

Elton, Edwin J./Gruber, Martin J./Blake, Christopher R. (1996): Survivorship Bias and Mututal Fund Performance, in: The Review of Financial Studies, Vol. 9, No. 4, 1996, pp. 1097-1120.

Epstein, Marc J./Pava, Moses L. (1993): How Useful Are Corporate Annual Reports, in: Business Credit, Vol. 95, No. 4, 1993, pp. 18-20.

Ernst & Young (2011): Excellence in Corporate Reporting 2011 – A survey of annual reports from South Africa's top 100 companies and top 10 state-owned entities, URL: http://www.sustainabilitysa.org/Portals/0/Documents/EY%20Excellence%20in%20 Corporate%20Reporting%202011.pdf (29.08.2016).

Evans, James D. (1996): Straightforward Statistics for the Behavioral Sciences, Pacific Grove, CA 1996.

EY (2013): EY's Excellence in Integrated Reporting Awards 2013 – A survey of integrated reports from South Africa's top 100 JSE listed companies and top 10 state owned companies, URL: http://www.ey.com/Publication/vwLUAssets/Eys_Excellence_in_Integrated_Reporting_Awards_2013/$FILE/EY%20Excellence%20in%20Integrated%20Reporting.pdf (29.08.2016).

EY (2014): Tomorrow's investment rules – Global survey of institutional investors on non-financial performance, URL: https://www.eycom.ch/en/Publications/20140502-Tomorrows-investment-rules-a-global-survey/download (29.08.2016).

EY (2015): Tomorrow's Investment Rules 2.0 – Emerging risk and stranded assets have investors looking for more from nonfinancial reporting, URL: http://www.ey.com/Publication/vwLUAssets/EY-tomorrows-investment-rules-2/$FILE/EY-tomorrows-investment-rules-2.0.pdf (29.08.2016).

F

Fama, Eugene F. (1965): The Behavior of Stock-Market Prices, in: The Journal of Business, Vol. 38, No. 1, 1965, pp. 34-105.

Fama, Eugene F. (1970): Efficient Capital Markets: A Review of Theory and Empirical Work, in: The Journal of Finance, Vol. 25, No. 2, 1970, pp. 383-417.

Fama, Eugene F. (1991): Efficient Capital Markets: II, in: The Journal of Finance, Vol. 46, No. 5, 1991, pp. 1575-1617.

Fama, Eugene F./Fisher, Lawrence/Jensen, Michael C./Roll, Richard (1969): The Adjustment of Stock Prices to New Information, in: International Economic Review, Vol. 10, No. 1, 1969, pp. 1-21.

Fama, Eugene F./French, Kenneth R. (1992): The Cross-Section of Expected Stock Returns, in: The Journal of Finance, Vol. 47, No. 2, 1992, pp. 427-465.

Fama, Eugene F./French, Kenneth R. (1993): Common risk factors in the returns on stocks and bonds, in: Journal of Financial Economics, Vol. 33, No. 1, 1993, pp. 3-56.

Fan, Steve/Yu, Linda (2013): Accrual Anomaly and Idiosyncratic Risk: International Evidence, in: The International Journal of Business and Finance Research, Vol. 7, No. 4, 2013, pp. 63-75.

Farrell, Joseph (1987): Cheap Talk, Coordination, and Entry, in: RAND Journal of Economics, Vol. 18, No. 1, 1987, pp. 34-39.

Farrell, Joseph/Gibbons, Robert (1989): Cheap Talk with Two Audiences, in: The American Economic Review, Vol. 79, No. 5, 1989, pp. 1214-1223.

Farrell, Joseph/Rabin, Matthew (1996): Cheap Talk, in: Journal of Economic Perspectives, Vol. 10, No. 3, 1996, pp. 103-118.

Faulkender, Michael/Petersen, Mitchell A. (2006): Does the Source of Capital Affect Capital Structure?, in: Review of Financial Studies, Vol. 19, No. 1, 2006, pp. 45-79.

Feldman, Ronen/Govindaraj, Suresh/Livnat, Joshua/Segal, Benjamin (2010): Management's Tone Change, Post Earnings Announcement Drift and Accruals, in: Review of Accounting Studies, Vol. 15, No. 4, 2010, pp. 915-953.

Ferreira, Daniel/Rezende, Marcelo (2007): Corporate strategy and information disclosure, in: RAND Journal of Economics, Vol. 38, No. 1, 2007, pp. 164-184.

Fertakis, John P. (1969): On Communication, Understanding, and Relevance in Accounting Reporting, in: The Accounting Review, Vol. 44, No. 4, 1969, pp. 680-691.

Financial Accounting Standards Board (FASB) (2001): Improving Business Reporting: Insights into Enhancing Voluntary Disclosures, URL: http://www.fasb.org/cs/ContentServer?c=Document_C&pagename=FASB%2Fdocument_C%2FdocumentPage&cid=1176156460184 (29.08.2016).

Financial Accounting Standards Board (FASB) (2013): Rules of Procedure – Amended and Restated through December 11, 2013, URL: http://www.fasb.org/cs/ContentServer?c=Document_C&pagename=FASB%2Fdocument_C%2FdocumentPage&cid=1176162391050 (29.08.2016).

Financial Accounting Standards Board (FASB) (2014): FASB Accounting Standards Codification – About the Codification (v 4.9), URL: https://asc.fasb.org/imageRoot/47/49128947.pdf (29.08.2016).

Financial Accounting Standards Board (FASB) (2016): Project Update – Conceptual Framework – Project Information Page, URL: http://www.fasb.org/jsp/FASB/FASBContent_C/ProjectUpdatePage&cid=900000011090&pf=true (29.08.2016).

Financial Accounting Standards Board (FASB) (n.d.a): Convergence with the International Accounting Standards Board (IASB), URL: http://www.fasb.org/intl/convergence_iasb.shtml&pf=true (29.08.2016).

Financial Accounting Standards Board (FASB) (n.d.b): Facts About FASB, URL: http://www.fasb.org/facts/index.shtml&pf=true#mission (29.08.2016).

Financial Accounting Standards Board (FASB)/International Accounting Standards Board (IASB) (2002): Memorandum of Understanding – "The Norwalk Agreement", URL: http://www.fasb.org/news/memorandum.pdf (29.08.2016).

Financial Reporting Standards Council (FRSC) (n.d.): Financial Reporting Standards Council – Rules of Procedure, URL: http://www.thedti.gov.za/business_regulation/docs/Rules_Procedure.pdf (29.08.2016).

Financial Services Board (FSB) (n.d.): About Us, URL: https://www.fsb.co.za/aboutUs/Pages/About-FSB.aspx (29.08.2016).

Financial Times Stock Exchange (FTSE) (2016): FTSE FACTSHEET – FTSE/JSE All-Share Index, URL: http://www.ftse.com/Analytics/FactSheets/Home/DownloadSingleIssue?issueName=J203 (29.08.2016).

Finch, Nigel (2006): Intangible Assets and Creative Impairment – An Analysis of Current Disclosure Practices by Large Australian Listed Firms, in: Journal of Law and Financial Mangement, Vol. 5, No. 2, 2006, pp. 18-24.

Fink, Christian/Kajüter, Peter/Winkeljohann, Norbert (2013): Lageberichterstattung – HGB, DRS und IFRS Practice Statement Management Commentary, Stuttgart, Germany 2013.

Flower, John (2015): The International Integrated Reporting Council: A story of failure, in: Critical Perspectives on Accounting, Vol. 27, 2015, pp. 1-17.

Foster, Taylor W. III/Jenkins, D. Randall/Vickrey, Don W. (1983): Additional Evidence on the Incremental Information Content of the 10-K, in: Journal of Business Finance and Accounting, Vol. 10, No. 1, 1983, pp. 57-66.

Frank, Ulrich (2003): Einige Gründe für eine Wiederbelebung der Wissenschaftstheorie, in: Die Betriebswirtschaft, Vol. 63, No. 3, 2003, pp. 278-292.

Frías-Aceituno, José-Valeriano/Rodríguez-Ariza, Lázaro/García-Sánchez, Isabel-María (2013a): The Role of the Board in the Dissemination of Integrated Corporate Social Reporting, in: Corporate Social Responsibility and Environmental Management, Vol. 20, No. 4, 2013, pp. 219-233.

Frías-Aceituno, José-Valeriano/Rodríguez-Ariza, Lázaro/García-Sánchez, Isabel-María (2013b): Is integrated reporting determined by a country's legal system? An exploratory study, in: Journal of Cleaner Production, Vol. 44, 2013, pp. 45-55.

Frías-Aceituno, José-Valeriano/Rodríguez-Ariza, Lázaro/García-Sánchez, Isabel-María (2014): Explanatory Factors of Integrated Sustainability and Financial Reporting, in: Business Strategy and the Environment, Vol. 23, No. 1, 2014, pp. 56-72.

Friedman, Benjamin M. (1979): Optimal Expectations and the Extreme Information Assumptions of 'Rational Expectations' Macromodels, in: Journal of Monetary Economics, Vol. 5, No. 1, 1979, pp. 23-41.

Frisch, Thomas/Kolaric, Sascha/Schiereck, Dirk (2014): Returns On large Stock Price Declines And Increases In The South African Stock Market: A Note On Market Efficiency, in: International Business & Economics Research Journal, Vol. 13, No. 3, 2014, pp. 581-592.

Fülbier, Rolf U. (2004): Wissenschaftstheorie und Betriebswirtschaftslehre, in: Wirtschaftswissenschaftliches Studium, Vol. 31, No. 5, 2004, pp. 266-271.

Funke Busayo, Oyebanji (2013): Earning News on Stock Liquidity and Post Earnings Announcement Drift in France, USA and South Africa: URL: http://wiredspace.wits.ac.za/bitstream/handle/10539/13076/Earning%20News%20on%20Stock%20Liquidity%20and%20Post%20Earnings%20Announcement%20Drift%20in%20France,%20USA%20and%20South%20Africa.pdf?sequence=1 (29.08.2016).

Furubotn, Eirik G./Richter, Rudolf (2005): Institutions and Economic Theory: The Contribution of the New Institutional Economics, 2nd edition, Ann Arbor, MI 2005.

G

García-Sánchez, Isabel-María/Rodríguez-Ariza, Lázaro/Frías-Aceituno, José-Valeriano (2013): The cultural system and integrated reporting, in: International Business Review, Vol. 22, No. 5, 2013, pp. 828-838.

Girdler, Reynolds (1963): 18,000,000 Books Nobody Reads, in: Saturday Review, Vol. 39, No. 15, 1963, pp. 71, 78.

Givoly, Dan/Lakonishok, Josef (1980): Financial Analysts' Forecasts of Earnings – Their Value to Investors, in: Journal of Banking and Finance, Vol. 4, No. 3, 1980, pp. 221-233.

Gleason, Christi A./Lee, Charles M. C. (2003): Analyst Forecast Revisions and Market Price Discovery, in: The Accounting Review, Vol. 78, No. 1, 2003, pp. 193-225.

Global Development and Environment Institute (2003): Five Kinds of Capital: Useful Concepts for Sustainable Development, URL: http://www.ase.tufts.edu/gdae/publications/working_papers/03-07sustainabledevelopment.PDF (29.08.2016).

Göbel, Elisabeth (2002): Neue Institutionenökonomik, Konzeptionen und betriebswirtschaftliche Anwendungen, Stuttgart, Germany 2002.

Gode, Dan/Mohanram, Partha (2003): Inferring the Cost of Capital Using the Ohlson-Juettner Model, in: Review of Accounting Studies, Vol. 8, No. 4, 2003, pp. 399-431.

Goerke, Björn (2009): Event-Studies, in: Albers, Sönke/Klapper, Daniel/Konradt, Udo/Walter, Achim/Wolf, Joachim (eds.), Methodik der empirischen Forschung, 3rd edition, Wiesbaden, Germany 2009, pp. 467-484.

Gompers, Paul/Ishii, Joy/Metrick, Andrew (2003): Corporate Governance and Equity Prices, in: The Quarterly Journal of Economics, Vol. 118, No. 1, 2003, pp. 107-155.

Gray, Rob/Kouhy, Rezy/Lavers, Simon (1995): Corporate social and environmental reporting: A review of the literature and a longitudinal study of UK disclosure, in: Accounting, Auditing & Accountability Journal, Vol. 8, No. 2, 1995, pp. 47-77.

Gray, Rob/Owen, Dave/Adams, Carol (1996): Accounting & Accountability – Changes and challenges in corporate social and environmental reporting, London, UK 1996.

Gray, Sidney J. (1988): Towards a Theory of Cultural Influence in the Development of Accounting Systems Internationally, in: Abacus, Vol. 24, No. 1, 1988, pp. 1-15.

Greinert, Markus (2004): Weitergehende Anforderungen an den Konzernlagebericht durch E-DRS 20 sowie das Bilanzrechtsreformgesetz, in: Zeitschrift für internationale und kapitalmarktorientierte Rechnungslegung, Vol. 4, No. 2, 2004, pp. 51-60.

Grice, H. Paul (1975): Logic and Conversation, in: Cole, Peter/Morgan, Jerry L. (eds.), Syntax and Semantics 3: Speech Acts, New York, NY 1975, pp. 41-58. Reprinted in: Grice, H. Paul (ed.), Studies in the Way of Words, Cambridge, MA 1989, pp. 22-40.

Griffin, John M./Kelly, Patrick J./Nadari, Federico (2010): Do Market Efficiency Measures Yield Correct Inferences? A Comparison of Developed and Emerging Markets, in: The Review of Financial Studies, Vol. 23, No. 8, 2010, pp. 3225-3277.

Griffin, Paul A. (2003): Got Information? Investor Response to Form 10-K and Form 10-Q EDGAR Filings, in: Review of Accounting Studies, Vol. 8, No. 4, 2003, pp. 433-460.

Grigaliuniene, Zana (2013): Investor Sentiment, Overreaction and Underreaction in Stock Market, in: Studies in Modern Society, Vol. 4, No. 1, 2013, pp. 32-42.

Grochla, Erwin (1978): Einführung in die Organisationstheorie, Stuttgart, Germany 1978.

Grünberger, David (2015): IFRS 2016 – Ein systematischer Praxisleitfaden, 13th edition, Vienna, Austria 2015.

Güleş, Nicki (2014): Way ahead – South Africa's pioneering introduction of integrated reporting has had far-reaching consequences, in: Accounting and Business Magazine, Vol. 17, No. 3, 2014, pp. 26-28.

Gunning, Robert (1952): The Technique of Clear Writing, New York, NY 1952.

H

Haller, Axel/Zellner, Paul (2014): Integrated Reporting Framework – eine neue Basis für die Weiterentwicklung der Unternehmensberichterstattung, in: Der Betrieb, Vol. 67, No. 22, 2014, pp. 253-258.

Hao, Si (2014): Corporate Integrated Reporting in Canada: Are the Businesses Ready?, URL: http://papers.ssrn.com/sol3/papers.cfm?abstract_id=2531522 (29.08.2016).

Hartmann-Wendels, Thomas (1989): Principal-Agent-Theorie und asymmetrische Informationsverteilung, in: Zeitschrift für Betriebswirtschaft, Vol. 59, No. 7, 1989, pp. 714-734.

Hasnas, John (1998): The Normative Theories of Business Ethics: A Guide for the Perplexed, in: Business Ethics Quarterly, Vol. 8, No. 1, 1998, pp. 19-42.

Havlová, Kristýna (2015a): Integrated Reporting: New Trend from the Perspective of Czech Companies, URL: http://msed.vse.cz/msed_2015/article/130-Havlova-Kristyna-paper.pdf (29.08.2016).

Havlová, Kristýna (2015b): What Integrated Reporting Changed: The Case Study of Early Adopters, in: Procedia Economics and Finance, Vol. 34, 2015, pp. 31-237.

Healy, Paul M. (1985): The Effect of Bonus Schemes on Accounting Decisions, in: Journal of Accounting and Economics, Vol. 7, No. 1-3, 1985, pp. 85-107.

Healy, Paul M./Palepu, Krishna G. (2001): Information asymmetry, corporate disclosure, and the capital markets: a review of the empirical disclosure literature, in: Journal of Accounting and Economics, Vol. 31, No. 1, 2001, pp. 405-440.

Heard, James E./Bolce, William J. (1981): The Political Significance of Corporate Social Reporting in the United States of America, in: Accounting, Organizations and Society, Vol. 6 No. 3, 1981, pp. 247-254.

Hewitt, Max R. (2007): Using Cognitive Load Theory to Explain the Accrual Anomaly, Dissertation, University of Washington, URL: https://dlib.lib.washington.edu/dspace/bitstream/handle/1773/8810/3265347.pdf?sequence=1 (29.08.2016).

Higgins, Colin/Stubbs, Wendy/Love, Tyron (2014): Walking the talk(s): Organisational narratives of integrated reporting, in: Accounting, Auditing & Accountability Journal, Vol. 27, No. 7, 2014, pp. 1090-1119.

Hirji, Zahra (2013): Most U.S. Companies Ignoring SEC Rule to Disclose Climate Risks, URL: http://insideclimatenews.org/print/28024 (29.08.2016).

Hirshleifer, David A. (2001): Investor Psychology and Asset Pricing, in: The Journal of Finance, Vol. 56, No. 4, 2001, pp. 1533-1598.

Hirshleifer, David A./Lim, Sonya S./Teoh, Siew H. (2009): Driven to Distraction: Extraneous Events and Underreaction to Earnings News, in: The Journal of Finance, Vol. 64, No. 5, 2009, pp. 2289-2325.

Hirshleifer, David A./Teoh, Siew H./Yu Jeff J. (2011): Short Arbitrage, Return Asymmetry and the Accrual Anomaly, in: The Review of Financial Studies, Vol. 24, No. 7, 2011, pp. 2429-2461.

Hirst, D. Eric/Hopkins, Patrick E. (1998): Comprehensive Income Reporting and Analysts' Valuation Judgments, in: Journal of Accounting Research, Vol. 36, No. 3, 1998, pp. 47-75.

Hofstede, Geert (2001): Culture's Consequences – Comparing Values, Behaviors, Institutions, and Organizations Across Nations, 2nd edition, Thousand Oaks, CA 2001.

Holland, Alan (1994): Natural Capital, in: Royal Institute of Philosophy Supplements, Vol. 36, 1994, pp. 169-182.

Holsti, Ole R. (1969): Content Analysis for the Social Sciences and Humanities, Reading, MA 1969.

Holthausen, Robert W./Watts, Ross L. (2001): The Relevance of Value-Relevance Literature for Financial Accounting Standard Setting, in: Journal of Accounting and Economics, Vol. 31, No. 1-3, 2001, pp. 3-75.

Hong, Harrison/Lim, Terrence/Stein, Jeremy C. (2000): Bad News Travels Slowly: Size, Analyst Coverage, and the Profitability of Momentum Strategies, in: The Journal of Finance, Vol. 55, No. 1, 2000, pp. 265-295.

Hong, Harrison/Stein, Jeremy C. (1999): A Unified Theory of Underreaction, Momentum Trading and Overreaction in Asset Markets, in: The Journal of Finance, Vol. 54, No. 6, 1999, pp. 2143-2184.

Hope, Ole-Kristian/Thomas, Wayne B./Vyas, Dushyantkumar (2013): Financial Reporting Quality of U.S. Private and Public Firms, in: The Accounting Review, Vol. 88, No. 5, 2013, pp. 1715-1742.

Horn, Laurence R. (1984): Toward a New Taxonomy for Pragmatic Inference: Q-based and R-based Implicature, in: Schiffrin, Deborah (ed.), Meaning, Form and Use in Context, Washington, D.C. 1984, pp. 11-42.

Horsch, Andreas (2005): Agency und Versicherungsintermediation, in: Horsch, Andreas/Meinhövel, Harald/Paul, Stephan/Crasselt, Nils/Fülbier, Rolf U./Gassen, Joachim/Jansen, Harald (eds.), Institutionenökonomie und Betriebswirtschaftslehre, Munich, Germany 2005, pp. 81-99.

Hou, Kewei/Moskowitz, Tobias J. (2005): Market Frictions, Price Delay and the Cross-Section of Expected Returns, in: Review of Financial Studies, Vol. 18, No. 3, 2005, pp. 981-1020.

HRH The Prince of Wales (2009): A speech by HRH The Prince of Wales at the Accounting for Sustainability project seminar, St James's Palace, URL: http://www.princeofwales.gov.uk/media/speeches/speech-hrh-the-prince-of-wales-the-accounting-sustainability-project-seminar-st (29.08.2016).

Huang, Yan (2007): Pragmatics, Oxford, UK 2007.

Huddart, Steven/Ke, Bin/Shi, Charles (2007): Jeopardy, non-public information, and insider trading around SEC 10-K and 10-Q filings, in: Journal of Accounting and Economics, Vol. 43, No. 1, 2007, pp. 3-36.

Hüfner, Bernd (2007a): MD&A- und OFR-Berichtsregelungen der U.S.-amerikanischen SEC, in: Betriebswirtschaftliche Forschung und Praxis, Vol. 59, No. 3, 2007, pp. 289-310.

Hüfner, Bernd (2007b): The SEC's MD&A: Does It Meet the Informational Demands of Investors? – A Conceptual Evaluation, in: Schmalenbach Business Review, Vol. 59, No. 1, 2007, pp. 58-84.

Hung, Mingyi/Li, Xi/Wang, Shiheng (2015): Post-Earnings-Announcement Drift in Global Markets: Evidence from an Information Shock, in: The Review of Financial Studies, Vol. 28, No. 4, 2015, pp. 1242-1283.

Hütten, Christoph (2000): Der Geschäftsbericht als Informationsinstrument, Düsseldorf, Germany 2000.

I

Iannaconi, Teresa E./Rouse, Robert W. (1996): MD&A: When and How to Report Trends?, in: The Journal of Corporate Accounting and Finance, Vol. 8, No. 1, 1996, pp. 65-73.

IFRS Foundation/Securities and Exchange Commission (SEC) (2016): IFRS Application Around the World – Jurisdictional Profile: United States of America, URL: http://www.ifrs.org/Use-around-the-world/Documents/Jurisdiction-profiles/United-States-IFRS-Profile.pdf (29.08.2016).

imug Beratungsgesellschaft mbH (imug) (2015): "Mind the Gap" – Integrated Reporting zwischen Anspruch und Umsetzung – imug Best-Practice-Analyse, Hannover, Germany 2015.

Institut der Wirtschaftsprüfer in Deutschland e.V. (IDW) (2013): Comment letter on the Consultation Draft of the International Integrated Reporting Framework, URL: http://integratedreporting.org/wp-content/uploads/2013/08/024_IDW-Comment-Letter.pdf (29.08.2016).

Institute of Chartered Accountants in England and Wales (ICAEW) (2014): UK Narrative Reporting: New Regulations, URL: http://www.icaew.com/~/media/corporate/files/technical/financial%20reporting/financial%20reporting%20faculty/narrative%20reporting%20faqs.ashx (29.08.2016).

Integrated Reporting Committee of South Africa (IRCSA) (2011a): MEDIA RELEASE – King unveils world-first integrated reporting guidelines – JSE's 400 listed companies could replace traditional annual report with integrated report, URL: http://www.integratedreportingsa.org/Portals/0/IRC%20Media%20Release.doc (29.08.2016).

Integrated Reporting Committee of South Africa (IRCSA) (2011b): South Africa's world-first Integrated Reporting Discussion Paper attracts global attention – Paper to be re-issued to reflect public comments received and international developments, URL: http://www.integratedreportingsa.org/Portals/0/Documents/Media%20release_SA_world1st_IR_20July2011l.docx (29.08.2016).

Integrated Reporting Committee of South Africa (IRCSA) (2011c): South Africa's IRC welcomes the release of the international Discussion Paper on integrated reporting, URL:https://www.saica.co.za/DesktopModules/EngagePublish/printerfriendly.aspx?itemId=3128&PortalId=0&TabId=695 (29.08.2016).

Integrated Reporting Committee of South Africa (IRCSA) (2014): Preparing an Integrated Report – A Starter's Guide, URL: http://www.integratedreportingsa.org/Portals/0/Documents/IRCSA_StartersGuide.pdf (29.08.2016).

Integrated Reporting Committee of South Africa (IRCSA) (2015): The octopus model, URL: http://www.integratedreportingsa.org/Home/Theoctopusmodel.aspx (29.08.2016).

International Accounting Standards Board (IASB) (2016): IFRS – Conceptual Framework, URL: http://www.ifrs.org/Current-Projects/IASB-Projects/Conceptual-Framework/Pages/Conceptual-Framework-Summary.aspx (29.08.2016).

International Integrated Reporting Committee (IIRC) (2010a): Terms of Reference of the IIRC, URL: http://integratedreporting.org/wp-content/uploads/2011/03/IIRC-Terms-of-Reference-July-2010.pdf (29.08.2016).

International Integrated Reporting Committee (IIRC) (2010b): Press Release – Formation of the International Integrated Reporting Committee (IIRC), URL: http://www.theiirc.org/wp-content/uploads/2011/03/Press-Release1.pdf (29.08.2016).

International Integrated Reporting Committee (IIRC) (2011a): Integrated Reporting Pilot Programme, URL: http://integratedreporting.org/wp-content/uploads/2011/06/BriefingIntegratedReportingPilotProgramme.pdf (29.08.2016).

International Integrated Reporting Committee (IIRC) (2011b): The world has changed – reporting must too, IIRC Press Release 12.09.2011, URL: http://theiirc.org/wp-content/uploads/2011/09/IR-Discussion-Paper-Sep2011-press-release.pdf (29.08.2016).

International Integrated Reporting Committee (IIRC) (2011c): IIRC Appoint Mervyn King as Chairman to Lead Next Steps of Integrated Reporting Framework, URL: http://integratedreporting.org/wp-content/uploads/2011/10/IIRC-Chairman-press-release11oct.pdf (29.08.2016).

International Integrated Reporting Committee (IIRC) (2011d): The IIRC Announces Appointment of Paul Druckman as CEO, URL: http://integratedreporting.org/wp-content/uploads/2011/10/Paul-Druckman-19-October-2011.pdf (29.08.2016).

International Integrated Reporting Committee (IIRC) (2011e): IIRC Announces Selection of Global Companies to Lead Unique Integrated Reporting Pilot Programme, URL: http://integratedreporting.org/wp-content/uploads/2011/10/Pilot-programme-26boctober2011cmr.pdf (29.08.2016).

International Integrated Reporting Committee (IIRC) (2011f): IIRC enters new phase of activity, URL: http://integratedreporting.org/news/iirc-enters-ambitious-new-phase-of-activity/ (29.08.2016).

International Integrated Reporting Council (IIRC) (2012a): Towards Integrated Reporting – Communicating Value in the 21st Century – Summary of the Responses to the September 2011 Discussion Paper and Next Steps, URL: http://www.theiirc.org/wp-content/uploads/2012/06/Discussion-Paper-Summary1.pdf (29.08.2016).

International Integrated Reporting Council (IIRC) (2012b): International Integrated Reporting Framework on track for publication in 2013, confirms IIRC., URL: http://integratedreporting.org/news/international-integrated-reporting-framework-on-track-for-publication-in-2013-confirms-iirc/ (29.08.2016).

International Integrated Reporting Council (IIRC) (2012c): Capturing the experiences of global businesses and investors – The Pilot Programme 2012 Yearbook, URL: http://integratedreporting.org/wp-content/uploads/2012/10/THE-PILOT-PROGRAMME-2012-YEARBOOK.pdf (29.08.2016).

International Integrated Reporting Council (IIRC) (2013a): GRI and IIRC Deepen Cooperation to Shape the Future of Corporate Reporting, URL: http://integratedreporting.org/news/gri-and-iirc-deepen-cooperation-to-shape-the-future-of-corporate-reporting/ (29.08.2016).

International Integrated Reporting Council (IIRC) (2013b): Summary of Significant Issues – International <IR> Framework, URL: http://www.theiirc.org/wp-content/uploads/2013/12/13-12-08-Summary-of-significant-issues-IR.pdf (29.08.2016).

International Integrated Reporting Council (IIRC) (2013c): Business and Investors explore the sustainability perspective of Integrated Reporting – IIRC Pilot Programme Yearbook 2013, URL: http://integratedreporting.org/wp-content/uploads/2013/11/IIRC-PP-Yearbook-2013.pdf (29.08.2016).

International Integrated Reporting Council (IIRC) (2013d): IIRC Pilot Programme Investor Network, URL: http://integratedreporting.org/wp-content/uploads/2013/11/IIRC-Pilot-Programme-Investor-Network-backgrounder-October-2013.pdf (29.08.2016).

International Integrated Reporting Council (IIRC) (2014a): IIRC Pilot Programme Business Network, URL: http://integratedreporting.org/wp-content/uploads/2014/03/IIRC-Pilot-Programme-Business-Network-backgrounder-March-2014.pdf (29.08.2016).

International Integrated Reporting Council (IIRC) (2014b): Creating Value – Value to the board, URL: http://integratedreporting.org/wp-content/uploads/2015/04/Value-to-the-Board.pdf (29.08.2016).

International Integrated Reporting Council (IIRC) (2014c): Strategy: The Breakthrough Phase 2014-17, URL: http://integratedreporting.org/wp-content/uploads/2015/02/IIRC-Strategy-Summary-2015.pdf (29.08.2016).

International Integrated Reporting Council (IIRC) (2015a): Creating Value – Value to investors, URL: http://integratedreporting.org/wp-content/uploads/2015/04/Creating-Value-Investors.pdf (29.08.2016).

International Integrated Reporting Council (IIRC) (2015b): Assurance on <IR> – Overview of feedback and a call to action, URL: http://integratedreporting.org/wp-content/uploads/2015/07/IIRC-Assurance-Overview-July-2015.pdf (29.08.2016).

International Integrated Reporting Council (IIRC) (2015c): International Integrated Reporting Council Constitution, URL: http://integratedreporting.org/wp-content/uploads/2015/09/IIRC-CONSTITUTION-2015-SEPTEMBER.pdf (29.08.2016).

International Integrated Reporting Council (IIRC) (2015d): Creating Value – Integrated Reporting <IR> and Investor Benefits, URL: http://integratedreporting.org/wp-content/uploads/2016/01/1323_CreatingValue_No3_8a-1.pdf (29.08.2016).

International Integrated Reporting Council (IIRC)/American Institute of Certified Public Accountants (AICPA) (2013): Materiality – Background Paper for <IR>, URL: http://www.theiirc.org/wp-content/uploads/2013/03/IR-Background-Paper-Materiality.pdf (29.08.2016).

International Integrated Reporting Council (IIRC)/Association of Chartered Certified Accountants (ACCA)/Netherlands Institute of Chartered Accountants (NBA) (2013) (IIRC et al. (2013b)): Capitals – Background Paper for <IR>, URL: http://www.theiirc.org/wp-content/uploads/2013/03/IR-Background-Paper-Capitals.pdf (29.08.2016).

International Integrated Reporting Council (IIRC)/Chartered Institute of Management Accountants (CIMA)/International Foundation of Accountants (IFAC)/PricewaterhouseCoopers (PwC) (2013) (IIRC et al. (2013a)): Business Model – Background Paper for <IR>, URL: http://www.theiirc.org/wp-content/uploads/2013/03/Business_Model.pdf (29.08.2016).

International Integrated Reporting Council (IIRC)/EY (2013): Value Creation – Background Paper for <IR>, URL: http://www.theiirc.org/wp-content/uploads/2013/07/IR-Background-Paper-Value.pdf (29.08.2016).

International Integrated Reporting Council (IIRC)/Global Reporting Initiative (GRI) (2013): Memorandum of understanding, URL: http://www.theiirc.org/wp-content/uploads/2013/02/MoU-IIRC-GRI-20130201-1.pdf (29.08.2016).

International Integrated Reporting Council (IIRC)/IFRS Foundation (2013): Memorandum of Understanding, URL: http://www.theiirc.org/wp-content/uploads/2013/02/MoU-IIRC-IFRS-FOUNDATION-20130204.pdf (29.08.2016).

International Integrated Reporting Council (IIRC)/International Federation of Accountants (IFAC) (2015): Materiality in <IR> – Guidance for the preparation of integrated reports, URL: http://integratedreporting.org/wp-content/uploads/2015/11/1315_MaterialityinIR_Doc_4a_Interactive.pdf (29.08.2016).

International Integrated Reporting Council (IIRC)/The Sustainability Accounting Standards Board (SASB) (2013): Memorandum of Understanding, URL: http://www.theiirc.org/wp-content/uploads/2014/01/MoU-IIRC-SASB-Final.pdf (29.08.2016).

International Integrated Reporting Council (IIRC)/World Intellectual Capital Initiative (WICI) (2013): Connectivity – Background Paper for <IR>, URL: http://www.theiirc.org/wp-content/uploads/2013/07/IR-Background-Paper-Connectivity.pdf (29.08.2016).

International Monetary Fund (IMF) (2015): World Economic Outlook – Adjusting to Lower Commodity Prices – October 2015, URL: http://www.imf.org/external/pubs/ft/weo/2015/02/pdf/text.pdf (29.08.2016).

Investor Responsibility Research Center Institute (IRRCI)/Sustainable Investments Institute (Si2) (2013): Integrated Financial and Sustainability Reporting in the United States, URL: http://irrcinstitute.org/wp-content/uploads/2015/09/FINAL_Integrated_Financial_Sustain_Reporting_April_20131.pdf (29.08.2016).

Iselin, Errol R. (1988): The Effects of Information Load and Information Diversity on Decision Quality in a Structured Decision Task, in: Accounting, Organizations and Society, Vol. 13, No. 2, 1988, pp. 147-164.

J

Jackson, Gregory (2010): Understanding Corporate Governance in the United States – An Historical and Theoretical Reassessment, URL: http://www.boeckler.de/pdf/p_arbp_223.pdf (29.08.2016).

Jamerson, Louis (2004): South African Labor and Government: Compromise or Conflict?, in: Social Policy, Vol. 35, No. 1, 2004, pp. 41-43.

Jegadeesh, Narasimhan/Titman, Sheridan (1993): Returns to Buying Winners and Selling Losers: Implications for Stock Market Efficiency, in: The Journal of Finance, Vol. 48, No. 1, 1993, pp. 65-91.

Jensen, Julia C./Berg, Nicola (2012): Determinants of Traditional Sustainability Reporting Versus Integrated Reporting. An Institutionalist Approach, in: Business Strategy and the Environment, Vol. 21, No. 5, 2012, pp. 299-316.

Jensen, Michael C./Meckling, William H. (1976): Theory of the Firm, in: Journal of Financial Economics, Vol. 3, No. 4, 1976, pp. 305-360.

Johannesburg Stock Exchange (JSE) (n.d.a): Listing on AltX, URL: https://www.jse.co.za/capital/altx (29.08.2016).

Johannesburg Stock Exchange (JSE) (n.d.b): Equity Market, URL: https://www.jse.co.za/trade/equity-market (29.08.2016).

Johannesburg Stock Exchange (JSE) (n.d.c): Main Board, URL: https://www.jse.co.za/capital/main-board (29.08.2016).

Johnen, Jürgen/Ganske, Torsten (2002): Management's Discussion and Analysis (MD&A), in: Ballwieser, Wolfgang/Coenenberg, Adolf G./Von Wysocki, Klaus (eds.), Handwörterbuch der Rechnungslegung und Prüfung, 3rd edition, Stuttgart 2002, columns 1520-1536.

Joiner, Therese A./Leveson, Lynne/Langfield-Smith, Kim (2002): Technical Language, Advice Understandability, and Perceptions of Expertise and Trustworthiness: The Case of the Financial Planner, in: Australian Journal of Management, Vol. 27, No. 1, 2002, pp. 25-43.

Jones, Michael J. (1988): Annual Corporate Reports: A waste of time and money?, in: Management Accounting, Vol. 66, No. 2, 1988, pp. 40-41.

Jones, Michael J./Shoemaker, Paul A. (1994): Accounting Narratives: A Review of Empirical Studies of Content and Readability, in: Journal of Accounting Literature, Vol. 13, 1994, pp. 142-184.

Jung, Jay H./Kang, Jun-Koo/Lim, Sonya S./Yoo, Choong-Yuel (2016): Firm Trustworthiness and Investor Underreaction to Earnings News, URL: http://papers.ssrn.com/sol3/papers.cfm?abstract_id=2544247 (29.08.2016).

K

Kajüter, Peter (2013): Aktuelle Entwicklungen in der Unternehmensberichterstattung – Konzernlagebericht nach DRS 20 – Management Commentary – Integrated Reporting, in: Freidank, Carl-Christian/Velte, Patrick (eds.), Unternehmenssteuerung im Umbruch – Internationale Reformen in Reporting und Corporate Governance, Berlin 2013, pp. 119-153.

Kajüter, Peter (2014a): Das Rahmenkonzept des IIRC zum Integrated Reporting – Revolution in der Unternehmensberichterstattung?, in: Deutsches Steuerrecht, Vol. 52, No. 5, 2014, pp. 222-226.

Kajüter, Peter (2014b): Nachhaltigkeitsberichterstattung nach den G4-Leitlinien der GRI, in: Die Wirtschaftsprüfung, Vol. 67, No. 12, 2014, pp. 599-607.

Kajüter, Peter/Bachert, Kristian/Blaesing, Daniel/Kleimanns, Herrmann (2010): Die DRS zur Lageberichterstattung auf dem Prüfstand – Empirische Befunde zur Beurteilung und Anwendungspraxis der DRS, in: Der Betrieb, Vol. 63, No. 9, 2010, pp. 457-465.

Kajüter, Peter/Blaesing, Daniel/Hannen, Stefan (2013a): "Connectivity of information" as a key principle of integrated reporting, in: Zeitschrift für Internationale Rechnungslegung, Vol. 8, No. 5, 2013, pp. 199-205.

Kajüter, Peter/Blaesing, Daniel/Hannen, Stefan (2013b): Der Consultation Draft des IIRC zum Integrated Reporting – Kritische Würdigung und Implikationen für die Praxis, in: Deutsches Steuerrecht, Vol. 51, No. 32, 2013, pp. 1680-1687.

Kajüter, Peter/Hannen, Stefan (2014): Integrated Reporting nach dem Rahmenkonzept des IIRC – Anforderungen, Anwendung und offene Fragen, in: Zeitschrift für internationale und kapitalmarktorientierte Rechnungslegung, Vol. 14, No. 2, 2014, pp. 75-81.

Kaplan, Robert S./Norton, David P. (1992): The Balanced Scorecard – Measures That Drive Performance, in: Harvard Business Review, Vol. 70, No. 1, 1992, pp. 71-79.

Kassarjian, Harold H. (1977): Content Analysis in Consumer Research, in: The Journal of Consumer Research, Vol. 4, No. 1, 1977, pp. 8-18.

Kenny, David A. (1979): Correlation and Causality, New York, NY 1979.

Kessler, Harald (2005): Ist der Fair Value fair?, in: Bieg, Hartmut/Heyd, Reinhard (eds.), Fair Value – Bewertung in Rechnungswesen, Controlling und Finanzwirtschaft, Munich, Germany 2005, pp. 57-81.

Keusch, Thomas/Bollen, Laury H. H./Hassink, Harold F. D. (2012): Self-serving Bias in Annual Report Narratives: An Empirical Analysis of the Impact of Economic Crises, in: European Accounting Review, Vol. 21, No. 3, 2012, pp. 623-648.

Kincaid, John P./Fishburne Jr., Robert P./Rogers, Richard L./Chissom, Brad S. (1975): Derivation of New Readability Formulas (Automated Readability Index, Fog Count and Flesch Reading Ease Formula) for Navy Enlisted Personnel, Research Branch Report 8-75, Millington, TN 1975.

King, Mervyn E. (2009): A speech by Professor Mervyn King at The Prince's Accounting for Sustainability Forum seminar, St James's Palace – 17th December 2009, URL: http://www.accountingforsustainability.org/wp-content/uploads/2011/10/Professor-Mervyn-King-17th-December-2009.pdf (29.08.2016).

King, Mervyn E./Roberts, Leigh (2013): Integrate: Doing Business in the 21st Century, Claremont, South Africa 2013.

Kirsch, Hans-Jürgen/Koelen, Peter/Olbrich, Alexander/Dettenrieder, Dominik (2012): Die Bedeutung der Verlässlichkeit der Berichterstattung im Conceptual Framework des IASB und des FASB, in: Die Wirtschaftsprüfung, Vol. 65, No. 14, 2012, pp. 762-771.

Kohut, Gary F./Segars, Albert H. (1992): The President's Letter to Stockholders: An Examination of Corporate Communication Strategy, in: The Journal of Business Communication, Vol. 29, No. 1, 1992, pp. 7-21.

Kornmeier, Martin (2007): Wissenschaftstheorie und wissenschaftliches Arbeiten – Eine Einführung für Wirtschaftswissenschaftler, Heidelberg, Germany 2007.

KPMG (2011): Disclosure Overload and Complexity: Hidden in Plain Sight, URL: http://www.kpmg.com/US/en/IssuesAndInsights/ArticlesPublications/Documents/disclosure-overload-complexity.pdf (29.08.2016).

KPMG (2013): The KPMG Survey of Corporate Responsibility Reporting 2013, URL: http://www.kpmg.com/Global/en/IssuesAndInsights/ArticlesPublications/corporate-responsibility/Documents/corporate-responsibility-reporting-survey-2013.pdf (29.08.2016).

KPMG (2014): The KPMG survey of business reporting – Better Business Reporting, URL: https://www.kpmg.com/IM/en/IssuesAndInsights/ArticlesPublications/Documents/kpmg-survey-business-reporting.pdf (29.08.2016).

KPMG (2015a): Survey of Integrated Reports in Japan 2014, URL: http://www.kpmg.com/jp/ja/knowledge/article/integrated-reporting-article/documents/integrated-reporting-20150628e.pdf (29.08.2016).

KPMG (2015b): Currents of change – The KPMG Survey of Corporate Responsibility Reporting 2015, URL: http://www.kpmg.com/CN/en/IssuesAndInsights/ArticlesPublications/Documents/kpmg-survey-of-corporate-responsibility-reporting-2015-O-201511.pdf (29.08.2016).

Kromrey, Helmut (2016): Empirische Sozialforschung – Modelle und Methoden der standardisierten Datenerhebung und Datenauswertung mit Annotationen aus qualitativ-interpretativer Perspektive, 13th edition, Konstanz and Munich, Germany 2016.

Krüger, Louis P. (2011): The impact of black economic empowerment (BEE) on South African businesses: Focusing on ten dimensions of business performance, in: Southern African Business Review, Vol. 15, No. 3, 2011, pp. 207-233.

Küpper, Hans-Ulrich/Friedl, Gunther/Hofmann, Christian/Hofmann, Yvette/Pedell, Burkhard (2013): Controlling – Konzeption, Aufgaben, Instrumente, 6th edition, Stuttgart, Germany 2013.

L

Lachnit, Laurenz/Müller, Stefan (2015): Integrated Reporting als Objekt der externen Informationsanalyse, in: Freidank, Carl-Christian/Müller, Stefan/Velte, Patrick (eds.), Handbuch Integrated Reporting, Berlin, Germany 2015, pp. 539-560.

Lai, Alessandro/Melloni, Gaia/Stacchezzini, Riccardo (2016): Corporate Sustainable Development – is 'Integrated Reporting' a Legitimation Strategy?, in: Business Strategy and the Environment, Vol. 25, No. 3, 2016, pp. 165-177.

Lambert, Richard A./Leuz, Christian/Verrecchia, Robert E. (2012): Information Asymmetry, Information Precision, and the Cost of Capital, in: Review of Finance, Vol. 16, No. 1, 2012, pp. 1-29.

Larrinaga-González, Carlos (2007): Sustainability reporting – Insights from neoinstitutional theory, in: Unerman, Jeffrey/Bebbington, Jan/O'Dwyer, Brendan (eds.), Sustainability Accounting and Accountability, Abingdon, UK 2007, pp. 150-167.

Larsen, Heine T./Bukh, Per N. D./Mouritsen, Jan (1999): Intellectual Capital Statements and Knowledge Management: "Measuring", "Reporting", "Acting", in: Australian Accounting Review, Vol. 9, No. 3, 1999, pp. 15-26.

Latané, Henry A./Jones, Charles P. (1977): Standardized Unexpected Earnings – A Progress Report, in: The Journal of Finance, Vol. 32, No. 5, 1977, pp. 1457-1465.

Lawrence, Alastair (2013): Individual Investors and Financial Disclosure, in: Journal of Accounting & Economics, Vol. 56, No. 1, 2013, pp. 130-147.

Lee, Kin-Wai/Yeo, Gillian H.-H. (2016): The association between integrated reporting and firm valuation, in: Review of Quantitative Finance and Accounting, forthcoming.

Lee, Yen-Jung (2012): The Effect of Quarterly Report Readability on Information Efficiency of Stock Price, in: Contemporary Accounting Research, Vol. 29, No. 4, 2012, pp. 1137-1170.

Lehavy, Reuven/Li, Feng/Merkley, Kenneth (2011): The Effect of Annual Report Readability on Analyst Following and the Properties of Their Earnings Forecasts, in: The Accounting Review, Vol. 86, No. 3, 2011, pp. 1087-1115.

Lerman, Alina/Livnat, Joshua/Mendenhall, Richard R. (2007): Double Surprise into Higher Future Returns, in: Financial Analysts Journal, Vol. 63, No. 4, 2007, pp. 63-71.

Leuz, Christian/Wysocki, Peter D. (2015): Economic Consequences of Financial Reporting and Disclosure Regulation: A Review and Suggestions for Future Research, URL: http://research.chicagobooth.edu/~/media/7628D551E7424DC08524879103870C12.pdf (29.08.2016).

Levy, Yehuda J. (2015): Limits to rational learning, in: Journal of Economic Theory, Vol. 160, 2015, pp. 1-23.

Li, Feng (2008): Annual report readability, current earning, and earnings persistence, in: Journal of Accounting and Economics, Vol. 45, No. 2-3, 2008, pp. 221-247.

Lingnau, Volker (1995): Kritischer Rationalismus und Betriebswirtschaftslehre, in: Wirtschaftswissenschaftliches Studium, Vol. 24, No. 3, 1995, pp. 124-129.

Linsley, Philip/Shrives, Philip/Kajüter, Peter (2008): Risk Reporting: Development, Regulation and Current Practice, in: Woods, Margaret/Kajüter, Peter/Linsley, Philip (eds.), International Risk Management. Systems, Internal Control and Corporate Governance, Oxford, UK 2008, pp. 185-207.

Lipunga, Andrew M. (2015): Integrated Reporting in Developing Countries – Evidence from Malawi, in: Journal of Management Research, Vol. 7, No. 3, 2015, pp. 130-156.

Litsoukov, Nikita (2015): BaFin and the SEC: An international comparison of supervisory practice, URL: https://www.bafin.de/SharedDocs/Veroeffentlichungen/EN/Fachartikel/2015/fa_bj_1510_bafin_und_sec_en.html?nn=7858612#doc7874308bodyText1 (29.08.2016).

Lorenzen, Paul (1974): Konstruktive Wissenschaftstheorie, Frankfurt am Main, Germany 1974.

Loughran, Timothy J./McDonald, Bill D. (2014): Measuring Readability in Financial Disclosure, in: Journal of Finance, Vol. 69, No. 4, 2014, pp. 1643-1671.

Lubbe, Ilse/Modack, Goolam/Watson, Alex (2014): Financial Accounting IFRS Principles, 4th edition, Cape Town, South Africa 2014.

Lydenberg, Steve/Rogers, Jean/Wood, David (2010): From Transparency to Performance – Industry-Based Sustainability Reporting on Key Issues, URL: http://www.sasb.org/wp-content/uploads/2012/03/IRI_Transparency-to-Performance.pdf (29.08.2016).

M

MacKinlay, A. Craig (1997): Event Studies in Economics and Finance, in: Journal of Economic Literature, Vol. 35, No. 1, 1997, pp. 13-39.

Madura, Jeff/Richie, Nivine (2004): Overreaction to Exchange-Traded Funds During the Bubble of 1998-2002, in: The Journal of Behavioral Finance, Vol. 5, No. 2, 2004, pp. 91-104.

Makiwane, Theophilus S./Padia, Nirupa (2013): Evaluation of Corporate Integrated Reporting in South Africa Post King III Release South Africa – An Exploratory Enquiry, in: Journal of Economic and Financial Sciences, Vol. 6, No. 2, 2013, pp. 421-438.

Malley, Alex (2014): Integrated reporting – tackling the director liability challenge, URL: https://intheblack.com/articles/2014/10/23/integrated-reporting-tackling-the-director-liability-challenge (29.08.2016).

Magretta, Joan (2002): Why Business Models Matter, in: Harvard Business Review, Vol. 80, No. 5, 2002, pp. 86-92.

Mammatt, Jayne (2009): Integrated Sustainability Reporting and Assurance, URL: http://www.chartsec.co.za/documents/speakerPres/JayneMammat/MammattIntegratedSustainabilityReportingandAssurance.pdf (29.08.2016).

Mangel, Marc/Samaniego, Francisco J. (1984): Abraham Wald's Work on Aircraft Survivability, in: Journal of the American Statistical Association, Vol. 79, No. 386, 1984, pp. 259-.267.

Maniora, Janine (2013a): Integrated Reporting – Vom Diskussionspapier zum Konsultationsentwurf des IIRC, in: Zeitschrift für internationale und kapitalmarktorientierte Rechnungslegung, Vol. 13, No. 7-8, 2013, pp. 360-369.

Maniora, Janine (2013b): Der GRI G4 Standard – Synergie oder Antagonismus zum IIRC-Rahmenwerk?, in: Zeitschrift für internationale und kapitalmarktorientierte Rechnungslegung, Vol. 13, No. 10, 2013, pp. 479-489.

Marston, Claire L./Shrives, Philip J. (1991): The Use of Disclosure Indices in Accounting Research: A Review Article, in: British Accounting Review, Vol. 23, No. 3, 1991, pp. 195-210.

Martinez, Carlos R. (2016): Does the level of alignment with the Integrated Reporting framework reduce information asymmetry?, URL: http://papers.ssrn.com/sol3/papers.cfm?abstract_id=2684784 (29.08.2016).

Marx, Ben/Mohammadali-Haji, Ahmed (2014): Emerging Trends in Reporting: An Analysis of Integrated Reporting Practices by South African Top 40 Listed Companies, in: Journal of Economic and Financial Sciences, Vol. 7, No. 1, 2014, pp. 231-250.

Maury, Benjamin/Pajuste, Anete (2005): Multiple large shareholders and firm value, in: Journal of Banking & Finance, Vol. 29, No. 7, 2005, pp. 1813-1834.

Maxwell, Scott E./Delaney, Harold D. (1993): Bivariate Median Splits and Spurious Statistical Significance, in: Psychological Bulletin, Vol. 113, No. 1, 1993, pp. 181-190.

McEwen, Ruth A./Hunton, James E. (1999): Is Analyst Forecast Accuracy Associated with Accounting Information Use?, in: Accounting Horizons, Vol. 13, No. 1, 1999, pp. 1-16.

McWilliams, Abagail/Siegel, Donald (1997): Event Studies in Management Research: Theoretical and Empirical Issues, in: The Academy of Management Journal, Vol. 40, No. 3, 1997, pp. 626-657.

Melloni, Gaia (2015): Intellectual capital disclosure in integrated reporting: an impression management analysis, in: Journal of Intellectual Capital, Vol. 16, No. 3, 2015, pp. 661-680.

Melloni, Gaia/Stracchezzini, Riccardo/Lai, Alessandro (2016a): The tone of business model disclosure: an impression management analysis of the integrated reports, in: Journal of Management & Governance, Vol. 20, No. 2, 2016, pp. 295-320.

Melloni, Gaia/Caglio, Ariela/Perego, Paolo (2016b): Saying more with less? Disclosure conciseness and completness in Integrated Reports. Paper presented at the 39th European Accounting Association Annual Congress 2016, 11-13 May 2016, Maastricht, Netherlands, URL: http://www.eaacongress.org/r/home (17.05.2016).

Merschdorf, Martin (2012): Der Management Approach in der IFRS-Rechnungslegung – Implikationen für Unternehmen und Investoren, Frankfurt am Main, Germany 2012.

Mervelskemper, Laura/Streit, Daniel (2016): Enhancing market valuation of ESG performance: is integrated reporting keeping its promise?, URL: http://papers.ssrn.com/sol3/papers.cfm?abstract_id=2625044&rec=1&srcabs=2583283&alg=1&pos=6 (29.08.2016).

Meyer, John W./Rowan, Brian (1977): Institutionalized Organizations: Formal Structure as Myth and Ceremony, in: The American Journal of Sociology, Vol. 83, No. 2, 1977, pp. 340-363.

Miller, Brian P. (2010): The Effects of Reporting Complexity on Small and Large Investor Trading, in: The Accounting Review, Vol. 85, No. 6, 2010, pp. 2107-2143.

Miller, George A. (1956): The Magical Number Seven, Plus or Minus Two: Some Limits on Our Capacity for Processing Information, in: The Psychological Review, Vol. 63, No. 2, 1956, pp. 81-97.

Miller, Paul B. W./Robertson, Jack (1989): A guide to SEC regulations and publications: Mastering the maze, in: Research in accounting regulation, Vol. 3, 1989, pp. 239-249.

Minney, Tom (2010): "South Africa is best regulated securities exchanges in the world" WEF Competiveness Report, URL: http://www.africancapitalmarketsnews.com/597/%e2%80%9csouth-africa-is-best-regulated-securities-exchanges-in-the-world%e2%80%9d-wef-competiveness-report/ (29.08.2016).

Mio, Chiara/Fasan, Marco (2014): The determinants of materiality disclosure in integrated corporate reporting, URL: http://virgo.unive.it/wpideas/storage/2014wp9.pdf (29.08.2016).

Mitchell, Mark L./Stafford, Erik (2000): Managerial Decision and Long-Term Stock Price Performance, in: The Journal of Business, Vol. 73, No. 3, 2000, pp. 287-329.

Mlonzi, V. F./Kruger, Jan/Nthoesane, Meya G. (2011): Share price reaction to earnings announcement on the JSE-AltX: A test for market efficiency, in: Southern African Business Review Vol. 15, No. 3, 2011, pp. 142-166.

Moehrle, Stephen/Reynolds-Moehrle, Jennifer (2011): United States, in: Previts, Gary J./Walton, Peter/Wolnizer, Peter (eds.), A Global History of Accounting, Financial Reporting and Public Policy: Americas, Bingley, UK 2011, pp. 105-144.

Mook, Laurie (2006): Integrating and Reporting an Organisation's Economic, Social and Environmental Performance, in: Schaltegger, Stefan/Bennett, Martin/Burrit, Roger (eds.), Sustainability Accounting and Reporting, Dordrecht, The Netherlands 2006, pp. 281-298.

Morgan Stanley Capital International Inc. (MSCI) (2014): Global Industry Classification Standard (GICS) – Factsheet, URL: https://www.msci.com/resources/factsheets/MSCI_Global_Industry_Classification_Standard.pdf (29.08.2016).

Moxter, Adolf (1976): Fundamentalgrundsätze ordnungsmäßiger Rechenschaft, in: Baetge, Jörg/Moxter, Adolf/Schneider, Dieter (eds.), Bilanzfragen. Festschrift zum 65. Geburtstag von Prof. Dr. Ulrich Leffson, Düsseldorf, Germany 1976.

Müller, Stefan/Stawinoga, Martin (2013): Integrierte Berichterstattung: Aufstellung und Prüfung eines integrierten Berichts vor dem Hintergrund aktueller Verlautbarungen des IIRC, in: Zeitschrift für internationale und kapitalmarktorientierte Rechnungslegung, Vol. 13, No. 6, 2013, pp. 303-309.

Müller, Stefan/Stawinoga, Martin (2014): Das erste offizielle Rahmenwerk für das Berichterstattungskonzept des Integrated Reporting, in: Zeitschrift für Corporate Governance, Vol. 9, No. 1, 2014, pp. 39-44.

Müller, Stefan/Stawinoga, Martin (2015): Entwicklungslinien des Integrated Reporting, in: Freidank, Carl-Christian/Müller, Stefan/Velte, Patrick (eds.), Handbuch Integrated Reporting, Berlin, Germany 2015, pp. 3-28.

Müller, Tobias/Wachira, Mumbi/Berndt, Thomas (2016): Alignment and Uniqueness of Integrated Reporting: A Cross Country Analysis. Paper presented at the 39th European Accounting Association Annual Congress 2016, 11-13 May 2016, Maastricht, Netherlands, URL: http://www.eaacongress.org/r/home (29.08.2016).

Muslu, Volkan/Radhakrishnan, Suresh/Subramanyam, K. R./Lim, Dongkuk (2015): Forward-Looking MD&A Disclosures and the Information Environment, in: Management Science, Vol. 61, No. 5, 2015, pp. 931-948.

Muth, John F. (1961): Rational Expectations and the Theory of Price Movements, in: Econometrica, Vol. 29, No. 3, 1961, pp. 315-335.

N

Nair, Raghavan D./Rittenberg, Larry E. (1990): Summary Annual Reports: Background and Implications for Financial Reporting and Auditing, in: Accounting Horizons, Vol. 4, No. 1, 1990, pp. 25-38.

Näsi, Juha/Näsi, Salme/Phillips, Nelson/Zyglidopoulos, Stelios (1997): The Evolution of Corporate Social Responsiveness – An Exploratory Study of Finnish and Canadian Forestry Companies, in: Business & Society, Vol. 36, No. 3, 1997, pp. 296-321.

Nelson, Karen K./Pritchard, Adam C. (2007): Litigation Risk and Voluntary Disclosure: The Use of Meaningful Cautionary Language, URL: http://papers.ssrn.com/sol3/papers.cfm?abstract_id=998590&download=yes (29.08.2016).

Nelson, Karen K./Pritchard, Adam C. (2016): Carrot or Stick? The Shift from Voluntary to Mandatory Disclosure of Risk Factors, in: Journal of Empirical Legal Studies, Vol. 13, No. 2, 2016, pp. 266-297.

Newey, Whitney K./West, Kenneth D. (1987): A Simple, Positive Semi-Definite, Heteroskedasticity and Autocorrelation Consistent Covariance Matrix, in: Econometrica, Vol. 55, No. 3, 1987, pp. 703-708.

Nienhaus, Martin (2015): Segment Reporting under IFRS 8 – Reporting Practice and Economic Consequences, Frankfurt am Main, Germany 2015.

Nkonki Inc. (2011): South African Insights Into Integrated Reporting – An analysis of the Top 40 and SRI companies listed in the JSE – 2010, URL: http://www.nkonki.com/images/integrated-reporting/Top_100_JSE_Listed/2011/South%20African%20Insights%20Into%20Integrated%20Reporting.pdf (29.08.2016).

Nkonki Inc. (2012): Insights into Top 100 Integrated Reporting Trends – An analysis of the Integrated Reporting of the JSE top 100 and SRI companies covering year ends between December 2010 and November 2011, URL: http://www.nkonki.com/images/integrated-reporting/Top_100_JSE_Listed/2012/FM%20Nkonki%20Top%20100%20Integrated%20Reporting%20Awards%2016%20Nov%202012.pdf (29.08.2016).

Nkonki Inc. (2013): Insights into Top 100 Integrated Reporting Trends – An analysis of the Top 100 JSE Listed Companies and those listed on the SRI, URL: http://www.nkonki.com/images/integrated-reporting/Top_100_JSE_Listed/2013/Insights%20into%20Top%20100%20Intergrated%20Reporting%20Trends%20-%202013.pdf (29.08.2016).

Nkonki Inc. (2014): Insights into Top 100 Integrated Reporting Trends – An analysis of the Top 100 JSE Listed Companies and those listed on the SRI, URL: http://www.nkonki.com/images/integrated-reporting/Top_100_JSE_Listed/2013/Exxaro%20Wins%20Nkonki%20Top%20100%20Integrated%20Reporting%20Awards.pdf (29.08.2016).

Nkonki Inc. (2015): Insights into the Top 100 JSE Listed Companies – Integrated Reporting Trends, URL: http://www.nkonki.com/images/insights/jse-listed-companies/151003_JSE_Nkonki_Top_100_report_email_version.pdf (29.08.2016).

Nobes, Christopher W./Parker, Robert (2012): Comparative International Accounting, 12th edition, Harlow, UK 2012.

Nolden, Peter/Richter, Nicole (2012): Schließt Integrated Reporting die Erwartungslücken der herkömmlichen Unternehmensberichterstattung und -prüfung? – Vorschläge des IIRC zur Weiterentwicklung der Unternehmensberichterstattung, in: Die Wirtschaftsprüfung, Vol. 65, No. 18, 2012, pp. 978-987.

O

Oberholster, Johan. I. (1999): Financial Accounting and Reporting in Developing Countries: A South African Perspective, in: South African Journal of Economic and Management Sciences, Vol. 2, No. 2, 1999, pp. 222-239.

Ocean Tomo (2010): Ocean Tomo's Intangible Asset Market Value Study, URL: http://www.oceantomo.com/2013/12/09/Intangible-Asset-Market-Value-Study-Release/ (29.08.2016).

O'Donovan, Gary (2002): Environmental disclosures in the annual report, in: Accounting, Auditing & Accountability Journal, Vol. 15, No. 3, 2002, pp. 344-371.

O'Dwyer, Brendan (2005): Stakeholder democracy: challenges and contributions from social accounting, in: Business Ethics: A European Review, Vol. 14, No. 1, 2005, pp. 28-41.

Oprisor, Tudor (2015): Auditing Integrated Reports: Are There Solutions to This Puzzle?, in: Procedia Economics and Finance, Vol. 25, Special Issue: 16th Annual Conference on Finance and Accounting, ACFA Prague 2015, 29th May 2015, 2015, pp. 87-95.

Orton-Jones, Charles (2015): Progress Report, in: CIMA Financial Management, Vol. 44, No. 2, 2015, pp. 36-38.

Ott, Christian (2016): Investors' Perceptions of Integrated Reporting, Paper presented at the 39th European Accounting Association Annual Congress 2016, 11-13 May 2016, Maastricht, Netherlands, URL: http://www.eaacongress.org/r/home (29.08.2016).

P

Panzer, Lena/Ergün, Ismail (2015): Integrated Reporting in der (inter-)nationalen Forschung, in: Freidank, Carl-Christian/Müller, Stefan/Velte, Patrick (eds.), Handbuch Integrated Reporting, Berlin, Germany 2015, pp. 517-538.

Pearce, David W./Markandya, Anil/Barbier, Edward (1989): Blueprint for a Green Economy, London, UK 1989.

Peñarrubia Fraguas, Susana (2015): Bedeutung der integrierten Berichterstattung für Finanzanlageentscheidungen, in: Freidank, Carl-Christian/Müller, Stefan/Velte, Patrick (eds.), Handbuch Integrated Reporting, Berlin, Germany 2015, pp. 591-622.

Penrose, John M. (2008): Annual Report Graphic Use, in: Journal of Business Communication, Vol. 45, No. 2, 2008, pp. 158-180.

Petersen, Karl/Bansbach, Florian/Dornbach, Eike (eds.) (2016): IFRS Praxishandbuch – Ein Leitfaden für die Rechnungslegung mit Fallbeispielen, 11th edition, Munich, Germany 2016.

Petty, Richard/Guthrie, James (2000): Intellectual capital literature review – Measurement, reporting and management, in: Journal of Intellectual Capital, Vol. 1, No. 2, 2000, pp. 155-176.

Pfaff, Dieter/Zweifel, Peter (1998): Die Principal-Agent Theorie – Ein fruchtbarer Beitrag der Wirtschaftstheorie zur Praxis, in: Wirtschaftswissenschaftliches Studium, Vol. 27, No. 4, 1998, pp. 184-190.

Phillips, Kevin (2013): An Apple-Pie-Issue, in: Accountancy SA, December 2013/ January 2014, p. 18.

Phillips, Thomas J./Daily, Cynthia M./Luehlfing, Michael S. (2007): A Note on the Readability of Professional Materials for Management Accountants, in: Advances in Management Accounting, Vol. 16, 2007, pp. 311-318.

Picot, Arnold (1991): Ökonomische Theorien der Organisation – Ein Überblick über neuere Ansätze und deren betriebswirtschaftliches Anwendungspotential, in: Ordelheide, Dieter/Rudolph, Bernd/Büsselmann, Elke (eds.), Betriebswirtschaftslehre und Ökonomische Theorie, Stuttgart, Germany 1991, pp. 143-170.

Pincus, Morton/Rajgopal, Shivaram/Venkatachalam, Mohan (2007): The Accrual Anomaly: International Evidence, in: The Accounting Review, Vol. 82, No. 1, 2007, pp. 169-203.

Popper, Karl R. (1934): Logik der Forschung – Zur Erkenntnistheorie der modernen Naturwissenschaft, 1st edition, Vienna, Austria 1934.

Popper, Karl R. (2005): Logik der Forschung, 11th edition, Tübingen, Germany 2005.

Porter, Michael E. (1979): How competitive forces shape strategy, in: Harvard Business Review, Vol. 57, No. 2, 1979, pp. 137-145.

Pozzoli, Matteo/Gesuele, Benedetta (2016): The Quality of Integrated Reporting in The Public Utilities Sector: First Empirical Impressions, in: International Journal of Business Research and Development, Vol. 5, No. 1, 2016, pp. 23-31.

Previts, Gary J./Merino, Barbara D. (1998): A History of Accountancy in the United States – The Cultural Significance of Accounting, Columbus, OH 1998.

PricewaterhouseCoopers (PwC) (2012a): El reporting integrado en las empresas del IBEX 35 – Del cumplimiento a la ventaja competitiva, URL: https://kc3.pwc.es/local/es/kc3/publicaciones.nsf/V1/07088C10E04A0FDEC12579B20059844D/$FILE/Informe%20repoting%20integrado%20Empresas%20IBEX_1.pdf (29.08.2016).

PricewaterhouseCoopers (PwC) (2012b): Integrated Reporting in Germany – The DAX 30 Benchmark Study, URL: http://www.pwc.de/de_DE/de/rechnungslegung/assets/pwc-studie-integrated-reporting-in-germany-2012.pdf (29.08.2013).

PricewaterhouseCoopers (PwC) (2013a): A benchmark study of Swedish Large Cap companies' reporting 2011, Stockholm, Sweden 2013.

PricewaterhouseCoopers (PwC) (2013b): Momento para la diferenciación – Las empresas del IBEX 35 avanzan hacia el reporting integrado, URL: https://www.pwc.es/es/publicaciones/auditoria/assets/reporting-integrado-ibex-35.pdf (29.08.2016).

PricewaterhouseCoopers (PwC) (2013c): The value creation journey – A survey of JSE Top-40 companies' integrated reports, URL: http://www.pwc.co.za/en_ZA/za/assets/pdf/integrated-reporting-august-2013.pdf (29.08.2016).

PricewaterhouseCoopers (PwC) (2013d): Integrated reporting in Germany. The DAX 30 benchmark survey 2013. An analysis of company reporting in terms of the IIRC's consultation draft of the International (IR) framework, URL: http://www.pwc.de/de_DE/de/rechnungslegung/assets/pwc-studie_integrated-reporting-bei-den-dax-30-unternehmen.pdf (29.08.2016).

PricewaterhouseCoopers (PwC) (2013e): Integrated Reporting – Companies struggle to explain what value they create, URL: http://www.pwc.nl/nl/assets/documents/ir-opmars-geintegreerde-verslaggeving-stagneert.pdf (29.08.2016).

PricewaterhouseCoopers (PwC) (2013f): A benchmark study of Swedish Large Cap companies' reporting 2012, URL: https://www.pwc.se/sv/bolagsstyrning/assets/a-benchmark-study-of-swedish-large-cap-companies-reporting-2013.pdf (29.08.2016).

PricewaterhouseCoopers (PwC) (2014a): Corporate reporting for listed companies in Belgium – From compliance to competitive edge, URL: http://www.pwc.be/en/publications/2014/corporate_reporting_for_belgian_listed_companies_-_final.pdf (29.08.2016).

PricewaterhouseCoopers (PwC) (2014b): ¿Transmiten los informes el valor creado por las empresas? Análisis del estado del reporting integrado en las empresas del IBEX 35, URL: http://www.pwc.es/es/publicaciones/auditoria/assets/pwc-reporting-integrado-2013.pdf (29.08.2016).

PricewaterhouseCoopers (PwC) (2014c): The state of Integrated Reporting in Malaysia – An analysis of the Bursa Malaysia's top 30 companies' annual reports, URL: http://read.pwc.com/i/342680-the-state-of-integrated-reporting-in-malaysia (29.08.2016).

PricewaterhouseCoopers (PwC) (2014d): Value creation: The journey continues –A survey of JSE Top-40 companies' integrated reports, URL: http://www.pwc.co.za/en_ZA/za/assets/pdf/integrated-reporting-survey-2014.pdf (29.08.2016).

PricewaterhouseCoopers (PwC) (2014e): Towards more relevant reporting – An analysis of the Straits Times Index ("STI") constituents' annual reports, URL: http://read.pwc.com/i/385378-towards-more-relevant-reporting/49 (29.08.2016).

PricewaterhouseCoopers (PwC) (2014f): Integrated Reporting in Germany – The DAX 30 Benchmark Survey 2014, URL: https://www.pwc.de/de/rechnungslegung/assets/pwc-studie_integrated-reporting-bei-den-dax-30-unternehmen-langsam-aber-sicher-kommt-der-integrierte-bericht.pdf (29.08.2016).

PricewaterhouseCoopers (PwC) (2015a): En la senda de la integración – Análisis del estado del reporting integrado en las empresas del IBEX 35, URL: http://www.pwc.es/es/publicaciones/auditoria/assets/pwc-reporting-integrado-ibex-2014.pdf (29.08.2016).

PricewaterhouseCoopers (PwC) (2015b): Implementing Integrated Reporting, URL: https://www.pwc.nl/nl/assets/documents/pwc-integrated-reporting-practical-guide.pdf (28.08.2016).

PricewaterhouseCoopers (PwC) (2015c): Inspiring trust through insight – Integrated Reporting in Malaysia – An analysis of the reporting by Bursa Malaysia's Top 50 companies, URL: http://read.pwc.com/i/567317-inspiring-trust-throught-insight-integrated-reporting-in-malaysia (29.08.2016).

PricewaterhouseCoopers (PwC) (2015d): Integrated reporting – Where to next?, URL: http://www.pwc.co.za/en/assets/pdf/integrated-reporting-survey-2015.pdf (29.08.2016).

PricewaterhouseCoopers (PwC)/Vienna University of Economics and Business (WU) (2014): Integrated Reporting – Die Zukunft der Unternehmens-berichterstattung in Österreich, URL: https://www.pwc.at/publikationen/integrated-reporting.pdf (29.08.2016).

Q

Qi, Daqing/Wu, Woody/Haw, In-Mu (2000): The Incremental Information Content of SEC 10-K Reports Filed under the EDGAR System, in: Journal of Accounting, Auditing and Finance, Vol. 15, No. 1, 2000, pp. 25-46.

R

Raffée, Hans (1974): Grundprobleme der Betriebswirtschaftslehre, Göttingen, Germany 1974.

Ramanathan, Kavasseri V. (1976): Toward A Theory of Corporate Social Accounting, in: The Accounting Review, Vol. 51, No. 3, 1976, pp. 516-528.

Ramsey, James B. (1969): Tests for Specification Errors in Classical Linear Least-squares Regression Analysis, in: Journal of the Royal Statistical Society. Series B (Methodological), Vol. 31, No. 2, 1969, pp. 350-371.

Ratcliffe, Thomas A. (2003): OCBOA Financial Statements, in: Journal of Accountancy, Vol. 196, No. 4, 2003, pp. 71-75.

Reimsbach, Daniel/Hahn, Rüdiger/Gürtürk, Anil (2016): Integrated Reporting and Assurance of Sustainability Information: An Experimental Study on Professional Investors' Information Processing. Paper presented at the 39th European Accounting Association Annual Congress 2016, 11-13 May 2016, Maastricht, Netherlands, URL: http://www.eaacongress.org/r/home (29.08.2016).

Rensburg, Ronél/Botha, Elsamari (2014): Is Integrated Reporting the silver bullet of financial communication? A stakeholder perspective from South Africa, in: Public Relations Review, Vol. 40, No. 2, 2014, pp. 144-152.

Reuter, Marek/Messner, Martin (2015): Lobbying on the integrated reporting framework – An analysis of comment letters to the 2011 discussion paper of the IIRC, in: Accounting, Auditing & Accountability Journal, Vol. 28, No. 3, 2015, pp. 365-402.

Roberts, Leigh (2011): Integrated Reporting the status quo, in: Accountancy SA, December 2011/January 2012, pp. 11-12.

Roberts, Leigh (2014): The New Integrated Reporting Framework, in: Accountancy SA, March 2014, pp. 28-29.

Roberts, Leigh (2015): A Quality Integrated Report, in: Accountancy SA, December 2015/January 2016, pp. 36-37.

Robertson, Fiona A./Samy, Martin (2015): Factors affecting the diffusion of integrated reporting – a UK FTSE 100 perspective, in: Sustainability Accounting, Management and Policy Journal, Vol. 6, No. 2, 2015, pp. 190-223.

Rose, Jacob M. (2002): The Effects of Cognitive Load on Decision Aid Users, in: Advances in Accounting Behavioral Research, Vol. 5, 2002, pp. 115-140.

Rose, Jacob M./Wolfe, Christopher J. (2000): The effects of system design alternatives on the acquisition of tax knowledge from a computerized tax decision aid, in: Accounting, Organizations and Society, Vol. 25, No. 3, 2000, pp. 285-306.

Ross, Stephen A. (1973): The Economic Theory of Agency: The Principal's Problem, in: The American Economic Review, Vol. 63, No. 2, 1973, pp. 134-139.

S

Schmidt, Robert/Sutherland, Philip/Van Schalkwyk, Christiaan J./Lowe, Thomas/Bockmann, Roland (2011): Monitoring and enforcement of financial reporting standards in South Africa and Germany: A comparative assessment, in: Namibia Law Journal, Vol. 3, No. 1, 2011, pp. 55-83.

Schneider, Alan J. (1988): Summary annual reporting: has the concept been accepted?, in: Financial Executive, Vol. 4, No. 4, 1988, pp. 20-24.

Schnell, Rainer/Hill, Paul B./Esser, Elke (2013): Methoden der empirischen Sozialforschung, 10th edition, Munich, Germany 2013.

Schroeder, Nicholas/Gibson, Charles (1988): Improving Annual Reports by Improving the Readability of Footnotes, in: The Woman CPA, Vol. 50, No. 2, 1988, pp. 13-16.

Schroeder, Nicholas/Gibson, Charles (1990): Readability of Management's Discussion and Analysis, in: Accounting Horizons, Vol. 4, No. 4, 1990, pp. 78-87.

Schroeder, Nicholas/Gibson, Charles (1992): Are Summary Annual Reports Successful?, in: Accounting Horizons, Vol. 6, No. 2, 1992, pp. 28-37.

Schultz, Birl E. (1936): Stock Exchange Procedure, New York, NY 1936.

Schultz, Theodore W. (1961): Investment in Human Capital, in: The American Economic Review, Vol. 51, No. 1, 1961, pp. 1-17.

Schweitzer, Marcell (1978): Wissenschaftsziele und Auffassungen in der Betriebswirtschaftslehre – Eine Einführung, in: Schweitzer, Marcell (ed.), Auffassungen und Wissenschaftsziele der Betriebswirtschaftslehre, Darmstadt, Germany 1978, pp. 1-14.

Securities and Exchange Commission (SEC) (1998): A Plain English Handbook – How to create clear SEC disclosure documents, URL: http://www.sec.gov/pdf/handbook.pdf (29.08.2016).

Securities and Exchange Commission (SEC) (2007): About the Division of Enforcement, URL: https://www.sec.gov/divisions/enforce/about.htm (29.08.2016).

Securities and Exchange Commission (SEC) (2008): Final Report of the Advisory Committee on Improvements To Financial Reporting to the United States Securities and Exchange Commission, August 1, 2008 (SEC-Release No. 2008-166), URL: http://www.sec.gov/about/offices/oca/acifr.shtml (29.08.2016).

Securities and Exchange Commission (SEC) (2011): Annual Report, URL: http://edgar.sec.gov/answers/annrep.htm (29.08.2016).

Securities and Exchange Commission (SEC) (2013): The Investor's Advocate: How the SEC Protects Investors, Maintains Market Integrity, and Facilitates Capital Formation, URL: http://www.sec.gov/about/whatwedo.shtml (29.08.2016).

Serafeim, George (2015): Integrated Reporting and Investor Clientele, in: Journal of Applied Corporate Finance, Vol. 27, No. 2, 2015, pp. 34-51.

Setia, Neelam/Abhayawansa, Subhash/Joshi, Mahesh/Huynh, Anh Vu (2015): Integrated reporting in South Africa: some initial evidence, in: Sustainability Accounting, Management and Policy Journal, Vol. 6, No. 3, 2015, pp. 397-424.

Shefrin, Hersh (2002): Beyond Greed and Fear – Understanding Behavioral Finance and the Psychology of Investing, Oxford, UK 2002.

Shleifer, Andrei (2000): Inefficient Markets – An Introduction to Behavioral Finance, Oxford, UK 2000.

Shocker, Allan D./Sethi, S. Prakash (1973): An Approach to Incorporating Societal Preferences in Developing Corporate Action Strategies; in: California Management Review, Vol. 15, No. 4, 1973, pp. 97-105.

Simon, Herbert A. (1974): How Big Is a Chunk?, in: Science, Vol. 183, No. 4121, 1974, pp. 482-488.

Simpson, Kirsty (1997): Annual Reports: Glossy, expensive and useless?, in: Australian Accountant, Vol. 67, No. 8, 1997, pp. 16-18.

Sirois, Louis-Philippe/Bédard, Jean/Bera, Palash (2014): The Informational Value of Key Audit Matters in the Auditor's Report: Evidence from an Eye-tracking Study, URL: http://www.isarhq.org/2014_downloads/papers/ISAR2014_Sirois_Bedard_Bera.pdf (29.08.2016).

Slaper, Timothy F./Hall, Tanya J. (2011): The Triple Bottom Line: What Is It and How Does It Work?, in: Indiana Business Review, Vol. 86, No. 1, 2011, pp. 4-8.

Sloan, Richard G. (1996): Do Stock Prices Fully Reflect Information in Accruals and Cash Flows About Future Earnings?, in: The Accounting Review, Vol. 71, No. 3, 1996, pp. 289-315.

Smith, Clifford W./Watts, Ross L. (1983): The structure of executive contracts and the control of management, Unpublished manuscript, University of Rochester, Rochester, NY 1982.

Smith, James E./Smith, Nora P. (1971): Readability: A Measure of the Performance of the Communication Function of Financial Reporting, in: The Accounting Review, Vol. 46, No. 3, 1971, pp. 552-561.

Smith, Malcolm (2015): Research Methods in Accounting, 3rd edition, Los Angeles, CA 2015.

Smith, Malcolm/Taffler, Richard J. (1992): Readability and Understandability: Different Measures of the Textual Complexity of Accounting Narrative, in: Accounting, Auditing & Accountability Journal, Vol. 5, No. 4, 1992, pp. 84-98.

Smith, Malcolm/Taffler, Richard J. (1995): The Incremental Effect of Narrative Accounting Information in Corporate Annual Reports, in: Journal of Business Finance & Accounting, Vol. 22, No. 8, 1995, pp. 1195-1210.

Smith, Malcolm/Taffler, Richard J. (2000): The chairman's statement – A content analysis of discretionary narrative disclosures, in: Accounting, Auditing & Accountability Journal, Vol. 13, No. 5, 2000, pp. 624-646.

Snowball, Douglas A. T. (1979): Information Load and Accounting Reports: Too Much, Too Little or Just Right?, in: Cost and Management, May-June 1979, pp. 22-28.

Solomon, Jill F./Solomon, Aris/Norton, Simon D./Joseph, Nathan L. (2000): A Conceptual Framework for Corporate Risk Disclosure Emerging from the Agenda for Corporate Governance Reform, in: British Accounting Review, Vol. 32, No. 4, 2000, pp. 447-478.

Solstice Sustainability Works Inc. (Solstice) (2005): Integrated reporting – Issues and implications for reporters, URL: https://www.vancity.com/SharedContent/documents/IntegratedReporting.pdf (29.08.2016).

Speckbacher, Gerhard/Bischof, Juergen/Pfeiffer, Thomas (2003): A descriptive analysis on the implementation of Balanced Scorecards in German-speaking countries, in: Management Accounting Research, Vol. 14, No. 4, 2003, pp. 361-387.

Spence, A. Michael (1973): Job Market Signaling, in: The Quarterly Journal of Economics, Vol. 87, No. 3, 1973, pp. 355-374.

Spremann, Klaus (1987): Agent and Principal, in: Bamberg, Günther/Spremann, Klaus (eds.), Agency Theory, Information and Incentives, Berlin, Germany 1987, pp. 3-37.

Spremann, Klaus (1990): Asymmetrische Information, in: Zeitschrift für Betriebswirtschaft, Vol. 60, No. 5-6, 1990, pp. 561-586.

Stainbank, Lesley/Peebles, C. (2006): The usefulness of corporate annual reports in South Africa: perceptions of preparers and users, in: Meditari Accounting Research, Vol. 14, No. 1, 2006, pp. 69-80.

Stalnaker, Robert (2002): Common Ground, in: Linguistics and Philosophy, Vol. 25, No. 5, 2002, pp. 701-721.

Standard & Poor's Financial Services LLC (S&P) (n.d.): Market Capitalization Coverage of S&P U.S. Equities, URL: http://us.spindices.com/documents/additional-material/sp-500-trifold.pdf (29.08.2016).

Standard & Poor's Financial Services LLC (S&P) (2016): S&P 500 Factsheet, URL: http://us.spindices.com/idsenhancedfactsheet/file.pdf?calcFrequency=M&force_download=true&hostIdentifier=48190c8c-42c4-46af-8d1a-0cd5db894797&indexId=340 (29.08.2016).

Stawinoga, Martin (2015): Stakeholder als Informationsadressaten des Integrated Reportings, in: Freidank, Carl-Christian/Müller, Stefan/Velte, Patrick (eds.), Handbuch Integrated Reporting, Berlin, Germany 2015, pp. 183-213.

Stein, Carl (2011): The Most Significant Changes to South Africa's Company Laws Brought About by the Companies Act, 2008, URL: http://www.bowman.co.za/FileBrowser/ContentDocuments/NewCompanies-Act-Brochure.pdf (29.08.2016).

Steinmeyer, Volker (2008): Der Lagebericht als publizitätsorientiertes Instrument börsennotierter Aktiengesellschaften, Hamburg, Germany 2008.

Stent, Warwick/Dowler, Tuyana (2015): Early assessment of the gap between integrated reporting and current corporate reporting, in: Meditari Accounting Research, Vol. 23, No. 1, 2015, pp. 92-117.

Stevenson, Gelvin (1990): The Complete Return on Investment, in: The New York Times, 23 March 1990, URL: http://www.nytimes.com/1990/03/25/business/forum-the-complete-return-on-investment.html (29.08.2016).

Stewart, G. Bennett, III (1991): The Quest for Value – A Guide for Senior Managers, New York, NY 1991.

Stewart, Neil (2010): An audience with the GRI's Mervyn King, URL: http://www.irmagazine.com/articles/case-studies/16371/audience-mervyn-king/ (29.08.2016).

Stewart, Thomas A. (1997): Intellectual Capital: The New Wealth of Organizations, New York, NY 1997.

Stice, Earl K. (1991): The Market Reaction to 10-K and 10-Q Filings and to Subsequent The Wall Street Journal Earnings Announcements, in: The Accounting Review, Vol. 66, No. 1, 1991, pp. 42-55.

Stickel, Scott E. (1991): Common Stock Returns Surrounding Earnings Forecast Revisions – More Puzzling Evidence, in: The Accounting Review, Vol. 66, No. 2, 1991, pp. 402-416.

Stiglitz, Joseph E. (1975): The Theory of "Screening", Education, and the Distribution of Income, in: The American Economic Review, Vol. 65, No. 3, 1975, pp. 283-300.

Stiglitz, Joseph E./Weiss, Andrew (1981): Credit Rationing in Markets with Imperfect Information, in: The American Economic Review, Vol. 71, No. 3, 1981, pp. 393-410.

Stubbs, Wendy/Higgins, Colin/Milne, Markus/Hems, Les (2014): Financial Capital Providers' Perceptions of Integrated Reporting, URL: http://papers.ssrn.com/sol3/papers.cfm?abstract_id=2473426 (29.08.2016).

Subramanian, Ram/Insley, Robert G./Blackwell, Rodney D. (1993): Performance and Readability: A Comparison of Annual Reports of Profitable and Unprofitable Corporations, in: The Journal of Business Communication, Vol. 30, No. 1, 1993, pp. 49-61.

Suchman, Mark C. (1995): Managing Legitimacy: Strategic and Institutional Approaches, in: Academy of Management Review, Vol. 20, No. 3, 1995, pp. 571-610.

Sustainability Accounting Standards Board (SASB) (n.d.): Evolution of SASB, URL: http://www.sasb.org/sasb/vision-mission/#1470334393614-641257f4-8d58 (29.08.2016).

Swart, D. J./Hoffman, Alwyn J. (2013): Analysis of the post-earnings announcement drift anomaly on the JSE, in: Investment Analysts Journal, Vol. 42, No. 77, 2013, pp. 17-34.

Sweller, John (1993): Some cognitive processes and their consequences for the organisation and presentation of information, in: Australian Journal of Psychology, Vol. 45, No. 1, 1993, pp. 1-8.

Sweller, John (1994): Cognitive Load Theory, Learning Difficulty, and Instructional Design, in: Learning and Instruction, Vol. 4, No. 4, 1994, pp. 295-312.

Sweller, John/Ayres, Paul/Kalyuga, Slava (2011): Cognitive Load Theory, New York et al., NY 2011.

Sweller, John/Chandler, Paul (1994): Why Some Material Is Difficult to Learn, in: Cognition and Instruction, Vol. 12, No. 3, 1994, pp. 185-233.

Sweller, John/Van Merriënboer, Jeroen J. G./Paas, Fred G. W. C. (1998): Cognitive Architecture and Instructional Design, in: Educational Psychology Review, Vol. 10, No. 3, 1998, pp. 251-296.

T

Tan, Hun-Tong/Wang, Elaine Y./Zhou, Bo (2015): How Does Readability Influence Investors' Judgments? Consistency of Benchmark Performance Matters, in: The Accounting Review, Vol. 90, No. 1, 2015, pp. 371-393.

Tarmizi, Rohani A./Sweller, John (1988): Guidance During Mathematical Problem Solving, in: Journal of Educational Psychology, Vol. 80, No. 4, 1988, pp. 424-436.

The cost of doing nothing (The Economist) (2014), URL: http://www.economist.com/news/united-states/21605936-scorched-farms-flooded-homes-and-lower-productivity-cost-doing-nothing (29.08.2016).

The Energy Policy and Conservation Act (P.L. 94-163, 42 U.S.C. 6201) (1976), in: William & Mary Environmental Law and Policy Review, Vol. 1, No. 2, 1976, pp. 2-3.

The SIGMA Project (2003): The Sigma Guidelines – Putting Sustainable Development into Practice – A Guide for Organizations, URL: http://www.projectsigma.co.uk/Guidelines/SigmaGuidelines.pdf (29.08.2016).

Thompson, Pat A./Brown, Robert D./Furgason, John (1981): Jargon and Data Do Make a Difference: The Impact of Report Styles on Lay and Professional Evaluation Audiences, in: Evaluation Review, Vol. 5, No. 2, 1981, pp. 269-279.

Tversky, Amos/Kahneman, Daniel (1974): Judgment under Uncertainty: Heuristics and Biases, in: Science, Vol. 185, No. 4157, 1974, pp. 1124-1131.

U

Ullmann, Arieh A. (1985): Data in Search of a Theory: A Critical Examination of the Relationships Among Social Performance, Social Disclosure, and Economic Performance of U.S. Firms, in: Academy of Management Review, Vol. 10, No. 3, 1985, pp. 540-557.

University of Münster (2013): Comment letter on the Consultation Draft of the International Integrated Reporting Framework, URL: http://integratedreporting.org/wp-content/uploads/2013/08/135_University-of-M%C3%Bcnster-Chair-of-International-Accounting.pdf (29.08.2016).

V

Van Staden, Chris (2003): The relevance of theories of political economy to the understanding of financial reporting in South Africa: the case of value added statements, in: Accounting Forum, Vol. 27, No. 2, 2003, pp. 224-245.

Velte, Patrick (2008): Intangible Assets und Goodwill im Spannungsfeld zwischen Entscheidungsrelevanz und Verlässlichkeit – Eine normative, entscheidungsorientierte und empirische Analyse vor dem Hintergrund internationaler und nationaler Rechnungslegungs- und Prüfungsstandards, Wiesbaden, Germany 2008.

Velte, Patrick/Stawinoga, Martin (2016): Integrated reporting: The current state of empirical research, limitations and future research implications, in: Journal of Management Control, forthcoming.

Verhoef, Grietjie/Van Vuuren, Lucas (2012): South Africa, in: Previts, Gary J./Walton, Peter J./Wolnizer, Peter W. (eds.), A Global History of Accounting, Financial Reporting and Public Policy – Eurasia, the Middle East and Africa, Bingley, UK 2012, pp. 135-181.

Vermorken, Maximilian A. M. (2011): GICS or ICB, how different is similar?, in: Journal of Asset Management, Vol. 12, No. 1, 2011, pp. 30-44.

Victor, Peter A. (1993): Indicators of sustainable development: some lessons from capital theory, in: Ecological Economics, Vol. 4, No. 3, 1993, pp. 191-213.

Von Auer, Ludwig (2016): Ökonometrie: Eine Einführung, 7th edition, Berlin, Germany 2016.

W

Wald, Abraham (1943): Tests of Statistical Hypotheses Concerning Several Parameters When the Number of Observations is Large, in: Transactions of the American Mathematical Society, Vol. 54, No. 3, 1943, pp. 426-482.

Wald, Abraham (1980): A Method of Estimating Plane Vulnerability Based on Damage of Survivors (Reprint by the Center for Naval Analyses Operations Evaluation Group), Alexandria, VA 1980.

Walker, David/Meiring, Ina (2010): King Code and developments in corporate governance, URL: http://www.companylaw.uct.ac.za/usr/companylaw/downloads/legislation/WLB_2010-09_King_Code_and_Corporate_Governance.pdf (29.08.2016).

Watts, Ross L. (2003a): Conservatism in Accounting Part I: Explanations and Implications, in: Accounting Horizons, Vol. 17, No. 3, 2003, pp. 207-221.

Watts, Ross L. (2003b): Conservatism in Accounting Part II: Evidence and Research Opportunities, in: Accounting Horizons, Vol. 17, No. 4, 2003, pp. 287-301.

Watts, Ross L./Zimmerman, Jerold L. (1978): Towards a Positive Theory of the Determination of Accounting Standards, in: The Accounting Review, Vol. 53, No. 1, 1978, pp. 112-134.

Watts, Ross L./Zimmerman, Jerold L. (1986): Positive Accounting Theory, London, UK 1986.

Weber, Harry R. (2010): Time to scrap BP brand? Gas station owners divided, URL: http://www.nbcnews.com/id/38493212/ns/business-us_business/#.UTOKBVccPlk (29.08.2016).

Weil, Gotshal & Manges LLP (Weil) (2013a): International Comparison of Selected Corporate Governance Guidelines and Codes of Best Practice, URL: http://www.weil.com/~/media/files/pdfs/International_Comparison_2013.pdf (29.08.2016).

Weil, Gotshal & Manges LLP (Weil) (2013b): Comparison of Corporate Governance Principles & Guidelines: United States, URL: http://www.weil.com/~/media/files/pdfs/US_Active_Comparison_of_Corporate_Governance_Guidelines.pdf (29.08.2016).

Weißenberger, Barbara E. (2014): Integrated Reporting: Fragen (und Antworten) aus der Diskussion um die integrierte Rechnungslegung, in: Controlling, Vol. 26, No. 8, 2014, pp. 440-446.

West, Andrew (2009): The ethics of corporate governance – A (South) African perspective, in: International Journal of Law and Management, Vol. 51, No. 1, 2009, pp. 10-16.

White, Amanda (2016): SASB the Missing Link in ESG Integration, URL: http://www.top1000funds.com/analysis/2016/05/13/sasb-the-missing-link-in-esg-integration/ (29.08.2016).

White, Halbert (1980): A Heteroskedasticity-Consistent Covariance Matrix Estimator and a Direct Test for Heteroskedasticity, in: Econometrica, Vol. 48, No. 4, 1980, pp. 817-838.

Whittington, Geoffrey (2008): Fair Value and the IASB/FASB Conceptual Framework Project: An Alternative View, in: Abacus, Vol. 44, No. 2, 2008, pp. 139-168.

Wild, Susan/Van Staden, Chris (2013): Integrated Reporting: Initial analysis of early reporters – an Institutional Theory approach, URL: http://www.apira2013.org/proceedings/pdfs/K236.pdf (29.08.2016).

Woodward, David G./Edwards, Pam/Birkin, Frank (1996): Organizational Legitimacy and Stakeholder Information Provision, in: British Journal of Management, Vol. 7, No. 4, 1996, pp. 329-347.

Wooldridge, Jeffrey M. (2014): Introduction to Econometrics – Europe, Middle East and Africa Edition, 5th edition, Andover, Hampshire, UK 2014.

World Economic Forum (2014): The Global Competitiveness Report 2014-2015, URL: http://www3.weforum.org/docs/WEF_GlobalCompetitivenessReport_2014-15.pdf (29.08.2016).

Wu, Jin G./Zhang, Lu/Zhang, X. Frank (2010): The q-Theory Approach to Understanding the Accrual Anomaly, in: Journal of Accounting Research, Vol. 48, No. 1, 2010, pp. 177-223.

Wulf, Inge/Niemöller, Jens/Rentzsch, Natalia (2014): Development toward integrated reporting, and its impact on corporate governance: a two-dimensional approach to accounting with reference to the German two-tier system, in: Journal of Management Control, Vol. 25, No. 2, 2014, pp. 135-164.

Y

You, Haifeng/Zhang, Xiao-Jun (2007): Investor Under-reaction to Earnings Announcement and 10-K Report, URL: http://www8.gsb.columbia.edu/programs/sites/programs/files/accounting/XIAOJUNZHANG.pdf (29.08.2016).

You, Haifeng/Zhang, Xiao-Jun (2009): Financial reporting complexity and investor underreaction to 10-K information, in: Review of Accounting Studies, Vol. 14, No. 4, 2009, pp. 559-586.

Z

Zach, Tzachi (2003): Inside the 'Accrual Anomaly', URL: http://ssrn.com/abstract=417781 (29.08.2016).

Zeff, Stephen A. (2010): A Comment on 'Delegation', in: Accounting in Europe, Vol. 7, No. 1, 2010, pp. 123-125.

Zhang, Jieying (2008): The contracting benefits of accounting conservatism to lenders and borrowers, in: Journal of Accounting and Economics, Vol. 45, No. 1, 2008, pp. 27-54.

Zhou, Shan/Simnett, Roger/Green, Wendy (2016): Does Integrated Reporting Matter to the Capital Market, URL: http://papers.ssrn.com/sol3/papers.cfm?abstract_id=2600364 (29.08.2016).

List of cited annual (integrated) reports

A

AECI Limited (AECI) (2007): Annual report 2006 – Specialty products and service solutions, Woodmead, Sandton, South Africa 2007.

B

Baker Hughes Incorporated (2013): Well Connected – 2012 Annual Report, Houston, TX 2013.

C

City Lodge Hotels Limited (City Lodge) (2013): Integrated Report 2013, Bryanston, Sandton, South Africa 2013.

D

Datatec Limited (Datatec) (2013): Annual Report 2013 – Technology – Integration – Consulting, Sandown, Sandton, South Africa 2013.

DIRECTV (2013): Annual Report 2012, El Segundo, CA 2013.

I

Illovo Sugar Limited (Illovo) (2013): Integrated Report for the year ended 31 March 2013, Mount Edgecombe, Durban, South Africa 2013.

J

JSE Limited (JSE) (2015): Integrated Annual Report – Integrated Annual Report of the JSE Limited for the Year Ended 31 December 2014, Johannesburg, South Africa 2015.

P

PPG Industries, Inc. (PPG) (2013): 2012 PPG Annual Report and Form 10-K, Pittsburgh, PA 2013.

S

Sasol Limited (Sasol) (2013): annual integrated report 20 June 2013 – better together… we deliver, Johannesburg, South Africa 2013.

Sun International Limited (Sun) (2013): Integrated Annual Report 2013, Sandown, Sandton, South Africa 2013.

T

Target Corporation (Target) (2007): Expect More. Pay Less. Target Corporation Annual Report 2006, Minneapolis, MN 2007.

Target Corporation (Target) (2013): 2012 annual report, Minneapolis, MN 2013.

U

United Parcel Service, Inc. (UPS) (2013): We Shrink The Globe – UPS Annual Report 2012, Atlanta, GA 2013.

List of cited laws, regulations, standards and guidance materials

National laws, regulations, standards and guidance materials

Denmark

Guideline for Intellectual Capital Statements	A Guideline for Intellectual Capital Statements, issued by The Danish Agency for Trade and Industry Copenhagen, Denmark 2000, URL: http://www.juergendaum.com/articles/Danish_ICS.pdf (29.08.2016).
Intellectual Capital Statements – The New Guideline	Intellectual Capital Statements – The New Guideline, issued by The Danish Ministry of Science, Technology and Innovation, Copenhagen, Denmark 2003, URL: http://www.som.cranfield.ac.uk/som/dinamic-content/research/cbp/Intellectual%20Capital%20Statements%20-%20New%20Guidelines.pdf (29.08.2016).

Germany

GAS 15	German Accounting Standard (GAS) 15 "Management Reporting", published by the Federal Ministry of Justice on 7 December 2004, replaced by GAS 20 on 4 December 2012.
GAS 20	German Accounting Standard (GAS) 20 "Group Management Report", adopted by the Accounting Standards Committee of Germany on 2 November 2012, published by the Federal Ministry of Justice on 4 December 2012.
Intellectual capital statement – Made in Germany	Intellectual capital statement – Made in Germany – Guideline, issued by The Federal Ministry of Economics and Labour, Berlin, Germany 2004, URL: http://www.akwissensbilanz.org/Infoservice/Infomaterial/Leitfaden_english.pdf (29.08.2016).

South Africa

Companies Act No. 61	Companies Act No. 61 of 1973, Republic of South Africa, as amended by the Prevention and Combating of Corrupt Activities Act 12 of 2004, effective from 1 January 1974, replaced by the Companies Act. No. 71 of 2008 on 1 May 2011.
Companies Act No. 71	Companies Act No. 71 of 2008, Republic of South Africa, as amended by the Companies Amendment Act 3 of 2011, and Companies Regulations, 2011 (Regulations to the Companies Act No. 71 of 2008), effective from 1 May 2011.
IRCSA DP	Integrated Reporting Committee of South Africa Discussion Paper ("Framework for Integrated Reporting and the Integrated Report – Discussion Paper"), issued by the Integrated Reporting Committee (IRC) of South Africa, Johannesburg, South Africa 2011, URL: http://www.sustainabilitysa.org/Portals/0/IRC%20of%20SA%20Integrated%20Reporting%20Guide%20Jan%2011.pdf (29.08.2016).
JSE LR	Johannesburg Stock Exchange Listings Requirements (JSE LR), Johannesburg, South Africa 2015.
King I	King Report on Corporate Governance (including the Code of Corporate Practices and Conduct), issued by The Institute of Directors in Southern Africa and the King Committee, Johannesburg, South Africa 1994.
King II	King Report on Corporate Governance for South Africa 2002 (including the Code of Corporate Practices and Conduct), issued by The Institute of Directors in Southern Africa and the King Committee, Johannesburg, South Africa 2002.
King III	King Report on Governance for South Africa 2009 and King Code of Governance for South Africa 2009, issued by The Institute of Directors in Southern Africa and the King Committee, Johannesburg, South Africa 2009.

King IV	King IV Report on Corporate Governance for South Africa 2016 (including the King IV Code on Corporate Governance), issued by The Institute of Directors in Southern Africa and the King Committee, Johannesburg, South Africa 2016.

UK

Companies Act 2006 Regulations 2013	The Companies Act 2006 (Strategic Report and Directors' Report) Regulations 2013, as published by the Parliament of the United Kingdom, effective from 1 October 2013.

USA

AS 2710	Audit Standard (AS) 2710 "Other Information in Documents Containing Audited Financial Statements", issued by the Public Company Accounting Oversight Board (PCAOB), Washington, D.C. 2015, approved by the Securities and Exchange Commission (SEC) on 17 September 2015.
ASC Topic 205	Accounting Standards Codification (ASC) Topic 205 "Extractive Presentation of Financial Statements", issued by the Financial Accounting Standards Board (FASB), Norwalk, CT 2014.
ASC Topic 210	Accounting Standards Codification (ASC) Topic 210 "Balance Sheet", issued by the Financial Accounting Standards Board (FASB), Norwalk, CT 2013.
ASC Topic 810	Accounting Standards Codification (ASC) Topic 810 "Consolidation", issued by the Financial Accounting Standards Board (FASB), Norwalk, CT 2016.
ASC Topic 932	Accounting Standards Codification (ASC) Topic 932 "Extractive Activities – Oil and Gas", issued by the Financial Accounting Standards Board (FASB), Norwalk, CT 2014.

AT Section 701	Attestation Standards (AT) Section 701 "Management's Discussion and Analysis", issued by the American Institute of Certified Public Accountants (AICPA), Durham, CA 2001.
AU Section 550	Audit Standards (AU) Section 550 "Other Information in Documents Containing Audited Financial Statements", issued by the American Institute of Certified Public Accountants (AICPA), Durham, CA 2010.
AU Section 623	Audit Standards (AU) Section 623 "Special Reports", issued by the American Institute of Certified Public Accountants (AICPA), Durham, CA 1989.
Business Roundtable's Principles of Corporate Governance 2012	Principles of Corporate Governance 2012, issued by Business Roundtable, Washington, D.C. 2012, URL: http://businessroundtable.org/sites/default/files/legacy/uploads/studies-reports/downloads/BRT_Principles_of_Corporate_Governance_-2012_Formatted_Final.pdf (29.08.2016).
CF (FASB)	Statement of Financial Accounting Concepts No. 8 "Conceptual Framework for Financial Reporting", issued by the Financial Accounting Standards Board (FASB), Norwalk, CT 2010.
Dodd-Frank Wall Street Reform and Consumer Protection Act	Dodd-Frank Wall Street Reform and Consumer Protection Act, United States of America, effective from 21 July 2010, Washington, D.C.
Energy Policy and Conservation Act	Energy Policy and Conservation Act of 1975, United States of America, effective from 22 December 1975, Washington, D.C.
Exchange Act Rules and Regulations	17 CFR § 240, Code of Federal Regulations (CFR), Title 17, Chapter 2, Part 240 "General Rules and Regulations, Securities Exchange Act of 1934", issued by the Office of the Federal Register, Washington, D.C. 2016.

Financial Reporting Framework for Small- and Medium-Sized Entities	Financial Reporting Framework for Small- and Medium-Sized Entities, issued by the American Institute of Certified Public Accountants (AICPA), Durham, CA 2013, URL: http://www.aicpa.org/InterestAreas/FRC/AccountingFinancialReporting/PCFR/DownloadableDocuments/FRF-SME/FRF-SMEs-Framework.PDF (29.08.2016).
Findings and Recommendations of The Conference Board Commission on Public Trust and Private Enterprise	Findings and Recommendations – Part 1 Executive Compensation, Part 2 Corporate Governance, Part 3 Audit and Accounting, issued by The Conference Board Commission on Public Trust and Private Enterprise, New York, NY 2003, URL: https://www.conference-board.org/pdf_free/SR-03-04.pdf (29.08.2016).
Form 10-K	Form 10-K "Annual Reports Pursuant to Section 13 or 15(d) of the Securities Exchange Act of 1934", issued by the Securities and Exchange Commission (SEC), Washington, D.C. 2016.
Form 10-Q	Form 10-Q, issued by the Securities and Exchange Commission (SEC), Washington, D.C. 2016.
Form 20-F	Form 20-F "Registration Statement Pursuant to Section 12(b) or (g) of the Securities Exchange Act of 1934 or Annual Report Pursuant to Section 13 or 15(d) of the Securities Exchange Act of 1934 or Transition Report Pursuant to Section 13 or 15(d) of the Securities Exchange Act of 1934 or Shell Company Report Pursuant to Section 13 or 15(d) of the Securities Exchange Act of 1934", issued by the Securities and Exchange Commission (SEC), Washington, D.C. 2016.
NYSE Corporate Governance Guide	NYSE: Corporate Governance Guide, issued by the New York Stock Exchange (NYSE), London, UK 2014, URL: https://www.nyse.com/publicdocs/nyse/listing/NYSE_Corporate_Governance_Guide.pdf (29.08.2016).
NYSE Listed Company Manual	Listed Company Manual, issued by the New York Stock Exchange (NYSE), New York, NY 2016, URL: http://wallstreet.cch.com/LCM/ (29.08.2016).

PCC Private Company Decision-Making Framework	Private Company Decision-Making Framework – A Guide for Evaluating Financial Accounting and Reporting for Private Companies, issued by The Financial Accounting Standards Board Private Company Council (PCC), Norwalk, CT 2013, URL: http://www.fasb.org/jsp/FASB/Document_C/DocumentPage?cid=1176163703583&acceptedDisclaimer=true (29.08.2016).
Regulation S-K	17 CFR § 229, Code of Federal Regulations (CFR), Title 17, Chapter 2, Part 229 "Standard Instructions for Filing Forms under Securities Act of 1933, Securities Exchange Act of 1934 and Energy Policy and Conservation Act of 1975 – Regulation S K", issued by the Office of the Federal Register, Washington, D.C. 2016.
Regulation S-X	17 CFR § 210, Code of Federal Regulations (CFR), Title 17, Chapter 2, Part 210 "Form and Content of and Requirements for Financial Statements, Securities Act of 1933, Securities Exchange Act of 1934, Investment Company Act of 1940, Investment Advisers Act of 1940, and Energy Policy and Conservation Act of 1975", issued by the Office of the Federal Register, Washington, D.C. 2016.
Report of the NACD Blue Ribbon Commission on Director Professionalism	Report of the NACD Blue Ribbon Commission on Director Professionalism, issued by the National Association of Corporate Directors (NACD), Washington, D.C. 1996.
SAB 99	Staff Accounting Bulletin (SAB) No. 99 "Materiality", issued by the Securities and Exchange Commission (SEC) on 13 August 1999, Washington, D.C.
SAB 108	Staff Accounting Bulletin (SAB) No. 108, issued by the Securities and Exchange Commission (SEC) on 13 September 2006, Washington, D.C.
SASB CF	Conceptual Framework, issued by the Sustainability Accounting Standards Board (SASB), San Francisco, CA 2013, URL: http://www.sasb.org/wp-content/uploads/2013/10/SASB-Conceptual-Framework-Final-Formatted-10-22-13.pdf (29.08.2016).

SEC Financial Reporting Release No. 1	Securities and Exchange Commission (SEC) Financial Reporting Release No. 1 "Adoption of the Financial Reporting Release Series and Codification of Currently Relevant ASRs", 47 FR 21028, Washington, D.C. 1982.
SEC Release 33-6835	Securities and Exchange Commission (SEC) Release 33-6835 "SEC Interpretation: Management's Discussion and Analysis of Financial Condition and Results of Operations; Certain Investment Company Disclosures", Washington, D.C. 1989.
SEC Release 33-8124	Securities and Exchange Commission (SEC) Release 33-8124 "Final Rule: Certification of Disclosure in Companies' Quarterly and Annual Reports", Washington, D.C. 2002.
SEC Release 33-8182	Securities and Exchange Commission (SEC) Release 33-8182 "Final Rule: Disclosure in Management's Discussion and Analysis about Off-Balance Sheet Arrangements and Aggregate Contractual Obligations", Washington, D.C. 2003.
SEC Release 33-8221	Securities and Exchange Commission (SEC) Release 33-8221 "Policy Statement: Reaffirming the Status of the FASB as a Designated Private-Sector Standard Setter", Washington, D.C. 2003.
SEC Release 33-8350	Securities and Exchange Commission (SEC) Release 33-8350 "Interpretation: Commission Guidance Regarding Management's Discussion and Analysis of Financial Condition and Results of Operations", Washington, D.C. 2003.
SEC Release 33-8995	Securities and Exchange Commission (SEC) Release 33-8995 "Modernization of Oil and Gas Reporting", Washington, D.C. 2008.
SEC Release 33-9106	Securities and Exchange Commission (SEC) Release 33-9106 "SEC guidance regarding disclosure related to climate change", Washington, D.C. 2010.
SEC Release 33-10064	Securities and Exchange Commission (SEC) Release 33-10064 "Concept Release: Business and Financial Disclosure Required by Regulation S-K", Washington, D.C. 2016.

Securities Act	Securities Act of 1933, United States of America, effective from 27 May 1933, Washington D.C.
Securities Act Rules and Regulations	17 CFR § 230, Code of Federal Regulations (CFR), Title 17, Chapter 2, Part 230 "General Rules and Regulations, Securities Act of 1933", issued by the Office of the Federal Register, Washington, D.C. 2016.
Securities Exchange Act	Securities Exchange Act of 1934, United States of America, effective from 6 June 1934, Washington, D.C.
SOX	Sarbanes-Oxley Act of 2002 (SOX), United States of America, effective from 30 July 2002, Washington, D.C.
The American Law Institute's Principles of Corporate Governance	Principles of the Law – Corporate Governance: Analysis and Recommendations, Volumes 1 & 2, issued by The American Law Institute, Philadelphia, PA 1994.

International laws, regulations, standards and guidance materials

CD IR	Consultation Draft of the International <IR> Framework, issued by the International Integrated Reporting Council (IIRC), London, UK 2013, URL: http://integratedreporting.org/wp-content/uploads/2013/03/Consultation-Draft-of-the-InternationalIRFramework.pdf (29.08.2016).
CF (IASB)	The Conceptual Framework for Financial Reporting, issued by the International Accounting Standards Board (IASB), London, UK 2010.
Connected Reporting	Connected Reporting – A practical guide with worked examples, issued by Accounting for Sustainability (A4S), London, UK 2009, URL: http://www.accountingforsustainability.org/wp-content/uploads/2011/10/Connected-Reporting.pdf (29.08.2016).

DP IR	Discussion Paper Integrated Reporting ("Towards Integrated Reporting – Communicating Value in the 21st Century"), issued by the International Integrated Reporting Council (IIRC), London, UK 2011, URL: http://integratedreporting.org/wp-content/uploads/2011/09/IR-Discussion-Paper-2011_spreads.pdf (29.08.2016).
GRI G3	G3 "Sustainability Reporting Guidelines", issued by the Global Reporting Initiative (GRI), Amsterdam, The Netherlands 2006, URL: https://www.globalreporting.org/resourcelibrary/G3-Guidelines-Incl-Technical-Protocol.pdf (29.08.2016).
GRI G4	G4 "Sustainability Reporting Guidelines", issued by the Global Reporting Initiative (GRI), Amsterdam, The Netherlands 2013, URL: https://www.globalreporting.org/resourcelibrary/G4-Package.zip (29.08.2016).
IAS 1	International Accounting Standard (IAS) 1 "Presentation of Financial Statements", issued by the International Accounting Standards Board (IASB), London, UK 2014.
IAS 7	International Accounting Standard (IAS) 7 "Statement of Cash Flows", issued by the International Accounting Standards Board (IASB), London, UK 2016.
IAS 38	International Accounting Standard (IAS) 38 "Intangible Assets", issued by the International Accounting Standards Board (IASB), London, UK 2014.
IFRS 12	International Financial Reporting Standards (IFRS) 12 "Disclosure of Interests in Other Entities", issued by the International Accounting Standards Board (IASB), London, UK 2014.
IR F	The International <IR> Framework, issued by the International Integrated Reporting Council (IIRC), London, UK 2013, URL: http://integratedreporting.org/wp-content/uploads/2013/12/13-12-08-THE-INTERNATIONAL-IR-FRAMEWORK-2-1.pdf (29.08.2016).

PF IR	Prototype Framework Integrated Reporting ("Prototype of The International <IR> Framework"), issued by the International Integrated Reporting Council (IIRC), London, UK 2012, URL: http://integratedreporting.org/wp-content/uploads/2012/11/23.11.12-Prototype-Final.pdf (29.08.2016).
Practice Statement Management Commentary	IFRS Practice Statement Management Commentary – A Framework for Presentation, issued by the International Accounting Standards Board (IASB), London, UK 2010.
UN General Assembly Resolution 2202	Resolution 2202 (XXI). The policies of apartheid of the Government of the Republic of South Africa, adopted by The United Nations (UN) General Assembly, New York, NY 1966, URL: https://documents-dds-ny.un.org/doc/RESOLUTION/GEN/NR0/005/05/IMG/NR000505.pdf?OpenElement (29.08.2016).

Münsteraner Schriften zur Internationalen Unternehmensrechnung

Herausgegeben von Peter Kajüter

Band 1 Daniela Barth: Prognoseberichterstattung. Praxis, Determinanten und Kapitalmarktwirkungen bei deutschen börsennotierten Unternehmen. 2009.

Band 2 Tobias Dickmann: Controllingintegration nach M&A-Transaktionen. Eine empirische Analyse. 2010.

Band 3 Simon Esser: Produktorientiertes Kostenmanagement in der chemischen Industrie. Eine empirische Analyse. 2011.

Band 4 Christian Reisloh: Influence of National Culture on IFRS Practice. An Empirical Study in France, Germany and the United Kingdom. 2011.

Band 5 Matthias Moeschler: Cost Accounting in Germany and Japan. A Comparative Analysis. 2012.

Band 6 Martin Merschdorf: Der Management Approach in der IFRS-Rechnungslegung. Implikationen für Unternehmen und Investoren. 2012.

Band 7 Kristian Bachert: Fair Value Accounting. Implications for Users of Financial Statements. 2012.

Band 8 Daniel Blaesing: Nachhaltigkeitsberichterstattung in Deutschland und den USA. Berichtspraxis, Determinanten und Eigenkapitalkostenwirkungen. 2013.

Band 9 Christina Voets: Kulturelle Einflüsse auf die Anwendung des Impairment-Tests nach IAS 36. Eine experimentelle Untersuchung in Asien und Europa. 2013.

Band 10 Thomas Poplat: Foreign Investments in BRIC Countries. Empirical Evidence from Multinational Corporations. 2014.

Band 11 Moritz Schröder: Cost Accounting in Anglophone Subsidiaries. Empirical Evidence from Germany. 2014.

Band 12 Maximilian Saucke: Full IFRS and IFRS for SMEs Adoption by Private Firms. Empirical Evidence on Country Level. 2015.

Band 13 Martin Nienhaus: Segment Reporting under IFRS 8. Reporting Practice and Economic Consequences. 2015.

Band 14 Gregor Hagemann: Financial Reporting Quality in Emerging Economies. Empirical Evidence from Brazil and South Africa. 2017.

Band 15 Stefan Hannen: Integrated Reporting. Useful for investors? 2017.

www.peterlang.com